ST. JOHN'S LANE ELEMENTARY

Oh, the doors you will open!

STORYtown

HARCOURT SCHOOL PUBLISHERS

Winning Catch

Senior Authors
Isabel L. Beck • Roger C. Farr • Dorothy S. Strickland

Authors
Alma Flor Ada • Roxanne F. Hudson • Margaret G. McKeown
Robin C. Scarcella • Julie A. Washington

Consultants
F. Isabel Campoy • Tyrone C. Howard • David A. Monti

Harcourt
SCHOOL PUBLISHERS

www.harcourtschool.com

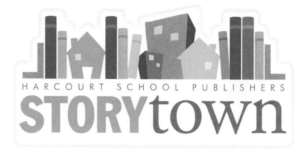

Winning Catch

SCHOOL PUBLISHERS

www.harcourtschool.com

Theme **1**
Facing Challenges

Contents

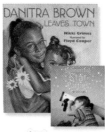

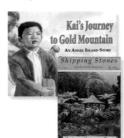

Theme ②
Getting the Job Done

Contents

Theme 3
Natural Changes

Contents

Paired Selections

Paired Selections

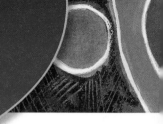

Theme **4**

Imagination at Work

Contents

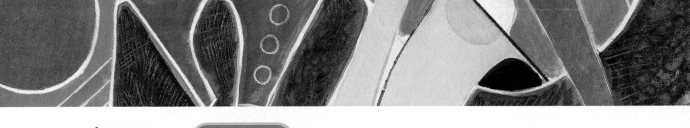

Theme 5
A New Home

Contents

Theme 6
Exploring Our World

Contents

14

Comprehension Strategies

Strategies for Reading

A **strategy** is a plan for doing something well. You can use strategies before, during, and after reading.

Before You Read

- **Preview the text** by looking at the title, headings, and photographs or illustrations.
- **Access prior knowledge** by thinking about what you already know about the topic or genre.
- **Predict** what the text will be about and what you might learn from reading it. Then **set a purpose** for reading.

While You Read

Think about what you understand and do not understand. Use the comprehension strategies on page 17 to help you understand the text and remember it later.

After You Read

Talk with a classmate about which strategies you used and why you used them.

Strategies to Use When Reading

- **Use Story Structure** Keep track of the characters, setting, and plot events to help you understand how a story is organized.

- **Summarize** Pause as you read to identify the most important ideas in the text.

- **Ask and Answer Questions** Ask yourself questions about what you do not understand in the text. Look for answers to questions as you read.

- **Use Graphic Organizers** Make charts and diagrams as you read to show how important ideas in the text are related.

- **Monitor Comprehension** When you do not understand a section of text, use one of these strategies to clarify the information.

  - **Reread**
  - **Read Ahead**
  - **Adjust Reading Rate**
  - **Self-Correct**

READING-WRITING
CONNECTION

Theme **1** Facing Challenges

▸ Glenna Goodacre, *Olympic Wannabes*

CONTENTS

Lesson 1

Genre: Realistic Fiction

The Hot and Cold Summer
illustrated by Mary GrandPré
by Johanna Hurwitz

Secret Talk
by Eve Merriam
illustrated by Catalina Estrada

Genre: Poetry

Focus Skill

Character's Traits and Motivations

A story is made up of characters, a setting, and plot events. A character's **traits** show what he or she is like. A character's **motivations** are the reasons he or she acts a certain way. Thinking about a character's traits and motivations will help you figure out why a character took a certain action in a story.

Character		
Traits	**Motivations**	**Actions**

Tip
To understand what a character is like, think about his or her thoughts, words, and actions.

Read the paragraph below. Then look at the graphic organizer. It shows how the character's traits and motivations can help you understand his actions.

James had been bragging for weeks about his science project. He was certain that his model volcano would win first prize, and he told everyone so. Two days before the science fair, he went to his classmate Paul's house. Paul had completed the most amazing model of the solar system that James had ever seen. It was much better than his own project. "You're not going to enter the science fair with that, are you?" James asked. "A model solar system is so boring!"

Character
James

Traits	Motivations	Actions
bragging, jealous	wants to win at the science fair	tells Paul his project is boring

Try This!

Look back at the paragraph. What is another action James might take, based on his traits and motivations?

 www.harcourtschool.com/storytown

23

Vocabulary

Build Robust Vocabulary

- pact
- queasy
- venture
- annoyed
- depriving
- foisted

Trading Chores

"We made a **pact**!" Charlie wailed. "I did the dishes for you, and you were supposed to take me to the ballpark today!"

"I know, I know, but I just don't feel well right now," said Charlie's older brother, Tyler. "I feel kind of **queasy**. I think I ate something bad." It was quite possible he had. He had just eaten a fish sandwich from his uncle's new diner. Tyler had wanted to support Uncle Stan's business **venture**, but now he was sorry he had done so.

"I can't miss this ball game! My friends are going to be there!" Charlie said, **annoyed** at Tyler.

"I'm not **depriving** you on purpose," Tyler replied. "I really don't feel well. I'll see if Liz can take you to the ball game." Tyler called their sister in and **foisted** the task on her. She was fine with the plan, as long as Tyler agreed to do her chores for a day.

"This just keeps getting more and more complicated," Tyler moaned, lying on the couch. "Maybe I can get Uncle Stan to help me with my chores, and then we'll all be happy!"

 www.harcourtschool.com/storytown

Word Detective

Your challenge this week is to find the Vocabulary Words outside your classroom. You might read them in a newspaper, hear them on the radio, or see them in an advertisement. Each time you see or hear a Vocabulary Word, write it in your vocabulary journal. Make sure you also record where you found the word.

Realistic Fiction

Genre Study

Realistic fiction has characters and events that are like people and events in real life. As you read, look for

- a setting that is familiar to most readers.

- realistic characters and events.

Characters	Setting
Plot Events	

Comprehension Strategy

Use story structure to help you understand how the characters, setting, and plot events in a story are connected.

The Hot and

Cold Summer

by Johanna Hurwitz

illustrated by Mary GrandPré

Best friends Rory and Derek have summer plans
that don't include a surprise visitor—a girl named
Bolivia. The boys make a pact not to speak to Bolivia but
soon find her hard to avoid. Derek and Bolivia become
friends, but Rory stubbornly tries to stay away from her.
Derek goes away to summer camp, leaving Rory and Bolivia
behind. The two become friends, even after Rory mistakenly
lets Bolivia's pet parrot, Lucette, out of her cage—and breaks
two toes trying to catch her. Now Derek is returning from
camp. Will the three of them be able to stay friends?

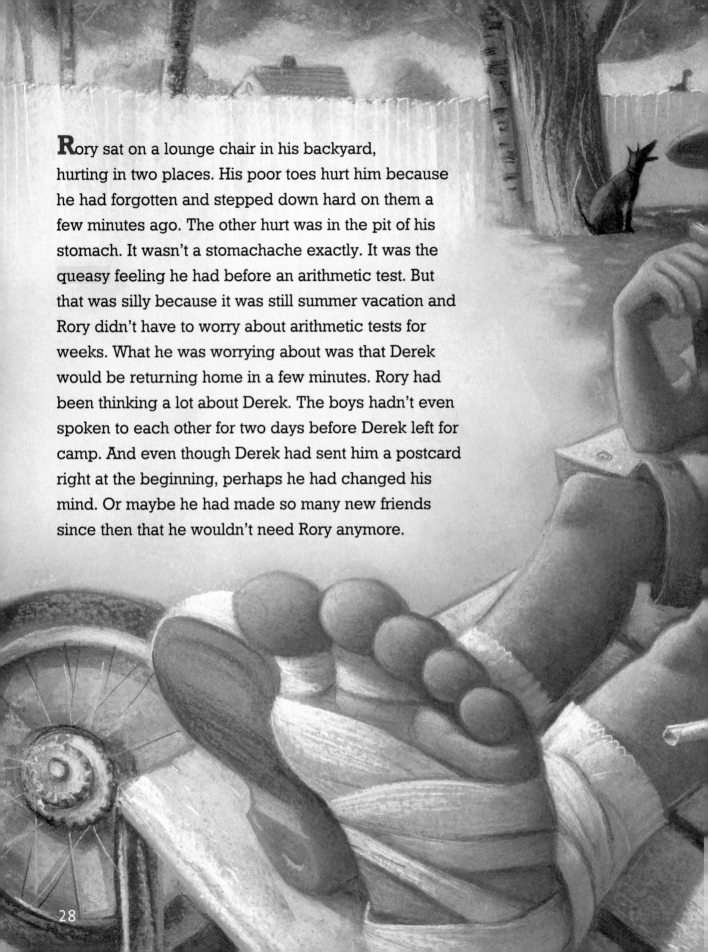

Rory sat on a lounge chair in his backyard, hurting in two places. His poor toes hurt him because he had forgotten and stepped down hard on them a few minutes ago. The other hurt was in the pit of his stomach. It wasn't a stomachache exactly. It was the queasy feeling he had before an arithmetic test. But that was silly because it was still summer vacation and Rory didn't have to worry about arithmetic tests for weeks. What he was worrying about was that Derek would be returning home in a few minutes. Rory had been thinking a lot about Derek. The boys hadn't even spoken to each other for two days before Derek left for camp. And even though Derek had sent him a postcard right at the beginning, perhaps he had changed his mind. Or maybe he had made so many new friends since then that he wouldn't need Rory anymore.

Rory moved his toes gingerly and thought about how it was before. Before the summer and before Bolivia. The two boys had so much fun together, and they had never argued about anything. Now he knew that Derek had been right. Bolivia was fun, too, even if she was a girl and had been foisted on them. He hadn't been very fair to her when she first came to Woodside. But how could he explain to Derek that he had changed his mind? Probably now that Derek was back, Bolivia would go bike riding or swimming with him and Rory would just have to sit still and rest his toes.

So Rory sat pretending to read the new comics that Mr. Golding had bought for him, but really he was listening for the Currys' car to drive up with Derek inside. He waited anxiously when he heard Derek's father pull into his driveway. The car doors opened and banged shut and Rory sat holding his breath. Would Derek come looking for him?

29

Minutes passed. I was right, thought Rory sadly. He didn't come running right over. He doesn't want to be my friend anymore.

Fifteen minutes later, Derek came running into the Dunn yard. He was tanned and taller than ever, and he was carrying his old comics. "I heard all about your foot," he said. "I thought you would want to borrow these."

Derek sat on the ground next to the lounge chair. "I can't stay long," he apologized. "My parents are taking me out to dinner. But tomorrow it will be like old times, being back home and doing things with you."

"I can't go to the pool or anything," said Rory sadly. "You'll probably want to go swimming."

"No," said Derek, shaking his head and standing up. "I haven't seen you in a long time. And, besides, I did plenty of swimming at camp."

The next day Derek and Bolivia and Rory spent most of the afternoon assembling a 500-piece puzzle on the bridge table that had served as their lemonade stand. Rory and Bolivia told Derek about their business venture.

"We made six dollars and five cents," said Rory proudly.

"And we didn't sell even a single cup of lemonade," said Bolivia.

"Except to each other," Rory reminded her.

"And Edna."

"We still haven't come up with a good way to spend the money," said Rory. It was upstairs in his bedroom underneath his T-shirts in a drawer. Bolivia said she trusted him with it, even after he had opened Lucette's cage.

When the puzzle was completed, they sat around trying to think of things to do. Derek got a deck of cards and showed them a couple of tricks that he had learned from one of the kids at camp. Gradually, the afternoon passed.

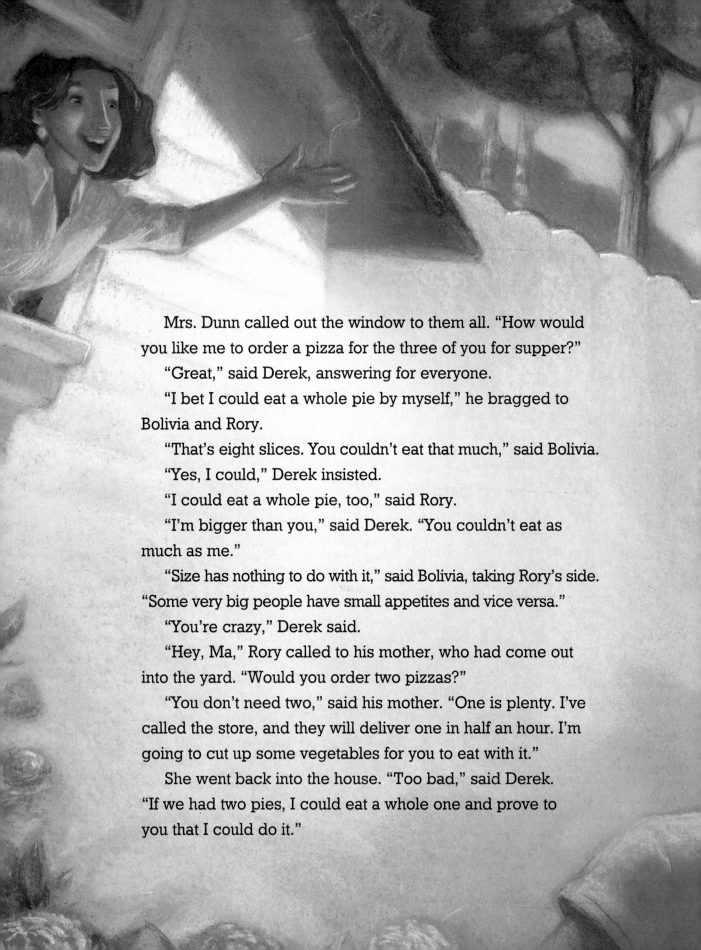

Mrs. Dunn called out the window to them all. "How would you like me to order a pizza for the three of you for supper?"

"Great," said Derek, answering for everyone.

"I bet I could eat a whole pie by myself," he bragged to Bolivia and Rory.

"That's eight slices. You couldn't eat that much," said Bolivia.

"Yes, I could," Derek insisted.

"I could eat a whole pie, too," said Rory.

"I'm bigger than you," said Derek. "You couldn't eat as much as me."

"Size has nothing to do with it," said Bolivia, taking Rory's side. "Some very big people have small appetites and vice versa."

"You're crazy," Derek said.

"Hey, Ma," Rory called to his mother, who had come out into the yard. "Would you order two pizzas?"

"You don't need two," said his mother. "One is plenty. I've called the store, and they will deliver one in half an hour. I'm going to cut up some vegetables for you to eat with it."

She went back into the house. "Too bad," said Derek. "If we had two pies, I could eat a whole one and prove to you that I could do it."

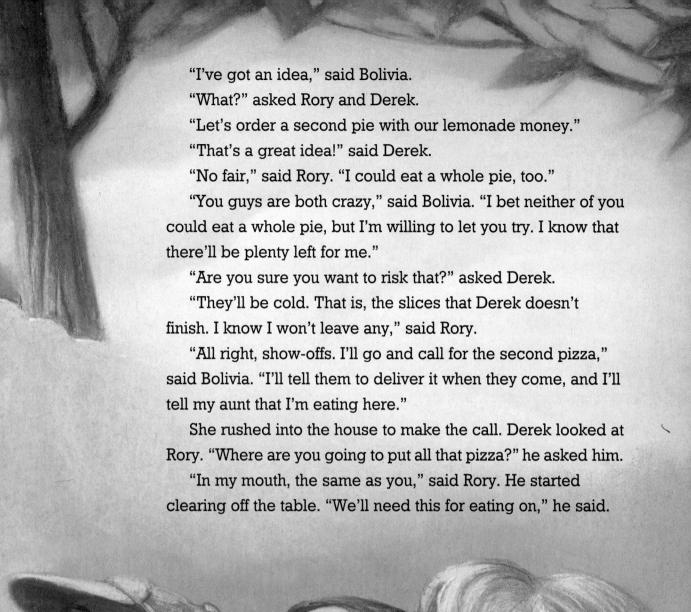

"I've got an idea," said Bolivia.

"What?" asked Rory and Derek.

"Let's order a second pie with our lemonade money."

"That's a great idea!" said Derek.

"No fair," said Rory. "I could eat a whole pie, too."

"You guys are both crazy," said Bolivia. "I bet neither of you could eat a whole pie, but I'm willing to let you try. I know that there'll be plenty left for me."

"Are you sure you want to risk that?" asked Derek.

"They'll be cold. That is, the slices that Derek doesn't finish. I know I won't leave any," said Rory.

"All right, show-offs. I'll go and call for the second pizza," said Bolivia. "I'll tell them to deliver it when they come, and I'll tell my aunt that I'm eating here."

She rushed into the house to make the call. Derek looked at Rory. "Where are you going to put all that pizza?" he asked him.

"In my mouth, the same as you," said Rory. He started clearing off the table. "We'll need this for eating on," he said.

"You better go into my house and get the money to pay for the pizza." He instructed Derek where to find the money in his room.

By the time the delivery truck pulled up forty-five minutes later, Mrs. Dunn had brought out napkins, a pitcher of grape juice, and a plate of carrot, green pepper, and celery sticks. Neither Rory nor Derek touched any of the vegetables. They were saving room for the pizza.

"Two pies?" asked Mrs. Dunn when the delivery boy came up the walk with two boxes. "There must be a mistake. I only ordered one."

"Dunn, 26 Dogleg Lane?" said the fellow. "It says two pies here," he said, holding out a slip.

"The second one is mine," said Bolivia, rushing forward to pay with the lemonade money that Derek had given her.

"You'll never be able to eat all that," said Mrs. Dunn sharply.

"It was my idea," said Bolivia apologetically. "I made a bet with Derek and Rory."

Rory knew that even if she were annoyed, his mother wouldn't scold Bolivia. He was right. Instead, she said, "Edna is having scrambled eggs for supper because I'm fixing chicken livers for Mr. Dunn and myself. If there is a slice left, she would love it."

34

"There won't be any left," said Rory.

"Sorry, Mrs. Dunn," said Derek.

"I'll bring it inside to her," promised Bolivia.

"Stop talking and open the boxes," said Rory. "The pizza will be cold."

There wasn't room for two pizza pies on the card table.

"I can rest my box right on the ground," said Derek. "It will be empty in a few minutes anyhow."

"Okay. On your mark, get set, go," shouted Bolivia. She reached for a carrot stick and began chewing on it as she watched the competitors.

"I'm sorry that you won't be getting any, Bolivia," said Derek, chewing away on his first slice. "I'm really going to pig out today."

"Don't worry about me," she told him.

"No fair, Rory," said Derek, pointing to the crusts that his friend had thrown into the box as he grabbed his second slice.

"I never eat those," complained Rory. "They're too boring."

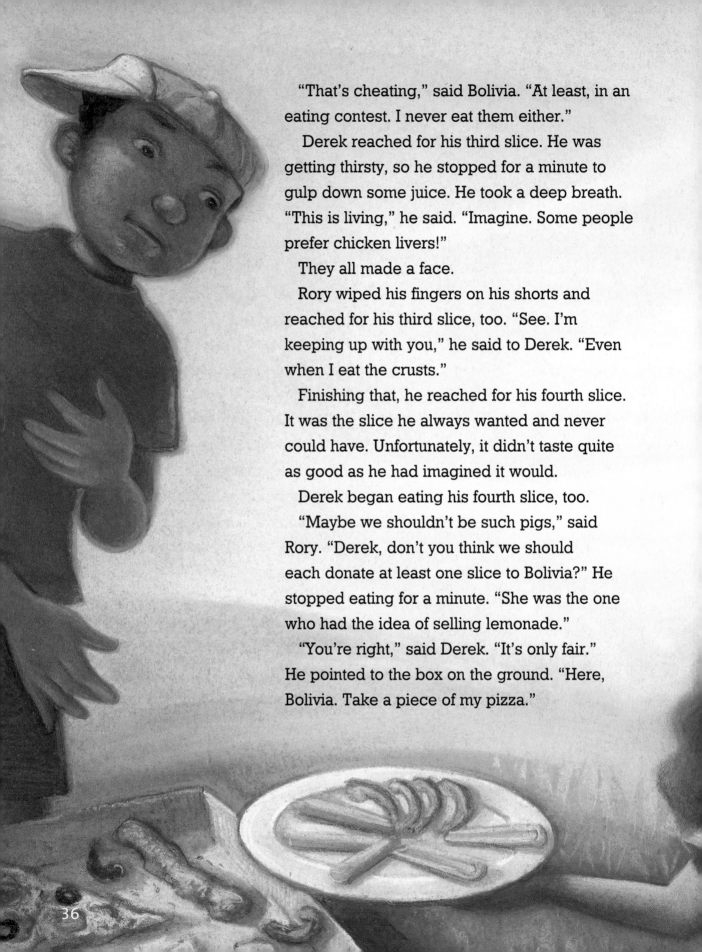

"That's cheating," said Bolivia. "At least, in an eating contest. I never eat them either."

Derek reached for his third slice. He was getting thirsty, so he stopped for a minute to gulp down some juice. He took a deep breath. "This is living," he said. "Imagine. Some people prefer chicken livers!"

They all made a face.

Rory wiped his fingers on his shorts and reached for his third slice, too. "See. I'm keeping up with you," he said to Derek. "Even when I eat the crusts."

Finishing that, he reached for his fourth slice. It was the slice he always wanted and never could have. Unfortunately, it didn't taste quite as good as he had imagined it would.

Derek began eating his fourth slice, too.

"Maybe we shouldn't be such pigs," said Rory. "Derek, don't you think we should each donate at least one slice to Bolivia?" He stopped eating for a minute. "She was the one who had the idea of selling lemonade."

"You're right," said Derek. "It's only fair." He pointed to the box on the ground. "Here, Bolivia. Take a piece of my pizza."

"Oh, I wouldn't think of depriving you," said Bolivia. She was chewing on a piece of green pepper.

Rory reached for his fifth slice. There were still three more slices in the box. "Bolivia," he insisted, "fair's fair. You worked hard selling the lemonade."

"You forgot. We didn't sell any lemonade," said Bolivia. "Most of the money was the reward you got for finding Mrs. Tillinghast's coin purse. So by rights you should eat all the pizza." She smiled and crunched down on a piece of celery.

"Too many vegetables will make you too healthy," said Derek. "Have a slice of pizza. Please."

"The nicest thing about eating celery is that chewing it makes a good noise," said Bolivia, munching away.

"I guess lying around all day because of my broken toes has kept me from having my usual appetite," Rory admitted. He was still nibbling at his fifth slice. He wasn't certain that he would be able to finish it.

"Confess that you're full," said Bolivia.

"I'm not full. Are you full, Derek?" Rory asked.

"Nope," said Derek. He was holding on to his fifth slice, too. "But I sure am not hungry either."

"Well, maybe I will do you guys a favor," said Bolivia. She reached into Derek's box and took out a slice.

"Hey, what about mine?" asked Rory.

Bolivia took a slice from Rory's box and placed it on top of the slice she was already holding. The tomato and cheese from each slice stuck together and the plain crusts were on the outside. "I'm having a pizza sandwich," she said as she began eating the two slices together.

Even though she was eating two slices at once, she finished them quickly. But she didn't eat the end crusts.

"Hey, you're supposed to eat those," said Rory, pointing to the crusts that she put down on the table.

"Why? I'm not in the contest," said Bolivia. "Aren't you guys eating any more?" she asked. They both shook their heads. Bolivia fixed herself another pizza sandwich.

"Delicious," she said. "I like it better cold. That way I don't burn my mouth." She finished her second sandwich except for the crusts and reached for another slice.

"Aren't you going to make another sandwich?" asked Rory.

"Nope," said Bolivia. "The last slice is for Edna. I promised to save it for her." She began chewing away on her fifth slice.

"Well, I guess it's a three-way tie," said Bolivia, wiping her hands on a napkin. "We each ate five slices."

"Yeah? You didn't eat your crusts," pointed out Rory.

"That's right," said Derek. At least the honor of boys against girls should be kept intact.

"True," agreed Bolivia, "but you didn't eat any salad." She pushed the plate of vegetables toward Derek and Rory, but both boys waved her away. Neither had any room at all.

"Derek, take this slice inside to Edna," said Bolivia, "and I'll put these crusts to good use." She picked up the crusts from her five slices.

"What are you going to do with them?" asked Rory.

"I'm going to bring them to Lucette," said Bolivia. "In all her life she never had as many pizza crusts as she wanted. She's going to break her record tonight, too."

"Don't talk about pizza records," said Rory, who felt as if pizza was coming out of his ears. "I may never be able to eat again." But though his stomach and his toes hurt him, he felt very good. It was great to have friends like Derek and Bolivia.

Think Critically

1. Why is Rory so worried about Derek's return?

    NOTE DETAILS

2. Rory and Derek remain friends even though they had a disagreement. Describe a time when you and a close friend had a disagreement and the way it was solved. MAKE CONNECTIONS

3. Why does Bolivia order a second pizza?

    CHARACTER'S TRAITS AND MOTIVATIONS

4. Why do Rory and Derek offer slices of their pizzas to Bolivia? MAKE INFERENCES

5. READ THINK EXPLAIN **WRITE** Bolivia says she isn't in the pizza-eating contest, yet she finds a way to prove to the boys that she can eat just as much as they can. Explain how she does this. SHORT RESPONSE

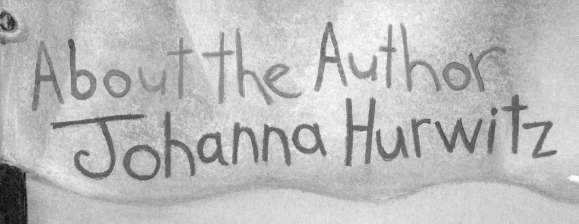

About the Author
Johanna Hurwitz

Johanna Hurwitz always knew that she wanted to be a writer. When she was young, she told stories to her younger brother and wrote stories in notebooks. When her parents told her she should also have a second career, she decided she would become a librarian, and she did. Johanna has worked as a librarian for more than thirty years and has written more than five dozen books. She enjoys writing realistic fiction for young readers. Johanna Hurwitz says she gets her ideas for books "partly from my own childhood, partly from my children, and from watching the children at the library."

About the Illustrator Mary GrandPré

Mary GrandPré has been drawing since she was five. As a child, she drew pictures of the photos in her encyclopedia. During her adult career as an artist, Mary GrandPré has created illustrations for children's books, films, ads, and magazines. She lives in Sarasota, Florida, with her husband, her dogs, Charlie and Chopper, and her cat, Jasper Cumulonimbus Cloud. She says, "Children are my favorite artists."

GO online www.harcourtschool.com/storytown

43

Language Arts

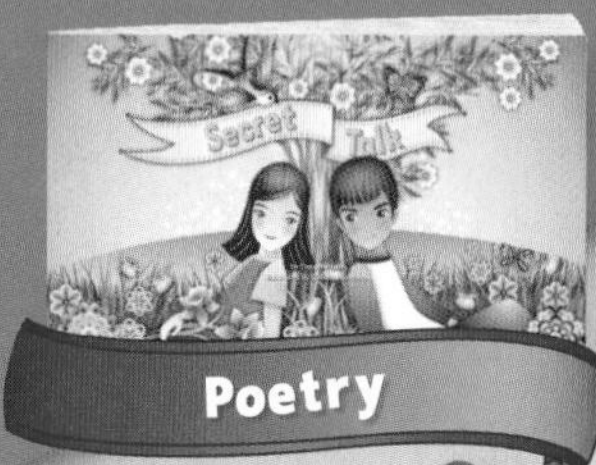

Secret

by Eve Merriam
illustrated by Catalina Estrada

I have a friend
and sometimes we meet
and greet each other
without a word.

We walk through a field
and stalk a bird
and chew a blade of
pungent grass.

Talk

We let time pass
for a golden hour
while we twirl a flower
of Queen Anne's lace
or find a lion's face
shaped in a cloud
that's drifting, sifting
across the sky.

There's no need to say,
"It's been a fine day"
when we say goodbye:
when we say goodbye
we just wave a hand
and we understand.

Connections

Comparing Texts

1. What can Rory and Derek's contest teach you about being boastful?

2. Compare the friendships in "The Hot and Cold Summer" with the friendship in "Secret Talk."

3. What is one lesson that "The Hot and Cold Summer" teaches about friendship?

Vocabulary Review

Rate a Situation

Work with a partner. Take turns reading aloud each sentence and pointing to the spot on the word line that shows how happy or unhappy you would feel.

Unhappy ——————————————— Happy
- You and a friend made a **pact** to stick together.
- You just had a great idea for a business **venture**.
- A challenging task was **foisted** on you.
- Your favorite relative became **annoyed** at you.

pact

queasy

foisted

venture

annoyed

depriving

Fluency Practice

Partner Reading

When you read with accuracy, you read each word correctly. Work with a partner. Choose a paragraph from "The Hot and Cold Summer." Read it aloud as your partner follows along. Ask your partner if you skipped any words or read words incorrectly. Then switch roles. Reread the paragraph until you can read it with complete accuracy.

Writing

Write About Characters

Write a paragraph about two friends who have a contest. Include details about why the characters have the contest and what each character says and does.

Characters:	
Traits:	
Motivations:	
Actions:	

My Writing Checklist

Writing Trait ▷ Voice

✔ I used a graphic organizer to plan my writing.

✔ I described each character's traits, motivations, and actions.

✔ I included vivid words to express my personal voice.

Analyze Writer's Craft: Narrative

A **narrative** is a story. It includes **characters**, a **setting**, and an **event** or series of events. When you write narratives, you can use the works of authors such as Johanna Hurwitz as writing models. Read the passage below from "The Hot and Cold Summer," and note how the author used **voice** and **word choice**. Look for ways to improve your own writing.

Writing Trait

VOICE
The author uses a kind **voice** to describe Rory. Phrases such as *his poor toes* express the author's positive feelings toward the character.

Writing Trait

WORD CHOICE
The author uses **vivid words** such as *queasy* to describe the character's strong feelings.

Rory sat on a lounge chair in his backyard, hurting in two places. His poor toes hurt him because he had forgotten and stepped down hard on them a few minutes ago. The other hurt was in the pit of his stomach. It wasn't a stomachache exactly. It was the queasy feeling he had before an arithmetic test. But that was silly because it was still summer vacation and Rory didn't have to worry about arithmetic tests for weeks. What he was worrying about was that Derek would be returning home in a few minutes.

Personal Narrative

In a **personal narrative**, a writer tells about an experience in his or her life, and his or her feelings before, during, and after the experience. As you read this personal narrative written by Akina, notice the humor and honesty in the writer's **voice.**

Student Writing Model

From the City to the Farm
by Akina H.

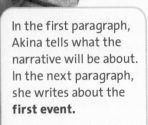

I had my summer all planned out. I was going to enjoy the city. I would play baseball with my friends, go swimming at the public pool, and visit the zoo. It was a perfect plan, right? Wrong! My parents had a different idea. They said I would be going to my grandparents' farm for a whole month. I was so upset I almost fainted. What could possibly be fun to do in the country?

When we arrived at the farm, it was so hot I thought I'd melt! Grandpa took me to a shady creek and showed me a wide place that formed a pool. He called it the "old swimming hole." It felt great to jump into the cool, clear water. I began to think the country wasn't so bad, after all.

49

The next day, Grandma gave me a bucket and sent me out to pick blackberries. I'd never picked wild berries before. The berries were so good that a lot of them disappeared before they reached my bucket. Back at the house, I helped Grandma make blackberry jam. Later, I picked huge sweet peaches from a tree in the yard. Grandma taught me how to make a fantastic peach pie!

I didn't get to visit a zoo, but I got an up-close look at pigs, goats, cows, and chickens. I fed the goats, milked the cows, and collected fresh eggs. I even saw a red fox running through the vegetable garden!

My summer wasn't what I had expected. I was prepared to hate farm life, but I loved it! I was sad that I had to leave. I learned so many new things. Now I know where to swim, how to tell when fruit is ripe, and how to take care of animals. I still love living in the city, but I learned that trying new things can be a lot of fun, too.

Now look at what Akina did to prepare to write her personal narrative.

Brainstorming

Akina asked questions to identify the characters, setting, and events in her narrative. Then she asked questions about how she felt before, during, and after visiting the farm.

> **Who are the characters?**
> me and my mother, father, and grandparents
>
> **What is the setting?**
> Grandma and Grandpa's farm
>
> **What events do I remember?**
> • took care of farm animals
> • went swimming at the creek
> • picked fruit, made jams, made pies
>
> **How did I feel before, during, and after?**
> At first I hated the idea of going to the farm. Then I loved being there. Afterward I was sad to leave.

Planning the Narrative

Akina used a sequence chart to organize her narrative. She decided what to include in her opening and closing paragraphs, and she listed the events of her narrative in order.

> **BEGINNING**
> my plans for the summer, my parents' plans
> I didn't want to go.

> **MIDDLE**
> 1. My parents drove me to the country.
>   I went swimming on the first day.
> 2. I picked fruit and learned to make jam.
> 3. I took care of animals.

> **END**
> I was sad that I had to leave but glad that I learned so much. I didn't want to leave.

CONTENTS

Lesson 2

Genre: Biography

MIGHTY JACKIE

THE STRIKE-OUT QUEEN

By Marissa Moss   Illustrated by C

The New Kid

by Mike Makley

illustrated by Kirsten Ulve

Genre: Poetry

Focus Skill

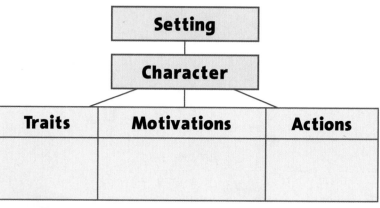 **Character's Traits and Motivations**

You have learned that thinking about a character's **traits** and **motivations** can help you figure out why that character takes certain actions. The **setting** of a story tells when and where it takes place. Sometimes a story's setting or situation affects a character's actions. For example, a warm, sunny day might cause a character to play outside.

Setting		
Character		
Traits	**Motivations**	**Actions**

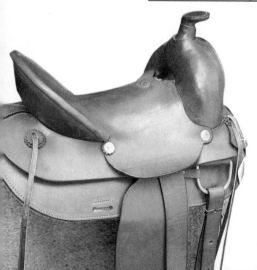

Tip

As you read, pay attention to the story setting and to a character's words, thoughts, and actions.

Read the paragraph below. Then look at the graphic organizer. It shows how the character's actions can be affected by the setting and by her traits and motivations.

Amy's older brother would frown when Amy saddled her pony and galloped off into the hills. "That is not fitting behavior for a girl," Jack would say. In the 1870s, girls were expected to sew and cook. Jack's comments made Amy even more determined to live her life in her own way. Besides, she loved the everyday work of a cattle ranch. By the time Amy was fifteen, she could ride and rope as well as any cowhand on the ranch—including her brother.

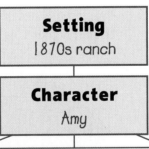

Setting
1870s ranch

Character
Amy

Traits	Motivations	Actions
determined, independent, strong-willed	Amy loves the work on a cattle ranch. She wants to live her life her own way.	Amy learns to ride and rope very well.

Try This!

Read the paragraph again. How does the setting affect Amy's thoughts and actions?

Vocabulary

Build Robust Vocabulary

glared

legendary

muttered

gaped

flinched

fluke

snickering

stunned

Table Tennis Shake-Up

Walter gripped his paddle and **glared** at his opponent. On the other side of the wide green table stood Rodney, **legendary** in the table tennis club for his great serves.

"You're going to get a surprise," Walter **muttered** under his breath. He had been taking lessons from his friend Mike's dad and knew that his playing had improved a lot recently.

Rodney served first, putting a lot of spin on the ball. Walter solidly returned the serve. Rodney, not expecting it to come back, **gaped** at the ball as it bounced and flew past his ear.

On the next serve, Walter lost sight of the ball and missed. He **flinched** when the ball hit his arm, wondering if his first successful shot had just been a **fluke**. Then he looked over at Rodney, who was **snickering** quietly about the miss, and Walter's determination grew.

Both boys played well, but Walter had an edge. After many hard volleys and many shots won and lost, Walter won the game. **Stunned** by the results, Rodney shook Walter's hand, and both players sat down to rest.

GO
online   www.harcourtschool.com/storytown

Word Champion

Your challenge this week is to use the Vocabulary Words outside your classroom. Keep the list of words in a place at home where you can see it. Use as many of the words as you can when you speak with family members and friends. For example, you might ask your sister why she is snickering. At the end of each day, write in your vocabulary journal the sentences you spoke that contained the words.

Award Winner

MIGHTY JACKIE
THE STRIKE-OUT QUEEN

Jackie Mitchell

by Marissa Moss Illustrated by C. F. Payne

Biography

Genre Study

A biography tells about a person's life and is written by another person. As you read, look for

- opinions and personal judgments based on facts.

- information about why the person is important.

Setting:		
Character:		
Traits	Motivations	Actions

Comprehension Strategy

Use story structure to help you understand the characters, setting, and plot events in a story.

MIGHTY JACKIE
The Strike-Out Queen

by Marissa Moss ◆ illustrated by C.F. Payne

It was April 2, 1931, and something amazing was about to happen. In Chattanooga, Tennessee, two teams were about to play an exhibition game of baseball.

One was the New York Yankees, a legendary team with famous players—Babe Ruth, Lou Gehrig, and Tony Lazzeri.

The other was the Chattanooga Lookouts, a small team, a nothing team, except for the pitcher, Jackie Mitchell.

Jackie was young, only seventeen years old, but that's not what made people sit up and take notice. Jackie was a girl, and everyone knew that girls didn't play major-league baseball.

The *New York Daily News* sneered that she would swing "a mean lipstick" instead of a bat. A reporter wrote that you might as well have "a trained seal behind the plate" as have a woman standing there. But Jackie was no trained seal. She was a pitcher, a mighty good one. The question was, was she good enough to play against the New York Yankees?

As long as she could remember, Jackie had played ball with her father. She knew girls weren't supposed to. All the kids at school, all the boys in her neighborhood told her that. When one boy yelled at another one, "You throw like a girl!" it was an insult—everyone knew girls couldn't throw. Or that's what they thought.

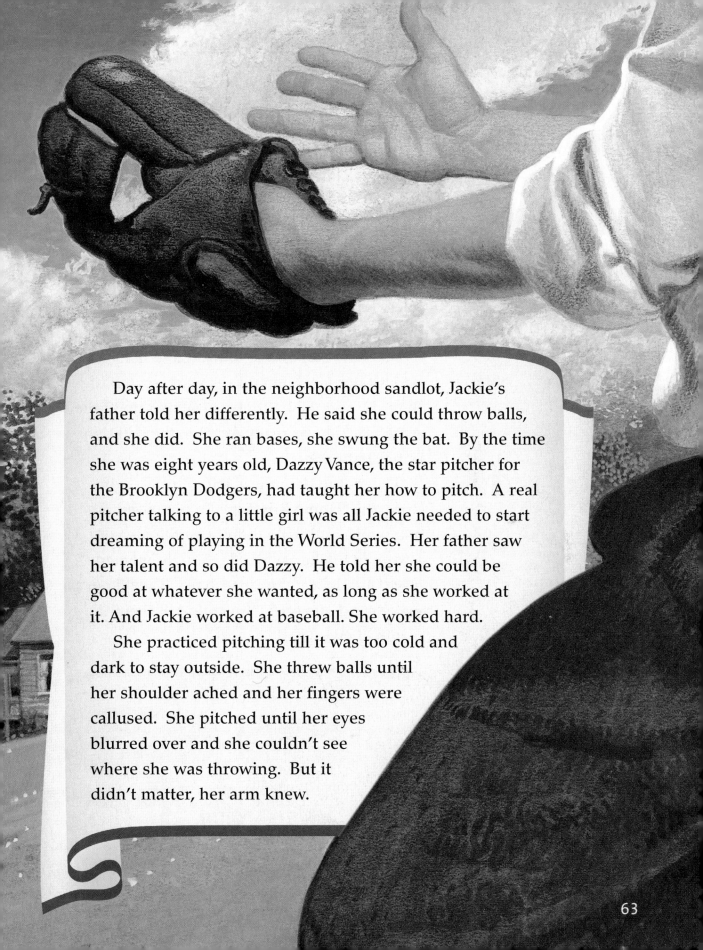

Day after day, in the neighborhood sandlot, Jackie's father told her differently. He said she could throw balls, and she did. She ran bases, she swung the bat. By the time she was eight years old, Dazzy Vance, the star pitcher for the Brooklyn Dodgers, had taught her how to pitch. A real pitcher talking to a little girl was all Jackie needed to start dreaming of playing in the World Series. Her father saw her talent and so did Dazzy. He told her she could be good at whatever she wanted, as long as she worked at it. And Jackie worked at baseball. She worked hard.

She practiced pitching till it was too cold and dark to stay outside. She threw balls until her shoulder ached and her fingers were callused. She pitched until her eyes blurred over and she couldn't see where she was throwing. But it didn't matter, her arm knew.

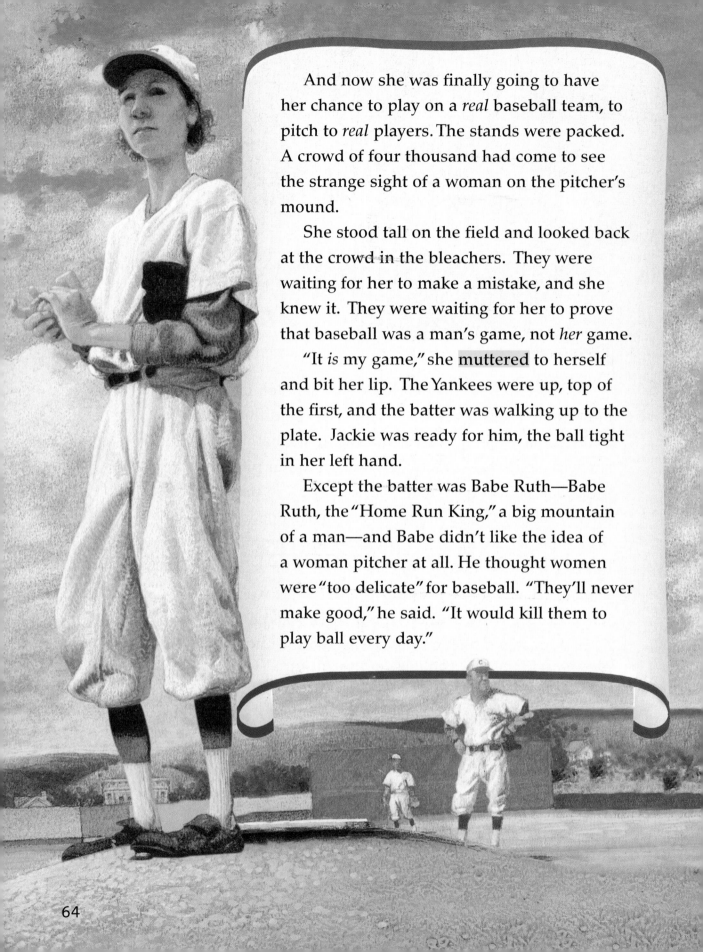

And now she was finally going to have her chance to play on a *real* baseball team, to pitch to *real* players. The stands were packed. A crowd of four thousand had come to see the strange sight of a woman on the pitcher's mound.

She stood tall on the field and looked back at the crowd in the bleachers. They were waiting for her to make a mistake, and she knew it. They were waiting for her to prove that baseball was a man's game, not *her* game.

"It *is* my game," she muttered to herself and bit her lip. The Yankees were up, top of the first, and the batter was walking up to the plate. Jackie was ready for him, the ball tight in her left hand.

Except the batter was Babe Ruth—Babe Ruth, the "Home Run King," a big mountain of a man—and Babe didn't like the idea of a woman pitcher at all. He thought women were "too delicate" for baseball. "They'll never make good," he said. "It would kill them to play ball every day."

He walked to the plate and tipped his cap at Jackie. But if she thought he was going to go easy on her, she could forget it! He gripped the bat and got ready to slam the ball out of the ballpark.

Jackie held that ball like it was part of her arm, and when she threw it, she knew exactly where it would go. Right over the plate, right where the Babe wasn't expecting it, right where he watched it speed by and *thwunk* into the catcher's mitt.

"STRRRRIKE ONE!"

Babe Ruth gaped—he couldn't believe it! The crowd roared. Jackie tried to block them out, to see only the ball, to feel only the ball. But Babe Ruth was facing her down now,

determined not to let a girl make a fool out of him. She flinched right before the next pitch, and the umpire called a ball.

"Hmmmph," the Babe snorted.

"You can do it!" Jackie told herself. "Girls can throw—show them!"

But the next pitch was another ball.

Now the crowd was hooting and jeering. The Babe was snickering with them.

Jackie closed her eyes. She felt her fingers tingling around the ball, she felt its heft in her palm, she felt the force of her shoulder muscles as she wound up for the pitch. She remembered what her father had told her: "Go out there and pitch just like you pitch to anybody else."

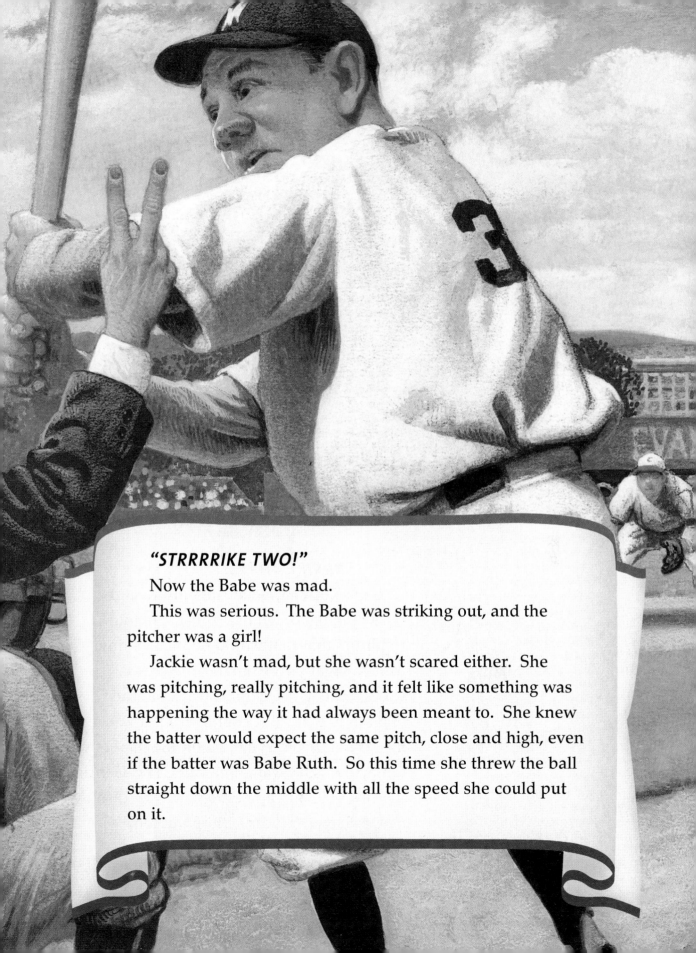

"STRRRRIKE TWO!"

Now the Babe was mad.

This was serious. The Babe was striking out, and the pitcher was a girl!

Jackie wasn't mad, but she wasn't scared either. She was pitching, really pitching, and it felt like something was happening the way it had always been meant to. She knew the batter would expect the same pitch, close and high, even if the batter was Babe Ruth. So this time she threw the ball straight down the middle with all the speed she could put on it.

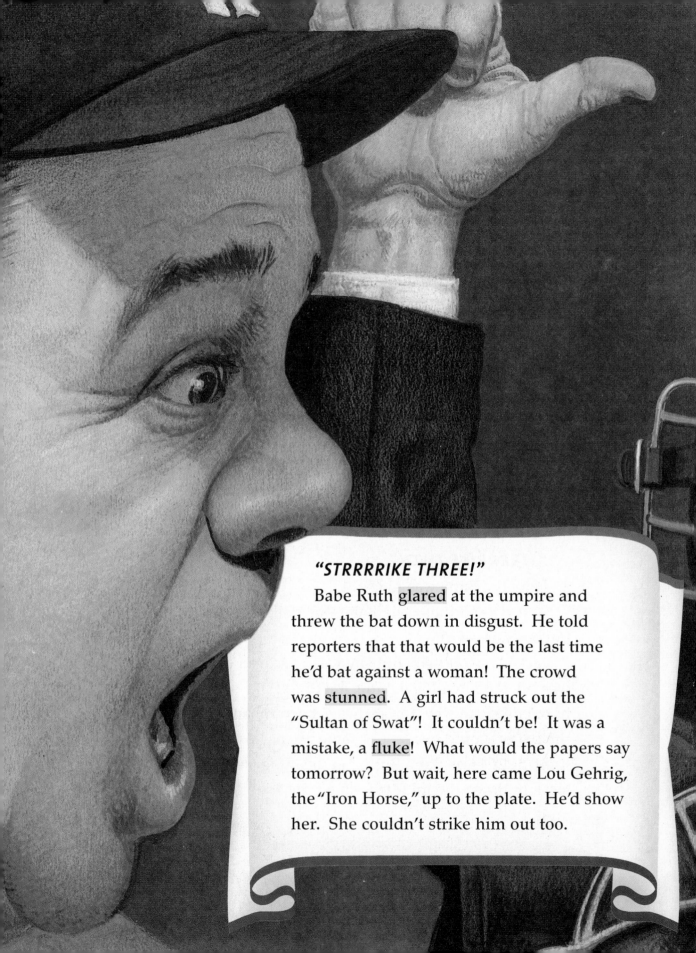

"STRRRRIKE THREE!"

Babe Ruth glared at the umpire and threw the bat down in disgust. He told reporters that that would be the last time he'd bat against a woman! The crowd was stunned. A girl had struck out the "Sultan of Swat"! It couldn't be! It was a mistake, a fluke! What would the papers say tomorrow? But wait, here came Lou Gehrig, the "Iron Horse," up to the plate. He'd show her. She couldn't strike him out too.

Lou Gehrig swung with a mighty grunt, but his bat hit nothing but air.

"STRRRRIKE ONE!"

He looked stunned, then dug in his heels and glared at Jackie.

"STRRRRIKE TWO!"

Jackie grinned. She was doing what she'd worked so hard and long to do, and nothing could stop her.

She pitched the ball the way she knew best, a lefty pitch with a low dip in it. No one could touch a ball like that when it was thrown right.

"STRRRRIKE THREE!"

The crowd, so ready to boo her before, rose with a roar, clapping and cheering like crazy. Back to back, Jackie had struck out two of baseball's best batters, Babe Ruth and Lou Gehrig. She'd proven herself and now the fans loved her for it.

But Jackie didn't hear them. She was too proud and too happy. She'd done what she'd always known she could do. She'd shown the world how a girl could throw—as hard and as fast and as far as she wanted.

THINK CRITICALLY

1 How did Jackie Mitchell become a talented pitcher? NOTE DETAILS

2 How does the author show Jackie's personality? What were her motives for playing against the Yankees? CHARACTER'S TRAITS AND MOTIVATIONS

3 Why do you think the fans' feelings about Jackie changed during the course of the game? DRAW CONCLUSIONS

4 Do you think Jackie Mitchell was a brave person? Tell why you think as you do. PERSONAL RESPONSE

5 **WRITE** Jackie Mitchell made history when she pitched against the New York Yankees. Use information and details from the selection to explain:
- how she felt before the game against the Yankees, and
- how she felt during and after the game.

EXTENDED RESPONSE

MARISSA MOSS

As a child, Marissa Moss was constantly making up stories and drawing pictures to go along with them. She says she loved the way that stories allowed her to make things happen the way she wanted them to. She began her career as a picture-book illustrator and then started writing as well. She says that when she painted, "What kept coming out were humorous watercolors that were stories in themselves. I realized I was making single-page children's books and that I wanted to tell stories."

C.F. PAYNE

C.F. Payne says that he wants his drawings to capture the personality and emotion of each character in a story. His art appears regularly in magazines and other publications. He has also created five stamps for the U.S. Postal Service and painted a hundred-foot-long mural for a theater.

C.F. Payne also teaches at colleges and universities. He lives with his family in Cincinnati, Ohio.

www.harcourtschool.com/storytown

73

The New Kid

by Mike Makley

illustrated by Kirsten Ulve

Our baseball team never did very much,
we had me and PeeWee and Earl and Dutch.
And the Oak Street Tigers always got beat
until the new kid moved in on our street.

The kid moved in with a mitt and a bat
and an official New York Yankee hat.
The new kid plays shortstop or second base
and can outrun us all in any place.

The kid never muffs a grounder or fly
no matter how hard it's hit or how high.
And the new kid always acts quite polite,
never yelling or spitting or starting a fight.

We were playing the league champs just last week;
they were trying to break our winning streak.
In the last inning the score was one-one,
when the new kid swung and hit a home run.

A few of the kids and their parents say
they don't believe that the new kid should play.
But she's good as me, Dutch, PeeWee, or Earl,
so we don't care that the new kid's a girl.

Connections

Comparing Texts

1. Jackie Mitchell struck out two baseball legends. If you could have a chance to triumph over an expert, who would it be and what would you do?

2. Compare the girl in "The New Kid" with Jackie Mitchell in "Mighty Jackie: The Strike-Out Queen."

3. In Jackie Mitchell's day, people did not think women should play professional sports. How has this attitude changed?

Vocabulary Review

She gaped at me, stunned at my question.

Word Pairs

Work with a partner. Write the Vocabulary Words on separate index cards. Place the cards face down. Take turns flipping over two cards and writing a sentence that uses both words. Read the sentence aloud to your partner. If you use the words correctly in the sentence, keep the cards. The student with the most cards at the end wins.

legendary

muttered

gaped

flinched

snickering

glared

stunned

fluke

Fluency Practice

Partner Reading

Work with a partner. Choose two paragraphs from "Mighty Jackie: The Strike-Out Queen." Read the two paragraphs aloud to your partner as he or she follows along. Then listen and follow along as your partner reads aloud. Give each other feedback about accuracy by pointing out missed or misread words. Reread the paragraphs until you can read them with complete accuracy.

Writing

Write a Newspaper Feature

Imagine that you have just met Jackie Mitchell after watching her strike out Babe Ruth and Lou Gehrig. Write a short newspaper feature describing Jackie's amazing feat.

Who? Jackie Mitchell
What?
Where?
When?
Why?
How?

My Writing Checklist

Writing Trait ▷ Voice

✓ I answered the questions Who? What? Where? When? Why? and How?

✓ I organized my information in a chart.

✓ I restated the information in my own words.

CONTENTS

Genre: Narrative Poetry

DANITRA BROWN
LEAVES TOWN

Nikki Grimes
illustrated by
Floyd Cooper

Summertime
Star
Parties
by Noreen Grice

Genre: Expository Nonfiction

Compare and Contrast

When you **compare** two or more things, you tell how they are alike. When you **contrast** two or more things, you tell how they are different. Comparing the people, places, or things in a story can help you understand what you are reading.

BOTH

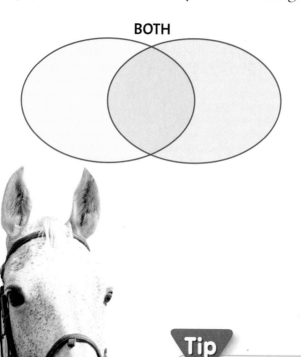

Tip

A Venn diagram helps you compare and contrast two things. Write differences in the outer parts of the circles. Write how the two things are alike in the middle.

Read the paragraph below. Then look at the Venn diagram. It shows how the two sisters described in the paragraph are alike and how they are different.

My sister Kate is taller than I am, even though she is a year younger. Kate has dark hair, while I have light hair. Also, my sister makes friends easily, but I am shy. When we meet new people, I sit quietly until I'm used to the new faces. Kate, however, starts making friends right away. People might not guess that we're sisters—until they hear us talk! Our voices sound exactly alike. We even have the same giggle!

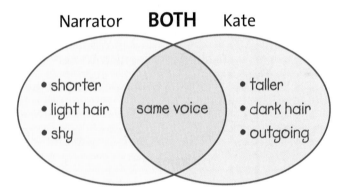

Narrator   **BOTH**   Kate

- shorter
- light hair
- shy

same voice

- taller
- dark hair
- outgoing

Try This!

Reread the paragraph. Find another way the sisters are alike and another way they are different. Add this information to the Venn diagram.

Go online   www.harcourtschool.com/storytown

Vocabulary

Build Robust Vocabulary

- stroll
- sizzles
- particular
- clusters
- surrender
- sparkling

Eggs the Hard Way

It was Saturday morning. Eva rubbed her eyes and read the note taped to her mirror. It said, "Eva, I've gone for a **stroll** and will be back soon. There are eggs in the fridge for breakfast. Use the microwave to heat them. Love, Mom."

Eva loved eggs for breakfast. She put on her slippers, went into the kitchen, and found the carton of eggs. She placed an egg on a plate, put it in the microwave, and set the timer for two minutes. "I suppose it will be done when it **sizzles** inside the shell," she thought.

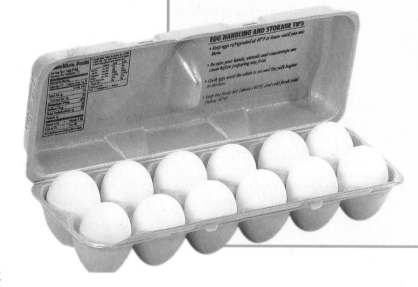

While the microwave hummed, Eva thought about her day. She had no **particular** plans. Suddenly she heard a loud pop. She ran to the microwave and opened it. **Clusters** of shiny egg white and bright yellow yolk stuck to every surface! Eva almost yelled out the door for her mother. Then she decided that she would not **surrender** her independence so easily.

Eva found some paper towels. Ten minutes later, the microwave was **sparkling**. As Eva opened the fridge to get out another egg, she noticed a plate of scrambled eggs covered with plastic wrap. "Aha!" she said to herself. "That's what Mom meant!"

 www.harcourtschool.com/storytown

Word Scribe

This week, your task is to use the Vocabulary Words in your writing. In your vocabulary journal, write sentences to show the meanings of the words. For example, you could write about a stroll you took with a friend. Use as many Vocabulary Words as you can. Share your writing with your classmates.

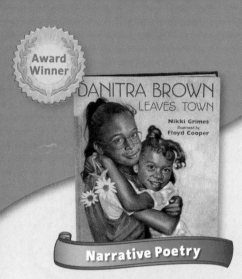

Award Winner

DANITRA BROWN
LEAVES TOWN

Nikki Grimes
Illustrated by
Floyd Cooper

Narrative Poetry

Genre Study

A narrative poem is a poem that tells a story. As you read, look for

- characters, a setting, and plot events.

- rhythm and rhyming words.

Characters	Setting

Plot Events

Comprehension Strategy

Answer questions you have about a story by looking in the text and thinking about what you already know.

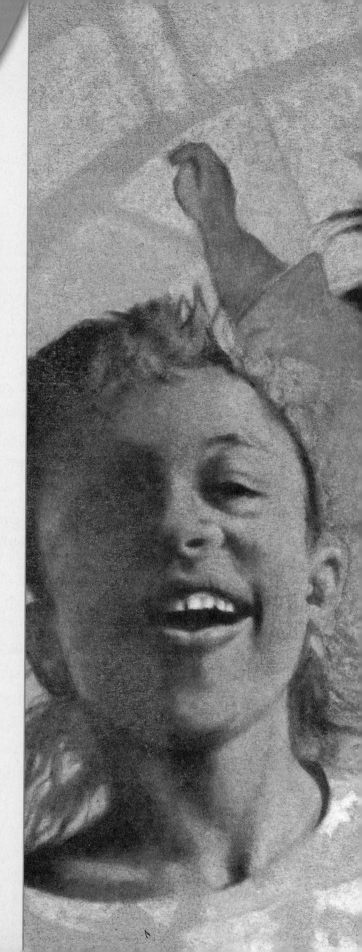

Danitra Brown Leaves Town

by Nikki Grimes

illustrated by Floyd Cooper

Big Plans

School is out soon
and Danitra's advice is:
surrender
to
summer,
to
raspberry ices
and
pink lemonade
and
walks on the beach
and
at least
one
trip to the zoo,
one
Ferris wheel ride,
one
family barbecue,
one
Sunday school picnic,
but
never a lick
of
homework to spoil
one
afternoon.

The Bad Good-bye

Danitra talked a blue streak
about her summer trip
all week.
And now that she is on her way,
she has the nerve to call and say
which station she is leaving from,
as though expecting me to come.

"I have better things to do," I blurt.
The phone is silent. Danitra's hurt.
But why am I supposed to care
when my supposed-to-be best friend
is leaving me, and loving it?

Noticing Nina

Summer insisted on starting
for no good reason that I could see.
I was alone, with nowhere particular to be.

One day Nina from the neighborhood
said she wondered if we could
play a little handball. I'm famous for the game,
but I never knew that Nina liked it too.

She and I spent hours slamming that ball
against the corner drugstore wall
wearing a hole in the bricks.

Later, we talked and laughed awhile,
and after we said good-bye, I wondered why
I'd never noticed Nina before.
Maybe the summer wouldn't be such a bore.

The Letter

I sat frowning by my window
when the mail truck came today
with a letter from Danitra
who is many miles away.

I said mean things when she left me.
I was so mad at her then.
Was she writing to forgive me,
or to say I'm not her friend?

I ripped Danitra's letter open,
in spite of my worst fear.
I bit my lip until I read
"I wish that you were here."

First Night

Dear Zuri,

I wish that you were here.
I camped out my first night
in my aunt's backyard.
Sleeping was hard
with all the sparkling beauty
hanging overhead.

Night-lights, Zuri, everywhere!
Clusters of fireflies
dancing 'round my head,
keeping me from bed
for hours.

And the sky! I've never seen one
so blue-black, like a thick overcoat
all buttoned up with stars.
At midnight, I stretched my arms out
to slip the darkness on,
and opened my eyes again
at dawn.

Block Party

Dear Danitra,

Tomorrow you're going to miss
those giant speakers
hissing and blasting
loud, fast music
into the crowded street.
There'll be no sense in my
trying to keep still.
You know how
that hot, hot dance beat
sizzles up through the concrete,
grabbing hold of my feet.
In a blink I become
a hip-swinging,
head-bobbing,
foot-stomping,
fancy-dancing
fool.

The Dare

Dear Zuri,

The kids here pretend to be tougher than they are.
I ignore it mostly, 'cause they're nice in their own way.
Besides, I think they may just be trying to impress the "city kid."

Today they dared me to climb up into a tree, and, of course, I did.
Then they yelled, "Okay, Miss Big-Town Brown, jump down."
Now, my mother taught me to use my head for more than a
hat rack.

So, I climbed back down and said, "A dare is fine with me,
but jumping from a tree is stupid, and I'm no fool."
Then I heard someone whisper, "She's pretty cool—
for a city girl."

Zuri at Bat

Dear Danitra,

At the softball game last week,
smart mouth J. T. snickered loud and said,
"What makes you think a puny girl like you can help us win?"
"Exactly where you been?" I asked him, stepping in.
When the pitch came, I slammed the ball so far,
it ripped through the clouds and headed for a star.
I strutted 'round the bases, took my own sweet time.
My new friend, Nina, laughed and bet J. T.
he couldn't hit a ball as far as me.
He can't, and that's a fact.

A Different Danitra

Dear Zuri,

You'd probably laugh
if you saw me now.
I'm not exactly behind a plow,
but still—here I am, in the dirt
on hands and knees,
yanking weeds,
watering roses,
dodging man-eating wasps
and one stubborn dragonfly,
who I'm convinced
wants me for lunch.
I have a hunch
you'd like it here.

Zuri's Fourth of July

We had the day
all to ourselves,
to search for seashells
on the beach.
To eat corn dogs
and candied apples.
To stroll awhile and talk
and skip along the boardwalk—
just Mom and me.
Seeing my mom skip
was worth the stuffy subway trip
it took to get there.

The holiday
seemed barely
long enough
to measure,
but I loved spending the day
with my mom next to me,
the pretty brownness
of her eyes and face
glistening in the light
of the late-night
fireworks.

Danitra's Family Reunion

On the Fourth of July,
my cousins and I
ran sack races,
played kickball
and tug-of-war
before
we heard
our stomachs
growl.

We stopped for
deviled eggs,
buttered corn,
coleslaw,
fried chicken,
potato salad, and
Strawberry Pie Jubilee.

We sipped lemonade
and listened to
Grandma Brown's stories
of when our folks were little.
Then Uncle Joe
handed out prizes
for this year's graduates
and for the best all-round student,
which I won.

By the time
the day was done,
I was full of fun
and food
and warm feelings,
knowing that I am more
than just me.
I am part
of a family.

Dream Places

Dear Danitra,

Since you left,
I've put a map on my bedroom wall.
I stick gold stars on all the places
I'll travel to someday:
Zaire, Hong Kong, Bombay.
I find each city in my geography book,
look up the facts and figures,
and write them down in the diary
I keep beside my bed. I lay my head
back on the pillow, close my eyes,
and see myself, a little older,
walking down an African street,
soaking in the heat of the sun.

Home Again

A good hello
is knowing
when we're far apart,
at heart
we're still together,
and being glad
you're home again
'cause that is ten times better.

Think Critically

1. Compare and contrast the way Danitra and Zuri spend their summer. **COMPARE AND CONTRAST**

2. How does Zuri feel before she reads Danitra's first letter? How does she feel after she reads it? **CHARACTER'S EMOTIONS**

3. Do you think Danitra and Zuri will stay friends if one of the girls moves to a new city? Explain. **PERSONAL RESPONSE**

4. The author uses many rhyming words to tell the story of Danitra and Zuri. How would the story be different if it had no rhyming words? **AUTHOR'S CRAFT**

5. **WRITE** Explain what Zuri learns about friendship while Danitra is away. Use details from the story to support your answer. **SHORT RESPONSE**

About the Author
Nikki Grimes

Nikki Grimes has written books and poetry about African American characters that many people can identify with. As a child, she dreamed of writing books about children like herself. Nikki Grimes began her writing career by writing poetry. She says that the challenge of painting a picture or telling a story in only a few words fascinated her. Nikki Grimes writes about things she knows—her feelings, fears, and dreams that have filled her imagination.

About the Illustrator
Floyd Cooper

Floyd Cooper drew his first picture
when he was only three. It was a huge
duck drawn on a wall in his family's
house—and it stayed on the wall, despite
many washings. Floyd Cooper studied
fine arts in Oklahoma and started his
artistic career illustrating ads and greeting
cards. After moving to New York City, he
discovered the world of children's book
illustration. He says that when he begins
to illustrate a children's book, he is drawn
into the story. He says, "I want to bring
the viewer along with me and feel the
story in the same way that I feel it when
I read the story."

 www.harcourtschool.com/storytown

Expository Nonfiction

Summertime Star Parties

by Noreen Grice

The summer months are a great time to introduce yourself to the wonders of the night sky. Plan to attend an organized star party offered by an astronomy club. You can even plan your own party! Star parties are often held at schools, in parks, and even in backyards. Check with your local planetarium or astronomy club for upcoming events.

Organized star parties are a great way to see the moon and planets. You'll meet amateur astronomers with telescopes pointed at different targets. They are usually very excited about astronomy. Many are even willing to offer you a view through their scopes. In some cases, they have built the telescopes they are using.

You'll find that some people prefer to observe the sky through binoculars. Some mount their binoculars on a tripod. Others just hold and point them at the sky. Compare a view of the moon through binoculars and a telescope. Which view do you like best?

If you can't find a star party near you, organize your own. If you don't own a telescope or binoculars, that's okay. You can see objects such as constellations and planets. A star party makes a great ending to a family outing on a clear night. The sky is your personal planetarium. Let the show begin!

Here are a few activities you might enjoy.

- Pass around empty paper towel tubes. Ask your audience to look at different parts of the sky through a tube. It won't magnify, but it will offer a new, interesting view.

- Check out different areas of the sky. Count the stars you see. What is the most crowded part of the sky? It's the Milky Way, the plane of our galaxy! Can your audience find it?

There is a lot of sky to share, so enjoy your star party!

Connections

Comparing Texts

1. Describe how you would feel if your best friend went away for the summer.

2. Compare "Danitra Brown Leaves Town" with "Summertime Star Parties." What ideas about summer do you get from both selections?

3. In what ways do Danitra and Zuri act as friends do in real life?

Vocabulary Review

Word Webs

Work with a small group. Take turns choosing one Vocabulary Word from the list and writing it in the center of a web. In the outer circles, write words and phrases that are related to the word. Explain your choices.

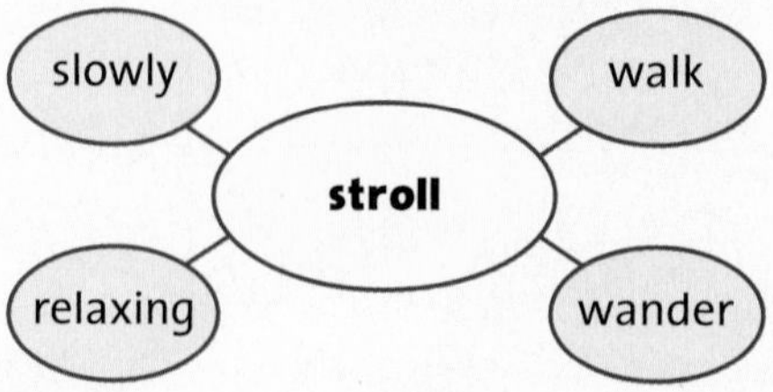

surrender

particular

sparkling

clusters

sizzles

stroll

slowly   walk

stroll

relaxing   wander

Fluency Practice

Partner Reading

Your reading rate is how quickly you are able to read a text correctly. Work with a partner. Choose one of the poems in "Danitra Brown Leaves Town" to reread aloud. Read the text as your partner listens. Have your partner use a wall clock to time your reading and to give you feedback on your accuracy. Then switch roles. Repeat the activity several times to increase your reading rate.

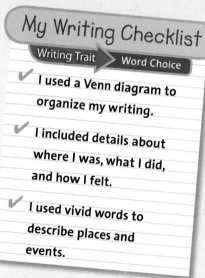

Writing

Write a Poem

Think about two activities you did last summer. Then write a poem that compares and contrasts the activities. Share your poem with the class.

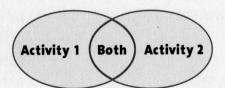

Activity 1 | Both | Activity 2

My Writing Checklist

Writing Trait ▶ Word Choice

✔ I used a Venn diagram to organize my writing.

✔ I included details about where I was, what I did, and how I felt.

✔ I used vivid words to describe places and events.

CONTENTS

Lesson 4

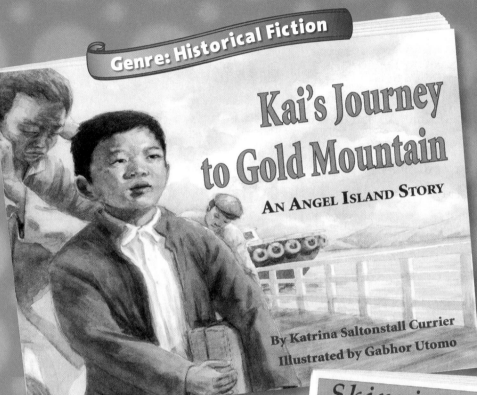

Kai's Journey to Gold Mountain

AN ANGEL ISLAND STORY

By Katrina Saltonstall Currier

Illustrated by Gabhor Utomo

Skipping Stones

Vol. 12, No. 5   A Multicultural Magazine

Nov. – Dec. 2000
US: $4.75; CAN: $5.75

Traditions • Celebrations

Focus Skill

 ## Compare and Contrast

You have learned that to **compare** is to tell how two or more things are alike. To **contrast** is to tell how they are different. Authors sometimes organize the ideas in their stories to show how two or more people, places, or things are alike and different.

BOTH

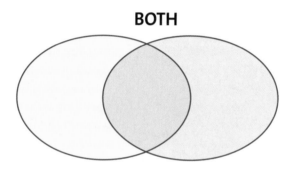

Tip

Words such as *and*, *also*, and *too* signal a comparison. Words such as *although*, *while*, and *but* signal a contrast.

Read the story below. Then look at the Venn diagram. It shows the differences between campfire pancakes and pancakes made at home. The space where the circles overlap shows what both kinds of pancakes have in common.

Kenji looked down at the tin plate he was holding. The three black discs piled up in a neat stack were pancakes that Dad had cooked over the campfire. Their smoky smell wasn't bad. It was just different from the sweet smell of the golden pancakes Dad made on the stove at home.

Kenji bit into a crunchy pancake. It tasted good. It just didn't taste like the soft, fluffy pancakes at home. Kenji wondered how pancakes that had the same ingredients could turn out so differently.

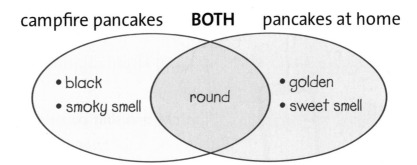

campfire pancakes   **BOTH**   pancakes at home

- black
- smoky smell

round

- golden
- sweet smell

Try This!

Look back at the story. Find another way the pancakes are alike and another way they are different. Where would you put these details in the diagram?

GO online   www.harcourtschool.com/storytown

Vocabulary

- solemnly
- accusing
- interrogation
- averted
- stern
- fury
- cringed
- craned

Last-Minute Scare

Chris's family had been planning this trip for months. At last, it was time to leave. Dad **solemnly** checked the travel folder one last time. "All right," he mumbled. "Traveler's checks . . . passports. . . ." Then he paused. "Where are the tickets?"

"I didn't take them!" Chris blurted out.

"I'm not **accusing** you, son," Dad said. "This is not an **interrogation**. We do need to find our tickets, however."

Chris **averted** his gaze. He hadn't meant to be rude. "The leather case they were in was in the kitchen. I saw it just before I let Max out."

Dad's look grew suddenly **stern**. "Where is that dog?" he demanded. Chewing and digging were Max's favorite activities. Dad and Chris bolted out the door and into the yard. Max was digging with a **fury**.

"Max, no!" Chris shouted. Max stopped digging. Chris **cringed** as they approached the hole. He dropped to his knees beside it. Chris **craned** his neck to see what Max had buried. Stirring through the dirt, he uncovered the case that held the tickets. "Found it!" he yelled.

 www.harcourtschool.com/storytown

Word Detective

Your goal this week is to look for the Vocabulary Words outside the classroom. You may find them in a book you are reading or in a newspaper. Each time you see a Vocabulary Word, write it in your vocabulary journal. Write down where you found each word.

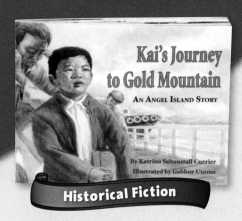

Kai's Journey to Gold Mountain
AN ANGEL ISLAND STORY

By Katrina Saltonstall Currier
Illustrated by Gabhor Utomo

Genre Study

Historical fiction is set in the past and portrays people, places, and events that did happen or could have happened. As you read, look for

- a setting that is a real time and a real place in the past.

- realistic characters and events.

Characters	Setting

Plot Events

Comprehension Strategy

Think about what you know to help you **answer questions** about what you read.

KAI'S JOURNEY TO GOLD MOUNTAIN

by Katrina Saltonstall Currier

illustrated by Gabhor Utomo

It's 1934. Twelve-year-old Kai is traveling alone by steamship from his home in China to Gold Mountain—the Chinese name for the United States. Kai's father is in San Francisco and has sent for him by letter. Only the sons of United States residents may immigrate to the United States from China. An immigrant must answer many questions to prove his father is a resident. Kai worries about answering the questions correctly. While on the steamship, Kai meets Young, a boy his age. When they arrive in San Francisco, Kai and the other Chinese immigrants are escorted by guards, or *luk yi*, to Angel Island. After a long night, Kai faces his first day in this strange, new place.

Kai awoke with a start to a bellowing gong. Bunks squeaked and men sighed as they climbed down and pulled on their baggy trousers. Kai shivered in the morning's chill and damp. He tried not to disturb the old man below him as he stepped over him and made his way into the crowd flocking towards what, he hoped, was the place to eat. He saw Young in line and nudged his way forward so that they were standing shoulder to shoulder. Dark circles hung beneath Young's eyes.

The mess hall was a large room lined with long tables. As they took their seats, servers slammed down big bowls of rice porridge on each table. Starving, Kai dug in quickly. But it was watery and lukewarm—no better than the food on the ship. Kai forced it down, bite by bite, only by focusing on the memory of Mother's thick, steamy rice porridge. Utensils clanged against bowls, and the older men chattered, but Kai and Young ate quietly. They averted their eyes from the *luk yi* patrolling the aisles.

When Kai returned to the barracks after breakfast he noticed sunlight pouring through the door in the wall next to his bunk. He dashed over to it, hoping to take a walk and explore his new surroundings, free from the watchful eyes of the men in green. Instead he found only a small yard enclosed by a high, metal fence topped with sharp, pointy wire. A few older boys pushed past him and ran into the yard tossing a ball to each other. Kai called Young, and together they watched the game all morning. "They're trying to throw the ball into that basket on a pole," Young observed.

"Yes, and the other boys are blocking them. I am not tall like that basket, but I have good aim. And you are quick. We must learn this new game, Young," vowed Kai.

One day melted slowly into another on the island. Every night when Kai went to sleep he assured himself that he wouldn't be here much longer. He couldn't be. Every morning he awoke to the echoing gong. He ate breakfast. He learned to play basketball. More soggy rice with overcooked vegetables for lunch. Card games or *mah jong* all afternoon. Soggy rice with leftover vegetables for dinner. Lights out by 9:00. Scratchy phonographs of Chinese opera as he fell asleep. Day after day after day. This was not the life Kai had expected to find in Gold Mountain.

Kai wondered when his turn would come to be questioned by the immigration officers. After all, wasn't that why he was here? His father must be worried about him, but Kai had no way to contact him.

On some days the *luk yi* entered the barracks and called a name followed by the words *"ho sai gai."* Whoops and cheers told Kai that someone had been released to land in San Francisco. On other days Kai watched the *luk yi* lead out men whose eyes flashed with the fury of caged tigers. Kai suspected that these men were being sent back to China.

夜靜微聞風嘯聲，
形影傷情見景詠。
雲霧漠漠也暗天，
蟲聲唧唧月微明，
天芳相連天相遠。

The mood of the barracks rose and fell with each day's news. The Chinese men in this room, though strangers, all shared the dream of reaching *Gum San*. For Kai, the worst part was the endless waiting. The man in the bunk below him had been on the island for twelve weeks, Kai learned. His graying head hung lower every day, and he rarely left his bunk.

One night Kai tossed and turned to the sounds of wind whistling through the bars outside his moonlit window. He awoke with a start to a noise like a rat scratching its claws against the wall. He peered nervously down to the bunk below, holding his breath. What was this? Kai's bunkmate was etching something into the wall behind their bed. How strange! He was working so intently that he didn't notice Kai. What could the old man be writing? Relieved that it wasn't a rat, but puzzled, Kai lay awake listening through the night.

In the morning Kai waited until the old man had left for breakfast. As soon as the barracks were empty he looked on the wall behind his bunk and found it covered in Chinese script. His eyes followed the rows of the old man's poem down the wall:

> *In the quiet of the night, I heard,*
> *faintly, the whistling of wind.*
> *The forms and shadows saddened*
> *me;*
> *The floating clouds, the fog, darken*
> *the sky,*
> *The moon shines faintly as the*
> *insects chirp.*
> *The sad person sits alone, leaning*
> *by a window.*

Kai sat very still contemplating Angel Island. Father had said nothing in his letter about this locked room with sad poetry on its walls. Kai dragged his feet down the covered walkway to breakfast, aching for home and feeling terribly alone.

One sunny morning several weeks later, Kai was playing basketball with Young and the other boys in the yard. As he shot the ball towards the basket, something caught his eye beyond the tall fence: a tree with purple fruits dangling from its branches. Plums! He ran over to the fence and jumped to reach one of the fruits, but he missed. Kai thought of his boring diet of soggy rice and overcooked vegetables. He dreamed of the plum sauce he would have with duck at Father's restaurant. The plums swayed in the breeze just beyond his grasp. Sweet and tempting. "Hmm," Kai thought. "There must be a way. . . . "

He ran inside to his bunk and grabbed a pair of old trousers. Hurrying back to the yard, he tied knots at the cuffs of the pants to make them into a sack. He called Young and whispered his plan into his friend's ear. Young grinned. Then they took the pants and pushed them under the fence near the fruit tree. They rejoined the game of basketball, and as soon as Kai got the ball, he winked at Young and threw the ball up and over the fence towards the plum tree. "Hey, *luk yi!*" he cried to the guard lounging by the gate. Kai motioned towards the ball with his arms, shrugged his shoulders, and with a questioning glance, asked the guard to help.

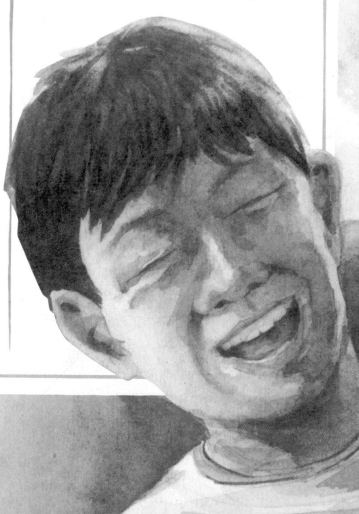

The lazy guard barked something that Kai didn't understand, but he unlocked the gate and pointed to Kai and Young to get the ball. With innocent looks on their faces, they sped around behind the fence where they found their sack on a carpet of ripe, fallen plums. Scrambling, they filled their bag with fruit in moments. They squeezed it under the fence, found the basketball under the tree, and returned to the gate before the guard became suspicious. Once inside, the boys scurried to the fence, retrieved the bag of fruits, and snuck it into the barracks to feast upon the sweet, purple plums. Sticky juice ran down their chins, as they laughed and laughed.

Five weeks passed. Every day Kai clung to the hope of being released. "Just one more day," he assured himself. "Don't give up on me, Father," he wished as he fell asleep each night, fingering the tattered letter under his pillow.

One foggy morning in August when Kai was playing basketball, he heard his name called in an unfamiliar voice. Dropping the ball, he raced inside to find a guard waiting by the door. The time for his interrogation had finally come! He fumbled on his buttons as he quickly changed into his gray suit from Hong Kong. He smoothed his black hair with his hand.

Taking a deep breath, he reminded himself not to worry. He was a legitimate son of a citizen and had nothing to fear. Young's glance revealed a tinge of envy as Kai passed his bunk, half-running to meet the *luk yi*, whose black boot tapped impatiently by the door.

Kai's interrogation began smoothly. A tall, stern white man wearing a wool suit asked all the questions in English. A Chinese man, also dressed in a suit, translated everything the tall man said to Kai. A uniformed guard hovered nearby. A white woman, the first Kai had seen, sat clicking her fingertips on a black machine while Kai and the men spoke.

They began with basic questions. What were all his names? How old was he? What was the name of his village? What were the names of all his family members? How old were they? For how long had his father been in America? Where did he live? What was his job? After answering their many questions with ease, Kai began to relax. Surely he would pass.

But suddenly the questions became more difficult. "How many chairs were in your house in China?"

"What a strange question," Kai puzzled. It was a small house. Four people lived in it. Plus his father when he visited. So there were probably five chairs. "Five," Kai guessed.

"What did the chairs look like? Were their backs round or square?"

"Square," replied Kai. He clasped and unclasped his sticky palms in his lap.

The interrogator shot Kai an accusing look. "Interesting," he replied, tapping his pen on the desk. "That's not what your father said." Kai's heart leapt. These men had spoken with his father! The thought of Father strengthened him. Taking a deep breath, he replied again.

"Sir, to the best of my knowledge, the chairs were square." Kai remembered how Father had warned him not to cause trouble. But he knew that one mistake could fail his interrogation. Could send him back to China. Oh, the shame this would cause Father. Kai thought of his grandmother's words, "Be a good boy."

He searched the interrogator's face for a sign of understanding. "I apologize for arguing, sir, but I lived in that house and sat on those chairs every day. My father lives here in America and only returns to China every four years. Who do you think knows the chairs better—him or me?" He swallowed. "Believe me. They're square."

With that, the interrogator raised his eyebrows to the guard and the translator. They looked at the small, bold boy sitting erect in his chair. And gradually a smile broke out on the interrogator's face. The translator glanced sideways at him and chuckled. Even the guard joined in their laughter and winked at Kai. Kai didn't dare smile in the presence of the white men, but relief washed over him.

After his interrogation Kai waited and waited. He tossed restlessly at night. He perched on the edge of his bunk during the day. He didn't even play basketball for fear of missing his news. Then, on the morning of the fourth day of waiting, a guard entered the barracks after breakfast and looked down towards Kai's bunk in the corner. "Wong Kai Chong?" Kai looked up. A ray of sunlight streamed in from the open door. The room fell silent. "*Ho sai gai!*"

Kai paused in disbelief. Me? I have been landed?

He scrambled down from the top bunk. The old man below stood to face Kai and gently squeezed his shoulders. The boys from the bunks nearby swarmed around him patting him on the back and congratulating him. Kai was overjoyed. His knees shook. But a nagging feeling held him back.

Kai could see an envious longing in the boys' faces, despite their generous smiles. He was free to go home to his father, but they were staying behind. Some might even be sent back to China. Kai bowed to each of them solemnly.

Once he had his gray suit on, his few belongings packed, and his suitcase in hand, he turned to face the guard waiting for him by the open door. But wait! Where was Young? He looked towards Young's bunk and saw his friend sitting cross-legged staring out the barred window. The guard cleared his throat impatiently. Kai called Young's name, but Young wouldn't look up. Kai understood. He whispered, "Goodbye. Good luck to you, my friend," even though Young probably wouldn't hear him. He hoped that Young would hear the call "*Ho sai gai*" soon. Maybe they would meet again. He turned to the open door, and the guard ushered him out of the barracks into the sunshine.

Kai jogged to keep up with the guard's strides. Down on the docks he saw the same small boat that had brought him to this island six long weeks ago. He was on his way to San Francisco to find his father, at last.

Kai looked back at Angel Island disappearing behind a bank of fog. In his mind he could hear the nighttime sounds of scratchy Chinese opera, creaking metal bunks, and sniffling. He remembered the old man etching his sad poem onto the wall. He cringed remembering all the soggy rice. The embarrassing medical exam. The boredom. He smiled thinking of basketball, especially the day he and Young discovered the plums. Shuddering at the thought of his friend having to stay behind on Angel Island, he hoped that Young would pass the interrogation soon.

Kai's heart pounded as the ferry approached the docks in San Francisco. He pushed his hair out of his eyes. He tugged at his new suit's sleeves, which were already getting too short. He inhaled the salty air deeply and pushed back his shoulders, wanting to show his father how much he had grown. Squinting into the sunlight, he searched for Father among the small crowd of people on the pier. Would he be there? Kai craned his neck to find him.

Just then he saw a figure running along the wharf waving a black, felt hat. He heard a jolly laugh. "Kai! Wong Kai Chong!"

"Father!" Kai cried. He pulled the letter from his pocket and waved it in the air.

The boat seemed to take forever to land. Finally, the railing was lifted. Kai leapt off the ferry's ramp, pushed through the crowd, and stood face to face with his father. He bowed respectfully, but Father stepped towards him and took him into his arms. Protective, familiar arms. And as they stood there amidst the bustle of the docks, Kai knew, at last, that he had found Gold Mountain.

THINK CRITICALLY

1. **Why do Kai and Young deliberately throw their ball over the fence?** CAUSE AND EFFECT

2. **Why does the author have Kai keep the tattered letter from his father under his pillow?** AUTHOR'S CRAFT

3. **Think about a time when you had to wait a long time for something you really wanted. How can this experience help you understand Kai's feelings as he waits at Angel Island?**

   IDENTIFY WITH CHARACTERS

4. **Compare and contrast the way Kai feels and behaves on Angel Island before and after his interrogation.**

   COMPARE AND CONTRAST

5. **WRITE** Kai spends several weeks on Angel Island. Use details and information from the story to explain how Kai spends his days on Angel Island. SHORT RESPONSE

ABOUT THE AUTHOR
KATRINA CURRIER

Katrina Currier lives in Mill Valley, California, not far from the modern ferryboat stop for Angel Island. Before she moved to California, Katrina Currier taught fourth grade in Massachusetts. One of the things she taught her students about was Angel Island. When she moved to San Francisco, she started researching Angel Island's history and met Albert "Kai" Wong, whose experiences she wrote about in *Kai's Journey to Gold Mountain*.

ABOUT THE ILLUSTRATOR
GABHOR UTOMO

Gabhor Utomo lives in San Francisco, where he moved from Indonesia to study art. Gabhor Utomo used watercolors to paint illustrations for *Kai's Journey to Gold Mountain*, his first picture book for young people. A thirteen-year-old boy whom the artist knows served as the model for his pictures of Kai.

 www.harcourtschool.com/storytown

Skipping Stones
A Multicultural Magazine

Narrative Nonfiction

My Japanese Sister

by Emily Bernier

I always wanted to have an exchange student from another country. I dreamed of learning another language, and getting to teach the student English. I never considered how I might grow to love her, or how sad I would be when she left.

Yuu Tagawa (yoo tah•kah•wah) stayed with my family for four months, and I really miss her now. Yuu is from Japan. Since we have only three bedrooms, and Yuu made the fifth family member, we ended up doing a huge "musical chairs" with our furniture; some went up to the attic and some came down. My sister and I had to share a room for four months.

Yuu taught me Japanese reading and writing, and taught us a little Japanese culture. We taught her American sayings and culture.

One very interesting part of the learning process for Yuu was her trouble with everyday expressions, such as "make sure." How do you *make* sure? What is it made of?

It was also interesting to see the simple things which Yuu had never heard of or seen before. One weekend, we stayed at our home in the Catskill Mountains in New York. When we opened the door, Yuu gasped. The fireplace! She had heard of them, but never in her life had she actually seen one. That evening, we all sat around the fireplace, playing cards and talking. I noticed that Yuu wasn't doing either—she was relaxing on the couch, just watching the fire.

Yuu had also never seen or tasted peanut butter before. One morning, my mother was listing the usual choices for breakfast. When she mentioned toast with peanut butter, Yuu tilted her head to one side like she did when she was confused. My mother showed her the peanut butter, and she looked at it from every angle. Yuu burst out laughing at the look on my mother's face when Yuu told her she had never seen peanut butter before.

One day, Yuu gave my sister and me each a kimono (a Japanese formal dress). There is a special ribbon that goes around your middle, and she said she had to take classes to learn how to tie it! It took Yuu two full minutes to complete the tie. We put on our kimonos, and Yuu took a picture of us. The picture is still on our mantelpiece.

One thing I loved about Yuu was her sense of humor. It took her a few weeks to learn to express it in English, but it was an amazing accomplishment. As my mother remarked later, it's very hard to have a sense of humor in another language. You don't know what is considered funny, and what is considered insulting. Yuu was a natural; she had us in stitches sometimes.

Yuu was like a sister to me. When I heard that she had to go, I cried and was very upset for a while. I miss her very much. Still, I think many more people should have exchange students. You could have a friend, or a sister, for life.

◀ The ribbon that wraps around your waist is called an *obi* (oh●bee).

◀ Kimonos are the traditional garments of Japan.

Connections

Comparing Texts

1. Kai and Young learn to play basketball on Angel Island. How could playing sports help you get along with others?

2. Compare Kai's experience with Yuu Tagawa's experience.

3. One man at Angel Island expresses his feelings by writing poems on the walls. What is another way people express their feelings through the arts?

Vocabulary Review

Word Sort

Sort the Vocabulary Words into categories about feelings such as *angry* or *frightened*. Work with a small group to compare your sorted words. Then choose two Vocabulary Words in each category and write a sentence that shows why they belong in the same category.

> Anger: When someone is accusing me, I may feel fury.

averted

fury

interrogation

stern

accusing

solemnly

cringed

craned

Fluency Practice

Timed Reading

Remember that your reading rate is how quickly you can read text correctly. Reread three paragraphs from "Kai's Journey to Gold Mountain." Then read them again, using a stopwatch to time yourself. Record your time on a sheet of paper. Then read the passage again, and try to improve your reading rate. Compare the times you recorded. How much did your reading rate improve?

Writing

Write a Letter

Imagine that you are Kai and you have not yet left Angel Island. Write a letter to your mother back home in China. Explain how your experience has been the same and different from what you had expected.

Expected Experience — Both — Actual Experience

My Writing Checklist

Writing Trait ▸ Word Choice

✔ I used a Venn diagram to plan my writing.

✔ I compared and contrasted my experiences.

✔ I used vivid words to describe events.

CONTENTS

Readers' Theater
REALISTIC FICTION

PEDRO
Puts On a Play

illustrated by Marc Burckhardt

RAUL'S
AFTER-School Snack

by Joyce Styron Madsen

Reading for Meaning
REALISTIC FICTION

culinary

downcast

consternation

vivid

extensive

serenely

reminiscent

pensive

recruit

commenced

Characters

Narrator
Mrs. Lloyd
Naomi
Class
Raymond
Pedro's mother
Pedro
Miguel, Pedro's brother
Pedro's grandfather
Pedro's father

Reading for Fluency

When reading a script aloud,

- Practice reading each word correctly until you can read your lines with **accuracy**.

- Make sure that your **reading rate** is neither too fast nor too slow.

PEDRO
Puts On a Play
illustrated by Marc Burckhardt

Narrator: It is Friday afternoon in Mrs. Lloyd's fourth-grade classroom.

Mrs. Lloyd: Before I dismiss you, I have a homework assignment for you.

Naomi: Homework?

Mrs. Lloyd: Yes, but I'm not depriving you of fun this weekend. I think this project will be fun for everyone.

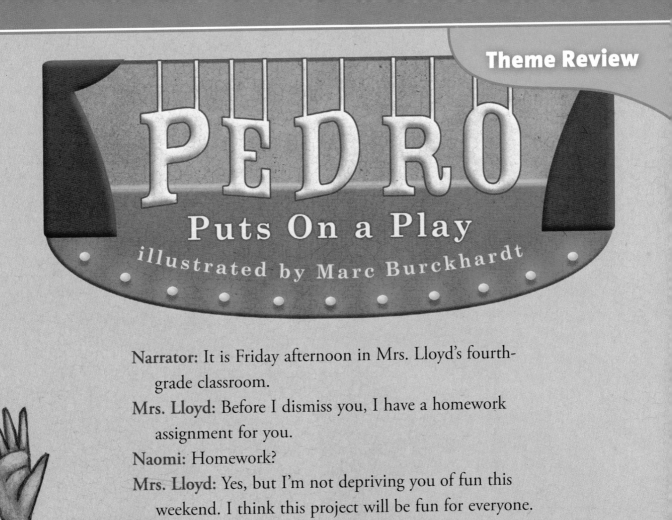

Class: What is this fun project, Mrs. Lloyd?

Mrs. Lloyd: For Monday, please prepare a creative presentation about your family's cultural heritage. Can anyone explain what *cultural heritage* is?

Naomi: Your cultural heritage is passed down through your family, from grandparents to parents to children. It can include stories, songs, or even recipes.

Mrs. Lloyd: You are absolutely correct, Naomi. You can sing a song, teach a game, or tell us about a culinary tradition from your culture.

Raymond: My mom is from Haiti. I could teach the class a Creole song I know.

Mrs. Lloyd: Great idea, Raymond. I'm looking forward to all your presentations on Monday!

Narrator: It is Friday evening at Pedro's house. Pedro and his grandfather, father, mother, and brother, Miguel, are eating dinner. *Abuelo* Eduardo, Pedro's grandfather, is visiting Pedro's family. His home is in Mexico City. Pedro feels downcast. He is looking down at the floor solemnly.

Pedro's mother: Pedro, why aren't you eating? You never lose your appetite. Do you feel queasy?

Narrator: Pedro averts his eyes from his mother's look of consternation. He mutters when he speaks, his voice soft and low.

Pedro: I'm not hungry.

Miguel: That's all right, *Mami*. There's more for me!

Narrator: Pedro's mother reaches across the table and feels Pedro's forehead.

Pedro's mother: You don't feel as if you have a fever.

Pedro: I'm not sick, *Mami*. Mrs. Lloyd wants us to give a presentation about our family's cultural heritage. I don't have anything to share.

Pedro's grandfather: *Áy*, Pedro! There are many exciting customs in your Mexican heritage.

Pedro's mother: I'm sure your *papí* and your *abuelo* can help you.

Pedro: Do you have any ideas, *Abuelo*?

Pedro's grandfather: I do have an idea for you, Pedro. You can show your class a Mexican mariachi band in sparkling silver and black costumes!

Pedro: How will I find a mariachi band? The assignment is due on Monday.

Pedro's father: Your ideas are always great, *Abuelo*, but this particular one isn't very practical.

Pedro's grandfather: My son, have you forgotten *los títeres*?

Pedro and Miguel: *Los títeres*?

Pedro's grandfather: *Títeres* means "puppets." They are handmade Mexican marionettes. They are painted in vivid colors and dressed as traditional Mexican characters.

Pedro's father: *Abuelo* had an extensive collection of *títeres*. When I left Mexico and immigrated to the United States, he gave them to me.

Pedro's grandfather: I remember a cowboy puppet, a dancer with a swirling skirt. . . .

Pedro's father: . . . and mariachi musicians!

Pedro and Miguel: Where are they now, *Papi*?

Pedro's father: They're upstairs in the attic.

Narrator: After dinner, Pedro and Miguel find an old wooden chest in the attic. Their father, mother, and grandfather watch. Pedro reaches inside and pulls out a brightly painted puppet. Pedro gapes at the puppet. He is stunned and unable to speak at first.

Pedro: *Abuelo*, it's beautiful!

Pedro's grandfather: It's a musician with a silver and black costume, just as I said.

Pedro's father: Look at the strings.

Miguel: There's one string to make each arm move, one to make each leg move, and one to make his head turn!

Narrator: Pedro's grandfather reaches into the chest. He picks up several puppets and smiles serenely.

Pedro's grandfather: How exciting to see these again after so many years. They are reminiscent of my childhood in Mexico!

Pedro: *Abuelo*, did you really play with these when you were young?

Pedro's grandfather: Yes! My brother and I used to put on plays for our friends. In our neighborhood, our theatrical skills were legendary!

Narrator: Pedro looks pensive. Suddenly, there is an excited look in his eyes.

Pedro: *Abuelo*, I have a great idea! I can put on a puppet show for my class.

Pedro's grandfather: Perfect!

Fluency Tip

To improve your reading rate, practice reading portions of text that have unfamiliar words.

Pedro's father: Maybe you can recruit your brother to help you.

Pedro: Miguel, will you help me put on a play?

Miguel: Sure! What's the play about?

Pedro: It's about a boy who learns about his family's Mexican heritage, thanks to his *papí* and his *abuelo*.

Narrator: Pedro's father embraces *Abuelo* Eduardo.

Pedro's father: I'm glad we saved the *títeres*. They are a family treasure.

Pedro's grandfather: Pedro and Miguel will be the third generation in our family to bring these puppets to life!

Narrator: It is Monday morning in Mrs. Lloyd's classroom. The cultural festival has commenced. Pedro and Miguel stand in front of the class and finish their puppet play. They bow as the class applauds. They move the puppets' strings to make them bow, too.

Class: That was a great play!

Naomi: Where did you get those puppets, Pedro?

Pedro: From our father.

Raymond: How did you learn how to make them move?

Pedro: Our *abuelo* taught us.

Class: We like the cowboy!

Naomi: I like the dancer!

Raymond: Will you teach us how to make them move?

Pedro: Sure!

Miguel: It's not hard.

Class: Let's put on another play!

Narrator: Mrs. Lloyd steps up to the front of the class.

Mrs. Lloyd: Pedro, your presentation was wonderful. Miguel, thank you.

Miguel: You're welcome.

Mrs. Lloyd: You are two very skilled puppeteers!

Pedro: Thanks, Mrs. Lloyd! We inherited our skill from our *abuelo*. It runs in the family!

COMPREHENSION STRATEGIES
Review

Reading Fiction

Bridge to Reading for Meaning Realistic fiction has characters, settings, and events that are like people, places, and events in real life. The notes on page 145 point out some text features of realistic fiction, including characters, setting, and plot events. How can recognizing these features help you understand the realistic fiction you read?

Review the Focus Strategies

If you do not understand what you are reading, use the comprehension strategies you learned about in this theme.

 ### Use Story Structure

All stories are organized in a similar way. This is called story structure. Use story structure to help you understand how the

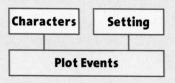

characters, setting, and plot events in a story fit together.

 ### Answer Questions

Answer questions about a story by looking in the text and thinking about what you already know.

As you read "Raul's After-School Snack" on pages 146-149, think about where and how to use comprehension strategies.

CHARACTERS

Characters are the people and animals who appear in a story. The main character may be like someone we know. He or she may change or learn a lesson by the end of a story.

RAUL'S AFTER-SCHOOL SNACK

by Joyce Styron Madsen
illustrated by Maryn Roos

"Mom!" Raul called as he tossed his jacket and backpack onto the kitchen countertop. "I'm home!"

Silence. The only sound was the tip-tap-tip of Scruffy's claws as she bounced along the back hallway to welcome Raul home from a long day at school.

"Hi, girl! How's it going?" Raul reached down to give Scruffy a pat on the nose and a scratch on the chin. "At least *you're* here to greet me."

Then Raul noticed a note on the refrigerator.

Raul,
Gone to pick up books from the library.
Be back soon.
Love, Mom

P.S. Please don't leave your things on the kitchen countertop.

Raul looked guiltily over his shoulder. Quickly grabbing his jacket and backpack, he hung them up on the hallway coat rack. "Okay, that's done," he said to Scruffy. "Now, how about a snack?" Scruffy thumped her tail in agreement.

Raul reached for a glass and headed towards the refrigerator. Then he noticed that the oven door had been left slightly open, even though the oven temperature dial had been switched to "off." Curious, he peered inside and saw two large baking trays filled with delicately browned cookies.

"M-m-m-m," he said as he reached for an oven mitt and lifted three of the fragrant cookies onto a plate. "The perfect after-school snack!" he commented. Raul popped a cookie into his mouth while he poured himself a glass of milk. "Hm-m-m...tasty, but not very sweet. Mom must be trying to cut down on sugar."

SETTING

The setting is where and when a story takes place. An author of realistic fiction uses a time and a place that are or could be real.

PLOT EVENTS

Plot events are the actions in a story. In realistic fiction, the plot events are like those that could happen in real life.

Apply the Strategies Read this realistic fiction story about what happens after Raul gets home from school. As you read, use different comprehension strategies, such as using story structure, to help you understand the text.

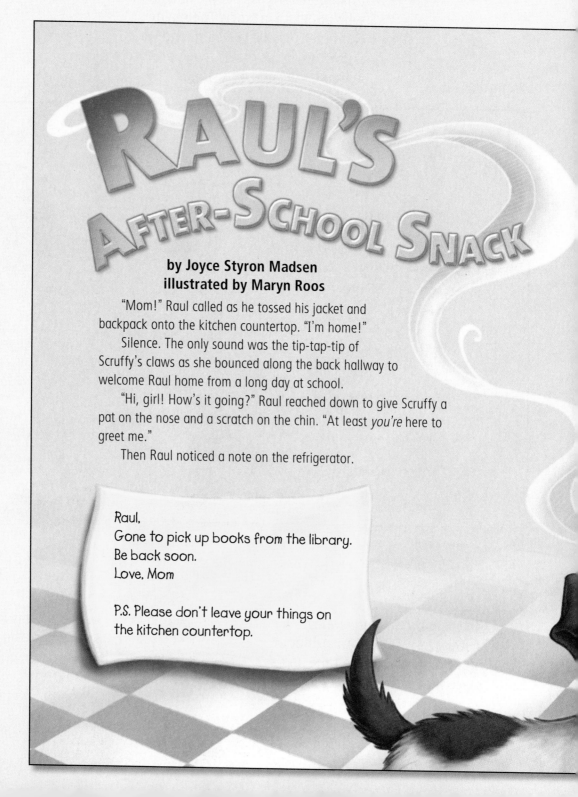

RAUL'S AFTER-SCHOOL SNACK

by Joyce Styron Madsen
illustrated by Maryn Roos

"Mom!" Raul called as he tossed his jacket and backpack onto the kitchen countertop. "I'm home!"

Silence. The only sound was the tip-tap-tip of Scruffy's claws as she bounced along the back hallway to welcome Raul home from a long day at school.

"Hi, girl! How's it going?" Raul reached down to give Scruffy a pat on the nose and a scratch on the chin. "At least *you're* here to greet me."

Then Raul noticed a note on the refrigerator.

Raul,
Gone to pick up books from the library.
Be back soon.
Love, Mom

P.S. Please don't leave your things on the kitchen countertop.

Stop and Think

Pay attention to the characters' words and actions to help you understand the plot events. **USE STORY STRUCTURE**

Raul looked guiltily over his shoulder. Quickly grabbing his jacket and backpack, he hung them up on the hallway coat rack. "Okay, that's done," he said to Scruffy. "Now, how about a snack?" Scruffy thumped her tail in agreement.

Raul reached for a glass and headed towards the refrigerator. Then he noticed that the oven door had been left slightly open, even though the oven temperature dial had been switched to "off." Curious, he peered inside and saw two large baking trays filled with delicately browned cookies.

"M-m-m-m," he said as he reached for an oven mitt and lifted three of the fragrant cookies onto a plate. "The perfect after-school snack!" he commented. Raul popped a cookie into his mouth while he poured himself a glass of milk. "Hm-m-m...tasty, but not very sweet. Mom must be trying to cut down on sugar."

Scruffy's eyes followed the movement of Raul's hand as he brought another cookie from the plate to his mouth. Crunch...crunch...crunch... Scruffy licked her chops longingly. Raul took a final slurp of milk and swallowed, just as his mom walked through the back door. Scruffy ran to dance at Mom's heels.

"Hi, Mom!" Raul said as he carried his plate and empty glass to the sink.

"Hello, kiddo," Mom replied, setting a stack of books down on the table. "You, too, Scruffo. Hope you're not spoiling your appetite with junk food."

"No, I just had a few of those cookies," Raul answered. "They're good, but they sure are hard to chew."

"Cookies?" Mom drew her eyebrows together. "What cookies?"

"The ones you left in the oven."

"Cookies..." Mom repeated, unblinking.

"Yeah, I didn't think you'd mind if I..." Raul paused when he noticed the dazed look on his mother's face.

Mom slowly pulled out a chair from the kitchen table and, inch by inch, lowered herself onto it. "Raul," she began, "those aren't cookies."

"What...what do you mean?"

Mom looked at the oven. Then she looked at Raul. Then she looked at Scruffy, who cocked her fuzzy head to the side in puzzlement.

Think about what you already know to answer questions about the story. **ANSWER QUESTIONS**

"They're homemade dog biscuits," Mom said, swallowing hard. "I made them as a special treat for Scruffy's birthday next week."

Raul gulped. Mom gulped in sympathy. Scruffy wagged her tail in appreciation.

Raul sat down across the table from Mom. "I *thought* they tasted a little...different," he said after a moment. "But Mom, they weren't shaped like dog bones or anything."

"I couldn't find the bone-shaped cutter so I just used regular cookie cutters," Mom explained. "Well, I guess there's no harm done. All the ingredients are healthy foods. There's nothing in them that should hurt you."

"Bow wow," said Raul.

READING-WRITING
CONNECTION

Theme ② Getting the Job Done

Xia Xueming, *Picking Fruit*

CONTENTS

Lesson 6

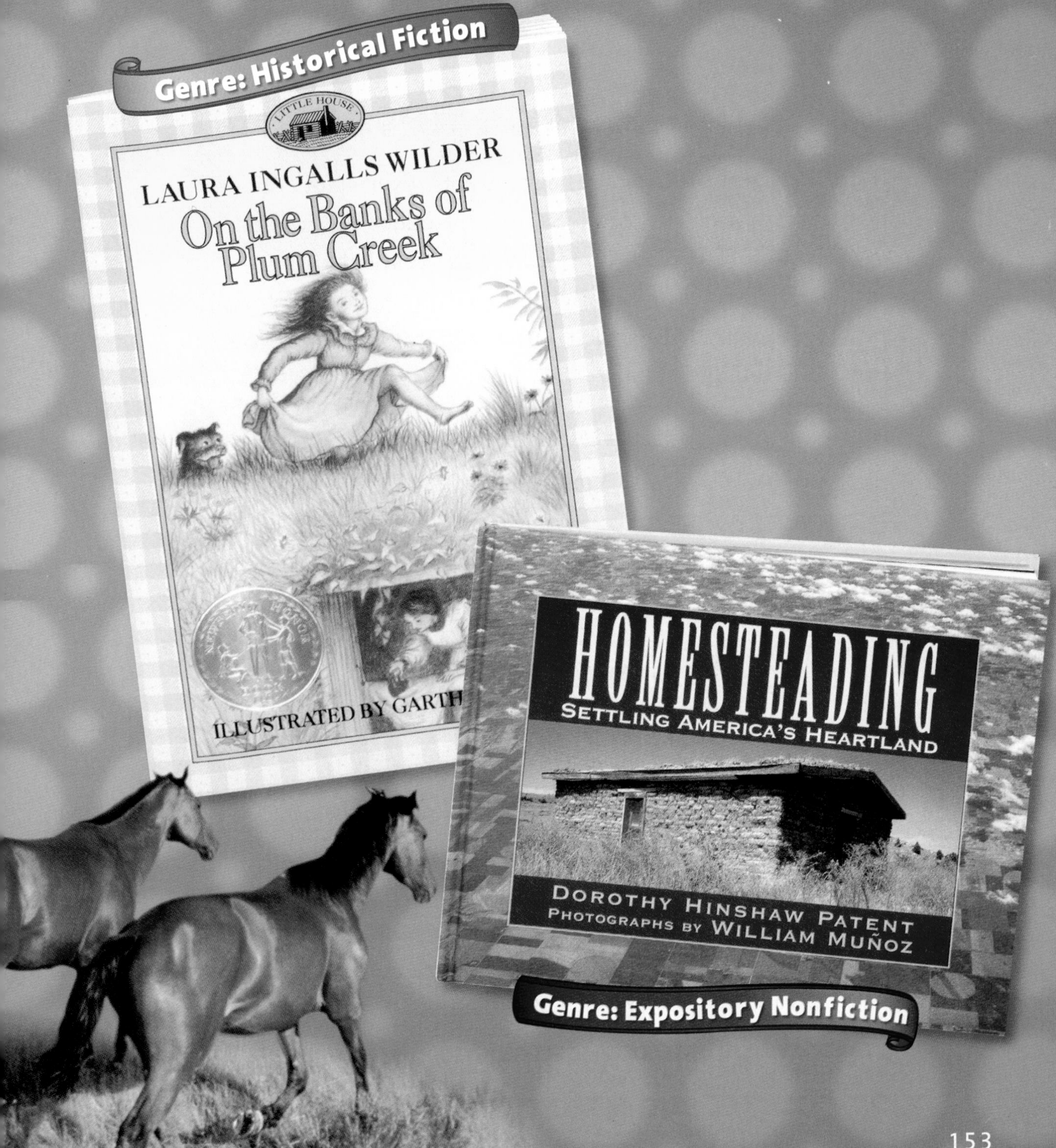

Genre: Historical Fiction
LITTLE HOUSE
LAURA INGALLS WILDER
On the Banks of Plum Creek
ILLUSTRATED BY GARTH
HOMESTEADING
SETTLING AMERICA'S HEARTLAND
DOROTHY HINSHAW PATENT
PHOTOGRAPHS BY WILLIAM MUÑOZ
Genre: Expository Nonfiction

Plot: Conflict and Resolution

All stories have a **plot**, or a series of events. Every plot contains a **conflict**, or problem. Authors often introduce the conflict early in a story. The plot events lead to the **resolution**, or solution. The resolution usually comes near the end of a story. Knowing how to identify the conflict in a story can help you better understand the plot.

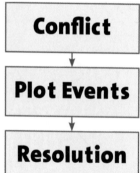

Conflict

↓

Plot Events

↓

Resolution

Tip

To recognize a story's conflict, look for a challenge that one of the characters faces.

154

Read the story below. Then look at the graphic organizer. It shows the conflict—the problem Luke faces in this story. The resolution is how Luke solves his problem.

Luke paddled more quickly. He did not like the look of the dark clouds ahead. He reached the shore just as the first raindrops fell. "What will I do if my gear gets soaked?" he wondered.

Luke pulled the canoe onto the rocks, quickly unpacked his gear, and turned the canoe upside down on top of it. "I may get wet, but my gear won't," he thought.

Conflict
Luke worries that his gear will get wet.

↓

Plot Events
- Luke paddles to shore.
- Luke pulls his canoe onto the rocks and unpacks his gear.

↓

Resolution
Luke covers his gear with his canoe to keep it dry.

Try This!

Look back at the story. What might be the next conflict Luke faces? How might it be resolved?

www.harcourtschool.com/storytown

Vocabulary

darted

swerved

responsible

contradicting

jostling

attentive

pounced

A Pioneer's Diary

June 24, 1868
We were driving the wagon into town today when, suddenly, a rabbit **darted** out in front of us. The horses got scared and started running. The wagon **swerved**, but Pa was able to keep it on the trail.

June 25, 1868
Today Pa told me I was old enough to help Jen bring the cattle to the barn for the night. He said that I was very **responsible** and that he trusted me to do a good job. That made me feel good. I feel very grown-up!

June 27, 1868

This morning, Jen and I saw a snake in the back field. I think it was a rattlesnake, but Jen said it was only a king snake. (She is always **contradicting** me.) The snake disturbed the cattle, and the cattle started **jostling** each other to get out of the way. Pa said he didn't know what kind of snake it was. He reminded us always to be **attentive** when we walk through the tall grass.

June 29, 1868

We spotted that snake again today. Our dog, Grace, **pounced** on it. It turned out to be only a king snake after all.

 www.harcourtschool.com/storytown

Word Detective

Your mission this week is to look for Vocabulary Words outside your classroom. You might read them in a book, or you might hear them in a movie or on the radio. Each time you see or hear a Vocabulary Word, write it in your vocabulary journal. Don't forget to tell where you found the word.

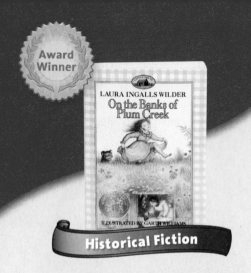

LAURA INGALLS WILDER

On the Banks of Plum Creek

ILLUSTRATED BY GARTH WILLIAMS

Historical Fiction

Genre Study

Historical fiction is based on a real time and a real place in the past. The events, characters, and other details may be imagined. As you read, look for

- realistic characters and events.

- details that show the story takes place in the past.

Characters	Setting
Conflict	
Plot Events	
Resolution	

Comprehension Strategy

Monitor comprehension while you read by **rereading** sections of the text you did not understand.

On the Banks of PLUM CREEK

by Laura Ingalls Wilder

illustrated by Garth Williams

additional illustrations by Grady McFerrin

Laura Ingalls and her family are pioneer settlers in Minnesota. The family includes Ma and Pa, sisters Mary, Laura, and Carrie, and their dog, Jack. The family lives in a dugout, a home dug into the raised side of Plum Creek. Mary and Laura enjoy playing in the warm grasses of the prairie and in the nearby creek. In preparation for the cold months, Pa has cut the prairie grasses and left them to dry into straw. The straw will feed their oxen, Pete and Bright, and their cow, Spot, during the winter. Now that winter is near, Pa needs to go into town for supplies. He takes Ma and baby Carrie with him. Mary and Laura, like other pioneer girls their age, stay behind to take care of their home.

THE INGALLS CHILDREN

Summer was gone, winter was coming, and now it was time for Pa to make a trip to town. Here in Minnesota, town was so near that Pa would be gone only one day, and Ma was going with him.

She took Carrie, because Carrie was too little to be left far from Ma. But Mary and Laura were big girls. Mary was going on nine and Laura was going on eight, and they could stay at home and take care of everything while Pa and Ma were gone.

For going-to-town, Ma made a new dress for Carrie, from the pink calico that Laura had worn when she was little. There was enough of it to make Carrie a little pink sunbonnet. Carrie's hair had been in curl-papers all night. It hung in long, golden, round curls, and when Ma tied the pink sunbonnet strings under Carrie's chin, Carrie looked like a rose.

Ma wore her hoopskirts and her best dress, the beautiful challis with little strawberries on it, that she had worn to the sugaring-dance at Grandma's long ago in the Big Woods.

"Now be good girls, Laura and Mary," was the last thing she said. She was on the wagon seat, with Carrie beside her. Their lunch was in the wagon. Pa took up the ox goad.

"We'll be back before sundown," he promised. "Hi-oop!" he said to Pete and Bright. The big ox and the little one leaned into their yoke and the wagon started.

"Good-by, Pa! Good-by, Ma! Good-by, Carrie, good-by!" Laura and Mary called after it.

Slowly the wagon went away. Pa walked beside the oxen. Ma and Carrie, the wagon, and Pa all grew smaller, till they were gone into the prairie.

The prairie seemed big and empty then, but there was nothing to be afraid of. There were no wolves and no Indians. Besides, Jack stayed close to Laura. Jack was a responsible dog. He knew that he must take care of everything when Pa was away.

That morning Mary and Laura played by the creek, among the rushes. They did not go near the swimming-hole. They did not touch the straw-stack. At noon they ate the corn dodgers and molasses and drank the milk that Ma had left for them. They washed their tin cups and put them away.

LAURA

Then Laura wanted to play on the big rock, but Mary wanted to stay in the dugout. She said that Laura must stay there, too.

"Ma can make me," Laura said, "but you can't."

"I can so," said Mary. "When Ma's not here, you have to do what I say because I'm older."

"You have to let me have my way because I'm littler," said Laura.

"That's Carrie, it isn't you," Mary told her. "If you don't do what I say, I'll tell Ma."

"I guess I can play where I want to!" said Laura.

Mary grabbed at her, but Laura was too quick. She darted out, and she would have run up the path, but Jack was in the way. He stood stiff, looking across the creek. Laura looked too, and she screeched, "Mary!"

The cattle were all around Pa's hay-stacks. They were eating the hay. They were tearing into the stacks with their horns, gouging out hay, eating it and trampling over it.

There would be nothing left to feed Pete and Bright and Spot in the winter-time.

Jack knew what to do. He ran growling down the steps to the footbridge. Pa was not there to save the hay-stacks; they must drive those cattle away.

"Oh, we can't! We can't!" Mary said, scared. But Laura ran behind Jack and Mary came after her. They went over the creek and past the spring. They came up on the prairie and now they saw the fierce, big cattle quite near. The long horns were gouging, the thick legs trampling and jostling, the wide mouths bawling.

Mary was too scared to move. Laura was too scared to stand still. She jerked Mary along. She saw a stick, and grabbed it up and ran yelling at the cattle. Jack ran at them, growling. A big red cow swiped at him with her horns, but he jumped behind her. She snorted and galloped. All the other cattle ran after her, and Jack and Laura and Mary ran after them.

But they could not chase those cattle away from the hay-stacks. The cattle ran around and around and in between the stacks, jostling and bawling, tearing off hay and trampling it. More and more hay slid off the stacks. Laura ran panting and yelling, waving her stick. The faster she ran, the faster the cattle went, black and brown and red, brindle and spotted cattle, big and with awful horns, and they would not stop wasting the hay. Some tried to climb over the toppling stacks.

Laura was hot and dizzy. Her hair unbraided and blew in her eyes. Her throat was rough from yelling, but she kept on yelling, running, and waving her stick. She was too scared to hit one of those big, horned cows. More and more hay kept coming down and faster and faster they trampled over it.

Suddenly Laura turned around and ran the other way. She faced the big red cow coming around a hay-stack.

The huge legs and shoulders and terrible horns were coming fast. Laura could not scream now. But she jumped at that cow and waved her stick. The cow tried to stop, but all the other cattle were coming behind her and she couldn't. She swerved and ran away across the plowed ground, all the others galloping after her.

Jack and Laura and Mary chased them, farther and farther from the hay. Far into the high prairie grasses they chased those cattle.

Johnny Johnson rose out of the prairie, rubbing his eyes. He had been lying asleep in a warm hollow of grass.

"Johnny! Johnny!" Laura screeched. "Wake up and watch the cattle!"

"You'd better!" Mary told him.

Johnny Johnson looked at the cattle grazing in the deep grass, and he looked at Laura and Mary and Jack. He did not know what had happened and they could not tell him because the only words he knew were Norwegian.

They went back through the high grass that dragged at their trembling legs. They were glad to drink at the spring. They were glad to be in the quiet dugout and sit down to rest.

All that long, quiet afternoon they stayed in the dugout. The cattle did not come back to the hay-stacks. Slowly the sun went down the western sky. Soon it would be time to meet the cattle at the big gray rock, and Laura and Mary wished that Pa and Ma would come home.

Again and again they went up the path to look for the wagon. At last they sat waiting with Jack on the grassy top of their house. The lower the sun went, the more attentive Jack's ears were. Often he and Laura stood up to look at the edge of the sky where the wagon had gone, though they could see it just as well when they were sitting down.

Finally Jack turned one ear that way, then the other. Then he looked up at Laura and a waggle went from his neck to his stubby tail. The wagon was coming!

They all stood and watched till it came out of the prairie. When Laura saw the oxen, and Ma and Carrie on the wagon seat, she jumped up and down, swinging her sunbonnet and shouting, "They're coming! They're coming!"

"They're coming awful fast," Mary said.

Laura was still. She heard the wagon rattling loudly. Pete and Bright were coming very fast. They were running. They were running away.

The wagon came bumpity-banging and bouncing. Laura saw Ma down in a corner of the wagon box, hanging on to it and hugging Carrie. Pa came bounding in long jumps beside Bright, shouting and hitting at Bright with the goad.

He was trying to turn Bright back from the creek bank.

He could not do it. The big oxen galloped nearer and nearer the steep edge. Bright was pushing Pa off it. They were all going over. The wagon, Ma, and Carrie were going to fall down the bank, all the way down to the creek.

Pa shouted a terrible shout. He struck Bright's head with all his might, and Bright swerved. Laura ran screaming. Jack jumped at Bright's nose. Then the wagon, Ma, and Carrie flashed by. Bright crashed against the stable and suddenly everything was still.

Pa ran after the wagon and Laura ran behind him.

"Whoa, Bright! Whoa, Pete," Pa said. He held on to the wagon box and looked at Ma.

"We're all right, Charles," Ma said. Her face was gray and she was shaking all over.

Pete was trying to go on through the doorway into the stable, but he was yoked to Bright and Bright was headed against the stable wall. Pa lifted Ma and Carrie out of the wagon, and Ma said, "Don't cry, Carrie. See, we're all right."

Carrie's pink dress was torn down the front. She snuffled against Ma's neck and tried to stop crying as Ma told her.

"Oh, Caroline! I thought you were going over the bank," Pa said.

"I thought so, too, for a minute," Ma answered. "But I might have known you wouldn't let that happen."

"Pshaw!" said Pa. "It was good old Pete. He wasn't running away. Bright was, but Pete was only going along. He saw the stable and wanted his supper."

But Laura knew that Ma and Carrie would have fallen down into the creek with the wagon and oxen, if Pa had not run so fast and hit Bright so hard. She crowded against Ma's hoopskirt and hugged her tight and said, "Oh, Ma! Oh, Ma!" So did Mary.

"There, there," said Ma. "All's well that ends well. Now, girls, help bring in the packages while Pa puts up the oxen."

They carried all the little packages into the dugout. They met the cattle at the gray rock and put Spot into the stable, and Laura helped milk her while Mary helped Ma get supper.

At supper, they told how the cattle had got into the hay-stacks and how they had driven them away. Pa said they had done exactly the right thing. He said, "We knew we could depend on you to take care of everything. Didn't we, Caroline?"

They had completely forgotten that Pa always brought them presents from town, until after supper he pushed back his bench and looked as if he expected something. Then Laura jumped on his knee, and Mary sat on the other, and Laura bounced and asked, "What did you bring us, Pa? What? What?"

"Guess," Pa said.

They could not guess. But Laura felt something crackle in his jumper pocket and she pounced on it. She pulled out a paper bag, beautifully striped with tiny red and green stripes. And in the bag were two sticks of candy, one for Mary and one for Laura!

They were maple-sugar-colored, and they were flat on one side.

Mary licked hers. But Laura bit her stick, and the outside of it came off, crumbly. The inside was hard and clear and dark brown. And it had a rich, brown, tangy taste. Pa said it was horehound candy.

After the dishes were done, Laura
and Mary each took her stick of candy and
they sat on Pa's knees, outside the door in
the cool dusk. Ma sat just inside the dugout,
humming to Carrie in her arms.

The creek was talking to itself under the
yellow willows. One by one the great stars
swung low and seemed to quiver and flicker
in the little wind.

Laura was snug in Pa's arm. His beard softly
tickled her cheek and the delicious candy-taste melted on her tongue.

After a while she said, "Pa."

"What, little half-pint?" Pa's voice asked against her hair.

"I think I like wolves better than cattle," she said.

"Cattle are more useful, Laura," Pa said.

She thought about that a while. Then she said, "Anyway, I like wolves
better."

She was not contradicting; she was only saying what she thought.

"Well, Laura, we're going to have a good team of horses before long,"
Pa said. She knew when that would be. It would be when
they had a wheat crop.

CARRIE

Think Critically

1 What is the main conflict that Laura and Mary face in the story, and how is it resolved? 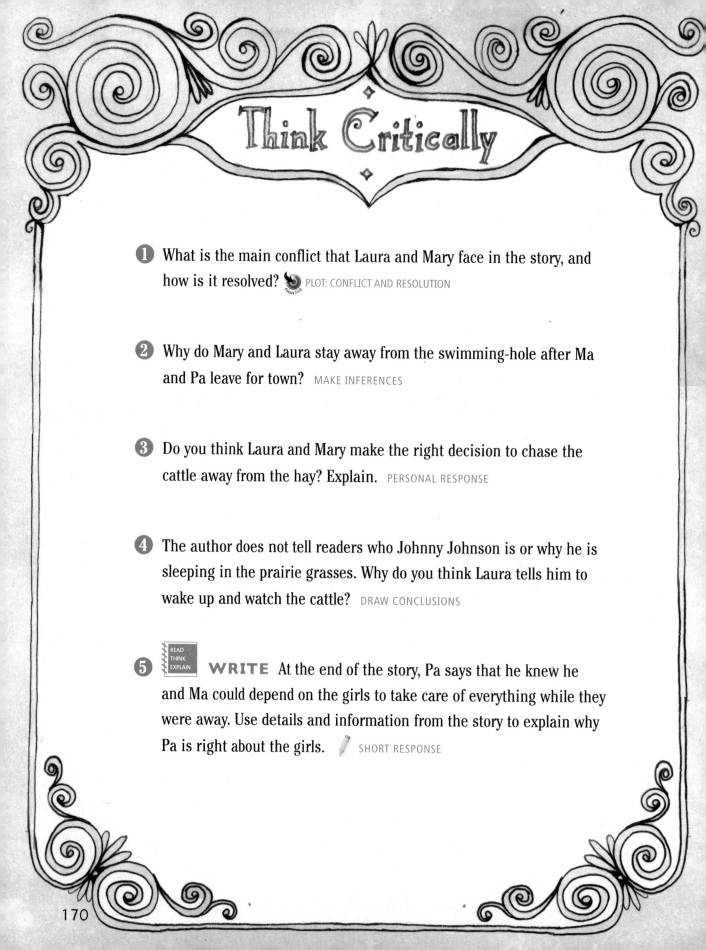 PLOT: CONFLICT AND RESOLUTION

2 Why do Mary and Laura stay away from the swimming-hole after Ma and Pa leave for town? MAKE INFERENCES

3 Do you think Laura and Mary make the right decision to chase the cattle away from the hay? Explain. PERSONAL RESPONSE

4 The author does not tell readers who Johnny Johnson is or why he is sleeping in the prairie grasses. Why do you think Laura tells him to wake up and watch the cattle? DRAW CONCLUSIONS

5 READ THINK EXPLAIN **WRITE** At the end of the story, Pa says that he knew he and Ma could depend on the girls to take care of everything while they were away. Use details and information from the story to explain why Pa is right about the girls. SHORT RESPONSE

170

Laura Ingalls Wilder

Laura Ingalls Wilder faced many challenges growing up as one of the early settlers of wild frontier land. Here are some things she wrote about her stories and her life.

I was born in the "Little House in the Big Woods" of Wisconsin on February 7 in the year 1867. I lived everything that happened in my books. . . . I wanted children now to understand more about the beginning of things, to know what is behind the things they see—what it is that made America as they know it. Today so many things have made living and learning easier. But the real things haven't changed. It is still best to be honest and truthful; to make the most of what we have; to be happy with simple pleasures and have courage when things go wrong.

GO online
www.harcourtschool.com/storytown

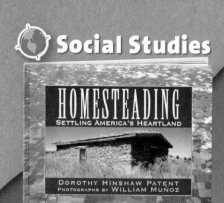

HOMESTEADING
SETTLING AMERICA'S HEARTLAND

DOROTHY HINSHAW PATENT
PHOTOGRAPHS BY WILLIAM MUÑOZ

Expository Nonfiction

SURVIVING ON THE PRAIRIES

by Dorothy Hinshaw Patent

During the mid-1800s, millions of Americans traveled westward to farm the prairie. The United States government permitted settlers, known as *homesteaders*, to each claim 160 acres of land. To claim their land, homesteaders had to dig a well, build a house, and plow at least 20 acres on which to grow crops. The settlers quickly learned that it took a great deal of hard work to make a new life on the prairie.

In the fall, families worked hard to put aside food for the harsh winter ahead. The men and older boys harvested the grain. The women and children dug the potatoes that would help the family survive the winter. They dried fruits and vegetables, smoked and salted meat, and turned cabbage into sauerkraut.

There were no refrigerators. For storing food, each homestead had a cellar that stayed cool even during the summer because it was underground. It had another important use. The prairie is tornado country. When a tornado threatened, the family hurried into the cellar for protection from the storm, just as prairie families do today.

The cellar could be a separate structure. It was used for storing food and as protection in case of a tornado.

Corn was a vital crop. The corn homesteaders grew was field corn, not the sweet corn we eat off the cob. The kernels of field corn are starchy rather than sweet. They can be dried and stored for months to serve as food throughout the year. Sometimes, corn was just about all there was to eat.

Field corn was used for cooking and feeding livestock. It dries on the plants before being harvested.

Salt pork was another mainstay of the diet. Salt pork comes from a pig's belly, just like bacon. It consists of layers of white fat mixed with thin strips of lean meat. Salting the pork preserves it so it can be stored for long periods of time in a cool place.

Laura Ingalls Wilder, author of the Little House books, wrote that her mother cooked thin slices of the pork in boiling water, drained it, coated it with flour, and fried it.

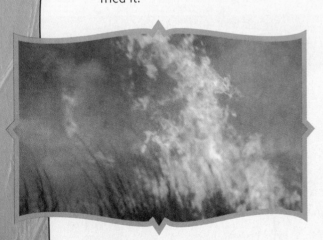

Prairie fires spread very fast as they burn through the dry grass. Fire was perhaps the most feared danger during homesteading times.

Homesteaders had to count on nature to provide weather good enough to grow a year's worth of food. Prairie fires, grasshopper plagues, and droughts were just some of the threats to successful farming. Trips to town were long, difficult, and infrequent. When their crops failed, so did many homesteaders. They had to abandon their hard-won claims and head back to the cities in hope of finding another way of making a living.

Connections

Comparing Texts

1. What have you learned about pioneer life from reading "On the Banks of Plum Creek"?

2. Compare and contrast the Ingalls family with the homesteaders in "Surviving on the Prairies."

3. How does daily life today compare with daily life in pioneer times, as described by Laura Ingalls Wilder?

Vocabulary Review

The attentive cat pounced on the mouse.

Word Pairs

Work with a partner. Write each Vocabulary Word on a separate index card. Place the cards face down. Take turns flipping over two cards and writing a sentence that uses both words. Read aloud the sentence to your partner. You must use the words correctly in the sentence to keep the cards. The student with more cards at the end wins.

responsible

darted

jostling

swerved

attentive

pounced

contradicting

Fluency Practice

Partner Reading

When you read aloud, your intonation should change to reflect changes in the mood in the text. Choose a section of "On the Banks of Plum Creek." Read aloud the text as your partner listens. Use intonation to reflect the changing tone of the story. Ask your partner for feedback. Then switch roles. Practice reading aloud until your intonation reflects the story's mood.

Writing

Write a Paragraph

In "On the Banks of Plum Creek," the girls face the challenge of chasing the cattle away from the hay-stacks. Write a paragraph about a person or a group of people who face a challenge or have a conflict that must be resolved.

Conflict
↓
Plot Events
↓
Resolution

My Writing Checklist

Writing Trait ▸ Ideas

✔ I used a graphic organizer to plan my writing.

✔ I included the most important details to keep my ideas focused.

✔ I included plot events that led to the resolution.

Reading-Writing Connection

Analyze a Narrative: Response to Literature

A **response to literature** explains what you think about a story you have read. Before you write a response to literature, ask yourself questions about the characters and events in the story. Form **opinions** about the story and think about how it **connects to your life**.

Read the passage below from "Danitra Brown Leaves Town." Think about the questions in the boxes.

> What is your opinion about the way Zuri acts toward Danitra?

Danitra talked a blue streak
about her summer trip all week.
And now that she is on her way,
she has the nerve to call and say
which station she is leaving from,
as though expecting me to come.
"I have better things to do," I blurt.
The phone is silent. Danitra's hurt.
But why am I supposed to care
when my supposed-to-be-best friend
is leaving me, and loving it?

> Did you ever have a close friend who went away? How did you feel about it?

Response to Literature

A student named Tina wrote this response to "Danitra Brown Leaves Town." As you read it, look for Tina's summary of the selection, her opinions about it, and how she connects it to her life. Note how she **focuses** on the main events and characters in the selection and how she **organizes** her response.

Student Writing Model

My Response to "Danitra Brown Leaves Town"
by Tina G.

In these poems, Danitra and Zuri learn about friendship. Danitra is excited about spending the summer in the country, but Zuri has to stay in the city. Zuri is angry because her friend is leaving her. She won't go to the station to say good-bye. Instead of being angry, Danitra writes to Zuri and says, "Wish you were here." The two friends keep writing to each other, and their friendship grows stronger.

Writing Trait

ORGANIZATION
In the first paragraph, Tina writes a brief summary of the selection. She describes the setting, the main characters, the main events, and what the characters learn.

In the next paragraph, Tina gives her opinion about an important event in the selection. She goes on to connect the selection to her own life.

I think Zuri is very rude when she tells Danitra "I have better things to do" than go to the station. Zuri acts angry, but I think she is really afraid. She says that Danitra is "leaving me." I think Zuri is worried that Danitra will find a new best friend in the country. I remember feeling the same way when my best friend went away for the summer.

Danitra and Zuri are very different characters. Danitra is very kind, because she forgives Zuri for getting angry. She writes to Zuri about her experiences in the country, such as camping and seeing fireflies. However, Zuri is not as kind. She tries to make Danitra jealous about her "new friend," Nina. Zuri wants to be like Danitra. She says that someday she will travel, as does Danitra. The two girls hug each other in the last picture in the book. Seeing this picture helped me understand that Danitra and Zuri will stay very good friends.

Writing Trait

IDEAS
Tina continues to focus on the two main characters. She uses details from the selection to compare and contrast the characters' actions.

In the conclusion, Tina restates what the characters learned.

Danitra and Zuri learn that friends can get angry without ending their friendship. They learn that traveling away from home can be exciting and that friendships can last even when friends are separated.

Now look at what Tina did to prepare her response to literature. First, she used a story map to help her write a summary of events.

Characters	Setting
Danitra, Zuri	city and country in summer

Plot Events

- Danitra goes to the country. Zuri is angry and won't say good-bye.
- Danitra writes to Zuri. She enjoys the country.
- Danitra comes home. She and Zuri are closer than ever.

Forming Opinions

As Tina read the selection, she formed opinions about the characters and events. She then wrote the characters' exact words to support her opinions. She made notes about how the selection connected to her life and about what the characters learned.

My opinion of characters and events:

Zuri is very rude at first. Danitra is kind and forgiving.

How this connects to my life:

When my friend went away last summer, I felt the way Zuri did.

What the characters learned:

Friendship can last even when friends are apart.

Organizing Information

Then Tina made a list to organize all the parts of her response to literature. The list shows what Tina planned to include in each paragraph.

1. Summarize the events.
2. State my opinions and connect to my life.
3. Compare Danitra and Zuri.
4. Tell what the characters learned.

179

CONTENTS

Lesson 7

JUSTIN and the BEST BISCUITS IN THE WORLD

MILDRED PITTS WALT

HOME ON THE RANGE

HATS OFF TO THE COWBOY

by Brewster Higley and Red Steagall
illustrated by Chris O'Leary

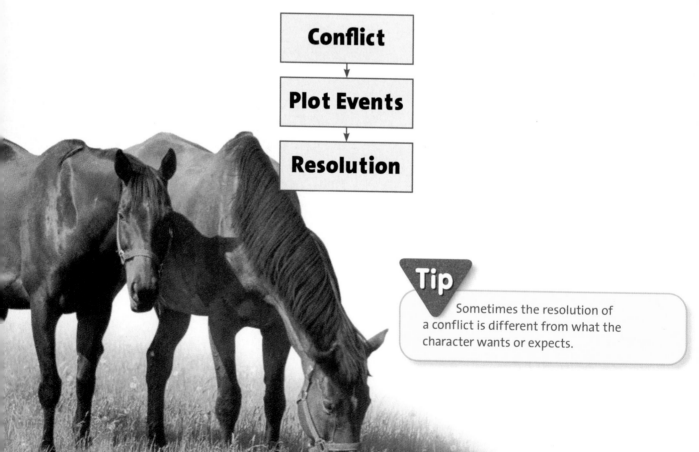

Focus Skill

Plot: Conflict and Resolution

The plot of a story contains a **conflict,** or problem, that the characters must solve. The **resolution** of the plot shows how the conflict is solved. As you read a story, look for challenges the characters face. Then look for the steps they take to solve them. Knowing how to recognize the conflict and resolution in a plot helps you better understand a story.

Conflict

↓

Plot Events

↓

Resolution

Tip

Sometimes the resolution of a conflict is different from what the character wants or expects.

Read the story below. Then look at the graphic organizer. The conflict is shown in the first paragraph. The conflict is resolved by the end of the story.

Jenna and Rick bounded toward the stable. Jared lagged behind his cousins. He hadn't told them he had never ridden a horse. A knot of fear rose in his throat.

Jenna must have guessed. "You can ride Old Pie," she said. "She's very gentle. We'll ride around the corral until you get used to her." Jared felt much better!

Conflict
Jared is worried because he has never ridden a horse.

Plot Events
- Jared lags behind because he is afraid.
- Jenna guesses that Jared has never ridden before.
- Jenna tells Jared he can practice riding a very gentle horse.

Resolution
Jared feels much better about riding a horse.

Try This!

Look back at the story. How do Jenna's character traits help her resolve the conflict?

www.harcourtschool.com/storytown

Vocabulary

Build Robust Vocabulary

inspecting

taut

untangled

rumpled

lurked

resounded

reluctant

surge

Just Another Day

Terry liked living on a ranch, but some days were a little too exciting. Last Friday, Terry noticed a calf was missing. He ran to get his father. The two of them began **inspecting** the fence to see where the calf could have escaped. They found the wires **taut** all the way to the creek. There, however, they found that a heavy tree branch had fallen across the fence, twisting the wires beneath it. Terry and his father worked together and **untangled** the fence wires.

After they moved the branch, they repaired the fence and crawled through it. Terry's father ran a hand through his **rumpled** hair. He knew that coyotes **lurked** in the hills. Their howls **resounded** across the land most evenings. A young calf would be easy prey.

Suddenly, Terry and his dad heard a sound coming from the gully. They ran toward it and found the calf trapped at the bottom. Though the calf was **reluctant** to move, Terry and his dad were able to pull it up to safety. Terry then felt a great **surge** of relief—the runaway calf was safe.

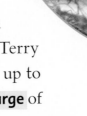

GO online www.harcourtschool.com/storytown

Word Detective

The search is on! Your mission this week is to look and listen for the Vocabulary Words outside your classroom. You might read them in a magazine, hear them on television, or find them in a book. Each time you see or hear a Vocabulary Word, write it in your vocabulary journal. Don't forget to note where you found the word.

Realistic Fiction

Genre Study

Realistic fiction has characters and events that are like people and events in real life. As you read, look for

- realistic characters and events.

- challenges and problems that might happen in real life.

Characters	Setting

Plot Events

Comprehension Strategy

Monitor comprehension by **rereading** sections of the text you did not understand.

Justin
and the
Best Biscuits
in the World

by MILDRED PITTS WALTER

illustrated by DON TATE

Justin lives in the city with his mother and his sisters, Evelyn and Hadiya. After hearing many complaints about the way he does chores around the house, Justin becomes convinced he can't do anything right, at least not the things his friend Anthony calls "women's work." In fact, while his grandfather is visiting, Justin gets so upset that he starts to cry. When Grandpa invites him to come spend some time on his ranch, Justin is eager to go.

The smell of coffee and home-smoked ham woke Justin. His grandpa was already up and downstairs cooking breakfast. Justin jumped out of bed and quickly put on his clothes.

Grandpa had hot pancakes, apple jelly, and ham all ready for the table. Justin ate two stacks of pancakes with two helpings of everything else.

After breakfast, Grandpa cleared the table, preparing to wash the dishes. "Would you rather wash or dry?" he asked Justin.

"Neither," Justin replied, quickly thinking how little success he had with dishes.

Grandpa said nothing as he removed the dishes from the table. He took his time, carefully measuring liquid soap and letting hot water run in the sink. Then he washed each dish and rinsed it with care, too. No water splashed or spilled. Soapsuds were not all over. How easy it looked, the way Grandpa did it.

After washing the dishes, Grandpa swept the floor and then went upstairs.

Justin stood around downstairs. He had a strange feeling of guilt and wished he had helped with the dishes. He heard Grandpa moving about, above in his room. Justin thought of going outside, down into the meadow, but he decided to see what was going on upstairs.

When he saw his grandpa busy making his own big bed, Justin went into his room. His unmade bed and his pajamas on the floor bothered him. But he decided that the room didn't look too bad. He picked up his pajamas and placed them on the bed and sat beside them. He waited.

Finally Grandpa came in and said, "Are you riding fence with me today?"

"Oh yes!"

"Fine. But why don't you make your bed? You'll probably feel pretty tired tonight. A well-made bed can be a warm welcome."

Justin moved slowly, reluctant to let Grandpa see him struggle with the bed. He started. What a surprise! Everything was tightly in place. He only had to smooth the covers. The bed was made. No lumps and bumps. Justin looked at Grandpa and grinned broadly. "That was easy!" he shouted.

"Don't you think you should unpack your clothes? They won't need ironing if you hang them up. You gotta look razor sharp for the festival." He gave Justin some clothes hangers.

"Are we *really* going to the festival every day?" Justin asked.

"You bet, starting with the judging early tomorrow and the dance tomorrow night." Grandpa winked at him.

Justin's excitement faded when he started unpacking his rumpled shirts. "They sure are wrinkled, Grandpa," he said.

"Maybe that's because they weren't folded."

"I can't ever get them folded right," Justin cried.

"Well, let's see. Turn it so the buttons face down." Grandpa showed Justin how to bring the sleeves to the back, turning in the sides so that the sleeves were on top. Then he folded the tail of the shirt over the cuffs, and made a second fold up to the collar. "Now you try it."

Justin tried it. "Oh, I see. That was easy, Grandpa." Justin smiled, pleased with himself.

"Everything's easy when you know how."

Justin, happy with his new-found skill, hurriedly placed his clothes on the hangers. He hoped the wrinkles would disappear in time for the festival.

"Now you'll look sharp," Grandpa said. Justin felt a surge of love for his grandpa.

He would always remember how to make a bed snug as a bug and fold clothes neatly. He grabbed Grandpa's hand. They walked downstairs, still holding hands, to get ready to ride fence.

Riding fence meant inspecting the fence all around the ranch to see where it needed mending. Riding fence took a great deal of a rancher's time. Justin and Grandpa planned to spend most of the day out on the plains. Grandpa said he'd pack a lunch for them to eat on the far side of the ranch.

Justin was surprised when Grandpa packed only flour, raisins, and chunks of smoked pork. Grandpa also packed jugs of water and makings for coffee.

The horses stood in the meadow as if they knew a busy day awaited them. While Grandpa saddled Pal, he let Justin finish the saddling of Black Lightning. Justin tightened the cinches on Black, feeling the strong pull on his arm muscles. With their supplies in their saddlebags, they mounted Pal and Black, leaving Cropper behind to graze in the meadow.

The early sun shone fiery red on the hilltops while the foothills were cast in shades of purple. The dew still lingered heavily on the morning. They let their horses canter away past the house through the tall green grass. But on the outer edge of the ranch where the fence started, they walked the horses at a steady pace.

The fence had three rows of taut wire.

"That's a pretty high fence," Justin said.

"We have to keep the cattle in. But deer sometimes leap that fence and eat hay with the cattle." When it got bitter cold and frosty, Grandpa rode around the ranch dropping bales of hay for the cattle. It took a lot of hay to feed the cattle during the winter months.

"I didn't think a cow could jump very high," Justin said.

"Aw, come on. Surely you know that a cow jumped over the moon." Grandpa had a serious look on his face.

"I guess that's a joke, eh?" Justin laughed.

Justin noticed that Grandpa had a map.

When they came to a place in the fence that looked weak, Grandpa marked it on his map. Later, helpers who came to do the work would know exactly where to mend. That saved time.

Now the sun heated up the morning. The foothills were now varying shades of green. Shadows dotted the plains. Among the blackish green trees on the rolling hills, fog still lingered like lazy clouds. Insects buzzed. A small cloud of mosquitoes swarmed just behind their heads, and beautiful cardinals splashed their redness on the morning air. Justin felt a surge of happiness and hugged Black with his knees and heels.

Suddenly he saw a doe standing close to the fence. "Look, Grandpa!" he said. She seemed alarmed but did not run away. Doe eyes usually look peaceful and sad, Justin remembered. Hers widened with fear. Then Justin saw a fawn caught in the wire of the fence.

Quickly they got off their horses. They hitched them to a post and moved cautiously toward the fawn.

The mother rushed to the fence but stopped just short of the sharp wire. "Stay back and still," Grandpa said to Justin.

"She doesn't know we will help her baby. She thinks we might hurt it. She wants to protect it."

The mother pranced restlessly. She pawed the ground, moving as close to the fence as she could. Near the post the fence had been broken. The wire curled there dangerously. The fawn's head, caught in the wire, bled close to an ear. Whenever it pulled its head the wire cut deeper.

Grandpa quickly untangled the fawn's head.

Blood flowed from the cut.

"Oh, Grandpa, it will die," Justin said sadly.

"No, no," Grandpa assured Justin.

"Lucky we got here when we did. It hasn't been caught long."

The fawn moved toward the doe. The mother, as if giving her baby a signal, bounded off. The baby trotted behind.

As they mounted their horses, Justin suddenly felt weak in the stomach. Remembering the blood, he trembled. Black, too, seemed uneasy. He moved his nostrils nervously and strained against the bit. He arched his neck and sidestepped quickly. Justin pulled the reins. "Whoa, boy!"

"Let him run," Grandpa said.

Justin kicked Black's sides and off they raced across the plain. They ran and ran, Justin pretending he was rounding up cattle. Then Black turned and raced back toward Grandpa and Pal.

"Whoa, boy," Justin commanded. Justin felt better and Black seemed calm, ready now to go on riding fence.

The sun beamed down and sweat rolled off Justin as he rode on with Grandpa, looking for broken wires in the fence. They were well away from the house, on the far side of the ranch. Flies buzzed around the horses and now gnats swarmed in clouds just above their heads. The prairie resounded with songs of the bluebirds, the bobwhite quails, and the mockingbirds mimicking them all.

The cardinal's song, as lovely as any, included a whistle.

Justin thought of Anthony and how Anthony whistled for Pepper, his dog.

It was well past noon and Justin was hungry. Soon they came upon a small, well-built shed, securely locked. Nearby was a small stream. Grandpa reined in his horse. When he and Justin dismounted, they hitched the horses, and unsaddled them.

"We'll have our lunch here," Grandpa said. Justin was surprised when Grandpa took black iron pots, other cooking utensils, and a table from the shed. Justin helped him remove some iron rods that Grandpa carefully placed over a shallow pit. These would hold the pots. Now Justin understood why Grandpa had brought uncooked food. They were going to cook outside.

First they collected twigs and cow dung.

Grandpa called it *cowchips*. "These," Grandpa said, holding up a dried brown pad, "make the best fuel. Gather them up."

There were plenty of chips left from the cattle that had fed there in winter. Soon they had a hot fire.

Justin watched as Grandpa carefully washed his hands and then began to cook their lunch.

"When I was a boy about your age, I used to go with my father on short runs with cattle. We'd bring them down from the high country onto the plains."

"Did you stay out all night?"

"Sometimes. And that was the time I liked most. The cook often made for supper what I am going to make for lunch."

Grandpa put raisins into a pot with a little water and placed them over the fire.

Justin was surprised when Grandpa put flour in a separate pan. He used his fist to make a hole right in the middle of the flour. In that hole he placed some shortening. Then he added water. With his long delicate fingers he mixed the flour, water, and shortening until he had a nice round mound of dough.

Soon smooth circles of biscuits sat in an iron skillet with a lid on top. Grandpa put the skillet on the fire with some of the red-hot chips scattered over the lid.

Justin was amazed. How could only those ingredients make good bread? But he said nothing as Grandpa put the chunks of smoked pork in a skillet and started them cooking. Soon the smell was so delicious, Justin could hardly wait.

Finally Grandpa suggested that Justin take the horses to drink at the stream. "Keep your eyes open and don't step on any snakes."

Justin knew that diamondback rattlers sometimes lurked around. They were dangerous. He must be careful. He watered Black first.

While watering Pal, he heard rustling in the grass. His heart pounded. He heard the noise again. He wanted to run, but was too afraid. He looked around carefully. There were two black eyes staring at him. He tried to pull Pal away from the water, but Pal refused to stop drinking. Then Justin saw the animal. It had a long tail like a rat's. But it was as big as a cat. Then he saw something crawling on its back. They were little babies, hanging on as the animal ran.

A mama opossum and her babies, he thought, and was no longer afraid.

By the time the horses were watered, lunch was ready. "*M-mm-m*," Justin said as he reached for a plate. The biscuits were golden brown, yet fluffy inside.

And the sizzling pork was now crisp. Never had he eaten stewed raisins before.

"Grandpa, I didn't know you could cook like this," Justin said when he had tasted the food. "I didn't know men could cook so good."

"Why, Justin, some of the best cooks in the world are men."

Justin remembered the egg on the floor and his rice burning. The look he gave Grandpa revealed his doubts.

"It's true," Grandpa said. "All the cooks on the cattle trail were men. In hotels and restaurants they call them *chefs*."

"How did you make these biscuits?"

"That's a secret. One day I'll let you make some."

"Were you a cowboy, Grandpa?"

"I'm still a cowboy."

"No, you're not."

"Yes, I am. I work with cattle, so I'm a cowboy. "

"You know what I mean. The kind who rides bulls, broncobusters. That kind of cowboy."

"No, I'm not that kind. But I know some."

"Are they famous?"

"No, but I did meet a real famous Black cowboy once. When I was eight years old, my grandpa took me to meet his friend Bill Pickett. Bill Pickett was an old man then. He had a ranch in Oklahoma."

"Were there lots of Black cowboys?"

"Yes. Lots of them. They were hard workers, too. They busted broncos, branded calves, and drove cattle. My grandpa tamed wild mustangs."

"Bet they were famous."

"Oh, no. Some were. Bill Pickett created the sport of bulldogging. You'll see that at the rodeo. One cowboy named Williams taught Rough Rider Teddy Roosevelt how to break horses; and another one named Clay taught Will Rogers, the comedian, the art of roping." Grandpa offered Justin the last biscuit.

When they had finished their lunch they led the horses away from the shed to graze. As they watched the horses, Grandpa went on, "Now, there were some more very famous Black cowboys. Jessie Stahl. They say he was the best rider of wild horses in the West."

"How could he be? Nobody ever heard about him. I didn't."

"Oh, there're lots of famous Blacks you never hear or read about. You ever hear about Deadwood Dick?"

Justin laughed. "No."

"There's another one. His real name was Nate Love. He could outride, outshoot anyone. In Deadwood City in the Dakota Territory, he roped, tied, saddled, mounted, and rode a wild horse faster than anyone. Then in the shooting match, he hit the bull's-eye every time.

The people named him Deadwood Dick right on the spot. Enough about cowboys, now. While the horses graze, let's clean up here and get back to our men's work."

Justin felt that Grandpa was still teasing him, the way he had in Justin's room when he had placed his hand on Justin's shoulder. There was still the sense of shame whenever the outburst about women's work and the tears were remembered.

As they cleaned the utensils and dishes, Justin asked, "Grandpa, you think housework is women's work?"

"Do you?" Grandpa asked quickly.

"I asked you first, Grandpa."

"I guess asking you that before I answer is unfair. No, I don't. Do you?"

"Well, it seems easier for them," Justin said as he splashed water all over, glad he was outside.

"Easier than for me?"

"Well, not for you, I guess, but for me, yeah."

"Could it be because you don't know how?"

"You mean like making the bed and folding the clothes."

"Yes." Grandpa stopped and looked at Justin. "Making the bed is easy now, isn't it? All work is that way. It doesn't matter who does the work, man or woman, when it needs to be done. What matters is that we try to learn how to do it the best we can in the most enjoyable way."

"I don't think I'll ever like housework," Justin said, drying a big iron pot.

"It's like any other kind of work. The better you do it, the easier it becomes, and we seem not to mind doing things that are easy."

With the cooking rods and all the utensils put away, they locked the shed and went for their horses.

"Now, I'm going to let you do the cinches again. You'll like that."

There's that teasing again, Justin thought.

"Yeah. That's a man's work," he said, and mounted Black.

"There are some good horsewomen. You'll see them at the rodeo." Grandpa mounted Pal. They went on their way, riding along silently, scanning the fence.

Finally Justin said, "I was just kidding, Grandpa." Then without planning to, he said, "I bet you don't like boys who cry like babies."

"Do I know any boys who cry like babies?"

"Aw, Grandpa, you saw me crying."

"Oh, I didn't think you were crying like a baby. In your room, you mean? We all cry sometime."

"You? Cry, Grandpa?"

"Sure."

They rode on, with Grandpa marking his map. Justin remained quiet, wondering what could make a man like Grandpa cry.

As if knowing Justin's thoughts, Grandpa said, "I remember crying when you were born."

"Why? Didn't you want me?"

"Oh, yes. You were the most beautiful baby. But, you see, your grandma, Beth, had just died. When I held you I was flooded with joy. Then I thought, *Grandma will never see this beautiful boy.* I cried."

The horses wading through the grass made the only sound in the silence. Then Grandpa said, "There's an old saying, son. 'The brave hide their fears, but share their tears.' Tears bathe the soul."

Justin looked at his grandpa. Their eyes caught. A warmth spread over Justin and he lowered his eyes. He wished he could tell his grandpa all he felt, how much he loved him.

Think Critically

1 Why does Justin feel guilty after he has breakfast with Grandpa? NOTE DETAILS

2 Why doesn't Justin want to do the chores around the house when he visits Grandpa? MAKE INFERENCES

3 What is one task that became easier for you as soon as you learned how to do it? PERSONAL RESPONSE

4 How does the author show that the conflict in the selection has been resolved? PLOT: CONFLICT AND RESOLUTION

5 **WRITE** Justin learns some things while visiting his grandfather. Use information from the story to explain:

- what Justin learns about his grandfather, and
- what Justin's grandfather teaches him about household work. EXTENDED RESPONSE

About the Author
Mildred Pitts Walter

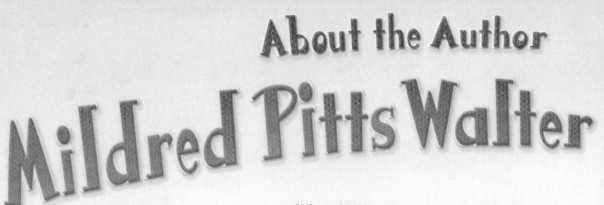

When Mildred Pitts Walter was teaching elementary school in Los Angeles, she could not find many children's books with African American characters.

"I contacted a publishing company and asked why, and they replied, 'Why don't you write them?'"

So she did.

Mildred Pitts Walter has traveled through Africa and Europe and has visited Russia, Turkey, and China. When she isn't traveling, she makes her home in Denver, Colorado.

About the Illustrator
Don Tate

Don Tate is from Des Moines, Iowa. He grew up making art of all kinds, from puppets to jewelry.

"In high school, when most of the other guys were trying to perfect their hoop skills, I was trying to perfect my drawing skills."

Don Tate's illustrations can be found in many places, including in theme parks and on greeting cards. His favorite kind of work is illustrating children's literature. He lives in Austin, Texas, with his wife and son.

 www.harcourtschool.com/storytown

Poetry

HOME ON THE RANGE

Oh! give me a home where the buffalo roam,
Where the Deer and the Antelope play;
Where never is heard a discouraging word,
And the sky is not clouded all day.

—Brewster Higley

HATS OFF TO THE COWBOY

The city folks think that it's over,
The cowboy has outlived his time—
An old worn-out relic, a thing of the past,
But the truth is, he's still in his prime.

The cowboy's the image of freedom,
The hard-ridin' boss of the range.
His trade is a fair one, he fights for what's right,
And his ethics aren't subject to change.

He still tips his hat to the ladies,
Lets you water first at the pond.
He believes a day's pay is worth a day's work,
And his handshake and word are his bond.

—**Red Steagall**

Connections

Comparing Texts

1. What did you learn from Justin's conversations with his grandfather that might help you solve a problem?

2. Compare the descriptions of cowboys in "Justin and the Best Biscuits in the World" with those in the poems "Home on the Range" and "Hats Off to the Cowboy."

3. Grandpa shows Justin the value of cooking, making a bed, and folding shirts. What is another valuable skill? How is it valuable?

Vocabulary Review

Word Webs

Work with a partner. Choose two Vocabulary Words. Create a web for each word. In the outer circles, write words and phrases that are related to the Vocabulary Word. Explain how each word or phrase is related to the Vocabulary Word.

reluctant

rumpled

surge

inspecting

taut

untangled

resounded

lurked

hesitate — shy — reluctant — doubtful — feel afraid

Fluency Practice

Partner Reading

When Grandpa mentions the festival, Justin is excited. Then the tone of the story changes. Work with a partner to take turns rereading aloud pages 190–191 of the story. As you read, use intonation to reflect the changing mood in the story. Give each other feedback about your reading. Repeat the activity until your intonation matches the story's mood.

Writing

Write a Journal Entry

Imagine that you are Justin. You have had a long day riding fence. Write a journal entry describing the events of your day.

The Day's Events
1.
2.
3.

My Writing Checklist

Writing Trait ▸ Ideas

✔ I used a graphic organizer to plan my writing.

✔ I described the events in sequence.

✔ I described only one day's events to keep my ideas focused.

CONTENTS

Lesson 8

Genre: Play

Three Little Cyberpigs

by Jane Tesh • illustrated by Nathan Jurevicius

The Three Little Pigs Revisited

by Kok Heong McNaughton

illustrated by Aaron Meshon

Genre: Fairy Tale

Focus Skill

 ## Author's Purpose and Perspective

Every author has a **purpose**, or a reason, for writing. An author may write to entertain, to inform, to persuade, or to teach a lesson. Authors may have more than one purpose for writing.

An author may also have a **perspective** in his or her writing. An author's perspective is how the author feels about the subject. Readers can use details in the text as clues to the author's purpose and perspective.

Author's Purpose	Author's Perspective	Details in the Text

Tip

To determine the author's purpose, ask yourself why the author wrote the text.

Read the paragraph below. The graphic organizer shows the details in the text that support the author's perspective.

A woodsman lived alone in a forest. One day, he saved the life of a princess. To thank him, the princess offered to grant him one wish. The woodsman wished to be king of the forest. The princess looked sad. She granted his wish, but the forest animals would not obey their new king. From then on, the woodsman was careful about his wishes.

Author's Purpose	Author's Perspective	Details in the Text
To teach a lesson	The woodsman wished for the wrong thing.	• The princess looked sad when the woodsman made his wish. • The animals would not obey their new king.

Try This!

Look back at the paragraph. What lesson does the author want to teach? Look at the last sentence for a clue.

 www.harcourtschool.com/storytown

impressed

slick

nimble

exist

fierce

cease

Next Stop: Internet

The mayor of Oak City has announced plans to install computers on city buses. Computer screens and large, simple keypads will be available on the backs of bus seats beginning next month. Many Oak City residents are **impressed** with the plan.

"That will be **slick**," said 30-year-old Jason Beck. "Now I'll be able to surf the Internet on my way to work."

Don Chen, 60, agreed. "My typing fingers aren't as **nimble** as they once were. The large keypad will make it easy to e-mail my grandson."

Aleesha Johnson, 15, also praised the plan. "I can't believe this didn't **exist** sooner," she said.

One citizens' group, however, has voiced **fierce** opposition. Its members say people already spend too much time on the Internet. This group promises to **cease** riding buses altogether if the city goes through with its plan.

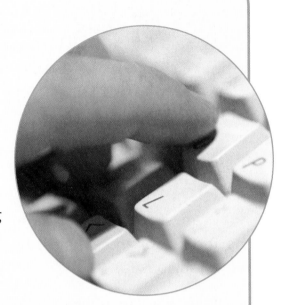

 www.harcourtschool.com/storytown

Word Scribe

Your challenge this week is to use the Vocabulary Words in writing. Write an e-mail to a friend in which you describe a slick car you have seen or a computer game that really impressed you. Use as many Vocabulary Words as you can in your e-mail. Send your e-mail to your friend.

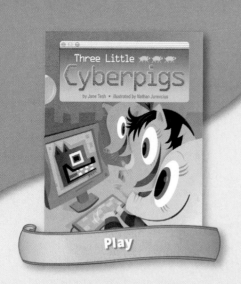

Three Little Cyberpigs

by Jane Tesh • illustrated by Nathan Jurevicius

Play

Genre Study

Plays are stories that can be performed for an audience. As you read, look for

- characters' names introducing dialogue.

- stage directions describing how the characters move on stage.

First
↓
Next
↓
Then
↓
Finally

Comprehension Strategy

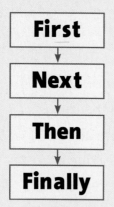 Use a sequence chart like the one above to help you **summarize** the text as you read.

Three Little Cyberpigs

by Jane Tesh • illustrated by Nathan Jurevicius

Characters

Three Little Pigs:

    PETE

    PATSY

    P.J.

BIG BAD WOLF

ANN, *a mouse*

HUMPTY DUMPTY

KING'S MEN

HORSES

MISS MUFFET

SPIDER

JACK BE NIMBLE

LITTLE BO PEEP

JACK

JILL

OLD KING COLE

THREE BLIND MICE

LITTLE JACK HORNER

MARY

COMPUTER VIRUS

(TIME: *The present.*

BEFORE RISE: PETE, PATSY, *and* P.J. *enter, cross stage.*)

PIGS: Three little pigs are we, we, we,

    Heading on down to the grocery!

(BIG BAD WOLF *jumps on stage.*)

WOLF: Hold on, piggies, not so fast!

PIGS: It's the Big Bad Wolf—alas!

WOLF: I couldn't blow down your house of brick,

    But now I'll catch you, quick, quick, quick! (*He chases* PIGS.)

PETE: We must run and get away,

    Or we'll be piggie stew today!

WOLF: Piggie stew! That sounds real fine.

    Three Little Pigs will soon be mine!

PATSY (*Pointing center*): Look! What's that over there?

P.J.: That's a new shop on the square.

PETE: It's worth a try, come on, let's run!

WOLF: Or barbecued piggies on a bun!

(WOLF *dashes off, missing* PIGS *as they run through curtain.*)

>>>

(SETTING: *Mother Goose Cybershop. Tables hold several computers, laptops, printers, etc. Sign on backdrop reads:* MOTHER GOOSE CYBERSHOP. SHOP HERE FOR ALL YOUR NURSERY RHYME COMPUTER NEEDS.

AT RISE: PIGS *look around in wonder at equipment. Seated on chairs at computer terminals are* HUMPTY DUMPTY, MISS MUFFET, JACK BE NIMBLE, LITTLE BO PEEP, JACK, JILL, OLD KING COLE, THREE BLIND MICE, LITTLE JACK HORNER, *and* MARY.)

PETE: Guess the wolf was not too quick.

PATSY: This looks neat!

P.J.: And really slick! All the latest techno-whiz. (ANN *enters.*) Tell me who this lady is.

ANN: You need a guide, and I'm the best. Let me tell you all the rest. I'm a mouse, my name is Ann. I'm your guide through Cyberland.

PETE: But the wolf is at the door.

ANN: He won't catch you any more.

PATSY: Can you help us?

ANN: Yes, I can. Come see the folks in Cyberland. (ANN *leads* PIGS *to* HUMPTY DUMPTY.)

HUMPTY DUMPTY: Humpty Dumpty sat on a wall, Couldn't get programs started at all.

(KING'S MEN *and* HORSES *enter. One of the* HORSES *presses reset button on computer.*)

KING'S MEN: All the king's horses and all the king's men, rebooted him up, got him started again.

(HUMPTY DUMPTY *looks at his computer, smiles, and shakes hands with* KING'S MEN *and* HORSES. ANN *leads* PIGS *to* MISS MUFFET.)

MISS MUFFET: Little Miss Muffet sat on a
tuffet,

Surfing the Internet way,

Along came a spider,

(SPIDER *enters and tries to use computer.*)

Who couldn't get by her,

Till WebCrawler showed him the way!

(MISS MUFFET *and* SPIDER *happily use
computer together.* ANN *leads* PIGS *to*
JACK BE NIMBLE.)

JACK BE NIMBLE: Jack be nimble,

Jack be quick,

Give your mouse a double click!

(JACK *jumps twice over his computer.*
ANN *and* PIGS *applaud.*)

PETE: This is really something grand!

PATSY: I like it here in Cyberland.

P.J.: But you know we cannot stay.

PETE: We will until the wolf's away.

ANN: Let me show you something more.

Customers just love our store.

(*Leads* PIGS *to* BO PEEP)

LITTLE BO PEEP: Little Bo Peep has lost
her sheep

And can't tell where to find them.

File them and save

Under "Sheep, you behave!"

And you'll always be able to find them.

(*She clicks on her computer and
"baaing" sounds are heard.*)

PETE: That's amazing!

PATSY: I should say!

P.J.: We are learning lots today!

(ANN *leads* PIGS *to* JACK *and* JILL.)

>>>

JACK *and* **JILL** (*Together*): Jack and Jill went
   up the hill
To see about a letter,
Jack came down and turned around
And said, "Email is better."
So Jack and Jill don't climb the hill
They stay at home; it's better
To use their own computer keys
To send an e-mail letter.
(JACK *and* JILL *show* PIGS *their e-mail
and* PIGS *nod,* impressed. ANN *leads* PIGS
to THREE BLIND MICE.)

THREE BLIND MICE: Three blind mice,
Three blind mice,
We click and drag and find all the files,
We open and close and enter and smile,
Have you ever seen such a sight in a while
As three blind mice?
(ANN *and* PIGS *applaud.* ANN *leads* PIGS
to OLD KING COLE.)

OLD KING COLE: Old King Cole was a merry
   old soul,
And a merry old soul was he!
He called for his disk,
(1ST BLIND MOUSE *brings him a disk.*)
And he called for his mouse,
(2ND BLIND MOUSE *sits on his lap.*)
And he called for his Windows Three.
(3RD BLIND MOUSE *brings him a set of
disks.* ANN *leads* PIGS *to* LITTLE JACK
HORNER.)

LITTLE JACK HORNER: Little Jack Horner
   sat in a corner,
Eating his Christmas pie.
Holidays were a flop,
Till he got a laptop,
And said, "What a good boy am I!"

PETE: Gee, I like the look of that,
A small computer, nice and flat!
(ANN *leads* PIGS *to* MARY.)

ANN: Mary, Mary, quite contrary,
How does your web page grow?

221

MARY (*Showing them*): With great new fonts and super ads
And graphics all in a row!
(PIGS *admire* MARY's *web page*.)

PATSY: I'd really like to learn some more!

P.J.: This is a great computer store!

MOTHER GOOSE CHARACTERS (*Together*):
Three, four, backup some more,
Five, six, edit, fix,
Seven, eight, repaginate!
Nine, ten, let's start again!

PETE: This is great! We're so impressed.
(*Loud knocking sounds are heard.*)

PATSY: But we're still three pigs in deep distress.

ANN: What's the matter?

P.J.: We must hide.
The Big Bad Wolf is still outside.

WOLF (*Offstage*): You can't stay in there all day!
Come on out for pig soufflé!

PETE: Oh, no, he really sounds upset!

PATSY: We might end up as pork chops yet.

WOLF (*Offstage*): I'll huff and puff and blow and blow
Until you're all off-line, ho, ho!

P.J.: Ann, perhaps we'd better split,
He'll ruin the store; you'll have to quit.

ANN: Oh, that old wolf is talking trash.
I know a way to make him crash.
Everybody, enter this:
Big Bad Wolf, cease to exist.
(*Characters type on keyboards.*)
Here's the way, and it's real neat,
Everybody, press "delete"!
(*Characters press delete buttons. There
is a whooshing sound.* PIGS *peer out center stage.*)

>>>

PETE: Wow, it worked! He isn't there!

PATSY: He simply vanished in thin air!

P.J.: Now we're safe from being snacks!

PETE: He didn't even leave his tracks.

ANN: So now you see what we can do.

PIGS: We all want computers, too!

(*Loud buzzing noise is heard offstage.*)

PETE: Say, what's that sound?

ANN: Oh, not again!

(COMPUTER VIRUS *enters.*)

Goodness me, who let you in?

VIRUS (*In a tough voice*): I am here to make a mess.

ANN: Oh, no, you won't. You're just a pest.

PIGS: He looks fierce. Is he all right?

ANN: His bark is much worse than his bite.

He thinks he's going to cause a fuss.

(*To* VIRUS) Go away! You don't scare us!

(VIRUS *exits, sulking.* ANN *turns to* PIGS.)

We'll get you set up right away.

PIGS: Pigs in Cyberland, hooray!

THE END

Think Critically

1 What computer knowledge do the pigs gain? NOTE DETAILS

2 How does the author feel about computers? Do you think the author's main purpose in writing the play is to inform, to persuade, or to entertain? How do you know? AUTHOR'S PURPOSE AND PERSPECTIVE

3 In your opinion, which character learns the most important thing about computers? Use details from the play to explain your answer. MAKE JUDGMENTS

4 When the pigs say that the virus looks fierce, Ann replies, "His bark is much worse than his bite." What does she mean? FIGURATIVE LANGUAGE

5 READ THINK EXPLAIN **WRITE** In the play, Humpty Dumpty has a problem with his computer. Use details from the play to describe the problem and explain how it was solved. SHORT RESPONSE

ABOUT THE AUTHOR
Jane Tesh

Jane Tesh lives in the small town of Mt. Airy, North Carolina. Before she retired, she was the media specialist at a local school for more than thirty years. She has written more than a dozen plays for children. Jane Tesh likes to travel. When she is not traveling, she spends some of her time playing the piano at the local theater.

ABOUT THE ILLUSTRATOR
Nathan Jurevicius

Nathan Jurevicius (Joor•ee•VISH•us) is an illustrator, animator, and toy designer. When he was six, he presented his first art show. He sold three art pieces, including one titled *Woman with a fly on her nose in a phonebox.* He decided at age fourteen to be an artist. Nathan Jurevicius has been inspired by many artists, including Dr. Seuss. He lives with his wife and children in Melbourne, Australia.

 www.harcourtschool.com/storytown

Fairy Tale

The Three Little Pigs Revisited

by Kok Heong McNaughton
illustrated by Aaron Meshon

226

Once there were three little pigs who lived in a country with a housing shortage. Vacant houses and apartments were very hard to find.

The three little pigs decided to build their own home. But knowing how working together might be hard, they thought it safer for each to build his own ideal home. This way, each could be creative without the others telling him that his ideas were dumb.

Unfortunately, in addition to a severe housing shortage, there were no more building materials. The three little pigs would have to use other materials.

The first little pig towed his wagon around every day collecting old newspapers. After a week, he had enough to build himself a house. It wasn't the most sturdy of homes, but the first little pig liked it because he could sit at home in the evenings and read the walls. One thing he had to be careful about, though, was building fires. He became an expert outdoor chef.

The second little pig collected aluminum cans. He built his home by stacking the cans together. His house was comfortable most of the time except during midday, when it would be as hot as an oven inside. The second little pig didn't mind. He loved the sound of raindrops falling on his tin roof. It made him feel luckier than his brother, whose newspaper house would collapse and have to be rebuilt every time it rained.

The third little pig learned how to make adobe bricks. For months he labored over making an adobe house. It was the dream house he had always wanted. It shielded him from the hot sun and kept him safe from wind and rain. When he was hungry, he nibbled on the straw sticking out of the wall, tidying his house as he ate.

One day, a wolf, who had been chased out of his apartment because he hadn't paid the rent for three months, came upon the first little pig's newspaper house.

"Little pig, little pig, let me come in!" he cried.

"Not by the hair of my chinny-chin-chin," the first little pig answered.

"Then I'll huff, and I'll puff, and I'll blow your house in!"

So he huffed, and he puffed, and he blew all the newspapers away, exposing the first little pig clutching the sports section to his chest.

The first little pig took one look at the wolf and ran. He ran as fast as his four short legs could carry him to his brother's aluminum house, with the wolf hot on his curly tail. Just in time, he reached his brother's home, and they slammed in the last few aluminum cans, sealing themselves inside.

Now that he had two little pigs instead of one to handle, the wolf cried, "Little pigs, little pigs, let me come in!"

"Not by the hair of my chinny-chin-chin," replied the two pigs.

"Then I'll huff, and I'll puff, and I'll blow your house in!"

So he huffed, and he puffed, and he scattered the aluminum cans all over the landscape. While the wolf stumbled over the cans, the two little pigs took off like two shots for their brother's adobe home.

The third little pig was sunning himself outside his adobe home when who should come running along but his two silly brothers who had built paper and aluminum houses.

"Oh, darn," he said to himself. "I knew they would have to move in with me one of these days. But couldn't they have waited a bit longer?"

Then, to his surprise, they told him that the wolf was going to eat them all up unless he saved them.

They ran inside the house, and the third little pig latched the door. Soon the wolf caught up and cried his familiar line, "Little pigs, little pigs, let me come in!"

"Not by the hair of my chinny-chin-chin," the three little pigs said together.

"Then I'll huff, and I'll puff, and I'll blow your house in!"

So the wolf huffed, and he puffed. He huffed, and he puffed again. And again. And again. But he couldn't blow that sturdy adobe house down.

The three little pigs stood by the window gleefully watching the wolf puffing himself silly. But suddenly, as they watched in horror, the wolf collapsed, clutching his chest.

"Oh, no!" said the first little pig. "What's wrong with him?"

"I think he's having a heart attack," said the second little pig.

"We must save him," said the third little pig. "We can't let him die!"

The three little pigs opened the door and went out to help the wolf. While the first little pig counted, the second and third little pigs performed CPR on the unconscious wolf. After a while, the wolf stirred and sat up.

When the three little pigs saw that the wolf had recovered, they made for the safety of the house once more. But before they could slam the door shut, the wolf said, "Why are you afraid of me?"

The three little pigs did a double take. "Pigs are supposed to be afraid of wolves," they said. "Don't you want to eat us up?"

The wolf guffawed. "Pork chops? No thanks, I'm a vegetarian."

"Oh? So why were you chasing us and

blowing our houses down?" asked the first little pig.

"I only wanted to move in with you," said the wolf. "And I wanted to find out if your house is solid enough for me. I see that this one is."

"If you wanted to move in with us, why didn't you just say so?" The second little pig threw up his front hooves in exasperation.

"But I did! I asked you to let me in," said the wolf.

"You didn't say please. And you shouldn't have asked so aggressively," the first little pig rebutted.

"He's right. And you should have said exactly what you meant. You shouldn't beat around the bush like that," the second little pig scolded.

"All right, all right," intervened the third little pig. "It's all a lack of communication. Let's start all over again, shall we?" He turned to the wolf. "Now say your line."

The wolf cleared his throat and said solemnly, "Little pigs, little pigs, may I move in with you?" He looked around at the three little pigs and when they didn't reply, he added, "Please?"

The three little pigs nodded.

So the wolf and the first two little pigs helped the third little pig remodel the adobe house so that there was room for all of them. They learned the importance of cooperation and communication, and they all lived together happily ever after.

Connections

Comparing Texts

1. How can you use computers to get information and solve problems?

2. Compare and contrast the wolf characters in "Three Little Cyberpigs" and in "The Three Little Pigs Revisited."

3. In the play, a mouse guides three pigs through a cybershop. How can people learn about computers?

Vocabulary Review

Rate a Situation

Work with a partner. Read aloud each sentence. Point to the spot on the word line that shows how comfortable you would feel in each situation.

Comfortable _____ **Uncomfortable**

- Your friend said your outfit looked **slick**.
- You saw a **nimble** person walk on the ice.
- Your teacher was **impressed** with your work.
- You had to **cease** playing your favorite game.

slick

nimble

impressed

cease

exist

fierce

Fluency Practice

Partner Reading

Phrasing is how readers group words when they read aloud. Choose a section from "The Three Little Pigs Revisited" to read aloud as your partner listens. Discuss with your partner how you used punctuation marks in the text to guide your phrasing. Switch places with your partner and repeat the process.

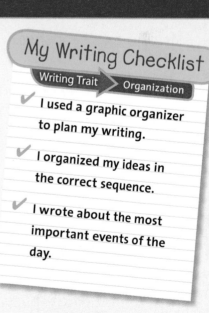

Writing

Write an E-Mail

Imagine you are Ann, the mouse, in "Three Little Cyberpigs." Write an e-mail to a friend about the day you met the wolf and the three pigs.

Event 1
↓
Event 2
↓
Event 3

My Writing Checklist

Writing Trait ▸ Organization

✓ I used a graphic organizer to plan my writing.

✓ I organized my ideas in the correct sequence.

✓ I wrote about the most important events of the day.

CONTENTS

Lesson 9

WEAVING A CALIFORNIA TRADITION

A Native American Basketmaker

by Linda Yamane/Photographs by Dugan

Wonder Weaver

by Ellen Holtzen • photos by Jackson Smith

Author's Purpose and Perspective

You know that an author has a **purpose** for writing, such as to entertain or to inform. Sometimes an author's purpose may be to change a law or to preserve a tradition. An author's **perspective**, or viewpoint, on a subject is often connected to his or her purpose. Details in the text are clues to the author's purpose and perspective.

Author's Purpose	Author's Perspective	Details in the Text

Tip

To figure out an author's perspective, ask yourself, *What is the author's opinion of the subject?*

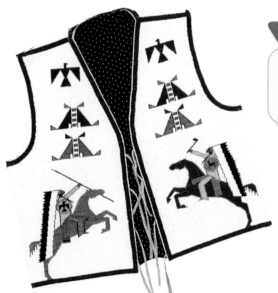

Read the paragraph below. Then look at the graphic organizer. The detail is a clue to the author's perspective. The author describes Native American culture as a "priceless treasure." This tells the reader that the author values that culture and believes it should be preserved.

Marcus Dewey is an outstanding Arapaho artist from the Wind River Reservation. He is famous for decorating very old horse saddles with beautiful beadwork. He creates beaded designs in traditional Arapaho colors—white, blue, red, and yellow. Artists such as Dewey help preserve the priceless treasure of Native American culture.

Author's Purpose	Author's Perspective	Details in the Text
To inform; to influence readers to preserve Native American culture	Native American culture should be preserved.	The author describes Native American culture as a priceless treasure.

Try This!

Look back at the paragraph. What is the author's perspective about Marcus Dewey? Which words are clues to the author's perspective?

 www.harcourtschool.com/storytown

Vocabulary

Build Robust Vocabulary

- unique
- delicate
- bond
- preserve
- infest
- inspires
- intervals
- flexible

Sand Painting

Sand painting is a **unique** tradition practiced by many Native Americans of the southwestern United States. Sand artists paint with **delicate** powders made from minerals. They sift the powders through their fingers to create colorful designs on the ground. Like other Native American traditions, sand painting reflects a special **bond** with nature. The designs often stand for natural objects.

An artist creates a traditional Native American sand painting.

In the past, native sand painters did not **preserve** their artworks. When a ceremony was over, the sand painting was destroyed. Today, many sand painters use glue to create permanent works on wood.

If you would like to make a sand painting, choose a flat piece of old, weathered wood. First, make sure that no insects **infest** the wood. Then, draw a scene that **inspires** you. Spread a thin layer of glue over your drawing, and then sprinkle sand over the glue. Change colors at regular **intervals** to create a pattern. You can attach a **flexible** piece of wire to the back of your artwork to hang it.

Some sand paintings are permanent.

 www.harcourtschool.com/storytown

Word Champion

 Your task this week is to use the Vocabulary Words outside your classroom. Keep a list of the words in a place at home where you can see it. Use as many words as you can in your daily conversations. For example, you might ask family members what inspires them. Be sure to write the words you used in your vocabulary journal.

Expository Nonfiction

WEAVING A
CALIFORNIA TRADITION
A Native American Basketmaker

by Linda Yamane/Photographs by Dugan Aguilar

Genre Study

Expository nonfiction gives you information about a topic. As you read, look for

- facts and details.

- photographs and captions.

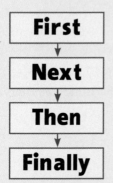

First
Next
Then
Finally

Comprehension Strategy

Use a sequence chart like the one above to help you **summarize** the text as you read.

For Carly Tex and her family, basketmaking is more than just a craft or a beautiful art form. They make baskets because that is what their family has always done. Carly is eleven years old and comes from a long line of Western Mono basketweavers. Carly lives with her mom and dad and her seven-year-old sister, Erin, in Dunlap, California, a small town in the foothills of the Sierra Nevada Mountains.

Weaving
A California
Tradition

by LINDA YAMANE

photographs by
Dugan Aguilar

Carly and her family are all involved in one way or another with basketmaking, but they also do many other things. Carly's mom, Julie Tex, has a college degree in anthropology and has recently returned to college to earn a graduate degree in social work. It's a lot of work going to school, studying, and taking care of her family.

Carly's older sister, Mandy Marine, also goes to college, at Fresno State University. She will graduate soon with a degree in anthropology.

Carly's dad, Dale Tex, is well known for his beadwork. He creates his own designs, using many colors. He made Carly's mom a belt with 18,000 beads in it!

The Western Monos are one of many California Indian tribes. You may have heard of the Cahuilla, Chumash, Pomo, Yurok, or Yokuts. There are nearly 60 tribes in California, and most of them are made up of many smaller tribal groups. For example, there are several Western Mono groups. Carly's mother, Julie, is Dunlap Mono. Carly's father, Dale, is North Fork Mono.

Carly, her sister Erin, and their parents, Dale and Julie, live in Dunlap, California. Carly's older sister, Mandy, doesn't live at home anymore. She goes to college in Fresno.

When most people think about what it takes to make a basket, they just think of the weaving. But a lot of hard work must be done before the weaving can begin. First, the proper plants must be gathered. Each plant is gathered at a certain time of the year.

The geography and climate of an area determine the kinds of plants that grow there. Generally, northern California baskets are made from different plants than those used by central California weavers. Still other plants are used in southern California. Within these regions, each tribal group has its own unique style.

Western Mono basketweavers use deergrass, chaparral, sourberry, redbud, sedge, and bracken fern. Deergrass is a bunch grass (a grass that grows in tufts). Deergrass has narrow flower stalks that are gathered in the fall and dried to use in baskets.

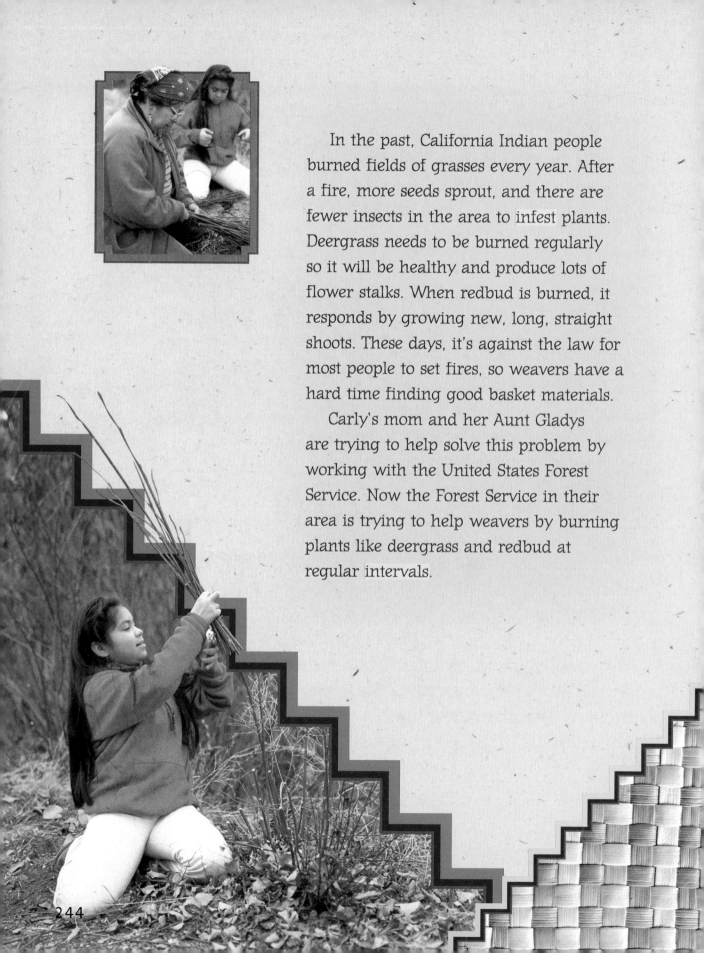

In the past, California Indian people burned fields of grasses every year. After a fire, more seeds sprout, and there are fewer insects in the area to infest plants. Deergrass needs to be burned regularly so it will be healthy and produce lots of flower stalks. When redbud is burned, it responds by growing new, long, straight shoots. These days, it's against the law for most people to set fires, so weavers have a hard time finding good basket materials.

Carly's mom and her Aunt Gladys are trying to help solve this problem by working with the United States Forest Service. Now the Forest Service in their area is trying to help weavers by burning plants like deergrass and redbud at regular intervals.

In the summer, Carly and her family also gather the red berries from the sourberry plant. Sourberries can be eaten fresh or dried. They are *really* sour—worse than a dill pickle! As Carly and the others walk among the sourberry bushes, they watch out for rattlesnakes. The strong scent of the sourberry plants fills the air. Many Western Mono people say the smell reminds them of their grandmothers, who were often busy scraping sourberry sticks for their baskets.

Carly is weaving her cradleboard from redbud, sourberry, and sedge. First she had to gather the materials and prepare them. Redbud, chaparral, and sourberry shoots are cut in late fall or early winter, after the first frosts have caused the leaves to fall from the plants. It's a cold time of the year in the mountains, but it's also beautiful.

Carly and her family enjoy spending this time together outdoors. They laugh and talk and sing songs as they cut enough sticks to last throughout the year. They look for sticks of the right length and thickness for different kinds of baskets.

Carly and her family have a good time gathering basket materials together.

They find some materials close to home, but sometimes they have to travel long distances to find the plants they need. Sometimes they gather on private land. Other times they find what they're looking for on public land or along roadsides. Carly and Erin remember a time when they went to gather redbud where they always had, but someone had built a house there. The redbud was gone.

When weavers collect plants, they are careful not to take too many or to destroy them. In fact, the cutting, trimming, and thinning benefits the plants. Sedge plants with underground runners that were crowded have room to spread out and grow long and straight. Redbud and other shrubs that are cut back will have less insects and grow healthy new shoots. Weavers take care of the plants and are taught to say "thank you" to the Creator, the plants, and the earth for what they take.

After the basketweaving plants are gathered, they are cleaned and tied together to dry.

246

Carly, Mandy, Gladys, and Julie enjoyed gathering basketry materials together.

After the weaving materials are gathered, they must be prepared—very soon after gathering, before they dry out. Sticks and roots usually need to be scraped or peeled to remove the bark. Sedge roots must be split lengthwise. It takes practice, patience, and a delicate touch to learn how to split roots properly. Bracken fern requires lots and lots of scraping and cleaning to remove the sticky material.

After the materials have been split, scraped, or peeled, they are tied into coils or bundles for drying. Basket materials usually must dry for six months to a year before they can be used.

Preparing for weaving involves a lot of hard work, but the jobs can be fun when done in a group. Carly and her family sometimes gather and prepare materials by themselves, but other times they share the work with people who are just learning to weave. This way they can pass along traditions that might otherwise be forgotten.

ast year, Carly gathered and prepared enough redbud to make a full-sized gathering basket called a *sumaya* (soo•MYE•yuh). It is oval in shape and gradually becomes deeper in the center. The sumaya is not tightly woven, but has spaces between the rows of weaving. It is made entirely of redbud, except for the rim, which is chaparral.

Carly's Aunt Gladys taught her that for a sumaya, she should look for short young redbud shoots without any nubs. These were for the basket's framework. She also looked for nice long sticks to split for the weavers, which are used to weave around the foundation or frame sticks. Carly had to find a special chaparral stick to use for the rim. It had to be long enough to curve around the whole edge of her sumaya.

California Indians have two ways of constructing baskets—*coiling* and *twining*. Cradleboards and sumayas are both twined baskets. Twined baskets have a framework of sticks. The weaver attaches these sticks together by twisting pairs of flexible weaving strands around them, row after row. Gladys taught Carly how to add new sticks to her sumaya frame to make the basket broader and deeper. Carly had to use her math skills to find the right places to add new sticks evenly. She counted the number of sticks in the basket and divided that by the number of new sticks she wanted to add. Then she knew the number of sticks that she should leave between each new one she added.

Shaping the sumaya was tricky, too, but Carly enjoyed doing it. Making the cradleboard was easier, she says, but the sumaya was more challenging, because she had to be patient and use more sticks.

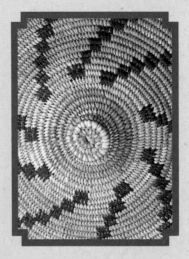

Detail of a coiled basket

Carly has worked hard to finish her sumaya in time for this year's California Indian Basketweavers Gathering. These annual gatherings are a time when basketmakers from throughout the state come to share their weaving skills and their love of baskets. Beginners, young or old, learn from more experienced weavers. There are many different tribal groups and styles of baskets, but the weavers all share a common bond.

This year's gathering is at the Tuolumne Rancheria, near Sonora. Carly is looking forward to entering her sumaya in the Basketweavers Showcase. The showcase is a display of baskets completed by California Indian basketweavers during the previous year. The showcase encourages weavers to find the time to work on their baskets, giving them a goal to work toward. It also inspires others to learn to weave.

Most California Indian baskets take a *very* long time to make. The amount of time depends on the type of basket and the size. A basket that is very tightly woven with fine weaving materials takes longer to make than an open-weave basket or one made with heavier materials. Because many weavers are busy working, going to school, or raising families, they are lucky to finish one or two baskets a year.

At this year's basketweavers gathering, people have come from near and far. Everyone is busy and excited. Carly's whole family is here, including some cousins.

During the first day of the gathering, weavers and their families and friends spend time together away from the public eye. It is a day for teaching and learning, and Carly does some of both. She sits next to her Aunt Gladys for a while, watching as Gladys begins a coiled basket. Carly and her cousin prepare deergrass for Gladys. As they work, Erin gives some helpful advice to a beginning weaver. Later, the girls prepare sedge strands by trimming them with a knife until they are nice and thin. These long strands will be wrapped and stitched around the deergrass foundation.

Carly watches Gladys weave a coiled basket.

251

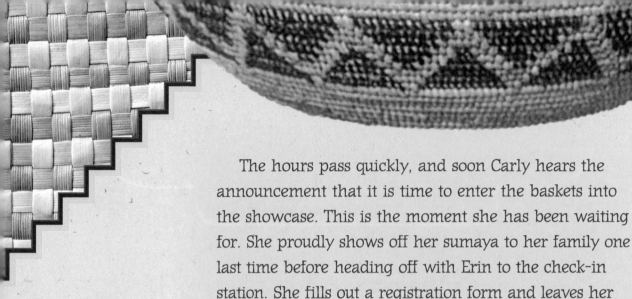

The hours pass quickly, and soon Carly hears the announcement that it is time to enter the baskets into the showcase. This is the moment she has been waiting for. She proudly shows off her sumaya to her family one last time before heading off with Erin to the check-in station. She fills out a registration form and leaves her basket there. It will be photographed, then arranged in the exhibit. The showcase won't be ready for viewing until tomorrow.

After the evening meal, as the warm night darkens, people begin getting up to share the stories and songs of their tribal areas. By bedtime, Carly and Erin are tired and ready for a good night's sleep.

The next morning, everyone gets up early. All the weavers help set up displays for the many visitors who will arrive soon, since the exhibit is open to the public.

All day long, Carly and the others demonstrate aspects of California Indian culture. Mandy shows how to make string from the silvery fibers found in the stem of the milkweed plant. She rolls and twists the long, soft fibers. In the old times, milkweed string was woven by hand into long sashes, which were used to tie babies into their cradleboards. Today most people use store-bought yarn to weave sashes, because making string by hand takes a long time. Still, people like Mandy try to preserve the old ways.

Carly and Erin also explain to visitors how to make clapper sticks, one of the instruments used in California Indian music. First, they peel the bark off a length of elderberry wood. Then they partially split it lengthwise, leaving a handle at the bottom. The soft inner pith is scooped out of the split section, and the whole instrument is sanded smooth. The split portion of the stick claps together when the player hits it against the palm of her hand. The sound of clapper sticks is a very ancient California sound.

Carly and Erin sing California Indian songs and use clapper sticks, a traditional instrument.

Carly & Erin Tex
W. Mono

Another instrument often used in traditional California Indian music is the deer-hoof rattle. Several deer hooves are hung with leather thongs or cords from a bone or wood handle. When shaken, the hooves clack together. Another kind of rattle is made from large moth cocoons. The cocoons are filled with tiny rocks and attached to a wooden handle.

Carly has been so busy she hasn't had a chance to visit the Basketweavers Showcase to see her sumaya and all the other baskets on display. In the exhibit are all shapes and sizes of baskets. One is covered with beads. Another has little quail feathers around the rim. There are sifting baskets and baby baskets, bowls and flat trays. There is even a fish-trap basket.

Carly is proud to see her sumaya on display with the other baskets at the Basketweavers Showcase.

Carly is proud to see her sumaya basket here among the others and wonders what kind of basket to make next year. She tells her mother she thinks she wants to make a redbud storage basket. It's a twined, deep, oval-shaped bowl. The outside will be red with a white design and the inside will be white with a red design.

Next year Carly will make her redbud storage basket. And the year after that she'll make another kind of basket . . . and the years and the baskets will go on and on. Carly likes to weave, and she wants to keep making baskets so she can carry on the tradition. "I want to keep learning and teach my own children so it can keep going through the generations," she says.

1994 California Indian Basketweavers Showcase

Carly Tex
Mono

Materials: Red Bud, split red bud, chapparel
Type of Basket: Twined Gathering

THINK CRITICALLY

1 How has the law against setting fires affected the California Indian basketweavers? CAUSE AND EFFECT

2 How are the basketmaking materials prepared for weaving after they have been gathered? NOTE DETAILS

3 Carly Tex is learning how to make the traditional baskets of her tribe. What have you learned about traditions that are important to your heritage?

USE PRIOR KNOWLEDGE

4 What is the author's perspective on Native American culture and traditions? How do you know? AUTHOR'S PURPOSE AND PERSPECTIVE

5 READ THINK EXPLAIN **WRITE** Summarize the events that take place at the California Indian Basketweavers Gathering. Use details and information from the selection to support your answer. SHORT RESPONSE

LINDA YAMANE

Linda Yamane is a singer, storyteller, and basketmaker. Her ancestors were the Rumsien Ohlone people from the central coast of California.

When she was growing up, Linda Yamane thought that all the baskets from her tribe had disappeared. As an adult, she found some of the baskets, studied them, and taught herself how to make them.

Linda Yamane now teaches other people about the baskets, culture, and history of the Rumsien Ohlone people.

Go online www.harcourtschool.com/storytown

Wonder Weaver

by Ellen Holtzen • photographs by Jackson Smith

Patrick Dougherty loves sticks! Wherever he goes, he makes wonderful weavings with them. In March 2001, he wove a great big teapot and three cups with the help of some kids.

THE TEAPOT TEAM

How did Patrick make the giant teapot? First he poked some strong curved branches into the ground. He turned them so that the tops met in the middle. Then he tied the tops of the branches together.

The kids helped weave sticks in and out of the branches. "That's the way," Patrick says. "Pull the sticks with one hand and push them with the other." While the kids wove the bottom of the teapot, Patrick used ladders and a scaffold to work on the top. Now the kids can play inside the teapot.

STUCK ON STICKS

"When I was a kid, I had a lot of fun with sticks. I made kid-sized nests for my brothers and sisters to crawl around in. And I used long, thin sticks for making tepees. That's why I'm always happy when kids enjoy helping with my weavings," Patrick explains.

STICK ART

Patrick has made stick buildings in lots of interesting shapes. He often weaves them in front of art museums, and he gets other people to help him.

Patrick really likes it when kids play in his buildings. Lots of kids crawled around in the funny jug faces. And the building was like a maze of arches. "Kids could run around and hide from each other in that one," Patrick says.

THE END

"After a while, my buildings start to fall apart, and that's OK," says Patrick. "The jug faces came to a really funny end. They were hit by heavy snow that slid off a nearby roof. When the snow melted, the flattened faces looked as if they were screaming for help!"

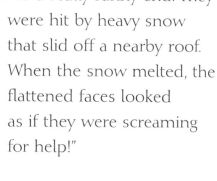

Connections

Comparing Texts

1. Carly learns how to make baskets from some of the older people in her family. Describe something you have learned from someone who is older than you are.

2. Use information from "Weaving a California Tradition" and "Wonder Weaver" to compare the ways that artists use natural materials.

3. Basketmaking is one kind of craft. Describe a handmade craft from another culture you know about.

Vocabulary Review

That delicate basket has a unique design.

Word Pairs

Work with a partner. Write each Vocabulary Word on a separate index card. Place the cards face down. Take turns flipping over the cards and writing a sentence that uses both words. Read aloud the sentence to your partner. You must use the words correctly in the sentence to keep the cards. The student with more cards at the end wins.

unique

infest

intervals

delicate

flexible

bond

inspires

preserve

Fluency Practice

Repeated Reading

When you use correct phrasing, your reading sounds natural. You can improve your phrasing with practice. Choose a three-paragraph passage from "Weaving a California Tradition." Read the passage aloud once. Use punctuation such as commas and periods to guide your phrasing. Reread the passage several times until your phrasing sounds natural.

Writing

Write a Paragraph

Write a paragraph that explains the author's perspective about basketweavers in "Weaving a California Tradition."

Author's Purpose	Author's Perspective	Details

My Writing Checklist

Writing Trait → Organization

✓ I used a chart to organize my ideas.

✓ I explained the author's perspective on the work of the basketweavers.

✓ I used details from the selection to explain the author's perspective.

CONTENTS

Lesson 10
Theme Review and Vocabulary Builder

Readers' Theater
INFORMATIONAL NARRATIVE

Emerald's Eggs

illustrated by Shino Arihara

YOUR
Social Studies
TEXTBOOK

Content-Area Reading
SOCIAL STUDIES TEXTBOOK

comprehend

pliable

solitary

scan

vulnerable

exuberant

mature

lumbers

encircle

nurture

Reading for Fluency

When reading a script aloud,

- Change your **intonation** to show the feelings of each character.

- Pay attention to punctuation as you read to improve your **phrasing**.

Emerald's Eggs

illustrated by Shino Arihara

CHARACTERS

Narrator 1	Ranger Melissa
Narrator 2	Sam
Ranger Jeff	Khaled
Jennifer	Cara
Chorus	Jorge

Narrator 1: A group of fourth-grade volunteers is at Padre Island National Seashore in south Texas. The volunteers are there to assist the rangers.

Narrator 2: The volunteers will be looking for sea turtles. If they are lucky, they will find a nest. First, the rangers want to know if the students comprehend the problems faced by sea turtles.

Ranger Jeff: Your teacher told us that you have studied sea turtles in class. Can anyone tell me how many species of sea turtles there are in the world?

Jennifer: There are seven species of sea turtles. All of them are endangered.

Ranger Jeff: That's right, Jennifer.

Chorus: Why are sea turtles endangered?

Ranger Melissa: There are many reasons. First, most fishing boats use large nets to catch many fish at one time. Turtles get caught in the nets and drown. Does anyone know another reason?

Sam: The places where turtles lay their eggs are being destroyed. That's why Padre Island is a protected area.

Ranger Jeff: Correct. Five out of the seven sea turtle species live right here. They come to Padre Island each spring to build their nests and lay eggs.

Khaled: Wow, I'm impressed.

Cara: We learned that hawksbills come to Padre Island.

Ranger Melissa: Yes, hawksbill turtles do come ashore here.

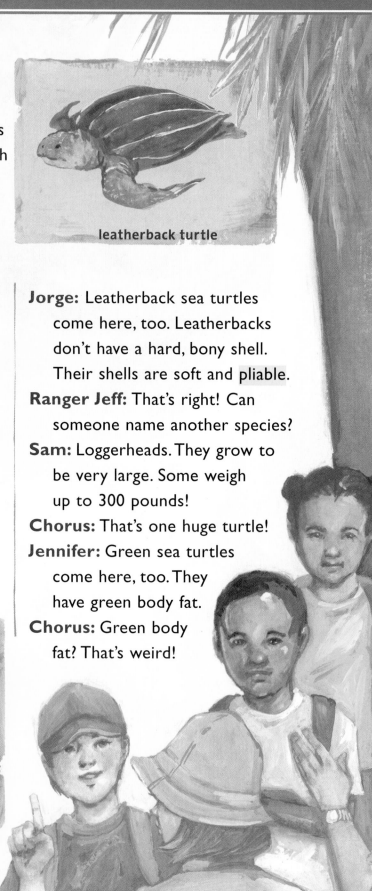

leatherback turtle

Jorge: Leatherback sea turtles come here, too. Leatherbacks don't have a hard, bony shell. Their shells are soft and pliable.

Ranger Jeff: That's right! Can someone name another species?

Sam: Loggerheads. They grow to be very large. Some weigh up to 300 pounds!

Chorus: That's one huge turtle!

Jennifer: Green sea turtles come here, too. They have green body fat.

Chorus: Green body fat? That's weird!

hawksbill turtle

Fluency Tip

When you see an exclamation point, change your **intonation** to show excitement.

Jennifer: Green sea turtles eat green algae, a tiny plant that grows in the ocean. That turns their body fat green.

green sea turtle

Ranger Melissa: Another characteristic of green sea turtles is that they are solitary most of the time. They may form groups to feed together.

Ranger Jeff: Does anyone remember the fifth species of turtle that comes to Padre Island?

Sam: The Kemp's ridley—my favorite! It's the smallest. It weighs between 80 and 100 pounds.

Khaled: Why is it called Kemp's ridley? That's an unusual name for a turtle.

Ranger Jeff: It is named after an American scientist, Richard Kemp. He first identified these turtles as a separate species.

Jorge: These turtles are the most endangered ones of all. If we don't help them, they could cease to exist.

Ranger Melissa: I hope that inspires you to look really hard for some nests. Come on, let's patrol the beach.

Kemp's ridley

267

Narrator 1: After a couple of hours, the students and rangers stop to rest.

Sam: We've been inspecting the beach, but we haven't found any nests yet. Still, I have a feeling that we'll be lucky today!

Ranger Melissa: You have a great attitude, team! Let's keep looking.

Narrator 1: The students and rangers continue searching.

Narrator 2: They climb a sand dune and use binoculars to scan the beach.

Narrator 1: While peering through his binoculars, Ranger Jeff walks into a giant heap of seaweed. He almost trips.

Ranger Jeff: Oops! I guess I'm not as nimble as I thought. I seem to be copying a characteristic of sea turtles—appearing awkward and being vulnerable on land.

Narrator 2: Ranger Jeff untangles himself from the seaweed, and the patrol continues to search.

Cara: Do you see that dark shape near that rock over there? It just hauled itself out of the water!

Jorge: I can see an olive-green shell.

Chorus: I see its flippers!

Narrator 1: Ranger Melissa looks through her binoculars. The students are exuberant at the arrival of the turtle.

Chorus: It's a Kemp's ridley!

Ranger Melissa: I'm a little reluctant to identify this turtle until we get a better look at it.

Narrator 2: The two rangers carefully approach the turtle while the students watch.

Ranger Jeff: There's a tag! She's number 251.

Khaled: What does the number mean?

Ranger Jeff: It identifies this individual turtle. From our records, we know that this turtle was first seen on Padre Island three years ago.

Ranger Melissa: Mature sea turtles lay eggs every two to three years.

Jennifer: I think we should name her.

Jorge: How about Jorge? That's my favorite name.

Khaled: Hmm, nice idea, Jorge. Don't forget that she's a female!

Cara: How about Emerald—like the green stone?

Sam: That's a great idea. Her shell is green.

Chorus: Let's call her Emerald!

Narrator 1: The volunteers and the rangers watch Emerald as she lumbers into a clump of sea grass.

Jennifer: I think she's going to make her nest there!

Ranger Jeff: If she does, she'll scoop out a hole in the sand and lay her eggs there. She will then cover up the hole and return to the sea.

Sam: What do we do now?

Ranger Melissa: You can help us put red flags in the sand to mark Emerald's tracks.

269

Use the correct **intonation** to express Ranger Jeff's concern for marking the tracks.

Ranger Jeff: Hurry! Those tracks are delicate. We don't want to forget where she came ashore.

Narrator 2: The volunteers each take a flag. They carefully mark Emerald's tracks. Then the rangers encircle Emerald's nest with more flags.

Narrator 1: The day is nearly over at Padre Island. The students are walking back across the beach with Ranger Melissa and Ranger Jeff.

Narrator 2: After watching Emerald make her nest, the students have more questions for the rangers.

Chorus: How many eggs will Emerald lay?

Ranger Jeff: She'll lay between eighty and one hundred small eggs. Their shells are flexible, like leather.

Khaled: What will happen after she lays her eggs?

Ranger Jeff: They'll be brought to the Padre Island laboratory. They'll be taken care of until they hatch. That takes about sixty days.

Jorge: What do the baby turtles look like?

Jennifer: I've seen pictures of them. They are tiny, about the size of a silver dollar. Their shells are black.

Ranger Jeff: You're right, Jennifer. They are tiny and helpless. That's why they stay in the lab, where we can nurture them for nine to eleven months.

Ranger Melissa: After that time, they're big enough to protect themselves. They'll be brought back to this same beach and released.

Ranger Jeff: After about two decades, the turtles will be mature adults.

Cara: Twenty years! It sure takes a sea turtle a long time to grow up. Think of how old we will be in two decades.

Ranger Melissa: Twenty years is a long time. But some sea turtles can live as long as eighty years. Do you know what happens once Emerald's babies are grown up?

Jorge: The turtles will swim back to this beach. Sea turtles always return to the beach where they were born.

Sam: How do they remember how to get to Padre Island?

Ranger Jeff: That's still a mystery. Scientists are trying to figure out how sea turtles remember the beach where they were born.

Narrator 1: The group is back at the parking lot. Everyone is tired but happy.

Chorus: Thank you, Ranger Melissa and Ranger Jeff.

Ranger Jeff: Do you think you'll remember this unique day twenty years from now—when Emerald's children return to Padre Island to lay their own eggs?

Chorus: We will! We will!

COMPREHENSION STRATEGIES
Review

Reading a Textbook

Bridge to Content-Area Reading Social Studies textbooks are examples of expository nonfiction. Expository nonfiction explains facts and information about real people, places, or events. The notes on page 273 point out some features of a social studies textbook. How can you use these features to skim and scan a social studies lesson?

Review the Focus Strategies

If you do not understand what you are reading, use the comprehension strategies you learned about in this theme.

Monitor Comprehension: Reread

Monitor comprehension while you read. If something in the text is unclear, reread to help you better understand the information.

Summarize

As you read, pause to summarize the most important ideas in the text. You can summarize after reading a paragraph, a section of text, or a complete text.

As you read the pages from a social studies textbook on pages 274–277, think about where and how you can use comprehension strategies.

HEADINGS

Headings give the topic of each section of text.

Lesson **3**

Local Governments

WHAT TO KNOW
How are California's local governments organized, and what do they do?

✔ Summarize how California's local governments are organized.

✔ Describe the function of each part of California's local governments.

✔ Explain the functions of California's special forms of local government.

VOCABULARY
county p. 481
county seat p. 481
board of supervisors p. 481
jury trial p. 482
municipal p. 483
city manager p. 484
special district p. 485
regional body p. 485
rancheria p. 486
sovereign p. 486

SUMMARIZE

YOU ARE THERE It's been several months since the city closed its park for repairs. Now you walk past the new playground and beds of freshly planted flowers to join a large group of people gathered in front of a stage. Soon the mayor arrives and gives a speech, thanking the many people who worked on the park. Then she cuts a ribbon, and the park is reopened.

❯ Lauren Hammond, Sacramento City Councilmember, listens to one of the city's residents.

County Governments

In addition to a state government, California also has county and city governments. These local governments make laws that apply only to the counties and cities. The highest level of local government is county government. A **county** is a section of a state.

The center of each county's government is called the county seat. A **county seat** is the city where the main government offices of the county are located.

The voters in each county elect a group of people to lead the government. This group is called the **board of supervisors**. In most counties, board members do the work of both the legislative and the executive branches. They make laws for the county and also decide how to spend tax money. County governments do a wide range of jobs, from running airports to picking up garbage.

READING CHECK ✦ **SUMMARIZE**
What does the board of supervisors in most county governments do?

California Counties

Alameda	36	Orange	55
Alpine	27	Placer	19
Amador	26	Plumas	12
Butte	11	Riverside	56
Calaveras	31	Sacramento	24
Colusa	15	San Benito	44
Contra Costa	29	San Bernardino	51
Del Norte	1	San Diego	57
El Dorado	25	San Francisco	34
Fresno	45	San Joaquin	30
Glenn	10	San Luis Obispo	49
Humboldt	4	San Mateo	35
Imperial	58	Santa Barbara	52
Inyo	48	Santa Clara	40
Kern	50	Santa Cruz	39
Kings	46	Shasta	6
Lake	14	Sierra	13
Lassen	7	Siskiyou	2
Los Angeles	54	Solano	23
Madera	42	Sonoma	20
Marin	28	Stanislaus	37
Mariposa	38	Sutter	16
Mendocino	8	Tehama	9
Merced	41	Trinity	5
Modoc	3	Tulare	47
Mono	33	Tuolumne	32
Monterey	43	Ventura	53
Napa	21	Yolo	22
Nevada	18	Yuba	17

Analyze Maps Of California's 58 counties, San Bernardino County is the largest in area. San Francisco County is the smallest.
◆ **Location** Which counties border the state of Oregon?

CAPTIONS

Captions help explain photographs and other graphics, and they support information in the main text.

MAPS

Maps show the place that you are reading about.

Apply the Strategies Read these pages about local governments in California from a social studies textbook. As you read, use comprehension strategies, such as rereading, to help you understand the text.

Lesson 3

Local Governments

💡 **WHAT TO KNOW**
How are California's local governments organized, and what do they do?

✔ Summarize how California's local governments are organized.

✔ Describe the function of each part of California's local governments.

✔ Explain the functions of California's special forms of local government.

VOCABULARY
county p. 481
county seat p. 481
board of supervisors p. 481
jury trial p. 482
municipal p. 483
city manager p. 484
special district p. 485
regional body p. 485
rancheria p. 486
sovereign p. 486

★ **SUMMARIZE**

🐻 California Standards
HSS 4.5, 4.5.3, 4.5.5

YOU ARE THERE It's been several months since the city closed its park for repairs. Now you walk past the new playground and beds of freshly planted flowers to join a large group of people gathered in front of a stage. Soon the mayor arrives and gives a speech, thanking the many people who worked on the park. Then she cuts a ribbon, and the park is reopened.

▶ Lauren Hammond, Sacramento City Councilmember, listens to one of the city's residents.

Stop and Think

If you don't understand the information about county governments, reread to clarify difficult concepts. **MONITOR COMPREHENSION: REREAD**

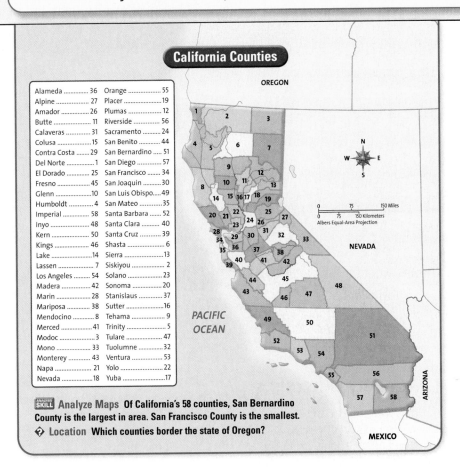

California Counties

Alameda	36	Orange	55
Alpine	27	Placer	19
Amador	26	Plumas	12
Butte	11	Riverside	56
Calaveras	31	Sacramento	24
Colusa	15	San Benito	44
Contra Costa	29	San Bernardino	51
Del Norte	1	San Diego	57
El Dorado	25	San Francisco	34
Fresno	45	San Joaquin	30
Glenn	10	San Luis Obispo	49
Humboldt	4	San Mateo	35
Imperial	58	Santa Barbara	52
Inyo	48	Santa Clara	40
Kern	50	Santa Cruz	39
Kings	46	Shasta	6
Lake	14	Sierra	13
Lassen	7	Siskiyou	2
Los Angeles	54	Solano	23
Madera	42	Sonoma	20
Marin	28	Stanislaus	37
Mariposa	38	Sutter	16
Mendocino	8	Tehama	9
Merced	41	Trinity	5
Modoc	3	Tulare	47
Mono	33	Tuolumne	32
Monterey	43	Ventura	53
Napa	21	Yolo	22
Nevada	18	Yuba	17

SKILL Analyze Maps Of California's 58 counties, San Bernardino County is the largest in area. San Francisco County is the smallest.

Location Which counties border the state of Oregon?

County Governments

In addition to a state government, California also has county and city governments. These local governments make laws that apply only to the counties and cities. The highest level of local government is county government. A **county** is a section of a state.

The center of each county's government is called the county seat. A **county seat** is the city where the main government offices of the county are located.

The voters in each county elect a group of people to lead the government. This group is called the **board of supervisors**. In most counties, board members do the work of both the legislative and the executive branches. They make laws for the county and also decide how to spend tax money. County governments do a wide range of jobs, from running airports to picking up garbage.

READING CHECK **SUMMARIZE**
What does the board of supervisors in most county governments do?

Chapter 12 ▪ 481

County governments provide services such as fire protection.

County Officials

Along with a board of supervisors, each county has other elected and appointed officials who perform a variety of jobs. These include enforcing laws, making sure elections are fair, and providing health care.

Each county has a sheriff chosen by voters to head the sheriff's department. The sheriff's job is to protect people and to make sure laws are obeyed in the county. The sheriff also runs the county jails.

Other county officials are the treasurer and the district attorney. The treasurer keeps track of the county's tax money and pays the county's bills. The district attorney represents the county in court cases.

Like state and federal governments, counties have a judicial branch. Each county has its own superior court. Superior court judges are elected by voters of the county.

Jury trials are often held in superior courts. In a **jury trial**, a group of citizens called a jury attends a trial and then decides whether the person on trial is guilty or not guilty.

Each county has an office of education headed by an elected superintendent of schools. The office of education works with both the state board of education and local school districts to provide quality education to all students in the county.

READING CHECK MAIN IDEA AND DETAILS
What are some of the jobs of people who work for county governments?

Stop and Think

Use the headings on these pages to help you summarize each section of text. **SUMMARIZE**

Municipal Governments

California has 478 communities that are set up as cities. More than three-fourths of all Californians live in cities. As a result, **municipal** (myu•NIH•suh•puhl), or city, governments often have the most direct effect on citizens' lives.

Municipal governments pass local laws and see that those laws are obeyed. They provide fire and police protection as well as many other services. They develop and maintain schools, libraries, parks, city jails, and other facilities. In addition, they run city recycling programs, keep local streets in good condition, and do many other important jobs.

Two kinds of cities described in the California Constitution are general law cities and charter cities. General law cities are organized by the state legislature and follow rules made by the state legislature. About three-fourths of California cities are general law cities.

Charter cities may form in communities of 3,500 people or more. The charter is an official document that tells how a city's government is set up. Unlike general law cities, charter cities set up their own rules for city government. General law cities usually follow the rules outlined in the state constitution.

READING CHECK **MAIN IDEA AND DETAILS**
What are the two kinds of cities described by the California Constitution?

▶ This officer (right) works for the San Francisco Police Department in an area of San Francisco known as Japantown. Garbage pickup (below) is another service that city governments provide.

277

▲ Andy Warhol, *Vesuvius*

CONTENTS

Lesson 11

WORLD OF WONDER

MIMICRY AND CAMOUFLAGE

BY MARY HOFF

lizards, frogs, and polliwogs

poems and paintings by
Douglas Florian

Text Structure: Cause and Effect

Knowing how an author has organized information can help you better understand and remember what you read. Authors of nonfiction texts organize information in what are called **text structures**. One kind of text structure is **cause and effect**. In texts that follow this structure, the author shows what happened (the effect) and the reason that it happened (the cause).

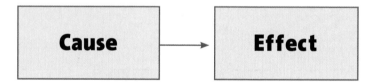

Tip

The words *because*, *if*, *when*, and *since* are clues to help you identify a cause-and-effect text structure.

Read the paragraph below. The graphic organizer shows the cause-and-effect relationship in the first sentence. The word *because* is a clue that this is a cause-and-effect relationship.

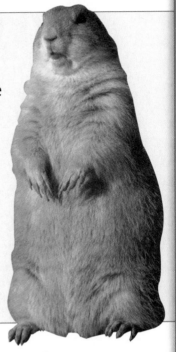

Prairie dogs live in large groups because it helps them survive. They live in underground tunnels that go on for miles. Some of the prairie dogs stand guard at the many entrances to the tunnels. If one of the guards senses danger, it barks. This sound tells other prairie dogs to hide in the tunnels. When the danger is gone, the guards use a different sound to tell the others. Because so many eyes are looking out for danger, the whole group of prairie dogs can stay safe.

Cause		Effect
Prairie dogs need a way to survive.	→	Prairie dogs live in large groups.

Try This!

Look back at the paragraph. What other cause-and-effect relationships can you find? What clue words helped you?

 www.harcourtschool.com/storytown

Vocabulary

Build Robust Vocabulary

predators

traits

lure

mimic

resembles

obvious

deceptive

avoid

Surprises in Nature

A plant called the Venus' flytrap is one of nature's surprising **predators**. One of the plant's most unusual **traits** is that it eats insects! The sweet-smelling leaves of the Venus' flytrap **lure** insects such as wasps, spiders, and flies. When an insect moves around on a Venus' flytrap leaf, it touches tiny hairs that signal the two parts of the leaf to close. Snap! In less than a second, the insect is trapped and becomes the plant's next meal.

It takes 8 to 10 days for the Venus' flytrap to digest an insect that it traps.

Amazing Sea Creatures

The puffer fish can **mimic** the appearance of a larger, dangerous-looking fish to disguise itself from enemies. When the puffer fish is calm, it **resembles** many other fish in the ocean. It doesn't look like an **obvious** danger. As soon as the puffer fish senses danger, however, it swallows water and grows to two or three times its normal size. The **deceptive** appearance keeps it safe from predators.

The puffer fish inflates itself to **avoid** being eaten by enemies in the ocean.

 online www.harcourtschool.com/storytown

Word Detective

 Your mission this week is to look for the Vocabulary Words outside your classroom. You might hear the words on television, read them in a magazine, or even find them in a science museum. Each time you see or hear a Vocabulary Word, write it in your vocabulary journal. Don't forget to record where you found the word.

WORLD OF WONDER
MIMICRY AND CAMOUFLAGE
BY MARY HOFF

Expository Nonfiction

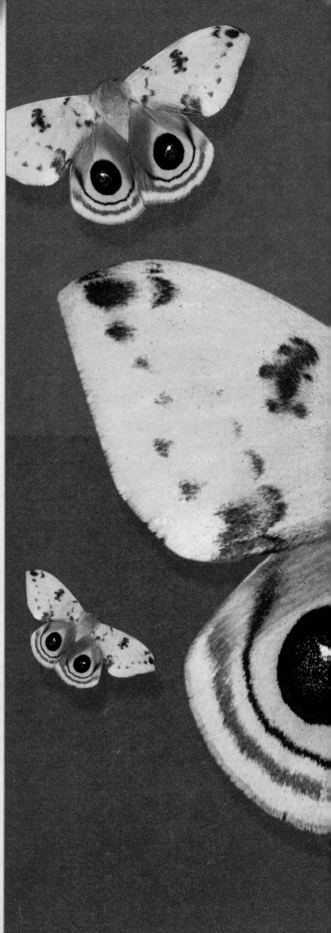

Genre Study

Expository nonfiction gives facts and information about a topic. As you read, look for

• photographs and captions.

• text structure—the way ideas are organized.

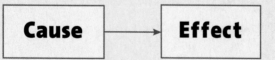

| Cause | → | Effect |

Comprehension Strategy

Use graphic organizers like the one shown above to write causes and effects.

286

MIMICRY
AND
CAMOUFLAGE

BY MARY HOFF

There are insects that look like flowers, flowers that look like insects, plants that smell like dead meat, and birds that sound like snakes. The world is full of creatures that are not what they seem to be. Some mimic other living things. Others are camouflaged, which means they blend in with their surroundings.

The surprises and disguises involved in mimicry and camouflage are all around us. In the forest, at the bottom of the sea, and in our own backyards, living things are constantly tricking each other. These tricks are not for fun, though. They are adaptations: traits that help plants and animals to survive.

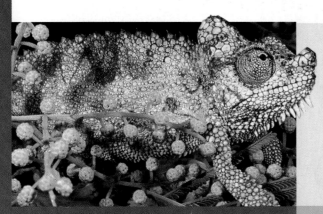

NATURE NOTE: *Chameleons are perhaps the most famous color-changing animals. Scientists think this ability helps them to communicate as well as hide.*

HIDDEN CRITTERS

In the corner of a yard is a pile of dead leaves. Suddenly, a bit of the pile hops away. What had seemed to be a dead leaf was really a blotchy brown toad. The toad's color and markings disguised it in a way that made it blend perfectly into its surroundings.

Camouflage, also known as cryptic coloration, helps some living things avoid becoming another creature's meal. Many birds' eggs have speckles and spots that make them harder for predators to see than a bright white egg would be. The dapples on the back of a white-tailed deer fawn allow it to blend into the pattern formed by sunlight filtering through tree leaves in the forest.

Of course, predators can play the hiding game, too. The stripes of a tiger help it blend into tall grass so it can sneak up on animals such as wild pigs and antelope. If a polar bear were black instead of white, it would have a much harder time surprising seals and other prey animals amid snow and ice.

NATURE NOTE: *A zebra's stripes help disguise it by making it hard for predators to tell where the zebra's body stops and its surroundings begin.*

There is a toad hidden
in this pile of leaves.

NATURE NOTE: Phasmid, *the scientific name for sticklike and leaflike insects, is related to the words* fantasy *and* fantastic.

STICKS AND STONES

Instead of coloring that helps them blend into the environment, some animals have disguises that make them look like other living or nonliving things. Some katydids (a kind of grasshopper) look almost identical to leaves. Insects known as phasmids look like sticks or leaves.

NATURE NOTE: *One phasmid, known as* Pharnacia serratipes, *grows to be a whopping 13 inches (33 cm) long!*

Six of these "rocks" are actually small plants.

The pebble plant, which grows in southern Africa, escapes the attention of ostriches and other animals that might like to eat it because it looks like stones scattered on the desert floor. Some species of spiders and moths escape enemies because they look like bird droppings. Some leaf beetles look like caterpillar droppings.

LOOKS LIKE TROUBLE

Some kinds of mimicry make an animal more obvious instead of less obvious. How does this help it to survive? By sending a message to predators and pests that says, "I'm trouble."

The common wasp stings animals that threaten it. Animals that get stung learn to avoid wasps. Hornet moths, wasp beetles, and hover-flies don't sting. But they don't have to. They have markings that mimic the markings of the common wasp. Animals that have learned to avoid wasps also avoid these harmless insects. Even though these insects are harmless, their ability to mimic the common wasp helps save them from becoming another animal's meal. A plant or animal that is not itself bothersome or dangerous, but wards off predators by looking like something that is, is called a Batesian (BAYT•see•un) mimic.

▲ *This harmless beetle mimics a dangerous wasp.*

▲ *This fly can't sting, but it looks as if it might.*

NATURE NOTE: *The larva, or wormlike young, of a hawk moth has large spots that make it look like a dangerous snake with scary eyes.*

TROUBLE TIMES TWO

Another kind of mimic is a Müllerian (myool•IR•ee•uhn) mimic. Müllerian mimics not only mimic a creature that is harmful or undesirable, they also are harmful or undesirable themselves. How does the mimicry help them? By increasing the likelihood that a predator will learn to leave creatures with that particular look alone.

The monarch butterfly is poisonous if eaten.

For example, butterflies called viceroys look like monarch butterflies. Both monarchs and viceroys contain chemicals that make birds that try to eat them sick to their stomachs. If a bird tries to eat a monarch, it quickly learns to avoid orange butterflies with black markings. If it tries to eat a viceroy, it learns the same lesson. Because birds get the same message from both kinds of butterflies, they learn to avoid them a lot faster than they would if only monarchs or only viceroys tasted bad.

NATURE NOTE: *Monarch-like viceroy butterflies were once considered an example of Batesian mimicry. But recently scientists discovered that viceroys taste bad, too.*

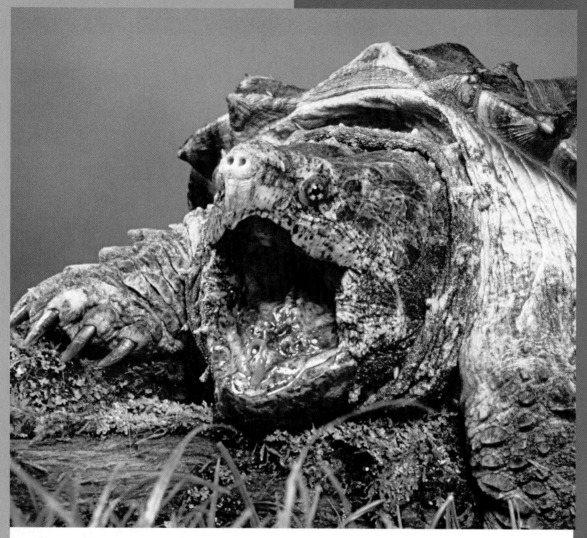

Fish swim right into the mouth of this turtle.

FATAL ATTRACTION

At the bottom of the Mississippi River, a little pink worm wiggles around. A fish swims up to it for a tasty bite. Then, suddenly, a pair of jaws snaps shut on it! The worm is not a worm, but part of the tongue of an alligator snapping turtle. By mimicking a worm, the turtle is able to lure fish right into its mouth.

The anglerfish mimics a worm to catch fish.

Some tropical fish also use this kind of foolery. Certain types of anglerfish have one fin that looks like a worm. When other fish come up to eat the "worm," the anglerfish sucks them into its mouth.

The African flower mantis, a type of large insect, plays a similar trick on land. The mantis looks like a bright flower. When an insect flies up to find nectar, a sweet liquid produced by flowers, it becomes the mantis's meal instead.

This mantis looks as harmless as a flower petal.

The rotten scent of skunk cabbage lures flies.

SCENTS AND LIGHTS

Deceptive odors can attract prey, too. The female bolas spider, found throughout much of North America, hangs a ball of sticky silk from a silky string. Then she gives off a scent that resembles that of a female moth. When male moths in the area catch the scent and fly in to find the female, the spider traps them by hitting them with the sticky ball.

The skunk cabbage, which grows in bogs and swamps, also uses odor to attract insects. The soil in which this plant grows doesn't have much nitrogen, a nutrient that plants need to grow. But the skunk cabbage has another way of getting nitrogen. It gives off heat and a stinky smell, like that of rotten meat. Flies and other insects in search of a dead animal on which to lay eggs fly in and get trapped in a little pool of water at the base of the skunk cabbage. As the insects decay, the plant gets the nitrogen it needs from their dead bodies.

A firefly's flash can attract a mate or a meal. ▶

Photuris (foh•TOOR•uhs) fireflies mimic behavior to get their meals. Fireflies flash in the night to attract mates. Each species has its own pattern of flashing. Female *Photuris* fireflies mimic the flashing pattern of other species of the genus *Photinus* (foh•TYN•uhs). The flashing attracts *Photinus* males. But instead of meeting a mate, they became a meal for the larger *Photuris* female.

LIKE A GLOVE

From plants that smell like dead meat to bears and hares that look like snow, the world is full of creatures that use mimicry or camouflage to make their way through life. Like a hand in a glove, these creatures fit perfectly into the environment around them.

NATURE NOTE: Photuris *fireflies can mimic the correct female flashing pattern response to the male flashes of several different species of* Photinus *fireflies.*

THINK CRITICALLY

1. Why do plants and animals use mimicry or camouflage? **Focus Skill** TEXT STRUCTURE: CAUSE AND EFFECT

2. What is the main idea of the section titled "Sticks and Stones"? What details support the main idea? MAIN IDEA AND DETAILS

3. What do you think is the strangest way an animal uses mimicry or camouflage? Use details from the selection to support your answer. PERSONAL RESPONSE

4. Imagine that you are standing in a thick forest. How might you camouflage yourself? MAKE CONNECTIONS

5. **WRITE** Tell how animals that use scents and animals that use lights are ALIKE and DIFFERENT. Use details and information from the selection to support your answer. SHORT RESPONSE

ABOUT THE AUTHOR
MARY HOFF

Mary Hoff divides her time between writing about science and enjoying her family. Her interest in science began in college. She had been studying science and working in laboratories. Mary Hoff soon decided that she wanted to be an author. She began writing about many different science topics.

Mary Hoff lives in Minnesota. She enjoys writing about the natural environment in her home state for a local magazine. Once she wrote about Minnesota animals that fool each other by using mimicry and camouflage.

GO online **www.harcourtschool.com/storytown**

lizards, frogs, and polliwogs

poems and paintings by Douglas Florian

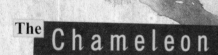

The Chameleon

Chameleon, comedian,

We never know which skin you're in.

Sometimes you're yellow,

Then you're green,

Turquoise blue, or tangerine.

Chameleon, you're hard to find.

Comedian, make up your mind!

The Glass Frog

Upon a tree
It's hard to see
Which part is leaf
And which is me
Which part is me
And which is leaf
I've lost myself again —
Good grief!

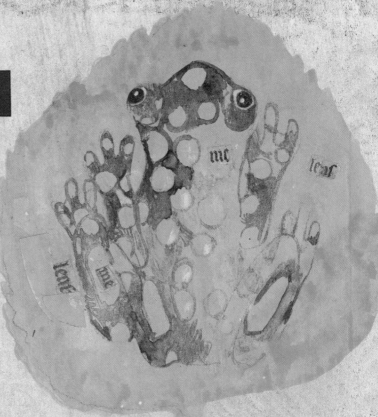

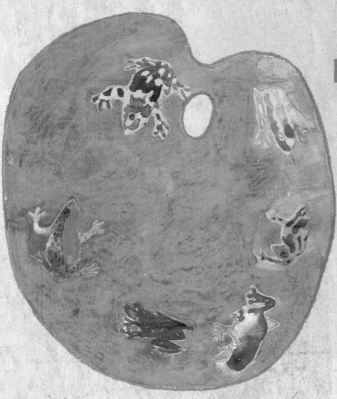

The Poison-Dart Frog

Brown with oval orange spots.
Crimson mottled black with blots.
Neon green with blue-black bands.
Tangerine with lemon strands.
Banana yellow.
Ultramarine.
Almost any color seen.
And though their poison
can tip a dart,
These frogs are Masters of Fine Art.

303

Connections

Comparing Texts

1. Some animals blend into their surroundings. Others stand out. Which type are you more like? Explain.

2. How are "Mimicry and Camouflage" and the poems from "lizards, frogs, and polliwogs" alike? How are they different?

3. What are some ways people, like animals, adapt to their environment?

Vocabulary Review

Creatures that mimic flowers can lure insects.

Word Pairs

Work with a partner. Write each Vocabulary Word on a separate index card. Place the cards face down. Take turns flipping over two cards and writing a sentence that uses both words. Read aloud the sentence to your partner. You must use the words correctly in the sentence to keep the cards. The student with the most cards at the end wins.

predators

traits

lure

mimic

resembles

obvious

deceptive

avoid

Fluency Practice

Partner Reading

Choose a section from "Mimicry and Camouflage." Read aloud the text as your partner listens and follows along. Your partner should give you feedback about your volume, your pacing, and your expression. Read the section aloud again, keeping in mind your partner's comments. Then switch roles and repeat.

Writing

Write a Scientific Description

Imagine that you are a scientist who is studying one of the animals or insects in "Mimicry and Camouflage." Then write a paragraph that tells about how the animal or insect behaves and why.

Cause → **Effect**

My Writing Checklist

Writing Trait ▸ Organization

✔ I used the text structure of cause-and-effect.

✔ I used a graphic organizer to plan my writing.

✔ I used information from the selection and one other resource.

Reading-Writing Connection

Analyze Writer's Craft: Expository Nonfiction

Expository nonfiction gives facts and information about a topic. It may include **headings**, **diagrams**, **photographs**, and **captions**. When you write expository nonfiction, you can use the work of authors such as Mary Hoff as writing models. Read the passage below from "Mimicry and Camouflage." Note how the author used conventions and a **cause-and-effect text structure**.

Writing Trait

SENTENCE FLUENCY
The **topic** is camouflage. The author begins with a **topic sentence**. Then she explains several **causes and effects**, such as *speckles make eggs harder to see*.

Writing Trait

CONVENTIONS
The author uses **commas** to set off the phrase *also known as cryptic coloration*. A phrase that helps define the term it follows is always set off by commas.

Camouflage, also known as cryptic coloration, helps some living things avoid becoming another creature's meal. Many birds' eggs have speckles and spots that make them harder for a predator to see than a bright white egg would be. The dapples on the back of a white-tailed deer fawn allow it to blend into the pattern formed by sunlight filtering through tree leaves in the forest.

Explanatory Essay

An **explanatory essay** is a kind of **expository nonfiction**. It explains how or why something happens. A student named Christine wrote the explanatory essay below. In it, she explains why butterflies are attracted to her garden. As you read Christine's essay, notice how she **organizes** her ideas.

Student Writing Model

Beautiful Attraction
by Christine G.

My family and I like to watch butterflies, so we made a butterfly garden in our backyard. We provide the right kinds of flowers, the right amount of light, and the right kind of water to attract butterflies.

Plant Them and They Will Come

Planting colorful flowering plants is the surest way to attract butterflies. Daisies and violets attract Red Admiral and Monarch butterflies. Large groups of plants attract more butterflies than single flowers. We planted lots of seeds, and they grew into a thick, lush butterfly haven!

Writing Trait

ORGANIZATION
Christine uses a **cause-and-effect text structure** to organize her essay. The **topic sentence** of each section states a cause-and-effect relationship.

Made in the Shade

A garden that has both sun and shade will keep butterflies happy. They are cold-blooded insects. Their body temperature changes, depending on their surroundings. Butterflies like to warm up in the sun and cool off in the shade. That's why we left one part of our garden open to direct sunlight and shaded the other part by planting shrubs.

Make a Splash

Butterflies gather at puddles after it rains, so water is an important attraction. We made a permanent puddle in our garden. We buried a bucket up to the rim, added some gravel, and filled the bucket with water. Sometimes we add a little fruit juice or a piece of fruit to the bucket. The nectar in the fruit attracts our fluttering friends.

We work hard to keep the right balance of plants, shade, and water in our garden. We love to watch butterflies floating above the flowers. It makes all our hard work worthwhile.

Now look at what Christine did to prepare to write her explanatory essay.

Organizing Ideas

First, she chose a subject she understands well: how to attract butterflies to a garden. Then she used a graphic organizer to help her organize the causes and effects in her essay.

Outlining

Christine wrote an outline to organize the three main causes she will explain in her essay. The outline shows her plan for writing an introduction, a paragraph explaining each main cause, and a conclusion.

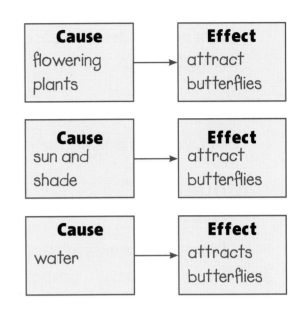

Cause	Effect
flowering plants	attract butterflies
sun and shade	attract butterflies
water	attracts butterflies

Title: Beautiful Attraction

I.   Introduction
    A. Our butterfly garden
    B. Three causes that attract
       butterflies

II. Cause #1 - Flowering Plants
    A. Daisies and violets
    B. Red Admirals and Monarchs

III. Cause #2 - Sun and Shade
    A. Butterflies are cold-blooded.
    B. Create sunny and shady areas.

IV. Cause #3 - Water
    A. Make a permanent puddle.
    B. Add fruit to the puddle.

V.   Conclusion
    A. Mention three causes again.
    B. Why we love our garden

CONTENTS

Lesson 12

Genre: Expository Nonfiction

MOUNTAINS
SEYMOUR SIMON

TO THE Top OF THE World

Genre: Magazine Article

Focus Skill

Text Structure: Cause and Effect

Authors of nonfiction texts may organize information in a **cause-and-effect text structure**. In texts with this structure, the author tells what happened (the effect) and why it happened (the cause). Sometimes a cause has more than one effect. You can use a graphic organizer like this one to keep track of the cause-and-effect relationships in the text.

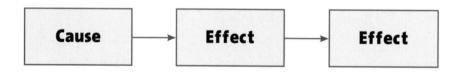

| Cause | → | Effect | → | Effect |

Tip

Phrases such as *due to* and *as a result* often signal a cause-and-effect relationship.

Read the paragraph below. The graphic organizer shows the cause-and-effect relationship in the last two sentences. The phrase *as a result* signals the effects.

Thousands of years ago, huge sheets of ice called glaciers covered parts of North America. When the glaciers began to melt, they moved slowly across the land. These rivers of ice cut deeply into the earth's surface because of their great weight. In some places, the ice scraped away parts of mountains. In time, the climate warmed. As a result, the ice melted away and left deep valleys and lakes in the land.

Cause	Effect	Effect
The climate warmed.	The ice melted away.	The land had deep valleys and lakes.

Try This!

Look back at the paragraph. Find another cause-and-effect relationship. What clue words helped you?

GO online www.harcourtschool.com/storytown

Vocabulary

Build Robust Vocabulary

- eruption
- constant
- immediate
- gradually
- depths
- revealed
- contract

The Double Volcano

Mexico's largest volcano, Popocatepetl (poh·puh·KA·tuh·peh·tuhl), is often called Popo. Its last big **eruption** occurred in 1947. In 1995, another eruption seemed likely. Smoke and ash started escaping from Popo. After two years, the smoke and ash stopped. Scientists now keep a **constant** watch on the volcano. They say that the people who live near Popo are not in **immediate** danger.

Popo is a volcano that formed on top of an older volcano.

314

Popo has an almost perfect cone shape. Its sides rise **gradually** for more than 16,000 feet. The crater at the top is shaped like an oval, and it is very deep. Peering into it is like looking into the **depths** of the earth. On one side of Popo, a smaller cone shape sticks out. There, the remains of an older volcano are **revealed**.

Popo's peak is covered with snow. In the icy air, rocks **contract** and break apart. On its lower slopes, forests grow. On a clear day, Popo is a beautiful sight.

No one knows when Popo will erupt again.

 www.harcourtschool.com/storytown

Word Detective

Your mission this week is to look for Vocabulary Words outside school. You may hear them on a television nature program, read them in a magazine, or find them in a library book. Each time you see or hear one of the words, write it in your vocabulary journal. Be sure to tell where you found each word.

Expository Nonfiction

Genre Study

Expository nonfiction gives facts and information about a topic. As you read, look for

- headings that begin sections of related information.

- photographs and captions.

Cause	→	Effect

Comprehension Strategy

Use graphic organizers like the one shown above to write causes and effects.

UNTAINS

by SEYMOUR SIMON

Mountains are a dramatic reminder of ages past and ages to come. They seem to be solid and unchanging, but they are not everlasting. Mountains are born, grow tall over the years, change their shapes, and are finally worn down and disappear into the earth from which they came.

THE HEIGHT OF MOUNTAINS

Mountains are tall, but just how tall does one have to be to be called a mountain? The Himalayan Mountains in central Asia have at least fourteen peaks over 26,000 feet. Mount Everest in the Himalayas is the highest mountain above sea level in the world, 29,028 feet. That's five and a half miles above sea level, taller than the world's twenty-six tallest skyscrapers stacked one atop another.

Mount Everest

The Jungfrau

The Alps of Europe, the Andes of South America, and the Rockies of western North America each have dozens of peaks taller than 10,000 feet. Air temperature drops about three degrees Fahrenheit for every one thousand feet of altitude, so the peaks of many tall mountains, such as the Jungfrau in the Alps, are always cold and are covered by snow year round.

The Appalachians are a group of old, worn mountains 200 miles long in the eastern United States. Only a few Appalachian peaks are as high as 6,000 feet and many are much lower. This hill in New York's Catskill Mountains is less than 3,000 feet above sea level. In the Himalayas or the Alps, mountains like this would be called foot- hills. Whether to call something a mountain seems to depend upon who is looking at it and how high its surroundings are.

Catskill Mountains

HOW MOUNTAINS FORM

Most mountains are not solitary peaks but part of long chains or ranges. The Himalayas are over 1,500 miles long and link up with other mountain ranges to stretch hundreds of miles farther.

Mountain ranges do not arise just anyplace. Most are formed when *plates*, giant pieces of the earth's crust, push and pull against each other. The United States, Canada, Mexico, and part of the North Atlantic Ocean are on the North American plate. The Rockies and the coast ranges of the western United States and Canada were formed where the North American plate pushed against the Pacific plate.

The Mid-Atlantic ridge, a 12,000-mile-long underwater mountain chain that stretches the length of the Atlantic Ocean, was formed where the North Atlantic plate pulled away from the Eurasian plate and the African plate. The islands of Iceland and Surtsey are actually the tops of volcanic mountain peaks reaching above the surface of the ocean, which covers most of the Mid-Atlantic ridge.

North American Plate

Juan De Fuca Plate

Pacific Plate

Cocos Plate

Nazca Plate

Antarctic Plate

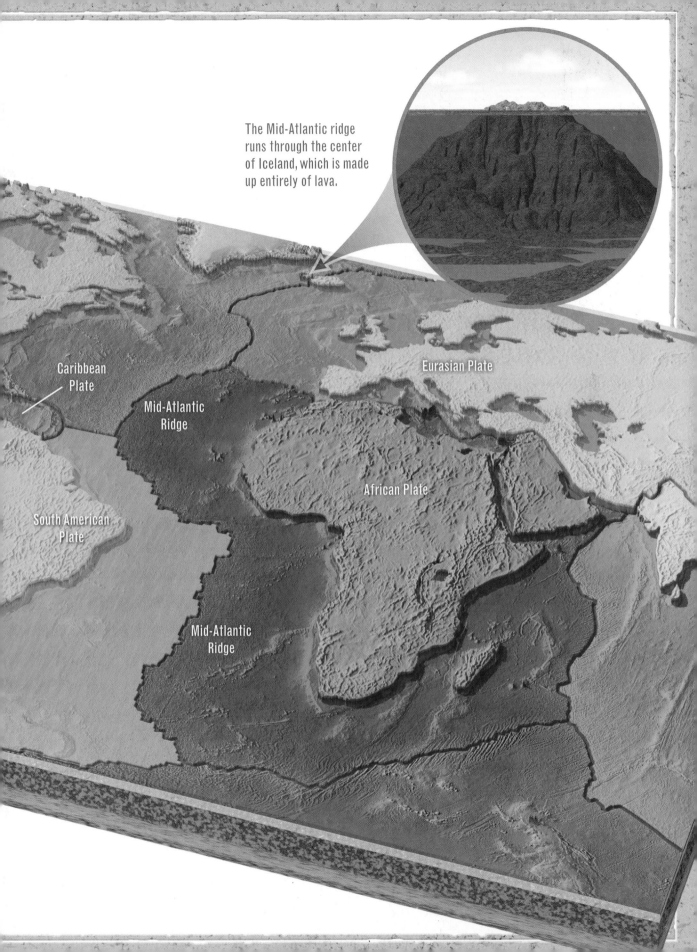

The Mid-Atlantic ridge runs through the center of Iceland, which is made up entirely of lava.

Caribbean Plate

Eurasian Plate

Mid-Atlantic Ridge

African Plate

South American Plate

Mid-Atlantic Ridge

STRATA   CRUST

▲ Folded peaks in the Rocky Mountains in Montana

Rocks are hard, but with time and pressure they can bend or fold. Hold a large piece of paper at either end and slowly push toward the middle. The pressure of your hands causes the paper to buckle and fold. In the earth's crust, pressure pushes sideways against the rocks. The rocks twist and bend, producing great folded mountain chains. It takes many thousands of years to bring about changes in the rocks of the earth's crust.

The Alps are folded mountains that formed as the Eurasian plate pushed against the African plate. Most of the great mountain chains on earth, including the Himalayas, the Andes, the Rockies, and the Appalachians, are folded mountains. When the bare mountainside is exposed, you can see the folds in the layers of rock, called *strata*, such as these folded peaks in the Rocky Mountains in Montana.

Another type of mountain is formed by the pulling apart or breaking of rocks. Faults are breaks in rock layers, and fault-block mountains form when one plate shifts or pulls away from another plate. Deep within the earth, hot currents of *magma*, molten rock, may well up and crack the weakened crust above. As the crust cracks, huge blocks of rock rise or fall, forming mountains. These mountains usually have a steep face on one side and a more gentle slope on the other side. The Sierra Nevada and the Grand Tetons of Wyoming (shown here) are examples of fault-block mountains.

CRUST   STRATA

Still other mountains are formed by the eruption of volcanoes. During a volcanic eruption, magma squeezes up through cracks in the earth's crust and explodes out as lava and ash. When huge amounts of hardening lava and cinders pile up around the vent, or opening, they form a volcanic mountain, such as Mount Hood in Oregon (above).

The Hawaiian Islands are the tops of volcanic mountains that rise 30,000 feet from the depths of the ocean, making them even taller than Everest if you measure from the ocean bottom. The aerial view of Hawaii below shows some of its volcanic cinder cones.

VENTS

MAGMA

CRUST

STRATA

STRATA CRUST MAGMA

▲ Half Dome in Yosemite National Park, California

Dome mountains are formed by the same kind of molten rock that forms volcanic mountains. Dome mountains do not act or even look like volcanoes. They too result from a welling up of magma from deep within the earth through a crack in the earth's crust. However, in dome mountains, the magma does not come to the surface. Instead, the molten rock pushes the ground up into a round or dome-shaped bulge, and the magma gradually hardens into rock. When the softer rocks above are worn away, the great dome of underlying rock is revealed.

The Adirondacks of New York and the Black Hills of South Dakota are dome mountains. Yosemite's Half Dome (above) is a dome mountain that was cracked in half when sheets of granite fell off one side and were carried away by a glacier thousands of years ago.

WEATHERING AND EROSION

As soon as mountains rise, they begin to be worn down steadily and slowly by the forces of erosion: wind, rain, moving water, and ice, as well as temperature and chemical changes. Some kinds of rocks, such as limestone, dissolve in water, but most water erosion on mountains is caused by streams and rivers that plunge down the steep sides, lifting up rocks and pushing them along to rub and scrape against other rocks. In cold climates, slowly moving rivers of ice, called *glaciers*, also carve away at mountains.

Rocks expand daily in the heat of the sun and then contract again during the cold nights. These constant temperature changes begin to crack the rock. Water gets into the tiny cracks, freezes at night, expands, and opens the cracks wider. Finally, the rock breaks off from the mountain. Sometimes the wind blows sand, which wears away mountains to produce towers such as in Zion National Park in Utah (above).

On steep mountain slopes, rocks tumble downhill, pulled by gravity. Sometimes a rain shower or a small earthquake can send rocks roaring down the mountainside in a rock slide or rock avalanche. Rock glaciers, like those shown on the slopes of Shivling Mountain in India (left), are rivers of small pieces of rock and soil frozen together that move slowly downhill like ice glaciers.

At the foot of a mountain, piles of broken boulders, smaller rocks, and soil often spread out in a fan-shaped pile called a *talus slope*. The material that makes up talus is called *sliderock*, and it continues to move downhill.

CLIMATE CHANGES

Mountains change shape slowly, but they have an immediate effect on weather and climate, especially on the amount of rainfall, the pattern of winds, and the movement of weather fronts. The reason for this is that mountains break up the flow of winds and force the air to move up or around. Air contains a certain amount of an invisible gas called *water vapor*. The cooler the air, the less water vapor it can hold. When air is forced to rise over a mountain, it gets colder and the water vapor condenses into tiny drops of water in clouds, mist, fog, and rain.

In the western United States, moisture-laden winds blow from the Pacific Ocean against the coastal mountain ranges of Washington, Oregon, and California. Clouds form and rain falls heavily on the rain forests of the western slopes.

On the eastern slopes of the mountains in these states, and in Wyoming, Montana, and Nevada, scarcely any rain falls at all. This is called the *rain shadow effect*. The driest deserts in America are separated from the wettest rain forests by only a few hundred miles.

Not many people live on mountains, but mountains are important to all of us. Mountains create rain forests and deserts. Mountains store water on their snowy peaks and release it in rivers that make the valleys below green and fertile. Many farms and cities depend on mountain lakes for their drinking water, and the rivers are often harnessed to manufacture electricity. Mountains offer a chance for people to climb or ski or just take pleasure from some of the most spectacular scenery in the world.

THINK CRITICALLY

1. What causes rock to expand during the day?

   TEXT STRUCTURE: CAUSE AND EFFECT

2. Are the earth's oldest mountains also its tallest mountains? How do you know? DRAW CONCLUSIONS

3. Where have you seen the effects of water or wind? MAKE CONNECTIONS

4. What might you find if you measured Mount Everest today and then measured it again a hundred years from now? MAIN IDEA

5. **WRITE** Different types of mountains form in different ways. Use information and details from the selection to explain:
   - how dome mountains form, and
   - how dome mountains are different from volcanic mountains. EXTENDED RESPONSE

About the Author

SEYMOUR SIMON

Seymour Simon taught science for twenty-three years. Often he couldn't find the right book on a topic he wanted to teach. So he began to write his own books.

"If you take a walk and really look, listen, and feel the world around you, it can be a strange experience," says Seymour Simon. "You begin to wonder about things that you've seen thousands of times—clouds, trees, rocks, machines. You ask questions: Why do some leaves turn red in the fall, while others turn yellow? What kind of rock has glittery little specks in it? How is an airplane able to fly? My books are full of questions." Seymour Simon's books have asked—and answered— thousands of questions.

 www.harcourtschool.com/storytown

331

TO THE TOP

by David Breashears

What would you do to stand at the top of the World? Brave temperatures as low as 40 below? Cross an ice gorge supported only by two aluminum ladders lashed together? Climb so high that your oxygen-deprived mind starts playing tricks on you?

All mountains are dangerous and feature unpredictable weather, but Mount Everest is the granddaddy of them all when it comes to risk. The wind whipping across the mountainside reaches 80 miles an hour— hurricane force.

With a single missed step, a climber can plunge into an icy crevasse. And even when they reach the top, climbers are usually too numb with exhaustion and oxygen deprivation to admire the glory of the view.

At Everest's altitude there is so little oxygen that the brain struggles to think. On Everest, even the smartest person has difficulty figuring out simple things, like which way to turn the valve on an oxygen tank to shut it off, or in which direction to walk.

Why do it, then? For filmmaker David Breashears, climbing is a passion, and climbing Everest is the ultimate. Breashears was asked about how he scaled Mount Everest in pursuit of amazing film footage. Here is what he said about the experience.

OF THE World

I left for work in the pitch of darkness. It was 38 degrees below zero. I walked out into a place where the air is so thin that a person could suffocate, where no animal or plant could survive. I was carrying a 40-pound movie camera nearly five and a half miles into the sky, to the top of the world.

My crew and I were on Mount Everest filming a movie in a special format called IMAX. IMAX creates movies that are viewed on huge screens and give viewers a feeling of really being there. This was my chance to show people what it's like to stand on top of the world.

I'm David Breashears, one of the world's few mountain-climbing filmmakers. I've seen it all at high altitude: joy, pain, excitement—and, sadly, death.

The Path to the Top

I was born in Fort Benning, Georgia. I grew up all over the world as my dad, an army major, was stationed in different places. Now I live in Newton, Massachusetts, when I'm not on location, making movies.

David Breashears uses his breath to keep his viewfinder free of ice.

Next, I want to make a movie about Kilimanjaro, Africa's tallest peak. I'm also writing a book on my experiences.

My love of mountain-climbing came before I decided to become a filmmaker. When I was 12, I saw a picture of Tenzing Norgay standing on top of Mount Everest. Sir Edmund Hillary, the New Zealand mountaineer and Norgay's climbing partner, had taken the picture. They were the first to climb Everest, back in 1953. The other climbers in their party had given up. Norgay and Hillary went on to the summit alone. That image of Norgay stuck with me and sparked my interest in climbing.

I started climbing in high school as an alternative to team sports, which I wasn't very good at. I was too skinny. But climbing built up my muscles, and it taught me many other things too.

Many things I learned as a Boy Scout in Troop 225, Cheyenne, Wyoming, have been vital in my climbing. Winter camping is one of the best things you can do. It teaches you what you need to survive.

I know about surviving: I've climbed Everest eleven times and led the trip four times. In 1983, I was the first to send TV pictures from the summit, and I was the first American to reach the summit twice.

Funny thing is, I don't like heights. But making movies at high altitudes is what I do. My climbing skills make it possible for me to make some amazing movies, like the IMAX film "Everest."

Survival Mode

You might think that once you get to the top of Everest, you give your climbing partners high-fives. Not true. When you're on Everest, you're in survival mode. Emotions take up a lot of energy, so you can't have strong emotions.

After all, reaching the summit isn't the end—it's only halfway. And walking downhill is dangerous; gravity's with you, and it's easy to fall. You have to remember that the finish line on any hike is back where you started.

An Extra Load

Climbing is a challenge in itself, and climbing with the IMAX camera is even more so.

The standard IMAX camera is big— it weighs 92 pounds—so we developed a lighter version to take up the mountain. The rolls of film are 500 feet long, weigh five and a half pounds, and shoot just 90 seconds of images.

Setting the camera up, filming, and taking it down took an hour altogether. I had to take off my gloves to load the film, but I had practiced by sticking my hands into a mountaintop snowbank for a minute to make sure I could do it.

The Importance of Learning

I didn't go to film school, unlike a lot of other filmmakers. Instead, I carried cameras, ran sound, and did the other behind-the-scenes tasks that go into making a movie. An apprenticeship— studying with people older and wiser than you—is a great way to learn.

If you want to succeed, I'd give you this advice: Have a passion, something you really want to do, like climbing mountains, making music, or building things. Then, learn everything you can about what you want to do. That way, you never forget—whether you're making a movie or trying to climb the world's tallest mountain. Remembering can save your life.

Connections

Comparing Texts

1. How are other mountains you know about similar to or different from those described in "Mountains"?

2. Compare and contrast the descriptions of Mount Everest in "Mountains" and in "To the Top of the World."

3. Mountains go through many changes. What kinds of changes do people go through during their lives?

Vocabulary Review

Word Sort

Work in a small group. Sort the Vocabulary Words into categories based on whether they describe "mountain changes" or "time." Some words fit more than one category. Discuss with your group why you put each word in a particular category. Then choose two Vocabulary Words in each category, and write a sentence that demonstrates why they belong in the same category.

eruption

depths

gradually

revealed

constant

contract

immediate

Fluency Practice

Partner Reading

Choose a section of text in "Mountains" to reread aloud while your partner follows along. Ask your partner to give you feedback about your pace. Reread the section, using your partner's feedback. Then switch roles and repeat the activity.

Writing

Write Captions

Choose a cause-and-effect relationship you read about in "Mountains." Draw a picture that illustrates the cause and one that illustrates the effect. Then write a caption to describe each picture.

My Writing Checklist

Writing Trait ➤ Conventions

✔ I used a graphic organizer to plan my writing.

✔ I used correct spelling, capitalization, and punctuation.

✔ I used words that signal causes and effects.

| Cause | → | Effect |

CONTENTS

Lesson 13

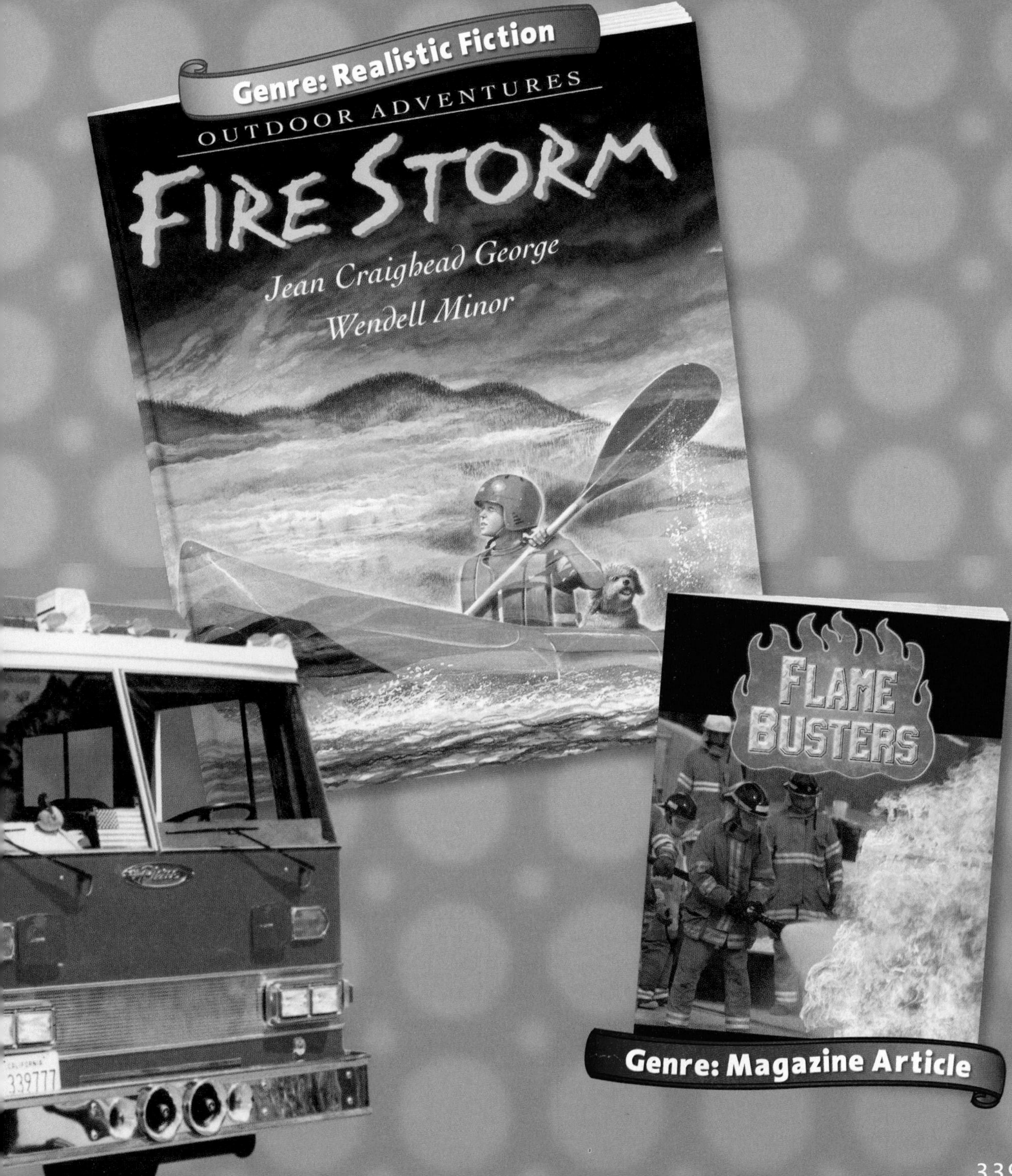

Genre: Realistic Fiction

OUTDOOR ADVENTURES

FIRE STORM

Jean Craighead George

Wendell Minor

FLAME BUSTERS

Genre: Magazine Article

Draw Conclusions

An author does not always explain everything in a story. Sometimes you must put together **story details** with **what you know** to understand what you are reading. This is called **drawing conclusions**.

Story Detail	What I Know	Conclusion

Tip

When you read a story, use what you know about people to help you understand each character's actions.

Read the paragraph below. Then read the information in the graphic organizer. It shows one detail from the paragraph and some information from real life. These are put together to draw a conclusion from the paragraph.

Fire season was coming. Maya spent one weekend trimming all the trees around her home. She spent another weekend clearing dead leaves from her roof. Next, she planned to remove all the dry weeds within 30 feet of her house. Maya wasn't about to take any chances. When fire season arrived, she would be prepared!

Story Detail	What I Know	Conclusion
Maya cleared dead leaves from the roof.	Dead leaves can burn easily.	Maya was working to protect her home from fire.

Try This!

Reread the paragraph. What kind of person is Maya? What details from the paragraph support your answer?

www.harcourtschool.com/storytown

Vocabulary

smoldering

plunge

treacherous

skeptically

altered

discouraged

scoffed

drudgery

A Town Transformed

Last summer, a three-alarm fire broke out in Greenwood. The fire left 15 stores in **smoldering** ruins. One year after the fire, we talked with fire chief Marcus Sanchez.

"Our firefighters did a great job," Chief Sanchez recalled. "To enter a burning building is to **plunge** into the unknown, and our firefighters met the challenge. They got everyone out quickly, and no one was hurt."

This is Greenwood after last summer's fire. Some buildings were closed due to **treacherous** conditions.

After the fire, the town needed to recover. "When we told people that their stores could be rebuilt," said Chief Sanchez, "most shook their heads **skeptically**. They thought the downtown area had been **altered** forever."

Mayor Leslie Oki told us, "At first, the community was very **discouraged**. Even though some people **scoffed** at the idea of rebuilding, everyone shared the **drudgery** of clearing away charred rubble. The store owners worked tirelessly to rebuild. Now look at what our citizens have accomplished. All 15 stores that burned have been rebuilt!"

 www.harcourtschool.com/storytown

Word Champion

Your challenge this week is to use the Vocabulary Words outside your classroom. Keep the list of words in a place at home where you can see it. Try to use as many of the words as you can when you speak to family members and friends. For example, you might ask family members what activity they would like to plunge into. At the end of each day, write in your vocabulary journal the sentences you spoke that contained the words.

OUTDOOR ADVENTURES

FIRE STORM

Jean Craighead George
Wendell Minor

Realistic Fiction

FIRE

Genre Study

Realistic fiction has characters and events that are like people and events in real life. As you read, look for

• realistic characters and events.

• a main character who faces a challenge.

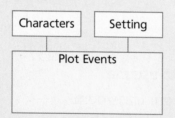

Characters	Setting
Plot Events	

Comprehension Strategy

Monitor comprehension when you do not understand what you are reading. **Read ahead** to find an explanation.

STORM

by Jean Craighead George
illustrated by Wendell Minor

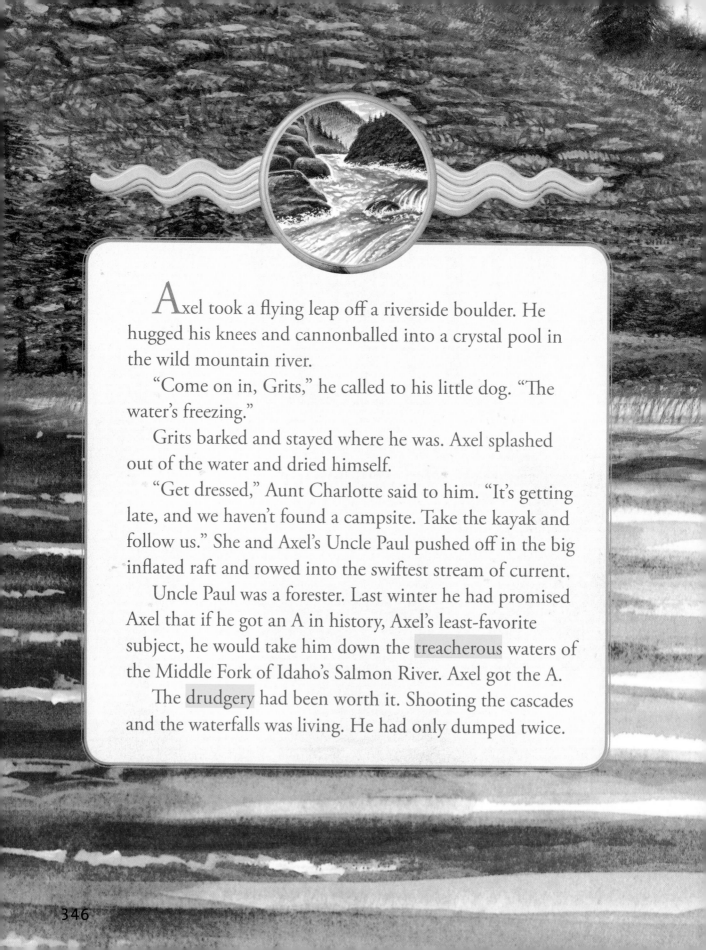

Axel took a flying leap off a riverside boulder. He hugged his knees and cannonballed into a crystal pool in the wild mountain river.

"Come on in, Grits," he called to his little dog. "The water's freezing."

Grits barked and stayed where he was. Axel splashed out of the water and dried himself.

"Get dressed," Aunt Charlotte said to him. "It's getting late, and we haven't found a campsite. Take the kayak and follow us." She and Axel's Uncle Paul pushed off in the big inflated raft and rowed into the swiftest stream of current.

Uncle Paul was a forester. Last winter he had promised Axel that if he got an A in history, Axel's least-favorite subject, he would take him down the treacherous waters of the Middle Fork of Idaho's Salmon River. Axel got the A.

The drudgery had been worth it. Shooting the cascades and the waterfalls was living. He had only dumped twice.

He followed the raft down a cascade, around two boulders, and into calm water. He looked up. A plume of black smoke was towering up from a distant mountain.

It was the summer of 2000, the driest summer in a hundred years. Fires were burning out of control all over the west.

"You won't have a fire problem," the fire warden had said when they started their float trip. "The fires are hundreds of miles from the Middle Fork."

For three days they had paddled in wild beauty. They had seen no cars, no roads, no telephone wires. Eagles, Rocky Mountain sheep, bears, and moose had been their companions.

Aunt Charlotte and Uncle Paul rowed to a boiling waterfall, then sped down it and into another calm eddy. Axel followed with his paddle held high. He let the current steer him right to them. They were staring at the smoke plume. "No threat," said Uncle Paul. "That fire is on the other side of the mountain."

Suddenly a bolt of dry lightning streaked from cloud to ground and hit the ridge above the river. No rain accompanied the strike. The tinder-dry pine needles exploded into flames. The flames raced up the trees.

"That's no Boy Scout campfire," Axel said to Grits, and kept close to the raft. An hour passed.

More dry lightning strikes started new fires. The mountain to the right of the rafting party crackled and roared. Smoke filled the river canyon.

Axel found his way by staying close to shore. When a wind cleared the air, he hurried to catch up with Aunt Charlotte and Uncle Paul. They were beached at White Sand campground, staring up at the flames. They were not setting up camp.

"We should get out of here," Uncle Paul said when Axel jumped from the kayak, "but it's risky. It's too smoky to see rocks and waterfalls downriver. They are dangerous even in broad daylight."

"Let's stay here," Axel said. "The fire's not burning on this side of the river."

"And it won't," said Uncle Paul. "There are too few trees on these rugged cliffs to fuel it." But Uncle Paul did not unpack the camping gear. He kept watching the fires.

Suddenly the wind changed. With a roar, the many fires hurricaned into one thundering fire storm. An orange wall of flame sped down the slope, jumped the river, and fired up the sage and trees behind the campsite.

As Axel and his family stood there, sand, sky, and river shone yellow-orange. Trees exploded like rifle shots. Burning sagebrush spiraled up into the fire storm and turned to dust. Grits whined.

"Let's go," Aunt Charlotte said.

"Wait," warned Uncle Paul. "It's better to sit still in the known than plunge into the unknown. A solution will present itself."

The three sat and waited for a solution. The sun set but darkness did not fall. The sky grew brighter, the air smokier. Aunt Charlotte dipped four bandanas in the river and handed them to Axel and Uncle Paul to tie over their noses and mouths.

Axel tied one on Grits and put him in the bottom of the kayak, where the air was fresher.

They waited. Flaming trees were sucked skyward by the winds that were created by the terrible heat. Black clouds mushroomed and billowed. Breathing became difficult.

Then the fire storm surrounded them. Axel saw no solution anywhere—except, perhaps, in the middle of the river. He located a deep pool where he thought he could survive. That thought calmed him.

Axel waded out into the water.

He leaned down and peered under the smoke.

"Does fire burn in the same place twice?" he called.

"No," Aunt Charlotte answered.

"I see a burned-out campsite not too far downriver."

"Good solution," said Uncle Paul. "Let's go for it." He and Aunt Charlotte jumped into the raft and quickly rowed out into the current. Axel and Grits followed in the kayak.

They pulled ashore at the blackened campsite. The trees and stumps were still smoldering, and the air was thick with smoke, but the fire had passed.

Uncle Paul tossed bailing buckets to Axel and Aunt Charlotte.

"Dump water on the smoldering tree stumps," he said. "We'll spend the night here."

When the last ember was out, they unrolled their sleeping bags and lay down, but Axel could not sleep.

The fire storm was noisy. Trees and even rocks exploded with loud booms. The towers of flames on the ridges whistled and screamed. Burning logs roared down the mountain and rolled to the edge of their campsite, where they slowly went out. There was nothing more to burn.

Looking back through a forest of black sticks that had once been green trees, Axel made out the White Sand campground. It was an inferno of flames.

The next morning the sun shone through dense smoke and colored the river, the boats, and the people a strange fluorescent orange. It was cold. Bandanas over their faces, their eyes watering, the little party cheered when the sun climbed higher. The air cleared, and they could see the river. They pushed off into the charred wilderness.

As Axel passed miles of smoldering trees and smoking stumps, he grew terribly sad. He paddled up to Uncle Paul and Aunt Charlotte's raft and clung to it.

"I can't look any longer," Axel said. "I want to cry for the lost forest."

"It's not lost," said Uncle Paul. "Just altered. It will come back and be healthier."

"No way!" said Axel.

"It's true," agreed Aunt Charlotte. "The forest is a phoenix, like that bird of legend. The phoenix burned itself to ashes and arose from those ashes to live again. The forest will, too."

"Tell me about it," Axel scoffed.

"A blade of grass will appear in the nutrient-rich ashes," she said. "Great swathes of fireweed will grow and blossom. Then a carpet of green shrubs will emerge from old roots. In the snowmelt of spring, little pine trees will push up."

"When I'm an old man," Axel grumbled.

"When we come back next summer," Uncle Paul said.

"That I want to see," said Axel skeptically. "It's a date."

After ten hours of hard paddling, the weary party pulled up at the Cache Creek takeout point.

A tired and discouraged Axel glanced up at the sky. A bald eagle, like the phoenix of legend, soared toward the ruins of the fire.

"I'll see you next summer," he said, and smiled.

THINK CRITICALLY

1 How does the setting affect the characters' actions?
NARRATIVE ANALYSIS

2 Why was the burned-out campsite a safe place to sleep? DRAW CONCLUSIONS

3 How do you think the author of the selection feels about the forest? How do you know? AUTHOR'S PERSPECTIVE

4 What part do wildfires play in the life cycle of a forest? MAKE CONNECTIONS

5 **WRITE** At the end of the story, what are Axel's feelings about the fire storm? Use details from the story to support your answer. SHORT RESPONSE

About the Author

JEAN CRAIGHEAD GEORGE

Jean Craighead George grew up in a family of nature lovers. Her father worked for the U.S. Forest Service and often took the family on weekend camping trips.

Jean Craighead George's adventure stories have been inspired by her family's experiences in nature. The idea for *Fire Storm* came from the real-life adventures of her nephew and his family. "Doing interesting things and then writing about them is the best way to become a good writer," she says. She has received many awards for her books, including the 1973 Newbery Medal for *Julie of the Wolves*.

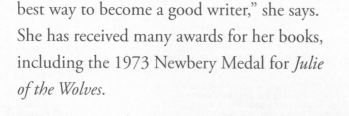

About the Illustrator
WENDELL MINOR

Wendell Minor grew up in Aurora, Illinois, and graduated from the Ringling School of Art and Design in Sarasota, Florida. In New York City, he began his career of creating art for book publishers. Minor's illustrations decorate the covers of more than 2,000 books, including many best-sellers.

Minor's illustrations show his love for the outdoors. He hopes that his art will inspire young people to explore the beauty of nature. "A good picture, like a good story, is timeless," he says. Minor wants his illustrations to accurately show the places described in the stories, so he often travels to the actual locations to take photographs and make sketches.

Minor has worked with Jean Craighead George on several picture books.

GO online **www.harcourtschool.com/storytown**

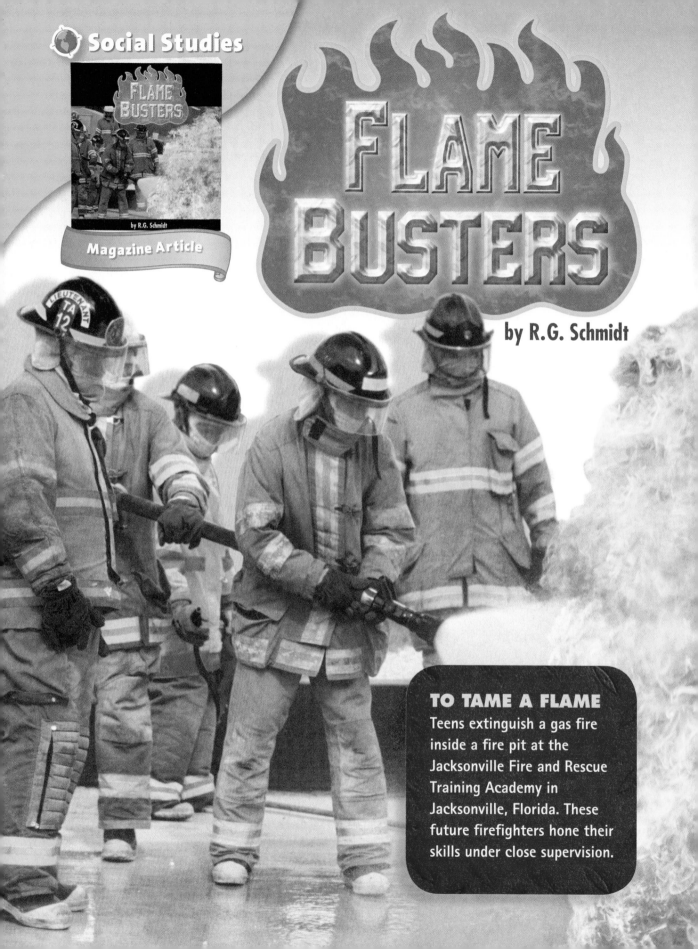

FLAME BUSTERS
by R.G. Schmidt

Magazine Article

FLAME BUSTERS

by R.G. Schmidt

TO TAME A FLAME
Teens extinguish a gas fire inside a fire pit at the Jacksonville Fire and Rescue Training Academy in Jacksonville, Florida. These future firefighters hone their skills under close supervision.

TEENS TRAIN TO BATTLE HEAT, FIRE, AND FEAR

With a huge roar, a gas flame shoots 50 feet high. Another flame leaps out 30 feet to the side. At about 900°F the burning gas is hot enough to melt lead. A team of teens moves in, determined to put it out.

"Step . . . step . . . step," commands Kim Balko, 17, the team leader. With each step the group moves closer to the blaze, taming it with a mist of water from a high-pressure hose. Finally Kim, wearing protective gloves, reaches in and shuts off the gas valve. The team backs away, still spraying water.

"Step . . . step . . . step," Kim repeats, making sure everyone moves in unison. "In a fire everyone has a job to do," she says. "Teamwork is important."

HOT HANDS
Suiting up to fight a fire, George Green, 17, of Jacksonville, Florida, slides on gloves to protect his hands from the fire's intense heat.

ROLLOUT

Bryan Bull, 18, rolls out a supply line, or hose, that will connect the apparatus, or fire truck, to the water hydrant.

The teens, all from Jacksonville, Florida, participate in Exploring, a program run by Learning for Life for young people 14 to 21 years old. The future firefighters gain knowledge and skills at the Jacksonville Fire and Rescue Training Academy. John Peavy, Explorer Post advisor and training officer, says the teens learn more than just how to spray water. "They learn the mechanics and the hazards of firefighting," he says. "Training includes math, chemistry, CPR, and first aid."

Explorers start their training by performing chores around a firehouse, where they also study procedures and firefighting terms. After several months they take a test; their scores and performance in the training exercises determine when each Explorer qualifies to go on a "ride-along" to a real fire.

CAREFUL CONNECTION

Kim Balko and Bryan Bull join two hoses. Firefighters must sometimes connect more than 20 hoses to get water to a fire.

SUPER SPRAY

Will Connor, 17, aims a hose that sprays 125 gallons of water each minute. In training he uses the hose to cool down a burning gas tank and nearby firefighters.

Although not allowed inside the "hot zone" where the fire is burning, Explorers have important jobs to do at the scene of a fire. "They help take equipment off the apparatus, or fire truck, and connect the hoses. They also help keep track of people, and even assist with crowd control," says Peavy.

Bill Harvey, 19, started training at age 14. He remembers one of his first ride-alongs. It was to a two-story house on fire. "I was nervous," he says. "I was afraid I would do something wrong. I knew the firefighters were counting on me, and I didn't want to let them down."

Bill's confidence has grown during his five years at the academy. "I feel more comfortable dealing with emergencies," he says. Todd Dunkley, 14, has just begun his training. He says he expects to learn a lot about teamwork and discipline. He won't be disappointed.

RESTING UP
After a difficult training exercise, the Explorers rest. Each may carry as much as 60 pounds of clothing and gear.

Connections

Comparing Texts

1. What can you learn from Axel's rafting trip that may help you when you face a challenge?

2. Compare what Axel learns about fire to what teens learn at the fire academy.

3. Describe a time when you had to "sit still and wait for a solution" as Axel did.

Vocabulary Review

Rate a Situation

Work with a partner. Read aloud each sentence and point to the spot on the line that shows how comfortable you would feel in each situation. Explain your choices.

Least
Comfortable ——————————————— Comfortable
Most

- You had to walk on a **treacherous** bridge
- You were told your chores would not be **drudgery**.
- You **plunged** into cold water on a hot day.
- Your favorite game had been **altered**.

treacherous

drudgery

plunge

smoldering

altered

scoffed

skeptically

discouraged

Fluency Practice

Movie Script

Work with a small group of classmates. Read aloud "Fire Storm" as if it were a movie script. Have each person in your group read the dialogue for one of the characters in the story. You may wish to divide the lines of the narrator between two group members. Practice reading your lines several times. Remember to match your expression to the feelings of the character in the story. Perform your movie script for other groups.

Writing

Newspaper Article

Imagine you are a reporter interviewing someone who was at the scene of a fire. Write a newspaper article to inform your readers about the fire.

Who?
What?
When?
Where?
Why?
How?

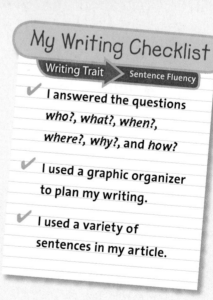

My Writing Checklist

Writing Trait ▶ Sentence Fluency

✓ I answered the questions who?, what?, when?, where?, why?, and how?

✓ I used a graphic organizer to plan my writing.

✓ I used a variety of sentences in my article.

CONTENTS

Lesson 14

Genre: Fantasy

THE STRANGER

A Place in the Sun

Genre: Atlas Entry

Draw Conclusions

Remember that authors do not always tell readers everything that happens in a story. Sometimes you must use **story details** and **what you know** to **draw conclusions** about what is happening in the text. When you draw conclusions, you figure out something an author has not directly explained.

Story Details	What You Know	Conclusion

Tip

As you read, ask yourself, *What has the author told me? What do I need to figure out for myself?*

Read the paragraph and the information in the graphic organizer. Notice how using story details with what you know can help you draw a conclusion about the paragraph.

Enrico walked quickly. It was snowing hard, and he still had three blocks to go. Suddenly, a glint of silver caught his eye. On the snowy sidewalk was a large silver coin. Curious, Enrico stopped to pick it up. He slipped off his mitten to pick up the coin—it was warm! "Strange," he thought, slipping it into his pocket. As Enrico stood up, he noticed fresh footprints leading away from the coin. Now he knew why the coin was warm.

Story Details	What You Know	Conclusion
A silver coin in the snow feels warm.	A coin in the snow should be cold.	The coin must have fallen out of someone's warm hand or pocket.

Try This!

Look back at the paragraph. What conclusion can you draw about when the coin was dropped? How did story details and your own knowledge help you?

peculiar

occasionally

drab

fascinated

hermit

timid

trembling

dashed

Mountain Mystery

TUESDAY MORNING

It's our first week of vacation in the mountains. One thing is **peculiar** about this place. **Occasionally**, early in the morning, we see a small dog in the woods nearby. The dog has a **drab** coat, but it looks as if it's being cared for. Dad says the dog must live in the woods.

WEDNESDAY AFTERNOON

I am **fascinated** by the dog. It never strays far from the woods. Mom thinks it might belong to a **hermit**.

THURSDAY EVENING

Today, we put food out for the dog. We left some slices of bacon at the edge of the woods. The dog seems very **timid**. I wonder if it will eat the bacon.

FRIDAY MORNING

The dog came back. I watched as it nibbled on the bacon. I spoke softly to the dog. It was **trembling** a bit, but it wagged its tail. Then it **dashed** back into the woods. I'm sure we'll see the dog again.

GO online www.harcourtschool.com/storytown

Word Scribe

This week your task is to use the Vocabulary Words in your writing. In your vocabulary journal, write sentences to show the meanings of the words. For example, you could write about something you found fascinating, or you could explain what makes a room look drab. Write about as many of the Vocabulary Words as you can. Share your writing with your classmates.

THE STRANGER

Fantasy

Award Winner

Genre Study

A fantasy is an imaginative story that may have unrealistic characters and events. As you read, look for

- story events that could not happen in real life.

- characters that may behave in an unrealistic way.

Characters	Setting

Plot Events

Comprehension Strategy

Monitor comprehension by **reading ahead** to look for an explanation for ideas you don't understand.

Focus Strategy

THE STRANGER

BY CHRIS VAN ALLSBURG

It was the time of year Farmer Bailey liked best, when summer turned to fall. He whistled as he drove along. A cool breeze blew across his face through the truck's open window. Then it happened. There was a loud "thump." Mr. Bailey jammed on his brakes. "Oh no," he thought. "I've hit a deer."

But it wasn't a deer the farmer found lying in the road, it was a man. Mr. Bailey knelt down beside the still figure, fearing the worst. Then, suddenly, the man opened his eyes. He looked up with terror and jumped to his feet. He tried to run off, lost his balance, and fell down. He got up again, but this time the farmer took his arm and helped him to the truck.

Mr. Bailey drove home. He helped the stranger inside, where Mrs. Bailey made him comfortable on the parlor sofa. Katy, their daughter, peeked into the room. The man on the sofa was dressed in odd rough leather clothing. She heard her father whisper ". . . must be some kind of hermit . . . sort of fellow who lives alone in the woods." The stranger didn't seem to understand the questions Mr. Bailey asked him. "I don't think," whispered Mrs. Bailey, "he knows how to talk."

Mr. Bailey called the doctor, who came and listened to the stranger's heart, felt his bones, looked in his eyes, and took his temperature. He decided the man had lost his memory. There was a bump on the back of his head. "In a few days," the doctor said, "he should remember who he is and where he's from." Mrs. Bailey stopped the doctor as he left the house. He'd forgotten his thermometer. "Oh, you can throw that out," he answered. "It's broken, the mercury is stuck at the bottom."

Mr. Bailey lent the stranger some clean clothes. The fellow seemed confused about buttonholes and buttons. In the evening he joined the Baileys for dinner. The steam that rose from the hot food fascinated him. He watched Katy take a spoonful of soup and blow gently across it. Then he did exactly the same. Mrs. Bailey shivered. "Brrr," she said. "There's a draft in here tonight."

The next morning Katy watched the stranger from her bedroom window. He walked across the yard, toward two rabbits. Instead of running into the woods, the rabbits took a hop in his direction. He picked one of them up and stroked its ears, then set it down. The rabbits hopped away, then stopped and looked back, as if they expected the stranger to follow.

When Katy's father went into the fields that day, the stranger shyly tagged along. Mr. Bailey gave him a pitchfork and, with a little practice, he learned to use it well. They worked hard. Occasionally Mr. Bailey would have to stop and rest. But the stranger never tired. He didn't even sweat.

That evening Katy sat with the stranger, watching the setting sun. High above them a flock of geese, in perfect V formation, flew south on the trip that they made every fall. The stranger could not take his eyes off the birds. He stared at them like a man who'd been hypnotized.

Two weeks passed and the stranger still could not remember who he was. But the Baileys didn't mind. They liked having the stranger around. He had become one of the family. Day by day he'd grown less timid. "He seems so happy to be around us," Mr. Bailey said to his wife. "It's hard to believe he's a hermit."

Another week passed. Farmer Bailey could not help noticing how peculiar the weather had been. Not long ago it seemed that autumn was just around the corner. But now it still felt like summer, as if the seasons couldn't change. The warm days made the pumpkins grow larger than ever. The leaves on the trees were as green as they'd been three weeks before.

One day the stranger climbed the highest hill on the Bailey farm. He looked to the north and saw a puzzling sight. The trees in the distance were bright red and orange.

But the trees to the south, like those round the Baileys', were nothing but shades of green. They seemed so drab and ugly to the stranger. It would be much better, he thought, if all trees could be red and orange.

The stranger's feelings grew stronger the next day. He couldn't look at a tree's green leaves without sensing that something was terribly wrong. The more he thought about it, the more upset he became, until finally he could think of nothing else. He ran to a tree and pulled off a leaf. He held it in a trembling hand and, without thinking, blew on it with all his might.

At dinner that evening the stranger appeared dressed in his old leather clothes. By the tears in his eyes the Baileys could tell that their friend had decided to leave. He hugged them all once, then dashed out the door. The Baileys hurried outside to wave good-bye, but the stranger had disappeared. The air had turned cold, and the leaves on the trees were no longer green.

Every autumn since the stranger's visit, the same thing happens at the Bailey farm. The trees that surround it stay green for a week after the trees to the north have turned. Then overnight they change their color to the brightest of any tree around. And etched in frost on the farmhouse windows are words that say simply, "See you next fall."

THINK CRITICALLY

1 How does the Bailey family meet the stranger? NOTE DETAILS

2 How do you know that the Baileys are a kind and generous family? CHARACTER'S TRAITS

3 How might things change at your home if the stranger visited you? MAKE CONNECTIONS

4 Who do you think the stranger is? DRAW CONCLUSIONS

5 **WRITE** Tell how the Baileys' farm is DIFFERENT after the stranger's visit. Use details from the story to support your answer. SHORT RESPONSE

ABOUT THE AUTHOR
CHRIS VAN ALLSBURG

Chris Van Allsburg starts a book by creating a picture in his mind. Then he asks himself questions about the picture. From his questions, a story forms. Chris Van Allsburg believes that good stories make readers wonder about what happens next. "I want my stories, my plots, to unfold as pieces of a puzzle."

Three of Chris Van Allsburg's books have been made into movies: *Jumanji*, *The Polar Express*, and *Zathura*. He lives in Providence, Rhode Island, with his wife and two daughters.

GO online www.harcourtschool.com/storytown

A place in the Sun

Without the Sun to light and heat it, Earth would be nothing more than a cold, dark, and lifeless rock. Orbiting at a distance of 93 million miles (150 million km) from the Sun, our planet is in an ideal position—between burning hot Venus and freezing cold Mars. With an average temperature of 59°F (15°C), Earth is the only planet known in our solar system that can support life. Because of Earth's shape — a gigantic ball that is slightly f lattened out—it does not receive the Sun's heat equally over its surface. Countries near Earth's equator get most of the Sun's rays, and so they have hot climates. Countries lying closer to the polar regions, as well as the North and South Poles, get the Sun's rays more indirectly. These regions all have much colder climates.

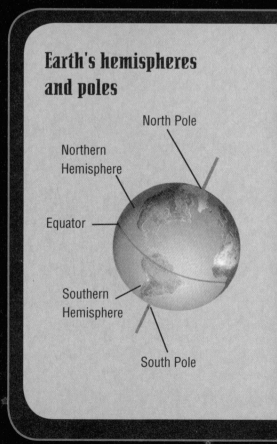

Earth's hemispheres and poles

North Pole

Northern Hemisphere

Equator

Southern Hemisphere

South Pole

The Cycle of the Seasons

Earth revolves around the Sun on a journey that takes one whole year to complete. It orbits in a slightly tilted position so that the North and South Poles are not sitting precisely at the top and bottom of the globe. This means that, depending on the time of year, either the Northern or the Southern Hemisphere is receiving more of the Sun's rays. It is the changes in Earth's position that are responsible for the seasons. In July, the Northern Hemisphere is tilted toward the Sun, giving North Americans their summer. At the same time of year, the Australians in the Southern Hemisphere are having their winter. Six months later, the opposite happens.

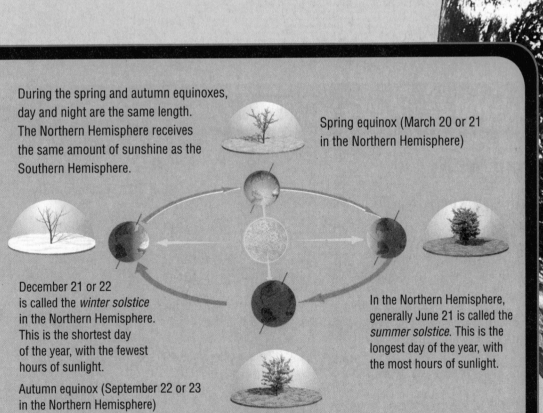

During the spring and autumn equinoxes, day and night are the same length. The Northern Hemisphere receives the same amount of sunshine as the Southern Hemisphere.

Spring equinox (March 20 or 21 in the Northern Hemisphere)

December 21 or 22 is called the *winter solstice* in the Northern Hemisphere. This is the shortest day of the year, with the fewest hours of sunlight.

Autumn equinox (September 22 or 23 in the Northern Hemisphere)

In the Northern Hemisphere, generally June 21 is called the *summer solstice*. This is the longest day of the year, with the most hours of sunlight.

Connections

Comparing Texts

1. Are you fascinated by the stranger? Explain.

2. What science concepts do you find in both "The Stranger" and "A Place in the Sun"?

3. What can you learn from "The Stranger" about helping people?

Vocabulary Review

Word Webs

Work with a partner. Choose two Vocabulary Words. Create a word web for each word. In your web, write words and phrases that are related to the Vocabulary Word. Discuss your word webs with your partner.

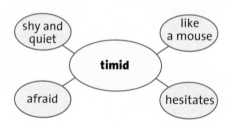

fascinated

occasionally

timid

hermit

peculiar

drab

trembling

dashed

Fluency Practice

Partner Reading

Choose your favorite part of "The Stranger." Reread the text aloud while your partner listens. After reading, ask your partner to give you feedback about how you used expression. Read the section aloud again, keeping in mind your partner's comments. Then switch roles and repeat the activity.

Writing

Write a Descriptive Paragraph

Imagine that you are on the Baileys' farm in autumn. Write a paragraph that describes your surroundings.

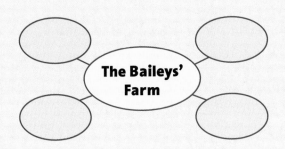

The Baileys' Farm

My Writing Checklist

Writing Trait ▸ Sentence Fluency

✔ I used a graphic organizer to plan my writing.

✔ I used a variety of sentence types in my paragraph.

✔ I used sensory details to describe the setting.

CONTENTS

Lesson 15
Theme Review and Vocabulary Builder

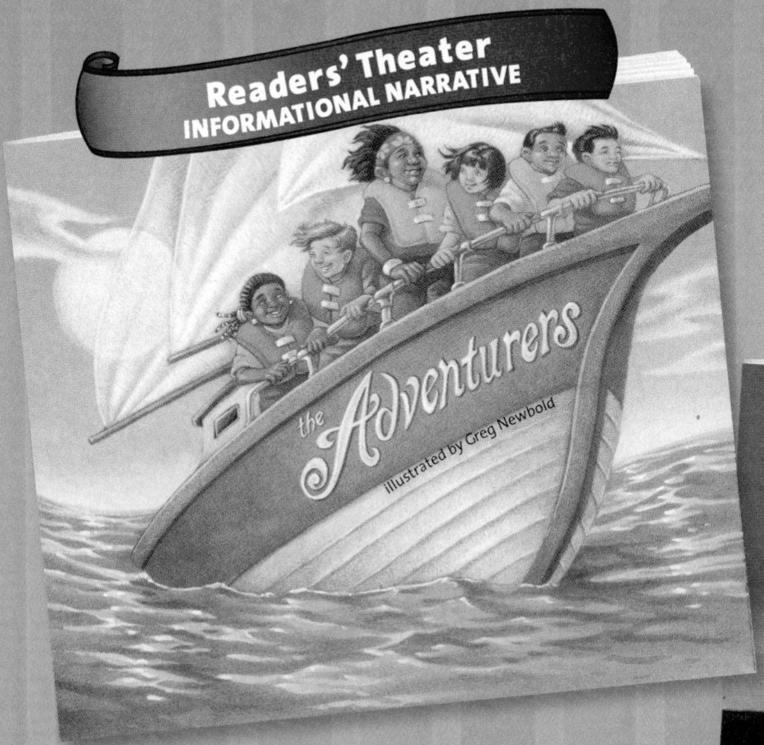

Readers' Theater
INFORMATIONAL NARRATIVE

the Adventurers

illustrated by Greg Newbold

ICEBERGS
Floating Snow Cones
by Ann Stalcup

Reading for Information
EXPOSITORY NONFICTION

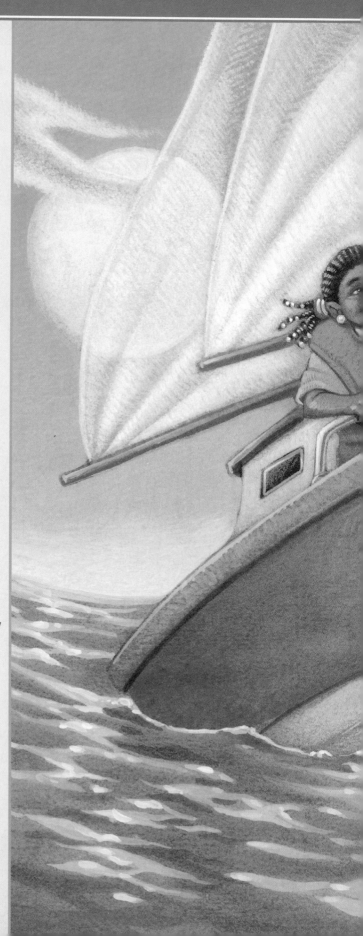

- intrepid
- seasoned
- guidance
- undoubtedly
- cherish
- hoist
- delectable
- pristine
- fragile
- privilege

Reading for Fluency

When reading a script aloud,

- Use punctuation marks to guide your **pace.**

- Read with **expression** to match the characters' emotions.

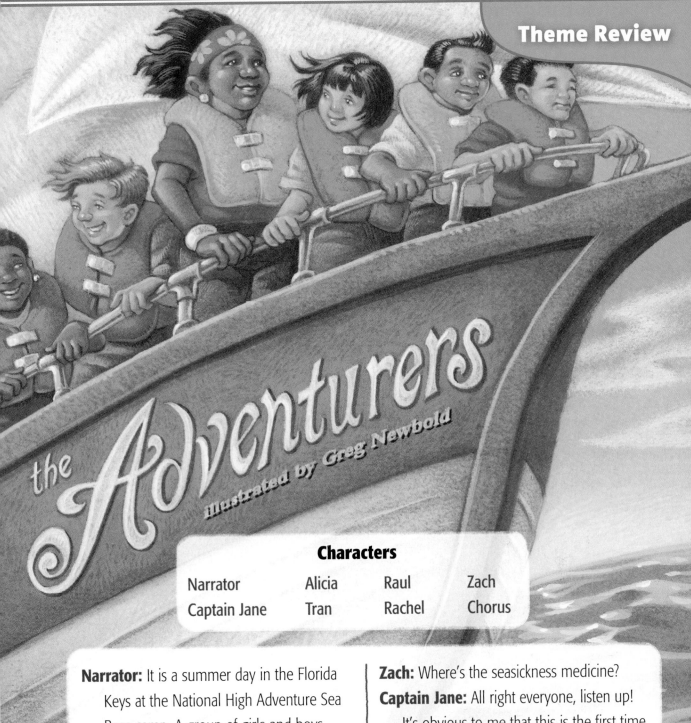

the Adventurers

illustrated by Greg Newbold

Characters

Narrator	Alicia	Raul	Zach
Captain Jane	Tran	Rachel	Chorus

Narrator: It is a summer day in the Florida Keys at the National High Adventure Sea Base camp. A group of girls and boys prepare to board the *Intrepid*, an 80-foot sailing ship.

Alicia: It's hot.

Raul: My backpack is weighing me down.

Zach: Where's the seasickness medicine?

Captain Jane: All right everyone, listen up! It's obvious to me that this is the first time on a sailing vessel for most of you. By the end of this trip, though, you'll all be seasoned sailors.

393

Tran: When do we start?

Captain Jane: Right now, Tran. I'm going to teach you every function of this ship, from the bow to the stern.

Rachel: I've never done anything like this before! Bow? Stern? What are those?

Alicia: The bow is the front of the ship. The stern is the back.

Captain Jane: As crew members, you'll be in constant motion. Look to me for guidance if you have any questions. One feature of this expedition will be a snorkeling trip over the coral reefs around Big Pine Key, so you will also learn how to snorkel.

Alicia: It's a good thing I love swimming!

Captain Jane: Undoubtedly, conditions will be uncomfortable at times. You should be prepared for that.

Raul: More uncomfortable than this backpack?

Captain Jane: I can promise you this, though—if you pay attention to what you're taught, and do your best, you will cherish this experience and want to do it again. Is everyone ready to venture forth into the unknown?

Chorus: AYE-AYE, CAPTAIN!

Captain Jane: Very well. It's time to put on life vests, hoist the anchor, and set sail!

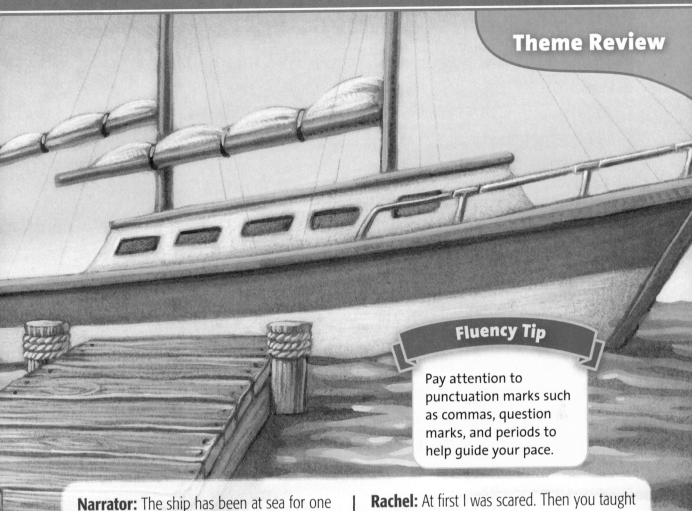

Fluency Tip

Pay attention to punctuation marks such as commas, question marks, and periods to help guide your pace.

Narrator: The ship has been at sea for one week. The boys and girls are taking turns at the helm of the ship.

Captain Jane: Hold the wheel steady, Rachel. You're doing very well!

Rachel: This is amazing! I never thought I could steer an 80-foot-long ship!

Zach: My big brother will be so jealous when he hears about this. He drives a car, but that's nothing compared to sailing a ship!

Raul: It feels great to plunge through the waves!

Captain Jane: Rachel, you seemed so timid when you first took the wheel.

Rachel: At first I was scared. Then you taught me how to guide the ship safely. Now I feel confident at the helm!

Captain Jane: You all are fast learners. You were landlubbers just a few days ago.

Tran: What's a landlubber, Captain Jane?

Captain Jane: Someone who knows nothing about the sea.

Alicia: We aren't landlubbers anymore!

Chorus: We're prepared!

Captain Jane: Now you're salty sea dogs.

Chorus: AYE-AYE, CAPTAIN!

Narrator: The ship is now anchored off Big Munson Key. The boys and girls have been here for five days. Captain Jane is helping them make a fire on the beach. Tran arranges twigs and driftwood in a fire pit. Captain Jane then carefully lights the wood with a match.

Captain Jane: No camp is complete without a roaring fire.

Tran: Now we need something to cook.

Zach: Raul is bringing over the rations.

Alicia: It's hard to believe we've spent twelve days without e-mail or TV!

Rachel: I thought once we hit dry land, we could eat at a restaurant on the island.

Captain Jane: You were all so shocked when we first arrived! Big Munson hasn't changed much in the past 150 years.

Zach: This place resembles those deserted islands you see in the movies.

Narrator: Raul approaches the group. He carries a box full of canned rations.

Raul: Are you guys ready for dinner?

Chorus: We're ready!

Tran: I can't believe how much we've all learned about survival.

Zach: At first, camping seemed like drudgery, but now I like it!

Narrator: Each camper opens a can of rations. Captain Jane puts the contents of all the cans into a pot over the fire. She adds water and then some spices from a small pouch in her survival kit. In a few minutes, dinner is ready.

Captain Jane: Stew is ready, everyone.

Alicia: It's a great idea to carry cooking spices in your survival kit, Captain Jane.

Captain Jane: It's just a matter of thinking ahead, Alicia. Adding spices to canned rations makes them taste a lot better!

Narrator: They all take out the bowls and spoons they carry in their backpacks. Captain Jane then fills each of their bowls with the steaming stew. Raul tries a spoonful.

Alicia: What do you think?

Raul: It's hot! But it's really good, too. This stew is delectable!

Narrator: The friends enjoy their dinner and later sit around the fire until it is smoldering.

Narrator: The *Intrepid* has now traveled south and docked at Big Pine Key, where the boys and girls have learned to snorkel. Now they board a smaller boat to go out to the reefs.

Captain Jane: All right, now, it's time to do some exploring. Remember, when you dive, water will get into your snorkel. What's the first thing you'll do when you come back to the surface?

Zach: Exhale hard through the snorkel.

Raul: The air we breathe out will push the water out of the snorkel so we can breathe in fresh air.

Fluency Tip

Use expression to show happiness, sadness, and other feelings your character has.

Tran: How deep is the water, Captain Jane?

Captain Jane: It's not very deep at all, Tran. If we were swimming to greater depths, we wouldn't be able to use snorkels. We would need scuba diving gear.

Alicia: I'm just happy we'll finally get to snorkel!

Rachel: I can't wait to see the reef up close. The pictures we've seen are so beautiful. Some of the fish looked so peculiar. They almost didn't seem real.

Captain Jane: You'll see they're all real once we're down there, Rachel. Now, what's the rule about getting close to the reef?

Tran: Look but don't touch.

Captain Jane: Very good! These reefs must remain in pristine condition to survive. Now, is everyone ready?

Chorus: AYE-AYE, CAPTAIN!

Narrator: Following the captain, the girls and boys lower themselves into the water. Below the surface, they see a beautiful coral reef. Brightly colored fish swim around them. After a half-hour of snorkeling, the group returns to the boat.

Tran: Wow, that was incredible!

Rachel: You said it! The reef is so wondrous and beautiful.

Zach: I wanted to touch it, but I didn't.

Captain Jane: Good for you! Coral is very fragile and will die if it's touched. It grows back very slowly—about a foot every one hundred years.

Raul: That's a long time.

Alicia: I'm glad we didn't see any sharks.

Rachel: Don't you remember our science class, Alicia? You won't find those kinds of predators in a coral reef. It's not their natural habitat.

Captain Jane: You did very well! It's time to head home.

Narrator: The *Intrepid* has now returned to its starting point at Key West. The voyage has ended.

Alicia: We're fully tied to the dock, Captain. We're ready to disembark.

Captain Jane: You all did very well. Be sure to collect all your gear before you leave the ship.

Tran: I'll cherish this trip forever.

Zach: It was a privilege to be a part of this adventure, Captain Jane.

Captain Jane: It was my privilege to sail with such a fine crew, Zach.

Alicia: Captain Jane, I want to sail on more adventures with you.

Rachel: Can't we stay aboard as your crew?

Zach: We can help train the next group.

Captain Jane: You need to get a few more voyages under your belts before you start teaching others how to sail.

Alicia: Yes, we learned so much on this trip, Captain Jane!

Captain Jane: There's always more to learn, Alicia. Keep studying and experiencing different parts of the marine world while you're here at Sea Base. Don't worry—I'm sure I'll be seeing you back aboard the *Intrepid* very soon. I see a ship captain in each and every one of you.

Raul: Let's do it again next year!

Captain Jane: You salty sea dogs will always be welcome!

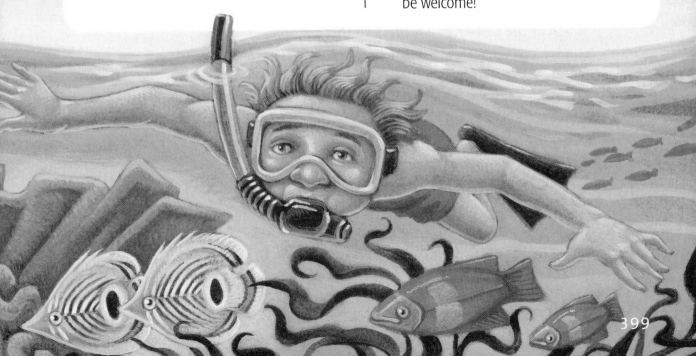

COMPREHENSION STRATEGIES
Review

Reading Nonfiction

Bridge to Reading for Information Expository nonfiction gives you accurate facts and information about a topic. The information should be clearly organized. The notes on page 401 point out some text features of expository nonfiction, including headings, photographs, and captions. How can these features help you read and understand the information presented?

Review the Focus Strategies

Use the strategies you learned about in this theme to help you understand what you are reading.

Use Graphic Organizers

Use graphic organizers to help you organize information as you read. You can use a graphic organizer like this to keep track of the causes and effects you find in paragraphs, sections of text, or the whole text.

Cause	→	Effect

Monitor Comprehension: Read Ahead

Monitor comprehension while you read. If you have questions about what you are reading, read ahead to find the answers.

As you read "Icebergs: Floating Snow Cones" on pages 402–405, think about where and how to use comprehension strategies.

HEADINGS
Headings tell you what a section of text is mostly about.

ICEBERGS
Floating Snow Cones

Every year, thousands of new icebergs are formed in the ocean around Greenland and Antarctica. Icebergs are giant blocks of freshwater ice that float in the sea. They come in many shapes, sizes, and colors. Some are deep blue or green. Some look like floating sculptures. Old icebergs that have been worn down by the weather sometimes look like columns of ice.

HOW ICEBERGS FORM

Icebergs begin and end in the ocean. First, moisture from the ocean rises into the air and moves up into Earth's atmosphere. Then the water falls as snow. As layers of snow develop over thousands of years, the heavy weight presses down and turns the snow to ice—lots of ice.

Large areas of ice called *ice sheets* and *glaciers* move slowly across the land toward the sea. When glaciers finally reach the coast, huge pieces split off into the ocean with a rumbling sound that echoes for miles. These are icebergs. The greatest number of icebergs split off into the ocean during the spring and summer months when the temperatures are warmer.

▲ An iceberg splits off into the ocean.

PHOTOGRAPHS
Photographs show you real places, people, or things.

CAPTIONS
Captions give you information about photographs and illustrations.

ICEBERGS
Floating Snow Cones

Every year, thousands of new icebergs are formed in the ocean around Greenland and Antarctica. Icebergs are giant blocks of freshwater ice that float in the sea. They come in many shapes, sizes, and colors. Some are deep blue or green. Some look like floating sculptures. Old icebergs that have been worn down by the weather sometimes look like columns of ice.

HOW ICEBERGS FORM

Icebergs begin and end in the ocean. First, moisture from the ocean rises into the air and moves up into Earth's atmosphere. Then the water falls as snow. As layers of snow develop over thousands of years, the heavy weight presses down and turns the snow to ice—lots of ice.

Large areas of ice called *ice sheets* and *glaciers* move slowly across the land toward the sea. When glaciers finally reach the coast, huge pieces split off into the ocean with a rumbling sound that echoes for miles. These are icebergs. The greatest number of icebergs split off into the ocean during the spring and summer months when the temperatures are warmer.

▲ An iceberg splits off into the ocean.

403

SIZE OF ICEBERGS

Scientists call the splitting of icebergs "calving." Icebergs are a lot larger than a calf, though. Icebergs as large as a ten-story building are not unusual. One of the largest Antarctic icebergs that formed recently is 185 miles long and 25 miles wide.

Usually, only about one-fifth of an iceberg appears above the surface of the water. The other four-fifths of the iceberg is hidden underwater, out of sight. Though all icebergs eventually melt, an Antarctic iceberg can last as long as 10 years. Wind and waves may bring an iceberg far away from where it first entered the ocean.

◀ Most of an iceberg extends below the surface of the water.

Stop and Think

Read ahead to clear up confusion you may have about the topic.
MONITOR COMPREHENSION: READ AHEAD

ICEBERGS CREATE DANGERS

Scientists study and track icebergs because they can be dangerous to ships, especially in foggy conditions. Sometimes, an iceberg has what is called a "foot," an extension that is completely under water. The *Titanic* was an extremely large ship that in 1912 hit an iceberg "foot" and sank in the Atlantic Ocean. Today radar, planes, and satellites are used to monitor where icebergs are moving and to warn ships that may cross paths with an iceberg.

READING-WRITING
CONNECTION

Theme (4) Imagination at Work

▶ Gil Mayers, *Portrait in Jazz*

407

CONTENTS

Lesson 16

From the creators of the Caldecott-winning SO YOU WANT TO BE PRESIDENT?

JUDITH ST. GEORGE

DAVID SMALL

SO YOU WANT TO BE AN INVENTOR?

MAKE a Movie MACHINE

Focus Skill

Focus Skill

Fact and Opinion

A **fact** is a statement that can be proved. An **opinion** is a statement of feeling or belief that cannot be proved. Authors of nonfiction text may include both facts and opinions about a topic. Knowing the difference between facts and opinions can help you judge the ideas in a nonfiction text. To decide whether a statement is a fact or an opinion, ask yourself:

- What evidence proves this statement is true?
- Does this statement include beliefs or feelings that cannot be proved?

Fact	Opinion
Evidence	Evidence

Tip

Some words that signal an opinion are *should, must, best, worst, I think*, and *I believe.*

Read the paragraph below. Then look at the graphic organizer. It shows one fact and one opinion from the paragraph.

Have you ever wondered what it would be like to ride a bicycle across a lake? On a water bike, you can find out. The water bike is an amazing invention. It looks like a floating bicycle with large, plastic wheels. As you pedal, paddles move back and forth under the water and push the bike forward. A water bike can travel at about six miles per hour. Everyone should ride a water bike!

Fact	Opinion
A water bike can travel at about six miles per hour.	The water bike is an amazing invention.
Evidence	**Evidence**
This can be proved by timing the water bike's speed.	This cannot be proved. Other people might not agree that water bikes are amazing.

Try This!

Look back at the paragraph. Find another fact and another opinion. Which word or words signal the opinion?

www.harcourtschool.com/storytown

Vocabulary

Build Robust Vocabulary

- quest
- barriers
- forged
- trampled
- hoaxer
- tinker
- perfect

Dad's Invention

My dad and I were on a **quest**. We had to find a way to keep our dog, Sam, out of the garden. We had surrounded it with **barriers**, but they did not keep him out. Sam always **forged** a new path into the rows of vegetables. He **trampled** the young plants under his big paws.

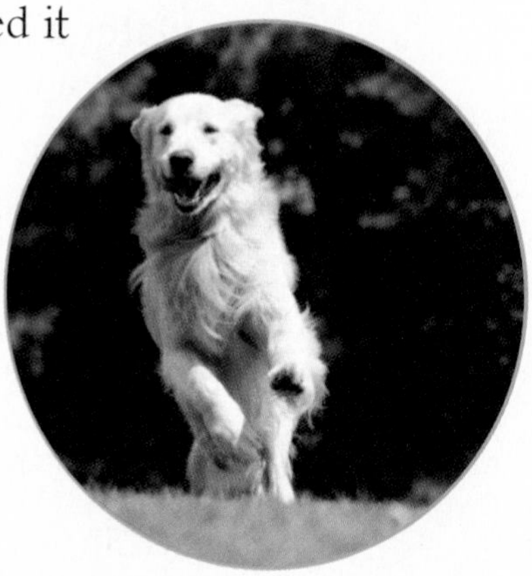

"I have to play a trick on Sam," Dad said. "I have to convince him that there is a cat in the garden."

Sam was afraid of cats.

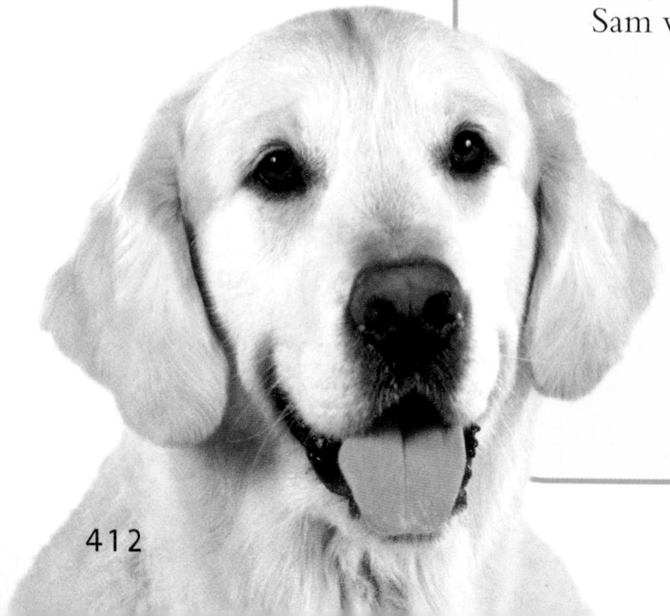

"I want to be a **hoaxer**, too!" I said.

I found a recording of loud, scary meows.

Dad began to **tinker** with a CD player and a motion sensor. Soon he was able to **perfect** his invention. When someone moved near the CD player, the meows began to play.

We hid the invention in the garden and waited. When Sam came near, he heard the meows and ran in the other direction.

 www.harcourtschool.com/storytown

Word Scribe

 This week your task is to use the Vocabulary Words in your writing. In your vocabulary journal, write sentences to show the meanings of the words. For example, you could write about an inventor who has to perfect an invention, or you could describe someone who goes on a quest.

Narrative Nonfiction

Genre Study

Narrative nonfiction tells about people, things, events, or places that are real. As you read, look for

- factual information that tells a story.

- illustrations or photographs of real people and places.

Facts	Opinions

Comprehension Strategy

Monitor comprehension while you read. **Adjust your reading rate** when you come to difficult sections of text.

So You Want to Be an Inventor?

BY
Judith St. George

Illustrated by
David Small

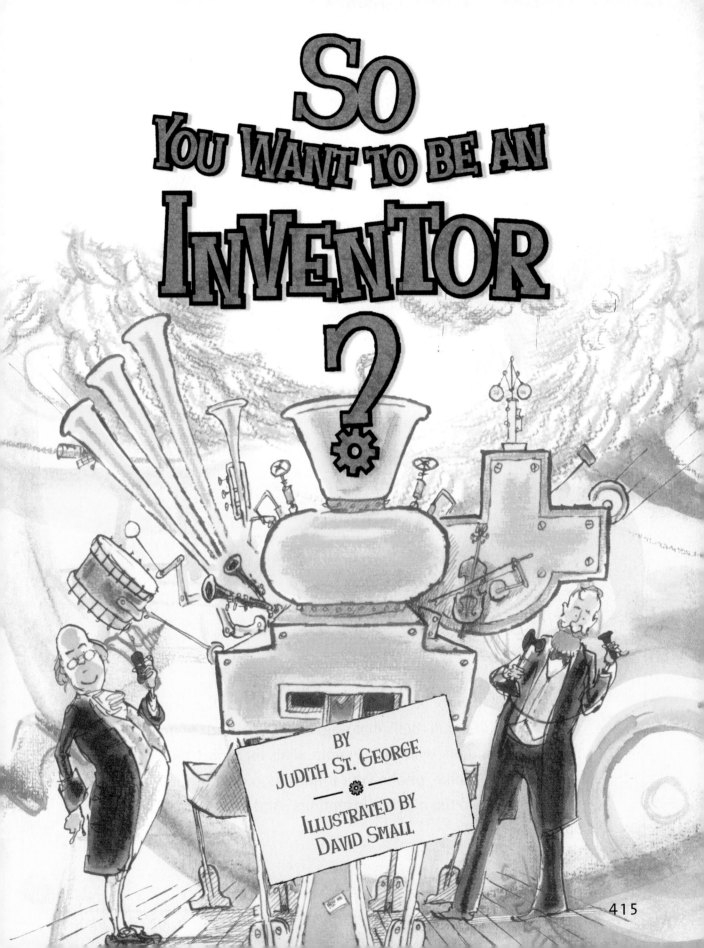

Are you a kid who likes to tinker with machines that clink and clank, levers that pull, bells that ring, cogs that grind, switches that turn on and off, wires that vibrate, dials that spin? You watch TV, ride a bike, phone your friends, pop popcorn in a microwave, go to the movies. Inventions! And you want to be an inventor, too?

You don't have to have white hair and wrinkles to be an inventor.

At twelve, **Benjamin Franklin** invented swim paddles for his hands and kick paddles for his feet. When he grew up, Ben Franklin invented the lightning rod, Franklin stove, fireplace damper, library stepstool and odometer to measure the distance that a vehicle travels. At seventy-seven, he invented bifocal glasses. (He probably needed them!)

If you want to be an inventor, find a need and fill it.

Cyrus McCormick got tired of reaping wheat on his family's farm with a hand scythe. It took forever! So in 1831, he invented a mechanical reaper. The flapping reaper frightened the horses. BUT it reaped in a few hours what three men could reap in a day.

The son of runaway slaves, **Elijah McCoy** was an oilman on a railroad. To oil the pistons, gears and bearings, the train had to be stopped. In 1872, he invented a lubricator that oiled the pistons, gears and bearings while the engine was running! Other workers wanted his invention for their engines. But they wanted "the real McCoy" lubricators or nothing!

If you want to be an inventor, be a dreamer.

As a boy in Scotland, **Alexander Graham Bell** had a "dreaming place." When he grew up, he dreamed of people talking across distances—maybe by electric signals. Electric signals it was! In 1876, he invented the telephone!

Young Russian **Igor Sikorsky** dreamed of a different way to fly—up, down, forward, backward, AND sideways. Igor's brother poked fun at him. "It will never fly!" He was wrong. With its three blades whirling, in 1939 Igor's dream helicopter took off.

If you want to be an inventor, keep your eyes open!

On a 1914 trip to Labrador, fur trader **Clarence Birdseye** watched the Inuit freeze fish on the ice. When the fish thawed, they tasted fresh. Would fast-freezing food between two metal plates work as well? It did! All those frozen dinners, pizzas and other frozen yummies come to you by way of Clarence Birdseye.

After a country walk with his dog in 1948, Swiss engineer **Georges de Mestral** picked cockleburs off his pants. Why, the cocklebur hooks gripped the wool loops in his pants. Hooks and loops! The perfect fastener! Georges' invention? Velcro!

An inventor has to be as stubborn as a bulldog.

Yankee **Charles Goodyear** spent ten years trying to make raw rubber usable. He spent all his money and was thrown into debtor's jail before he hit the jackpot in 1839 by treating raw rubber with sulphur under heat. Tires, tennis balls, and all sorts of other rubber goodies have been bouncing around ever since!

Thomas Edison spent more than a year looking for a thin thread called a *filament* that would glow without burning up when electricity passed through it. He tried platinum, nickel, gold, silver, fish line, cotton thread, coconut hair, people hair, wood shavings, cork and more. Carbonized bamboo was the answer! Edison's 1879 incandescent lamp (a lamp that stayed lit) brightened lives everywhere.

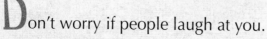

Don't worry if people laugh at you.

Everyone mocked **Robert Fulton's** steamboat, calling it "Fulton's Folly" and "a floating sawmill caught on fire." But the laughter lost steam in 1807 when Robert's *Clermont* chugged up the Hudson River from New York to Albany with paddle wheels churning and flags waving.

Newspapers laughed at **Robert Goddard** for trying to invent a space rocket. They called him "Moon Man." And a hoaxer. He was no hoaxer! Thanks to "Moon Man" Robert Goddard's 1926 invention of a liquid fuel rocket, the spacecraft *Apollo 11* landed Americans safely on the moon in 1969.

Inventors aren't all men!

Illinois homemaker **Josephine Cochran** figured other women were as fed up with washing dishes (and red hands) as she was. In 1886, she put together a wooden tub, wire basket and hand pump to invent the very first dishwasher.

Even Presidents can be inventors.

George Washington invented a sixteen-sided treading barn in 1792. Horses trampled over wheat, spread on the barn floor. The grain dropped through slots. Eureka! George Washington's wheat supply was dry, stored and ready to be ground into flour.

Thomas Jefferson invented a two-faced clock, one face inside (it told the day, hour, minute—and second) and one face outside (its Chinese gong could be heard three miles away). Jefferson wasn't called smart for nothing. The ropes holding the weights were so long that he cut holes in the floor to let the weights hang in the basement!

Maybe you like to work alone.

Alexander Graham Bell worked alone at night, every night, inventing an iron lung, kites to study flight and, of course, the telephone. "To take night from me is to rob me of life," he declared.

Nikola Tesla was world famous for inventing the alternating-current (AC) motor in the 1880s to produce huge amounts of electricity that could be sent over long distances. But Nikola lived in lonely New York hotel rooms, had no family, few friends, and only worked for himself.

Maybe you'd rather invent as part of a team.

Thomas Edison forged a crew of inventors who huddled day and night over clanking, hissing motors, smelly chemicals and machines that sent sparks flying. He—and his crew— came up with the incandescent lamp, the movie camera, the phonograph and more than a thousand other inventions!

One invention can lead to another.

In the early 1900s, **Henry Ford** jumped from Michigan Farmboy to King of the Road. He didn't invent the automobile, BUT he did perfect mass production and the moving assembly line that had workers slapping his Model T Ford cars together in a hurry.

Other inventors hopped on board. **Mary Anderson** invented windshield wipers. (Swish-swish!) **Garrett Morgan** came up with traffic lights. (Red—stop! Yellow—slow! Green—go!) **Elmer Wavering** invented car radios. (A little music, please!) More cars? More accidents? **Allen Breed's** air bags saved lives. (Whoosh!)

Wouldn't Henry Ford be amazed at what he had started!

Watch out! Your invention might scare people.

Swedish chemist **Alfred Nobel** invented dynamite in 1866 by mixing nitroglycerin with chalky soil. But when five workers were killed in an explosion, Alfred was ordered to work outside the city on a barge in the middle of a lake.

While experimenting in 1895, scientist **Wilhelm Roentgen** was shocked when he turned on an electric switch and saw light rays glowing from a screen he had treated with barium. X rays! People freaked out. Did seeing their own bones mean they would die? Or were X rays really death rays?

Some of **Orville and Wilbur Wright's** early-1900s flying machines landed safely and some didn't. Poor Orville! He was hurt in a glider crash, two airplane crashes and a plane crash that knocked him out and broke his leg and ribs! "Flying machine, cloth, and sticks in a heap, with me in the center," Orville wrote in his diary.

Keep a sharp eye on your invention—copycats are out there!

Joseph Henry invented a telegraph system in the 1830s that sent signals over short distances. In 1844, **Samuel F. B. Morse** jazzed up Joseph's invention, put together a Morse code dot-dash system, and was tapped as inventor of the telegraph.

Here's the bottom line! Whether your invention is named after you or not, whether you're a dreamer, a loner, are laughed at, work all night or put yourself in danger, your invention could change the world. It has happened!

Vladimir Zworykin's 1923 electronic tube led to television. Three U.S. scientists' 1947 transistor led to computers.

Even more important, **Johannes Gutenberg** invented a hand-operated printing press with movable metal type in the 1440s. A printer could print in a day what it took a year to write by hand. Result? Books! Books! Books! People decided it was time to learn to read. And they did!

In the end, being an inventor means pushing the limits of what human beings know and what human beings can do.

Because you're a risk taker and will be on a quest into the unknown, you have to be willing to try and fail, try and fail, try and MAYBE succeed.

One thing is certain: There will always be barriers to be broken, whether it's to find a new source of power, a different way to communicate, a machine that works medical miracles or something that we can't even imagine. It takes passion and heart, but those barriers could be broken by you!

THINK CRITICALLY

1 What examples does the author give to show that some new inventions frighten people? NOTE DETAILS

2 Why does the author call inventors "risk takers"? MAKE INFERENCES

3 Which invention described in the selection would be hardest for you to live without? Why? PERSONAL RESPONSE

4 Name one fact and one opinion from the selection. Tell how you know each statement is a fact or an opinion. FACT AND OPINION

5 **WRITE** Inventors are creative people who invent things they believe will help others. Use information and details from the selection to explain:

- the reasons why some inventors are successful, and
- two things you should do if you want to be an inventor. EXTENDED RESPONSE

ABOUT THE AUTHOR

JUDITH ST. GEORGE

Judith St. George says she wants the people in her books to come alive for her readers the way they come alive for her. Her special interest in history came about after living for a year in Longfellow House in Cambridge, Massachusetts—one of George Washington's headquarters during the Revolutionary War.

Judith St. George has written more than twenty books. She has also run story hours and reading programs for children. Judith St. George enjoys speaking to school groups and says she loves the challenge of helping children explore new worlds through books. She has four children and five grandchildren. Judith St. George lives with her husband in Old Lyme, Connecticut.

ABOUT THE ILLUSTRATOR

DAVID SMALL

David Small grew up in Detroit, Michigan. He was never an inventor, but he says that if he had been one as a child, he would have invented something to make himself invisible and to make his brother disappear. David Small had always dreamed of being an artist, but it was not until he had several works published that he began to say proudly, "I am an artist."

MAKE a Movie MACHINE

by Nick D'Alto

illustrated by Hal Mayworth

Did you know that a children's toy inspired Thomas Edison to make movies? The "phenakistoscope," or spindle viewer, was a popular toy during the mid- to late 1800s. It shows a movie by letting the viewer see a series of quickly moving pictures. You can make movies in a similar way, too!

YOU NEED

- drawing utensils (black marker for black-and-white movies; bright color markers for color movies)
- a pack of 3-inch-square self-stick notes
- cardboard
- a compass
- scissors
- a hole punch
- a thumbtack
- a pencil with an eraser

1 Draw a simple picture (an animal, a face, or even a stick figure) on one self-stick note, making sure you keep the pad's sticky part at the bottom. Then lay another self-stick note over that one and trace your first drawing, adding a slight movement to the second drawing. For example, move the figure's arm or leg up or down just a bit. Keep tracing and adding movement until you have 15 pictures on 15 self-stick notes.

2 Next, preview your film: Quickly flip your stack of self-stick notes at the edge, as if it were a deck of playing cards. Watch at the side—you will see your pictures move! Hollywood animators still use this flipbook method to test their cartoons.

3 Now you need to build your movie projector. To make a movie reel, use your compass to draw a circle that is 16 inches in diameter on the cardboard. Cut out this disk—it is your reel. Attach your pictures in order around the edge of the reel like flower petals, placing each picture about $\frac{1}{2}$ inch from the outside of the reel.

4 Use the hole punch to punch a hole through the cardboard between and slightly below each pair of pictures. Then, using the hole you punched as a starting point, cut away the cardboard by making slits about the width of the diameter of the hole.

5 Finally, poke the thumbtack through the center of your reel and push its point into your pencil's eraser.

It's Premiere Time!!!

To watch your film, hold your reel with the pictures facing a mirror. Then spin the reel and look at the mirror through the holes. You will see your pictures move!

Connections

Comparing Texts

1. Many old inventions were described in "So You Want to Be an Inventor?" Which one did you find most interesting?

2. Compare "So You Want to Be an Inventor?" with "Make a Movie Machine." What is the purpose of each selection?

3. An inventor uses his or her imagination. What other jobs require using one's imagination? Explain your answer.

Vocabulary Review

> The quest to perfect an invention takes a long time.

Word Pairs

Work with a partner. Write each Vocabulary Word on a separate index card. Place the cards face down. Take turns flipping over two cards and writing a sentence that uses both words. You must use the words correctly in the sentence to keep the cards. The student with the most cards at the end wins.

tinker

hoaxer

trampled

forged

perfect

quest

barriers

Fluency Practice

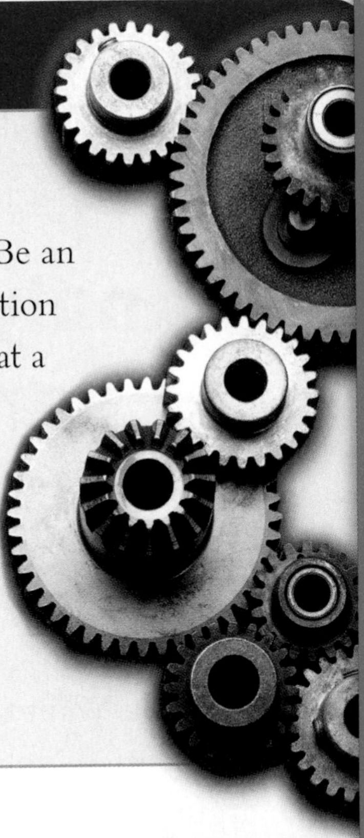

Partner Reading

Choose one of the inventions in "So You Want to Be an Inventor?" Read aloud the section about that invention while your partner listens and follows along. Read at a pace that is slow enough for listeners to understand the text and fast enough to keep them interested. When you have finished, ask your partner for feedback on your pace. Read the passage again, using your partner's feedback to improve your pace. Then switch roles.

Writing

Write a Fact-Opinion Paragraph

Choose an invention you read about in "So You Want to Be an Inventor?" Write a paragraph about how the invention affects people today.

Facts	Opinions

My Writing Checklist

Writing Trait → Voice

- ✔ I included facts as well as opinions to express my personal voice.
- ✔ I used information from the selection and another resource.
- ✔ I used a graphic organizer to plan my writing.

Reading-Writing Connection

Analyze Writer's Craft: Persuasive Writing

The purpose of **persuasive writing** is to **convince** readers of something the author **believes**. Authors give good reasons to support their arguments. They use powerful language to get their points across. Read this passage from "So You Want to Be an Inventor?" by Judith St. George. Notice how the author supports her argument.

Writing Trait

IDEAS
The writer clearly states her **opinion** in the first sentence. To support her opinion, she gives **examples** of an inventor's stubbornness.

Writing Trait

VOICE
The writer uses powerful words, such as *bulldog, thrown,* and *hit* to create a voice of authority that will help persuade the reader.

An inventor has to be as stubborn as a bulldog. Yankee Charles Goodyear spent ten years trying to make raw rubber usable. He spent all his money and was thrown into debtor's jail before he hit the jackpot in 1839 by treating raw rubber with sulphur under heat. Tires, tennis balls, and all sorts of other rubber goodies have been bouncing around ever since!

Persuasive Essay

A **persuasive essay** states an **opinion** and gives **reasons** supporting that opinion. If a writer wants to persuade a reader to do something, the essay may end with **a call to action**.

As you read this persuasive essay by a student named Megan, notice how she **focuses** on three main reasons to support her opinion. Pay attention to the **examples** she uses to support her reasons.

Student Writing Model

Do It Yourself!
by Megan S.

People should repair their own bicycles. Taking care of your own bike puts you in charge. It can also save you time and money.

When you are in charge of your bike, you get to know its parts and how they work. You can catch problems before they turn into disasters. For example, keeping the tires filled with the right amount of air helps you notice holes or leaks before you get a flat.

In the **introduction**, Megan states her **opinion**: People should repair their own bicycles. Then she mentions **three reasons** that support her opinion: It puts you in charge, it saves time, and it saves money.

Writing Trait

IDEAS
In the next paragraph, Megan focuses on her **first reason**: It puts you in charge. To support her reason, she gives the **example** of preventing flat tires.

435

Imagine how much time you could save by fixing your bike yourself! If a chain comes loose, you might waste hours carrying the bike to a shop. It might stay in the shop for days! Fixing the chain yourself only takes a few minutes. You could quickly solve the problem and be on your way.

Think of all the money you'll save once you start repairing your own bike! If you know which part needs to be fixed, you can shop around for the best price. For example, a new pedal is inexpensive, and you can install it with simple tools. You won't have to pay an expert, because you'll be the expert!

Bikes are not very complicated machines. You can learn everything you need to know by reading your owner's manual. You can also find bicycle repair books in the library. Take charge, save time, and save money. Learn to fix your own bike today!

Now look at what Megan did to prepare to write her persuasive essay.

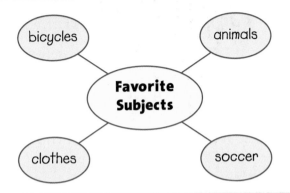

Brainstorming

First, Megan used an idea web to brainstorm subjects she is interested in. Then, she chose the subject about which she has the strongest opinions—bicycles.

Next, Megan listed her opinions about bicycles. She chose "People should fix their own bikes" as her topic because she had strong reasons and examples to support this opinion.

Outlining

Then, Megan created an outline to organize her opinions and supporting reasons. The outline shows the order in which Megan plans to present her ideas in her persuasive essay.

My Opinions About Bicycles

I think mountain bikes are best.

I think everyone should ride bikes.

I think people should fix their own bikes.

Title: Do It Yourself!

I. Introduction
   A. Opinion: People should fix their own bikes
   B. List three supporting reasons

II. Reason #1: Puts you in charge
   A. You get to know the parts
   B. Example

III. Reason #2: Saves time
   A. Saves time in repair shop
   B. Example

IV. Reason #3: Saves money
   A. Cost of parts and labor
   B. Example

V. Conclusion
   A. How to take action
   B. Call to action

CONTENTS

Lesson 17

Genre: Autobiographies

Just Like Me

Stories and Self-Portraits by Fourteen Artists

Edited by Harriet Rohmer

I Am an Artist

Pat Lowery Collins

illustrated by Jui Ishida

Genre: Poetry

Fact and Opinion

You have learned that a **fact** is a statement that can be proved and an **opinion** is a statement that expresses a feeling or a belief. When people write about their experiences, they usually include both facts and opinions. Knowing the difference between facts and opinions can help you understand what a writer tells you about his or her experiences.

Fact	Opinion
Evidence	Evidence

Tip

To test whether a statement is a fact, ask yourself, *Can this be proved to be true?* If the answer is no, the statement is probably an opinion.

Read the paragraph below. Then look at the graphic organizer. It shows a fact and an opinion from the paragraph.

I grew up on a small farm. I loved to draw, but I did not have many art supplies. I made charcoal pencils from the burned and blackened ends of sticks. For paint, I crushed blackberries into a purple liquid. I think that being practical is just as important as being creative. I received my first set of paints when I was nine. There is nothing more exciting than opening a new box of paints! Today, I carry paints and brushes with me wherever I go.

Fact	Opinion
I grew up on a small farm.	Being practical is as important as being creative.
Evidence	**Evidence**
This can be proved by asking the writer's family if it is true.	This statement cannot be proved. Some people might disagree.

Try This!

Look back at the paragraph. Find one more fact and one more opinion. Explain why one is a fact and the other is an opinion.

www.harcourtschool.com/storytown

participate

mischievous

exotic

graceful

brilliant

ancestors

The Coolest Show on Earth

Winters in Harbin, China, are long and cold. The air temperature stays well below freezing for months. Still, every year thousands of people visit Harbin during the winter. They go to see the Snow and Ice Festival.

Dozens of ice carvers **participate** in this event. These artists carve solid blocks of ice into many interesting forms. Visitors to Harbin might see a **mischievous** monkey or an **exotic** flower carved out of ice. They might even see a row of glittering, **graceful** swans.

This sculpture of the Great Wall of China doubles as an ice slide.

The ice sculptures are **brilliant** when the sunlight hits them. At night, colored lights shine on the ice sculptures, and they glow with color.

The people of Harbin welcome visitors to the Snow and Ice Festival. Their **ancestors** lived through the long winters without a festival or guests to entertain. Today, however, the city of Harbin is an unusual winter destination that is sure to be a memorable trip.

Gigantic snow sculptures such as this one are also a part of the festival.

 www.harcourtschool.com/storytown

Word Detective

 Be a word detective! Search for the Vocabulary Words outside your classroom. You might read them in a magazine, hear them on the radio or television, or find them in an advertisement. Each time you see or hear a Vocabulary Word, write it in your vocabulary journal. Make sure you also write where you found the word.

Just Like Me

Autobiographies

Genre Study

An autobiography is a person's account of his or her own life. As you read, look for

- the first-person point of view.

- the author's personal thoughts and feelings.

- facts and opinions about the author's life.

Facts	Opinions

Comprehension Strategy

Monitor comprehension while you read by **adjusting your reading rate** when you come to difficult sections of text.

444

Just Like Me

Me

edited by Harriet Rohmer

Tomie Arai

New York is a wonderful place to live because there is so much to look at. When I was a little girl, I would spend hours looking out the window of our apartment. I always thought that windows were a place to dream.

As I got older, I could walk for hours around the different neighborhoods of the city, and I started sketching the people I saw. I wanted to be like the painters Diego Rivera and Romare Bearden and the Japanese printmaker Hokusai, who really looked at the world around them and tried to record the way that people lived.

This is a picture of me looking out the window. Or maybe it is a picture that lets you look into a window at me. I am dreaming that I am a little girl again, surrounded by memories that float across the page like the people who pass me on the crowded streets of the city.

Most of my paintings are from my recollections of my childhood in south Texas, where I was born and raised. My memories of celebrations are very vivid because I usually had a new special outfit sewed by my mother. My favorite was the turquoise cotton organza dress she made for my graduation from elementary school. Every year she sewed new school clothes for all five of us kids, but the funniest were the flannel pajamas in our choice of colors and patterns.

When I was a young girl, I taught myself how to draw clothes for my paper dolls so they could have any dress I wanted—a flamenco dancer's dress or a dress from Mexico called a *China Poblana* with lots of shiny sequins. To this day, my favorite thing to paint is clothing.

My mother was the first person I saw paint. She was the one who inspired me to become an artist.

Carmen Lomas Garza

I was born in a poor village in China where everyone worked hard in the fields. I came to America at the age of five. My brothers and I did not have many toys, and our parents were too busy to pay much attention to us. I had to invent a world of my own through pictures. I used the brightest crayons I could find to create scenes from my imagination.

Nancy Hom

I like to draw flat shapes that fit together like jigsaw puzzles. My artwork is very simple and graceful, with curves like the edges of clouds. I am like that—soft, gentle, quiet, but strong at the same time. I express my strength through bold colors and patterns that jump out and grab your attention. This portrait has leaves of bamboo in it because bamboo also comes from China. It is strong but it can bend when it needs to, just like me.

448

George Littlechild

When I was a boy, people knew I was Indian (or First Nations, as we say in Canada) because I had the features of my Indian mother. As I got older, people weren't sure anymore. "You sure are exotic looking," they told me. "Are you Spanish? Italian? Portuguese?" I was looking more like my white father. But since both my parents were dead and I was living with my Dutch foster family, I was very confused about who I was. No one ever told me then that I was mixed-blood.

Sometimes I look Indian now, but sometimes I don't. My looks change according to my mood. That's why I've made these four different self-portraits. It took me many years to accept my features. Then one day I decided that I had to love myself just the way I am. I'm a rainbow man, with a half of this and a quarter of that, and a dash of a mixture of everything!

Stephen Von Mason

I always loved making art. My earliest drawings were of rodeo horses and cowboys—mainly because of a book I had read about rodeo riders. The book had many wonderful drawings, and I would copy them over and over.

In junior high I loved to draw football players, and my school would hang my pictures in the display cases. Those were real fun times for me because my friends and I were always busy making things. We made bows and arrows and crossbows. We carved heads and flutes out of wood. I painted model cars, and everyone wanted me to draw their portrait.

When I went to college I decided to be a painter and printmaker, and that's when I found out that making art was more than just reproducing what I saw in front of me. I started making abstract art and art from my imagination. I learned to be true to my vision, and I let the world know how I see things!

Welcome to my world! The dolphins are from my childhood in Australia, where they saved children from shark attacks. These fun-loving dolphins are chasing after a juicy tuna lunch!

My paintings have beauty and magic for me. The desert blooms with barely any water. The cacti have prickles to protect themselves. My Jewish face has laughter and sadness. Guido and Possum, my funny, mischievous cats, love sneaking into my paintings. My boyfriend, Guy, and I are laughing from a flying heart floating across a fake leopard-print shirt.

There's a family portrait on the table. My mother and father were Holocaust survivors who came to Australia after the war. When my mom gave me my first art supplies, she said, "I can't give you a beautiful world, but you can make one for yourself." Being an artist has brought me much happiness, which I try to share. I can't imagine anything more wonderful—other than maybe being a dolphin.

Mira Reisberg

Elly
Simmons

When I was little, my mother strolled me around museums to see art. The walls of our home were covered with her paintings, with colorful posters of Mexican art, and with prints by Ben Shahn showing people at work. These images stayed with me, shaping who I am.

I paint my love of life! I paint pomegranates, birds, mountains, and people. I paint what gives me joy, or makes me sad or angry.

When my daughter was born, brilliant suns burst into my paintings. Now I gather bright fabrics and photos to piece together a quilt of my Jewish family history. In this painting, my grandmother (as a baby) and my great-grandparents in the pomegranates honor my roots. My parents, in the yellow sun, are my source of life. They gave me love and the encouragement to celebrate life through art!

Daryl Wells

When I was growing up, I didn't understand why the crayon labeled "flesh" in my crayon box wasn't the color of my skin. As a way of proving that my color was also beautiful and real, I went through all my favorite storybooks and colored in the characters with the brown crayon. In this way I was able to relate to them as if they really were part of my world.

As I got older and became more interested in painting, I realized that there is no such thing as a single "flesh" color. Everybody's skin has many colors in it, and the way people look has a lot to do with how they're feeling at the time. I still love painting people, and I guess I'm still "coloring them in." My self-portrait is four different pictures of myself. I look different each time because I worked with four different kinds of artist's colors: oil paints, watercolors, colored pencils, and colored inks with oil pastels.

Michele Wood

As a child I often imagined myself as Sleeping Beauty, princess of the make-believe African kingdom of Koro. That's how I painted myself here. My hair is plaited in a royal crown of braids, and in my crown are six figures of me as paintbrushes showing different stages of my childhood. I'm playing with a hula hoop, riding a bike, reading storybooks, painting a picture, running track, and learning to sew.

The panels in the quilt show important times in my life. On the left, my mother is holding me as a baby. On the right, Mother and I are sitting on the kitchen floor playing jacks. I was an only child, and my mother would always participate in little games with me.

My character is a strong, fearless woman symbolizing the well-being of my people. I am free of fear, ready to forge ahead, hand in hand with my ancestors.

Think Critically

1. Who inspired Carmen Lomas Garza to become an artist?
NOTE DETAILS

2. Choose one of the artists in the selection. Name one fact and one opinion in the text. Explain how you can tell the fact from the opinion. FACT AND OPINION

3. Why do you think many of the artists in the selection chose to share childhood memories while talking about their art?
MAKE INFERENCES

4. Almost every portrait includes personal objects from the artist's life. What objects would you include in your own self-portrait? MAKE CONNECTIONS

5. **WRITE** In the selection, both Daryl Wells and George Littlechild included a portrait made up of four pictures of themselves. Write a paragraph that explains why these artists have done this. Use details from the selection in your paragraph. SHORT RESPONSE

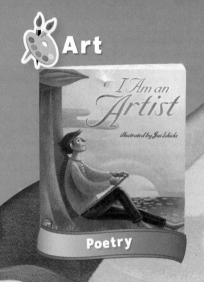

Poetry

I Am an Artist

by Pat Lowery Collins
illustrated by Jui Ishida

I am an artist when I follow a line where it leads me.
I am an artist when I find a face in a cloud
Or watch the light change the shape of a hill.

I am an artist when I discover shadows made by the moon
Or trace patterns in the sand
Or when I name the colors inside a shell.

I am an artist when I look through a sun shower for a rainbow.
I am an artist when I find one.

I am an artist when I notice that the sea is a mirror for the sky
And when I make something from the things that I collect.

I am an artist when I shoot water loops in the air with the hose
Or discover pictures in drops of rain.

I am an artist when I cut an apple to see the star inside
Or when I watch sunlight turn dust to glitter.

I am an artist when I crunch through crusted snow
And stop to gather winter's hush around me.

I am an artist when I look at a bird until I feel feathery too
And at an orange until I know what it is to be perfectly round.

I am an artist when I run my fingers over a shiny pod or across the
    rough bark of a tree
Or when I blow on a full-blown milkweed and it splinters into tiny
    white puffs
Or when I pick up a maple-tree seed and send it
Spinning back to earth by its twin propellers.

I am an artist when I see that the sun comes up in a soft haze
And goes down in a fiery blaze.

I am an artist when I wait for a star to streak through the night sky
Or when I sit very still in the woods and listen.

I am an artist whenever I look closely at the world
    around me.
And whenever *you* listen and search and see,
You are an artist too.

         — Pat Lowery Collins

Connections

Comparing Texts

1. Some of the artists in "Just Like Me" tell why they enjoy being an artist. Name something you enjoy doing, and tell why you like it.

2. Choose one of the artists in "Just Like Me." Compare and contrast how that artist and the artist in "I Am an Artist" are inspired.

3. Some artists paint pictures to express how they feel about a certain subject. Name some other things that people create to express their feelings.

Vocabulary Review

Word Webs

Create a word web for each of the Vocabulary Words. Write the Vocabulary Word in the center circle. In the other circles, write words and phrases that are related to the Vocabulary Word.

graceful

exotic

mischievous

brilliant

participate

ancestors

sly as a fox

tricky

mischievous

tease

gets into trouble

Fluency Practice

Partner Reading

When you read a passage aloud, try not to read too quickly or too slowly. Instead, read at a steady pace. Work with a partner. Choose an artist you read about in "Just Like Me." Take turns reading aloud the first two paragraphs of the passage. Give feedback on each other's pace by saying "too fast," "too slow," or "just right." Reread the passage aloud until the pace sounds right.

Writing

Write a Paragraph

Choose an artist you read about in "Just Like Me." Write a paragraph about that artist. Include both facts and your own opinions in your paragraph.

Artist:	
Facts	Opinions

My Writing Checklist

Writing Trait ▶ Voice

✔ I included the most important points from the artist's autobiography.

✔ I included both facts and opinions in my paragraph.

✔ I used a chart to organize my ideas.

CONTENTS

Genre: Fairy Tale

Hewitt Anderson's
Great Big
Life

Jerdine Nolen

illustrated by
Kadir Nelson

The
Little Fly
and the
Great Moose

A Native American Story Retold by JaNeen R. Adil

Genre: Pourquoi Tale

Focus Skill

Theme

All stories have a setting, characters, and a plot. Authors of fiction use these story elements to reveal a message, or **theme**. A story's theme is usually not stated directly. The reader can determine the theme by looking at the way story characters behave and what they learn.

Setting	Character's Actions	Character's Motives

Theme

Tip

To understand the theme of a story, ask yourself what the story tells you about life.

Read the story below. The graphic organizer shows how the story elements work together to reveal the theme.

One day, a woodcutter's ax fell into a lake. A fish offered to help him recover the ax. The fish dove down to find the ax. First, the fish brought up a golden ax. "Is this yours?" it asked. The woodcutter shook his head. Next, the fish brought up a silver ax. "Is this yours?" it asked. The woodcutter shook his head again. At last, the fish brought up an old, rusty ax. The woodcutter smiled and thanked the fish. Impressed with the woodcutter's honesty, the fish gave him the other axes as a gift.

Setting	**Character's Actions**	**Character's Motives**
a lake	A man refuses to take two axes that are more valuable than his own ax. A fish rewards him.	The man wants his own simple ax. The fish is impressed.

Theme
Always be honest.

Try This!

What might have happened if the woodcutter had taken the golden ax? How would the theme of the story change?

GO online   www.harcourtschool.com/storytown

Vocabulary

Build Robust Vocabulary

vast

bountiful

stature

intentions

inadvertently

relentless

resourceful

roused

The Giant

Long ago, a giant lived on a **vast** estate. Each day, he dined on the **bountiful** fruits and vegetables that his garden provided. Each night, he played sad songs on a huge fiddle. The giant had all the riches anyone could want, except one. He had no friends.

The giant knew that his **stature** frightened people. Though his **intentions** were always kind, he did clumsy things that scared people. Once, on a visit to town, he **inadvertently** knocked over a cart full of water barrels. The townspeople ran away in terror.

One winter, a **relentless** rain fell for three days. Streams and rivers filled to overflowing. Late at night, a dam broke. The giant saw a wall of water headed for the sleeping town. Luckily, he was **resourceful** as well as kind. He picked up his fiddle and played as loudly as he could. The music **roused** the sleeping townspeople, and all of them ran to safety.

The next day, the townspeople thanked the giant. He suddenly had more friends than he could count. From that day on, only joyful music came from the giant's fiddle.

 www.harcourtschool.com/storytown

Word Champion

Your challenge this week is to use the Vocabulary Words outside your classroom. Keep the list of words in a place at home where you can see it. Use as many of the words as you can when you speak to friends and family members. You might tell a friend he or she is resourceful for finding a clever solution to a problem. Write in your vocabulary journal the sentences you spoke that contained the words.

465

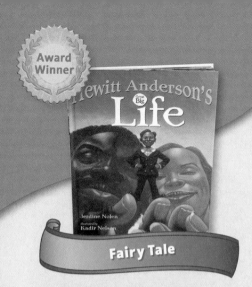

Hewitt Anderson's
Great Big
Life

Jerdine Nolen

Illustrated by
Kadir Nelson

Fairy Tale

Genre Study

A fairy tale is an imaginative story that may be passed down and retold in different forms. As you read, look for

- characters with traits that may not appear in real life.

- a happy ending.

Characters	Setting
Plot Events	

Comprehension Strategy

Monitor comprehension as you read by stopping to **self-correct** mistakes that make the meaning of the text unclear.

HEWITT ANDERSON'S
GREAT BIG
LIFE

by Jerdine Nolen
illustrated by Kadir Nelson

467

Hewitt Anderson lived with his parents in an enormous house at the edge of town. His parents believed *big things were best!* They boasted a grand and impressive residence overlooking the valley below.

Their house was marvelous for giving parties. The Andersons gave bountiful banquets, elegant teas, and glorious garden parties that sometimes lasted for days. And Hewitt celebrated many happy birthdays there with his loving family.

Hewitt Anderson lived happily and contentedly with his mother and father in the vast marvels of their home. A perfect house for giants—but alas, poor Hewitt was not. He was very, very small. While his parents loved him dearly, his size was a source of great worry and concern for the J. Carver Worthington Andersons. How could a normal-size boy be born to a family of giants?

Never in the entire generations of the J. Carver Worthington Anderson or C. Mable Luther Butters clans had anything like this ever occurred. "Small," "pint-size," and "miniature" had *never* been a part of their vocabularies or their lives. After all, they believed *big things were best.*

In fact, all of the Andersons' and Butters' relations and friends of their relations were giants. Ever since their great-great-great-grandmother Ida came to the valley after that business with the beanstalk, the family had been known as people of great stature and girth. Hewitt had many friends too— giants galore.

But nothing could change the fact that Mr. and Mrs. Anderson's own beloved son, Hewitt, was *so* very small. Teeny-weeny, in fact.

It was something Hewitt's parents had to live with and accept. For they loved their sweet, little bundle of joy, but oh—how they worried about his size.

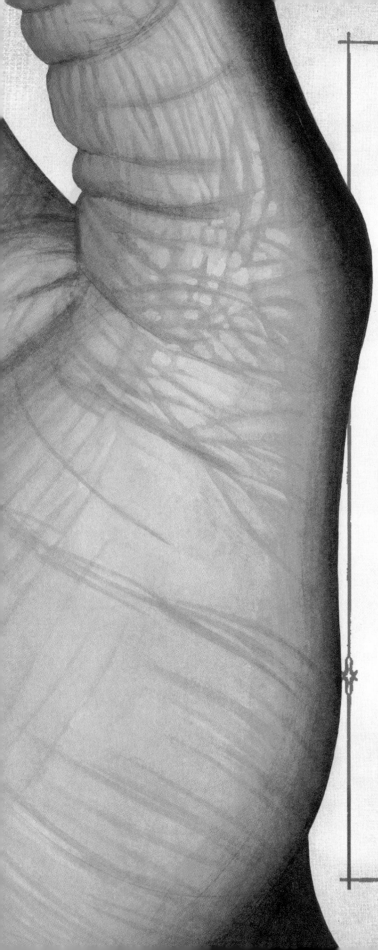

And Hewitt was hopelessly in love with them, too, of course. He loved the awe and wonder of them: the deep baritones of his father and the resounding, resplendent melodies of his mother. When his father chose to sing great operatic versions of nursery rhymes, his mother would join in, creating wonderful duets and harmonies that made Hewitt's liver quiver and tickled his funny bone right down to his shoes. He'd laugh endlessly after being serenaded for hours.

"Again, again, Papa and Mama, sing again. Sing again!" Hewitt squealed. Of course, they never disappointed their extraordinary son, and gave him more and more. Hewitt, so comforted while listening to the melodies, found it a perfect way to fall asleep, nestled in the deep well of his father's massive hands.

Hewitt loved riding around inside his father's shirt pocket or sightseeing from the perch of his mother's brimmed bonnet. It was impossible for the three of them to hold hands while out for their morning or afternoon walks, as did many families in their neighborhood. So, while his parents held hands, Hewitt sat in the folds of their entwined fingers, which made a nice hammock for him. He was gently lulled to sleep with the rhythm and motion of their walking. All the while his parents secretly hoped that Hewitt was getting the rest and nutrition he needed to grow. But . . . Hewitt was now five, and he wasn't much bigger than when he was born.

Amazingly it took a great deal of planning and preparation for Hewitt's parents to care for the mouselikeness of their child. At times it was like trying to find a needle in a haystack. Whenever Hewitt's parents swept the floor, though they always kept an eye out for him, once or twice Hewitt managed to avoid the broom just in time. Because Hewitt was small, he was able to hunker down between the floorboards, holding on until he was out of harm's way.

His parents tried not to be *too* concerned about Hewitt's safety and well-being. But the summer Hewitt turned seven, he suffered a rather close call. While preparing the seven-layer cake for Hewitt's birthday party, his mother, in her haste to create a fitting masterpiece, misplaced poor Hewitt. As Hewitt was trapped for an hour in a vat of flour, his parents began their relentless and public worry for the child they loved more than life itself. Finally Hewitt climbed out of the measuring cup. Hewitt told his parents repeatedly that he could take care of himself—oh, but worry they did.

Doctors were called in. Specialists from around the world made frequent visits to the Anderson home. But no one could explain the circumstances surrounding Hewitt's small and unimposing stature.

Dr. Gargantuan, a brilliant scientist and family friend, tried to calm their growing worries. "He will grow . . . he is just a bit late to bloom," he reassured them. "Or," he said, "perhaps this is the opposite of a growth spurt." Finally came his suggestion: "I *could* make Hewitt my life's work! Think of the fame, the celebrity for your family."

But his parents would not hear of such a thing! They adored their puny, frail, delicate bundle of joy. Believing *big was best*, they took it upon themselves to set things right: to see to it that Hewitt had a big life with big things in it!

The next morning, Mr. and Mrs. Anderson awoke in the best of spirits. Today would be Survival Lesson One—swimming. But in Mrs. Anderson's hurry to cheer her family on, she tripped and fell. Her tumble caused Mr. Anderson to miss an opportunity for a perfect-ten double-somersault pike. The two of them created quite a splash in the pond—a near tidal wave, in fact. And little Hewitt, who was already quite fond of water, was washed clear to the other end of the estate into the garden maze.

Quickly they rushed to him. But because Hewitt was small, he had already found his way out through a shortcut under the boxwood wall. Mr. and Mrs. Anderson, on the other hand, wandered aimlessly for a good part of the morning before Hewitt coached them to an exit. In the end all was served well, as Hewitt showed his talents in the art of solving giant puzzles.

For Survival Lesson Two, Mr. Anderson would show Hewitt how to climb a beanstalk in the event he would have to flee the path of an escaped rhinoceros from the nearby zoo. Mr. Anderson felt a surge of his youth again, climbing to the top of a giant Kentucky-wonder beanstalk with Hewitt tucked safely in his shirt pocket. But reaching the top paralyzed Mr. Anderson with great fear. Hewitt, being used to such heights, was not afraid at all.

Instantly Hewitt went into action. Just as a leaf from the mammoth beanstalk began to fall, Hewitt held on to the leaf's edge. He was able to float down on the breath of a helpful breeze. Upon landing he roused the emergency fire-and-rescue squad, who arrived minutes later with hooks and ladders and a safety net. Mr. Anderson was shaken by the experience but was more in awe of his perfectly resourceful son.

When it became clear that the lessons in survival training were not accomplishing their goals, Mr. and Mrs. Anderson decided to prepare for their dinner guest, Dr. Gargantuan.

Eager to discuss his plans for Hewitt, Dr. Gargantuan arrived before the dinner hour. He tried in earnest to convince Mr. and Mrs. Anderson that a life of scientific promise awaited Hewitt. He said that purpose could be made of Hewitt's small life after all. The Andersons listened politely but would hear nothing of it.

And so, to lighten the mood, they invited the doctor to view the family's golden egg collection. Inherited from Great-Great-Great-Grandmother Ida, their collection of golden eggs could not be duplicated: golden peacock eggs, golden goose eggs, and, of course, ostrich and emu eggs— all of solid, pure gold.

A family of big hearts and generous natures, the Andersons knew this trusted family friend had only the best of intentions for Hewitt. They thought it was only fitting to share something of value with Dr. Gargantuan—just not their beloved son.

In a moment of inspiration Mrs. Anderson reached for an egg, which was about the same size as Hewitt. "Dear Doctor, please accept this token with our thanks and appreciation for your dedication," she said, looking to her husband.

The good doctor was so overwhelmed and impressed by the generosity of the gift that, in a fit of excitement, he fell backward, causing the door to shut with such force that it locked them up good and tight. But the key had been inadvertently left in the keyhole. They all listened downheartedly as the key fell to the ground with a *clink*.

What would become of them? Would they ever be found? "My roast is in the oven!" cried Mrs. Anderson worriedly.

Then Hewitt had an idea. Because he was so small, he managed to climb into the keyhole, maneuver through the weights and gears to turn the tumblers to the lock, and set them all free. Once again it was up to Hewitt to save his parents—and now the good doctor, too. And as always, Hewitt came through.

Mr. and Mrs. Anderson watched Hewitt, in awe of his hidden talents. He was even more amazing than they had thought.

Spontaneously their voices rose in a beautiful aria, and a feeling of overwhelming joy brimmed deep within their hearts for Hewitt. Even the good doctor felt compelled to join in.

In that moment, the world in the Anderson household changed. Hewitt, standing in all his splendor and glory, seemed tall compared to his former self. Now his parents understood. Hewitt did indeed know how to live among gigantic things. And because he was small, Hewitt was just as he should be. For his parents realized that *big or small, either is best of all!*

And they could not have been more proud of Hewitt or loved him any more.

THINK CRITICALLY

① Why do Mr. and Mrs. Anderson worry about their son, Hewitt? NOTE DETAILS

② Why is Hewitt able to do some things his parents cannot do? Find examples from the story to support your answer. DRAW CONCLUSIONS

③ If you were Hewitt's size and you lived in a world of giants, what part of your daily routine would you find most challenging? IDENTIFY WITH CHARACTERS

④ What is the theme of "Hewitt Anderson's Great Big Life"? How does the author reveal the theme? THEME

⑤ **WRITE** Hewitt's parents realize that Hewitt is just the size he should be. Use details from the story to explain why they feel this way. SHORT RESPONSE

ABOUT THE AUTHOR
JERDINE NOLEN

When Jerdine Nolen was growing up, her mother encouraged her to collect words and was always eager to hear her favorites. One of her mother's favorite words was *cucumber*.

Jerdine Nolen says she cannot remember a time when she was not writing. Her story ideas come at any time—while driving a car, playing with her cats, doing laundry, and gardening. Hewitt Anderson isn't the only unusual character she has invented. She has also written about a farmer who grows balloons and a girl who raises a dragon.

ABOUT THE ILLUSTRATOR
KADIR NELSON

Kadir Nelson began drawing before he could write. His mother encouraged him to develop his talent. When he was sixteen, he began formal training as an illustrator with his uncle, who was an art teacher.

Kadir Nelson enjoys painting and drawing images of African-American history. In addition to illustrating books for both children and adults, Kadir Nelson has created artwork for sports magazines and newspapers. He lives in San Diego with his family.

www.harcourtschool.com/storytown

Pourquoi Tale

The Little Fly and the Great Moose

A Native American Story Retold by Janeen R. Adil
illustrated by Chris Sheban

The Pennacook (PEN•uh•kook), Pequawket (PIH•kwah•ket), and Winnipisauki (WIN•uh•puh•SAW•kee) peoples have long lived in what is now New Hampshire. This is their story of how a little fly defeated a great moose and turned the Merrimac into a rushing, noisy river.

A very long time ago, the Merrimac River flowed peacefully through the wooded hills. Many beavers made their homes in the river, and great schools of fish lived in its pure, clean waters. So delicious was the water that thirsty animals would come to drink at the river from far and wide.

Now, in this long-ago time, the largest of all the animals was Moose. Even bigger than the mighty bear, Moose stood as tall as the highest tree. When he walked, the ground shook beneath his heavy feet, and when he bellowed, birds flew before him in a panic.

One day, the giant creature learned of the Merrimac's sweet waters. I, too, will go there, Moose thought, and taste the water for myself.

When he reached the river, Moose immediately began to drink. The water pleased him, so he drank more and more. Soon the level of the water started to drop.

This made the beavers very nervous. What would happen to their homes, the dams they had worked so hard to build from mud and sticks?

"Help us," the beavers begged the rabbits. "We must stop Moose," they pleaded with the foxes. "Drive him away!" the beavers cried to the deer, but Moose was so big that no one—not even the bear—was brave enough to face him.

Meanwhile, Moose continued to drink from the river. The water dropped lower and lower, and now the fish were afraid. At least the beavers could move to a new home, but what would the fish do if the river dried up? And they, too, began to beg for help.

At last, one creature volunteered to chase Moose away. It was Fly. "You are the smallest of us all!" exclaimed the animals. "How can you possibly make that huge creature leave?" And they laughed at Fly, thinking it was a fine joke.

Little Fly, though, had a plan. First she landed on one of Moose's legs and bit him, but Moose simply brushed her off. Fly tried another leg, only this time she bit harder. Moose stamped his foot in annoyance. Then Fly buzzed quickly from spot to spot on Moose's brown hide, biting sharply as she went.

Moose was furious! He shook his immense head, snorted, stamped, and kicked. Up and down the riverbank he ran, trying to discover who was biting him, but since he couldn't see tiny Fly, Moose had no way to fight back. Finally he fled from the river as fast as he could run.

How proud little Fly was! She couldn't help boasting to the animals that she had driven Moose away. "You see," Fly told them, "my size didn't matter after all. I wasn't big enough or strong enough to fight Moose, but I *was* smart enough!"

Moose was gone, but beside the river were prints from his massive feet. Wherever he had stamped, the earth sank, and now the Merrimac came rushing in to fill the deep holes. No longer did the river flow quietly. Instead, it tumbled over falls and rushed noisily through rapids where Moose's feet had torn up the ground.

Connections

Comparing Texts

1. Imagine that you are Hewitt's size. Describe how you could use an everyday object in a completely new way.

2. Compare the characters and the theme of "The Little Fly and the Great Moose" with those of "Hewitt Anderson's Great Big Life."

3. Describe a situation in real life where you might want to tell someone that "bigger isn't always better."

Vocabulary Review

Rate a Situation

With a partner, take turns reading aloud each sentence and pointing to the spot on the word line that shows how you would feel in each situation.

Most
Happy _____ Least
Happy

- You were **roused** from a sound sleep.

- You were given a **vast** amount of money.

- Someone called you **resourceful**.

- You received **bountiful** homework.

vast

bountiful

stature

relentless

roused

resourceful

intentions

inadvertently

Lesson 19

Juan Verdades
The Man Who Couldn't Tell a Lie

retold by **Joe Hayes** • illustrated by **Joseph Da**

Hard Cheese
IN WHICH A FOX PERSUADES
A CROW OUT OF HIS LUNCH

Genre: Fable

Focus Skill

 **Theme**

You have learned that most stories have a **theme.** The theme of a story is the message the author wants readers to understand. You can figure out the theme of a story by thinking about what the main character does or learns.

The theme of a fable is called a **moral**. The moral is usually stated directly. It tells the lesson that is taught through the fable.

Setting	Character's Actions	Character's Motives

Theme

Tip

Put together story details about the characters, setting, and plot to figure out an unstated theme.

Read the story below. Then look at the graphic organizer. It shows how the story elements work together to reveal the theme.

One day, an ant went to the river to drink. She lost her balance and fell into the water. A dove saw the helpless ant and felt sorry for her. The dove dropped a wide leaf into the river. The ant climbed onto the leaf and floated to shore.

The next day, the ant saw that a hunter was about to catch the dove in a net. The ant stung the hunter on the ankle, and the dove flew to safety.

Setting
the bank of a river

Character's Actions
A dove saves an ant's life. The ant saves the dove from a hunter.

Character's Motives
kindness, pity, gratitude

Theme
Little friends may prove to be great friends.

Try This!

Look back at the story. What is another way you could state the theme? What other stories have you read that have a theme similar to the one in this story?

Go online www.harcourtschool.com/storytown

Vocabulary

Build Robust Vocabulary

declared

confidently

magnificent

distressed

gloated

insisted

anxiously

The New Ruler

One day, a queen called her six children into the palace garden. "It is time for me to choose a new ruler," she **declared**. "I will give each of you a seed to plant. One year from now, show me how your seed has grown. Then I will make my choice."

One year later, all but one child stood **confidently** before the queen. Each held a pot filled with a **magnificent** flowering plant. The sixth child looked **distressed**. His seed had not grown into anything.

One by one, the queen asked the children to speak. The first five bragged about their gardening skills. Each one **gloated**, certain that he or she had won the contest. The queen said nothing. Instead she called the sixth child forward. He **insisted** that he had cared for his seed as best he could.

The children waited **anxiously** for the queen's decision. At last, the queen said, "The seeds I gave you had been boiled. I knew that they wouldn't grow. Five of you exchanged your seed for another. Only one of you followed my instructions." She looked at the sixth child and smiled. "You, my honest child, shall be the new ruler."

 www.harcourtschool.com/storytown

Word Scribe

Your assignment this week is to use the Vocabulary Words in your writing. In your vocabulary journal, write sentences that show the meanings of the words. For example, you could write about something magnificent that you saw or about something that distressed you. Write sentences for as many of the Vocabulary Words as you can. Share your writing with your classmates.

Folktale

Genre Study

Folktales are stories that were first told orally. They show the customs and beliefs of a culture. As you read, look for

- a plot that teaches a lesson.

- a main character who shows the values of a culture.

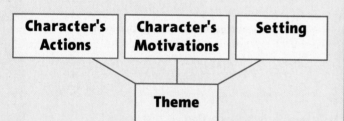

Character's Actions	Character's Motivations	Setting

| Theme |

Comprehension Strategy

Monitor comprehension as you read by stopping to **self-correct** mistakes that make the meaning of the text unclear.

JUAN VERDADES

THE MAN WHO COULDN'T TELL A LIE

retold by Joe Hayes • illustrated by Joseph Daniel Fiedler

One late summer day a group of wealthy rancheros was gathered on the village plaza, joking and laughing and discussing events on their ranches.

One of the men, whose name was don Ignacio, had a fine apple tree on his land. The rancher called the apple tree *el manzano real*—the royal apple tree—and was extremely proud of it. It had been planted by his great-grandfather, and there was something about the soil it grew in and the way the afternoon sun struck it that made the apple tree flourish. It gave sweeter and more flavorful fruit than any other tree in the country round about.

Every rancher for miles around knew about *el manzano real*, and each year they all hoped don Ignacio would give them a small basket of its sweet fruit. And so each of the ranchers asked don Ignacio how the fruit of the apple tree was doing. To each one don Ignacio replied, "It's doing beautifully, amigo, beautifully. My foreman takes perfect care of the tree, and every evening he reports how the fruit is ripening."

When don Ignacio said this to his friend don Arturo, the other man replied, "Do you mean to say, don Ignacio, that you don't tend your magnificent tree yourself? How can you have such faith in your employee? Maybe he's not doing all he says he is. Maybe he's not telling you the truth."

Don Ignacio wagged a finger at his friend. "*Mi capataz* has never failed me in any way," he insisted. "He has never told me a lie."

"Are you sure, *compadre*?" said don Arturo. "Are you sure that he has never lied to you?"

"Absolutely certain, *compadre*, absolutely certain. The young man doesn't know how to lie. His name is Juan Valdez, but everyone calls him Juan Verdades because he is so truthful."

"I don't believe it. There never was an employee who didn't lie to his boss. I'm sure I can make him tell you a lie."

"Never," replied the proud employer.

The two friends went on arguing good naturedly, but little by little they began to raise their voices and attract the attention of the other men on the plaza.

Finally don Arturo declared loudly, "I'll bet you whatever you want that within two weeks at the most I'll make this Juan Verdades tell you a lie."

"All right," replied don Ignacio. "It's a deal. I'll bet my ranch against yours that you can't make my foreman lie to me."

The other ranchers laughed when they heard that. "Ho-ho, don Arturo," they said, "now we'll see just how sure you are that you're right."

"As sure as I am of my own name," said don Arturo. "I accept the bet, don Ignacio. But you must allow me the freedom to try anything I wish." The two friends shook hands, and the other men in the group agreed to serve as witnesses to the bet.

The gathering broke up, and don Arturo and don Ignacio rode confidently away toward their ranches. But as don Arturo rode along thinking of what he had just done, he no longer felt so sure of himself. When he arrived home and told his wife and daughter about the bet, his wife began to cry. "What will we do when we lose our ranch?" she sobbed. And don Arturo began to think he had made a terrible mistake.

But his daughter, whose name was Araceli and who was a very bright and lively young woman, just laughed and said, "Don't worry, *Mamá*. We're not going to lose our ranch."

Araceli suggested to her father that he make up some excuse for them all to spend the next two weeks at don Ignacio's house. "If we're staying on don Ignacio's ranch," she said, "we'll surely discover a way to come out the winners."

503

The next day don Arturo rode to don Ignacio's ranch and told his friend, "My men are mending the walls of my house and giving them a fresh coat of whitewash. It would be more convenient for my family to be away. Could my wife and daughter and I stay at your house for a while?"

"Of course, my friend," don Ignacio answered. "Feel perfectly free."

That afternoon don Arturo and his family moved into don Ignacio's house, and the next morning Araceli rose at dawn, as she always did at home, and went to the ranch kitchen to prepare coffee. The foreman, Juan Verdades, was already there, drinking a cup of coffee he had made for himself and eating a breakfast of leftover tortillas. She smiled at him, and he greeted her politely: "*Buenos días, señorita*." And then he finished his simple breakfast and went off to begin his day's work.

That night don Arturo and his daughter made up a plan. Araceli rose before dawn the next day and went to the kitchen to prepare coffee and fresh tortillas for the foreman. She smiled sweetly as she offered them to Juan. He returned her smile and thanked her very kindly. Each morning she did the same thing, and Juan Verdades began to fall in love with Araceli, which was just what the girl and her father expected.

What Araceli hadn't expected was that she began to fall in love with Juan Verdades too and looked forward to getting up early every morning just to be alone with him. She even began to wish she might end up marrying the handsome young foreman. Araceli continued to work on the plan she and her father had made— but she now had a plan of her own as well.

Of course, Juan knew that he was just a worker and Araceli was the daughter of a wealthy ranchero, so he didn't even dream of asking her to marry him. Still, he couldn't help trying to please her in every way. So one morning when they were talking, Juan said to Araceli, "You're very kind to have fresh coffee and warm food ready for me every morning and to honor me with the pleasure of your company. Ask me for whatever you want from this ranch. I'll speak to don Ignacio and see that it's given to you."

This is exactly what the girl and her father thought would happen. And she replied just as they had planned. It was the last thing Juan expected to hear.

"There's only one thing on this ranch I want," she said. "I'd like to have all the apples from *el manzano real*."

The young man was very surprised, and very distressed as well, because he knew he couldn't fulfill her wish.

"I could never give you that," Juan said. "You know how don Ignacio treasures the fruit of that tree. He might agree to give you a basket of apples, but no more. I would have to take the fruit without permission, and then what would I say to don Ignacio? I can give you anything else from the ranch, but not what you're asking for."

With that the conversation ended and they separated for the day. In the evening Juan reported to don Ignacio, and they exchanged the exact words they said every evening:

"Good evening, *mi capataz*," the rancher said.

"Good evening, *mi patrón*," replied the foreman.

"How goes it with my cattle and land?"

"Your cattle are healthy, your pastures are green."

"And the fruit of *el manzano real*?"

"The fruit is fat and ripening well."

The next morning Juan and Araceli met again. As they sipped their coffee together, Juan said, "I truly would like to repay you for the kindness you've shown me. There must be something on this ranch you would like. Tell me what it is. I'll see that it's given to you."

But again Araceli replied, "There's only one thing on this ranch I want: the apples from *el manzano real*."

Each day they repeated the conversation. Araceli asked for the same thing, and Juan said he couldn't give it to her. But each day Juan was falling more hopelessly in love with Araceli. Finally, just the day before the two weeks of the bet would have ended, the foreman gave in. He said he would go pick the apples right then and bring them to the girl.

Juan hitched up a wagon and drove to the apple tree. He picked every single apple and delivered the wagonload of fruit to Araceli. She thanked him very warmly, and his spirits rose for a moment. But as he mounted his horse to leave, they sank once again. Juan rode away alone, lost in his thoughts, and Araceli hurried off to tell her father the news and then to wait for a chance to talk to don Ignacio too.

Juan rode until he came to a place where there were several dead trees.

He dismounted and walked up to one of them. Then he took off his hat and jacket and put them on the dead tree and pretended it was don Ignacio. He started talking to it to see if he could tell it a lie.

"Good evening, *mi capataz*," the rancher said.

"Good evening, *mi patrón*," replied the foreman.

"How goes it with my cattle and land?"

"Your cattle are healthy, your pastures are green."

"And the fruit of *el manzano real*?"

"The . . . the crows have carried the fruit away. . . ."

But the words were hardly out of his mouth when he heard himself say, "No, that's not true, *mi patrón.* I picked the fruit. . . ." And then he stopped himself.

He took a deep breath and started over again with, "Good evening, *mi capataz.*"

And when he reached the end, he sputtered, "The . . . wind shook the apples to the ground, and the cows came and ate them. . . . No, they didn't, *mi patrón.* I . . ."

He tried over and over, until he realized there was no way he could tell a lie. But he knew he could never come right out and say what he had done either. He had to think of another way to tell don Ignacio. He took his hat and coat from the stump and sadly set out for the ranch.

All day long Juan worried about what he would say to don Ignacio. And all day long don Ignacio wondered what he would hear from his foreman, because as soon as Araceli had shown the apples to her father he had run gleefully to tell don Ignacio what had happened.

"Now you'll see, *compadre*," don Arturo gloated. "You're about to hear a lie from Juan Verdades."

Don Ignacio was heartsick to think that all his apples had been picked, but he had agreed that don Arturo could try whatever he wanted. He sighed and said, "Very well, *compadre*, we'll see what happens this evening."

Don Arturo rode off to gather the other ranchers who were witnesses to the bet, leaving don Ignacio to pace nervously up and down in his house. And then, after don Ignacio received a visit from Araceli and she made a request that he couldn't deny, he paced even more nervously.

All the while, Juan went about his work, thinking of what he would say to don Ignacio. That evening the foreman went as usual to make his report to his employer, but he walked slowly and his head hung down. The other ranchers were behind the bushes listening, and Araceli and her mother were watching anxiously from a window of the house.

The conversation began as it always did:

"Good evening, *mi capataz*."

"Good evening, *mi patrón*."

"How goes it with my cattle and land?"

"Your cattle are healthy, your pastures are green."

"And the fruit of *el manzano real*?"

Juan took a deep breath and replied:

"Oh, *patrón*, something terrible happened today. Some fool picked your apples and gave them away."

Don Ignacio pretended to be shocked and confused. "Some fool picked them?" he said. "Who would do such a thing?"

Juan turned his face aside. He couldn't look at don Ignacio. The rancher asked again, "Who would do such a thing? Do I know this person?"

Finally the foreman answered:

"The father of the fool is my father's father's son.

The fool has no sister and no brother.

His child would call my father 'grandfather.'

He's ashamed that he did what was done."

Don Ignacio paused for a moment to think about Juan's answer. And then, to Juan's surprise, don Ignacio grabbed his hand and started shaking it excitedly.

The other ranchers ran laughing from their hiding places. "Don Arturo," they all said, "you lose the bet. You must sign your ranch over to don Ignacio."

"No," said don Ignacio, still vigorously shaking Juan's hand. He glanced toward the window where Araceli was watching and went on: "Sign it over to don Juan Verdades.

He has proved that he truly deserves that name, and he deserves to be the owner of his own ranch as well."

Everyone cheered and began to congratulate Juan. Don Arturo's face turned white, but he gritted his teeth and forced a smile. He shook Juan's hand and then turned to walk away from the group, his shoulders drooping and his head bowed down.

Araceli came running from the house and put her arm through her father's. "Papa," she said, "what if Juan Verdades were to marry a relative of yours? Then the ranch would stay in the family, wouldn't it?"

Everyone heard her and turned to look at the girl and her father. And then Juan spoke up confidently. "Senorita Araceli, I am the owner of a ranch and many cattle. Will you marry me?"

Of course she said she would, and don Arturo heaved a great sigh. "Don Juan Verdades," he said, "I'll be proud to have such an honest man for a son-in-law." He beckoned his wife to come from the house, and they both hugged Juan and Araceli.

The other ranchers hurried off to fetch their families, and a big celebration began. It lasted all through the night, with music and dancing and many toasts to Juan and Araceli. And in the morning everyone went home with a big basket of delicious apples from *el manzano real*.

THINK CRITICALLY

1 What is special about *el manzano real*? NOTE DETAILS

2 Why do you think Araceli asks Juan Verdades for all of the fruit from *el manzano real* after she falls in love with him? MAKE INFERENCES

3 What is the theme of this folktale? THEME

4 Think of a time when you or someone you know was rewarded for telling the truth. Explain what happened. PERSONAL RESPONSE

5 **WRITE** Araceli and her father, don Arturo, think of a plan to win the bet with don Ignacio. Use information and details from the story to explain their plan. SHORT RESPONSE

ABOUT THE AUTHOR
JOE HAYES

Joe Hayes grew up in a small town in Arizona, near the Mexican border. As a child, he learned to speak Spanish because many of his friends were Spanish speakers. As an adult, he moved to New Mexico. He was so fascinated with the folktales of this region that he became a professional storyteller. Today, he travels around the country, sharing the many stories he has collected. Hayes has written more than twenty books for children, and he has brought the art of storytelling to more than 1,500 schools.

ABOUT THE ILLUSTRATOR
JOSEPH DANIEL FIEDLER

In addition to illustrations for children's books, Joseph Daniel Fiedler has drawn many pictures for magazines and newspapers. Joseph Daniel Fiedler was born and raised in Pittsburgh, Pennsylvania. He spent several years living in the mountains of northern New Mexico. Today, he lives in Detroit, Michigan, with his cats, Iko and Obeah.

 www.harcourtschool.com/storytown

Fable

Hard Cheese

IN WHICH A FOX PERSUADES
A CROW OUT OF HIS LUNCH

retold and illustrated by Helen Ward

There once was a **CROW** sitting in a tree, holding a large, fresh cheese in his beak and feeling very pleased with himself. In fact, he was so pleased that he was just sitting there on his branch enjoying the all-round sense of well-being and smugness that the cheese was giving him when a **FOX** wandered into the story . . .

. . . A story that had begun when a freshly made cheese was left too close to an open window and the crow had stolen it. And would end, thought the Fox confidently, with the cheese safely in his mouth. Another opportunity for trickery (and lunch!), thought the fox.

So the fox sat under the tree and looked up at the crow until at last the crow looked uneasily down at the fox.

"I was just admiring your particularly fine feathers," said the fox. "Have you discovered some new birdbath on your travels? Your eyes seem particularly bright, too, and as for your toes . . . so dark and shiny . . . and your beak gleaming in the sunlight . . . so perfectly set off by the creamy whiteness of whatever that is you have a hold of. Quite magnificent!" The crow was becoming more astonished and pleased with himself by the moment.

"And," continued the fox, "a little bird was saying only this morning that you're not just a pretty face. I was told that you can sing beautifully, too. In fact, I understand you have the most remarkable singing voice for miles around . . . that you can move your audience from tears to laughter with a single note . . . that the nightingales hereabouts have all retired early . . ." Here the fox thought he had better stop, only adding, "How I would love to hear that mellifluous voice of yours. It would be such a privilege. A private performance—a mere verse or two? . . ."

The crow, so overwhelmed with flattery, felt a helpless urge to sing. He opened his beak . . ."Caw . . . CAW!" he went, unsweetly and tunelessly as only a crow can.

At the first note, the cheese fell, bouncing from branch to branch to plummet into the fox's wide open, waiting jaws. And that's where the story, as the fox predicted, ends.

BEWARE OF FALSE FLATTERY

Connections

Comparing Texts

1. Juan Verdades's most important quality is his honesty. What do you think is another important quality for a person to have? Why?

2. How are the themes in "Juan Verdades: The Man Who Couldn't Tell a Lie" and "Hard Cheese" alike? How are they different?

3. How would the world be different if more people were like Juan Verdades? Explain your answer.

Vocabulary Review

He confidently declared that he was the winner.

Word Pairs

Work with a partner. Write each Vocabulary Word on a separate index card. Place the cards face down. Take turns flipping over two cards and writing a sentence that uses both words. Read aloud the sentence to your partner. You must use the words correctly in the sentence to keep the cards. The student with more cards at the end wins.

magnificent

insisted

declared

confidently

distressed

gloated

anxiously

Fluency Practice

Partner Reading

Using correct phrasing makes reading aloud sound natural. Work with a partner to help you improve your phrasing. Listen as your partner reads aloud the first two paragraphs of "Juan Verdades: The Man Who Couldn't Tell a Lie." Follow along in your book, paying attention to where your partner pauses. Give your partner feedback about his or her phrasing. Then switch roles.

Writing

Write a Character Sketch

Juan Verdades shows that he has other good qualities in addition to honesty. Write a character sketch that describes Juan Verdades.

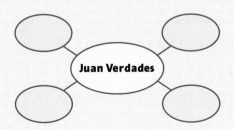

My Writing Checklist

Writing Trait ▶ Ideas

✔ I used a graphic organizer to plan my writing.

✔ I wrote my opinion of the character and his actions.

✔ I provided details from the story to support my ideas.

Juan Verdades

CONTENTS

Readers' Theater
MYSTERY

The Case of the Too-Hot Apple Cider

illustrated by Chris Buzelli

SEQUOYAH'S TALKING LEAVES

by Julie Doyle Durway
illustrated by Gina Triplett

Reading Nonfiction
BIOGRAPHY

ominous

confound

miserable

gracious

beams

self-assurance

monitor

exposed

installed

looming

Reading for Fluency

When reading a script aloud,

- Use a **pace** that fits the action in the story.

- Read words in meaningful groups so that your **phrasing** is smooth and natural.

The Case of the Too-Hot Apple Cider

illustrated by Chris Buzelli

Characters

Narrator One	Mom
Narrator Two	Noah
Narrator Three	Reggie, *Noah's robot*
Maggie	
Agatha, *Maggie's parrot*	

Narrator One: It is a dark and stormy night. At 227 Beaker Street, the home of ten-year-old detective Maggie Espinosa, a light burns in an upstairs window. Maggie sits at her desk.

Narrator Two: A sign on the desk reads "Maggie and Noah's Scientific Detective Agency." Agatha, Maggie's exotic pet parrot, is out of her cage. She is nestled comfortably next to Maggie's desk on what looks like a fuzzy nest.

Narrator Three: Lightning from the storm flashes outside the window. A moment later a loud, ominous thunderclap makes Maggie look up from her book.

Maggie: Wow! That one sounded pretty close, didn't it, Agatha?

Agatha: Pretty close! Pretty close!

Narrator One: Suddenly, Maggie hears a knock on the door.

Maggie: Who's there?

Mom: Maggie, Noah's here!

Noah: May I come in?

Maggie: What's the secret code?

Noah: Umm, wait a second . . . now I remember: "All tricksters, beware. Confound us if you dare!"

Mom: Good thing you remembered the code. When her cousins forget, she won't let them in!

Maggie: Come on in, Noah! What a miserable night!

Narrator Two: Noah walks in. He notices Maggie's stocking feet.

Noah: It's chilly in here, Maggie. Why aren't you wearing your purple bunny slippers?

Maggie: Agatha is sitting on them right now. She's warming them up for me. Say hello to Noah, Agatha.

Agatha: Hello, Noah!

Mom: Did you get very wet, Noah?

Noah: Only a little. Reggie held the umbrella. I hope you won't mind, but I brought him inside with me. I was afraid he'd get soaked out in the rain. If he gets rusty, I'll need to tinker with his gears again.

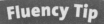

To improve your phrasing, read prepositional phrases such as *about Agatha's safety* as one group of words.

Maggie: No problem. Tell Reggie to come right in. I remember how many weeks it took you to perfect him the first time!

Noah: Reggie, you may enter. Please watch where you step. Last time you inadvertently almost trampled Agatha!

Mom: Noah, I'll get you a towel to dry Reggie.

Reggie: Maggie, please don't worry about Agatha's safety. I've just downloaded a new anti-trampling program.

Narrator Three: Reggie stomps into the room. He is covered with tiny rain droplets. He confidently extends his right arm to shake Maggie's hand.

Maggie: Nice to see you, Reggie.

Narrator One: Maggie shakes Reggie's outstretched hand. Agatha, still suspicious, shakes and ruffles her feathers.

Reggie: Noah said that this stormy night would be perfect for a mystery.

Narrator Two: Maggie's mom returns with a towel draped over her arm and two steaming cups in her hands.

Mom: I have hot apple cider here to warm you both up. Noah, here's that towel for Reggie.

Maggie: Thanks, Mom.

Noah: Thank you, Mrs. Espinosa.

Reggie: My circuits are most grateful for the towel. You are a gracious hostess, Mrs. Espinosa.

Mom: Did you program him to say that, Noah?

Narrator Three: Noah beams with self-assurance as he answers.

Noah: I sure did! Robots should have good manners.

Narrator One: Noah takes the towel and starts to dry Reggie. He sniffs the air and smiles.

Noah: That apple cider smells awfully good!

Maggie: Mom makes the best hot apple cider.

Reggie: Hot cider . . .
checking data banks . . .
apple cider heated to just
below the boiling point,
with cinnamon, orange peel,
nutmeg, cloves, and other spices
added.

Mom: I'm sorry the cups don't match.
They hold the same amount, though.

Noah: Oh! It's still pretty hot.

Narrator Two: Maggie cautiously touches
Noah's cup.

Maggie: Your cup does seem much hotter
than mine.

Mom: Well, that's surprising! I poured
equal amounts of apple cider into the
two cups.

Noah: That does seem strange. Why would
mine be hotter than yours?

Maggie: I would have thought that our
drinks would cool at the same rate. How
mysterious. . . .

Narrator Three: Maggie's mom sees the
thoughtful expression on her daughter's
face and smiles.

Mom: I think someone's getting excited
about a mystery to be solved.

Maggie: It's most curious, isn't it, Agatha?

Agatha: Most curious!

Reggie: I believe there is definitely a
science mystery to be solved here.

Maggie: Let's measure the temperature
of the cider in each cup. Agatha, please
bring the thermometers.

Narrator One: Agatha looks up at Maggie.
Although she clearly doesn't want to be
roused, she finally hops off the bunny
slippers.

Fluency Tip

Read at a pace that fits
your role. For example,
you should read a
narrator's lines more
slowly when they explain
a character's actions.

Narrator Two: Agatha waddles over to Maggie's backpack, which is lying open on the carpet. She finds two plastic thermometers, picks them up in her beak, and flies over to Noah.

Noah: Thank you, Agatha. Now let's measure the temperature in each cup.

Narrator Three: Noah puts the two thermometers into the cups. He and Maggie monitor them carefully.

Noah: My cider is 120 degrees Fahrenheit. It's still quite hot.

Narrator One: Maggie checks the thermometer in her cup. She frowns.

Maggie: My cider measures only 113 degrees Fahrenheit. It's much cooler than yours, even though both cups contain the same amount.

Reggie: Maggie's cider is 7 degrees cooler than Noah's.

Narrator Two: Maggie writes *7 degrees cooler* in her notebook.

Narrator Three: The detectives monitor the two thermometers for several more minutes. They call out the temperature of each cup of cider at one-minute intervals.

Mom: What temperatures do the thermometers read now?

Noah: Mine reads 117 degrees.

Maggie: My thermometer reads 109 degrees. Now the difference is 8 degrees!

Narrator One: Maggie jots down the temperature readings. Another minute passes.

Noah: Now my thermometer reads 116 degrees.

Maggie: Mine reads 107 degrees.

Reggie: The data suggest that Maggie's cider is cooling faster than Noah's.

Mom: Well, detectives, can you think of an explanation?

529

Noah: Let's review the facts. We should be able to figure out this puzzle.

Maggie: Hmm. Mom, you heated the cider and poured it into both cups at the same time. That means that the cider in both cups started at the same temperature, correct?

Mom: Correct.

Noah: You poured equal amounts of cider into the two cups, correct?

Mom: Correct. I did.

Reggie: Noah, what is the only difference between your cider and Maggie's?

Noah: Well, mine is in a narrower cup. Could that be the missing clue?

Maggie: I don't know. Every good detective knows that once you rule out the impossible, whatever's left, no matter how strange, has to be the answer.

Noah: You just made that up!

Reggie: That is incorrect, Noah. What Maggie said comes from a classic mystery story.

Noah: I know. I was just teasing her. But as my robot, you're supposed to agree with me!

Mom: I guess you didn't include that in his programming, Noah!

Narrator Two: They all laugh. Maggie continues to look at the cups and the thermometers, pondering the problem.

Maggie: You're right, Noah. My cup is much wider than yours. That has to be it.

Noah: Why would a wider cup make cider cool faster?

Maggie: It gives the cider a greater surface area. More cider is exposed to the air.

Noah: Now I get it! The more of it that is exposed to the cooler air, the faster the cider will lose heat.

Reggie: In Maggie's wide cup, air contacts more of the cider than it does in Noah's narrow cup.

Maggie: So, even though my cup contains exactly the same amount of cider as Noah's cup, mine allows the cider to lose heat faster.

Noah: Another mystery solved!

Narrator Three: Maggie and Noah shake hands.

Mom: Good job! You two make a magnificent team.

Agatha: Good job!

Narrator One: Lightning flashes across the sky. A second later, the sound of thunder shakes the room. Startled, Agatha flutters to the safety of Maggie's bunny slippers.

Narrator Two: The lights in the room flicker and then go out.

Maggie: Where's my flashlight?

Mom: Oh, dear!

Noah: Hang on, everyone. I can get us a little light.

Narrator Three: A moment later, two bright lights appear in the darkness. Reggie's eyes have lit up!

Noah: I knew these battery-powered lights I installed in Reggie's eyes would come in handy someday.

Mom: Very resourceful, Noah! That was good thinking.

Maggie: Well, it looks to me as if we have another mystery looming before us.

Noah: Oh, really? What mystery is that?

Maggie: The mystery of where I put my flashlight!

Reading a Biography

Bridge to Reading for Information A biography is the true story of a person's life, written by another person. The notes on page 533 point out some features of a biography, such as events in time order and facts about why the person is important. How can these features help you read a biography?

Review the Focus Strategies

If you do not understand what you are reading, use the comprehension strategies you learned about in this theme.

Monitor Comprehension: Adjust Reading Rate

Monitor comprehension as you read by adjusting your reading rate. When you come to difficult sections of text, read them more slowly.

Monitor Comprehension: Self-Correct

As you read, monitor your comprehension. Stop to correct any mistakes that make the meaning of the text unclear.

As you read "Sequoyah's Talking Leaves" on pages 534–537, think about where and how to use the strategies.

TIME ORDER
Events are usually presented in time order.

SEQUOYAH'S TALKING LEAVES

by Julie Doyle Durway
illustrated by Gina Triplett

Imagine creating a whole writing system by yourself. It seems like an enormous job for one person. But a Cherokee Indian named Sequoyah did it.

Sequoyah was born around 1780 in what is now Tennessee. A quiet boy who liked to draw, he grew up to be an artistic man who made things from silver. He was also concerned about the future of his people, the Cherokee Indians.

The Cherokees lived in the southeastern part of what became the United States. In the early 1800s, the Cherokees lost much of their land to white settlers. When Sequoyah tried to understand why, he decided that the power of the white settlers came from their ability to read and write. Unlike the whites, the Cherokee Indians had only a spoken language. Sequoyah decided he would invent a writing system so the Cherokees could read and write their own words.

FACTS
Facts are used to give details about the important places and events in the person's life.

OPINIONS
The author's opinions and personal judgments are based on his or her understanding of the facts.

Apply the Strategies Read this biography about Sequoyah.
As you read, use different comprehension strategies, such as
adjusting your reading rate, to help you understand the text.

SEQUOYAH'S
TALKING LEAVES

by Julie Doyle Durway
illustrated by Gina Triplett

Imagine creating a whole
writing system by yourself.
It seems like an enormous
job for one person. But a
Cherokee Indian named
Sequoyah did it.

Read more slowly sections of text that contain many facts and dates. **MONITOR COMPREHENSION: ADJUST READING RATE**

Sequoyah was born around 1780 in what is now Tennessee. A quiet boy who liked to draw, he grew up to be an artistic man who made things from silver. He was also concerned about the future of his people, the Cherokee Indians.

The Cherokees lived in the southeastern part of what became the United States. In the early 1800s, the Cherokees lost much of their land to white settlers. When Sequoyah tried to understand why, he decided that the power of the white settlers came from their ability to read and write. Unlike the whites, the Cherokee Indians had only a spoken language. Sequoyah decided he would invent a writing system so the Cherokees could read and write their own words.

535

Sequoyah began this great work by making pictures—pictograms—to stand for every word in the Cherokee language. But there were too many words in his language for this system to work well. So Sequoyah invented a writing system based on syllables, not words. (This is called a syllabary.) He needed 86 symbols—phonograms, each one the sound of a syllable in the Cherokee language. Sequoyah used the 26 letters of the English alphabet, as well as letters from other alphabets, and signs he invented himself. He called his syllabary "talking leaves."

Finally, after many years of hard work, the Cherokee language could be written down. At first, other Cherokees didn't believe Sequoyah's writing system would work. But Sequoyah soon proved them wrong. His writing system was so easy to learn that most of the Cherokee people could read and write within a few months. In 1828, the Cherokees printed their own newspaper.

Be sure to stop and correct any mistakes you make as you read.
MONITOR COMPREHENSION: SELF-CORRECT

Unfortunately, Sequoyah's system did not prevent the Cherokee people from continuing to lose their land to white settlers. Today, the Cherokee people use the English alphabet, although Sequoyah's system is sometimes used. The United States government did recognize Sequoyah's accomplishment, however. In 1849, the giant redwood trees that grow in California were named *sequoias*, in honor of Sequoyah. In 1890, Sequoia National Park was named for this amazing man.

SEQUOIA NATIONAL PARK

READING-WRITING
CONNECTION

Lesson 21 ▶

Lesson 22 ▶

SELECTION TITLES	**Because of Winn-Dixie** Decoding Dog Speak	**My Diary from Here to There** Moving *and* There's an Orange Tree Out There
Comprehension Strategies	Use Story Structure	Use Story Structure
Focus Skills	Character, Setting, and Plot	Character, Setting, and Plot

Theme (5) A New Home

▲ Mercedes McDonald, *City Scene*

CONTENTS

Lesson 21

NEWBERY HONOR BOOK

Because of
Winn-Dixie

Kate DiCamillo

Decoding
Dog Speak

by Ruth Musgrave

Genre: Expository Nonfiction

541

Focus Skill

Character, Setting, and Plot

Every story includes one or more **characters**, a **setting**, and **plot events**. The characters and the setting affect the plot events. Each event in the plot is affected by the event that happened before it.

Characters	Setting

Plot Events

Tip

The characters and the setting can shape the plot events.

Read the paragraph below. Then look at the graphic organizer. It shows the characters, setting, and plot events.

Molly was living at the animal shelter when the Webbers came to visit. They talked softly to her and petted her gently. Molly wanted them to keep playing with her, but they turned to another dog. Molly followed the Webbers, wagging her tail. At last, the Webbers turned back to her. They were going to take Molly home!

Characters	**Setting**
a dog named Molly the Webbers	the animal shelter

Plot Events
- The Webbers visit the animal shelter.
- The Webbers play with Molly and another dog.
- Molly follows the Webbers and wags her tail.
- The Webbers decide to take Molly home.

Try This!

Look back at the paragraph. How does the setting affect the plot events?

www.harcourtschool.com/storytown

Vocabulary

Build Robust Vocabulary

prideful

snatched

select

intends

recalls

consisted

Greensville: Best Town

Visitors passing through Greensville will have to excuse residents if they appear to be a bit **prideful**. This town of 50,000 people recently earned the title of "Best Town" in the state. Livingston, a town to the east, had held the title for three straight years, but then Greensville **snatched** away the honor. As a result, Greensville became one of the **select** few towns to be visited by the governor on his "Small Town Improvement" tour.

Greensville's mayor, Betty Chen, is proud of her town. "We invest a lot in our schools and parks," she said. "Next year, the town **intends** to expand the computer center in the library."

Greensville has grown rapidly in recent years. Lee Parker **recalls** a time when it was barely a dot on the map. "Back then, the town **consisted** of a general store, a schoolhouse, and a dozen homes. That was it!" Some say that Greensville should not be called a small town anymore. However, Greensville is still small enough to win the "Best Town" award.

 www.harcourtschool.com/storytown

Word Champion

 Your challenge this week is to use the Vocabulary Words in conversations outside the classroom. Post a list where you will see the words often. Use as many of the words as you can when you talk with family members or friends. For example, you might tell a friend what your dinner consisted of. At the end of each day, write in your vocabulary journal the sentences you spoke that contained the words.

Because of Winn-Dixie
Kate DiCamillo

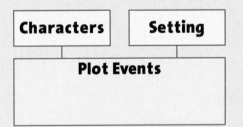

Realistic Fiction

Genre Study

Realistic fiction has characters and events that are like people and events in real life. As you read, look for

- a setting that could be a real place.

- realistic characters and events.

Characters	Setting
Plot Events	

Comprehension Strategy

Use story structure to keep track of the characters, setting, and plot events.

Because of
Winn-Dixie

by **Kate DiCamillo**

Ten-year-old India Opal Buloni and her father are the newest residents of Naomi, Florida. When her father sends Opal out one summer day for groceries, she comes home instead with a big, ugly, happy dog. She names the dog Winn-Dixie, after the supermarket where they met. At first, Opal's father doesn't want to keep Winn-Dixie, but he soon recognizes that this very friendly dog is a stray in need of a good home. He lets Opal keep Winn-Dixie, and she gains a wonderful friend in her new home.

"It all started with Winn-Dixie…"

I spent a lot of time that summer at the Herman W. Block Memorial Library. The Herman W. Block Memorial Library sounds like it would be a big fancy place, but it's not. It's just a little old house full of books, and Miss Franny Block is in charge of them all. She is a very small, very old woman with short gray hair, and she was the first friend I made in Naomi.

It all started with Winn-Dixie not liking it when I went into the library, because he couldn't go inside, too. But I showed him how he could stand up on his hind legs and look in the window and see me in there, selecting my books; and he was okay, as long as he could see me. But the thing was, the first time Miss Franny Block saw Winn-Dixie standing up on his hind legs like that, looking in the window, she didn't think he was a dog. She thought he was a bear.

This is what happened: I was picking out my books and kind of humming to myself, and all of a sudden, there was this loud and scary scream. I went running up to the front of the library, and there was Miss Franny Block, sitting on the floor behind her desk.

"Miss Franny?" I said. "Are you all right?"

"A bear," she said.

"A bear?" I asked.

"He has come back," she said.

"He has?" I asked. "Where is he?"

"Out there," she said and raised a finger and pointed at Winn-Dixie standing up on his hind legs, looking in the window for me.

"Miss Franny Block," I said, "that's not a bear. That's a dog. That's my dog. Winn-Dixie."

"Are you positive?" she asked.

"Yes ma'am," I told her. "I'm positive. He's my dog. I would know him anywhere."

"...that's
not
a bear.
That's
a
dog."

"...can Winn-Dixie come in and listen, too?"

Miss Franny sat there trembling and shaking.

"Come on," I said. "Let me help you up. It's okay." I stuck out my hand and Miss Franny took hold of it, and I pulled her up off the floor. She didn't weigh hardly anything at all. Once she was standing on her feet, she started acting all embarrassed, saying how I must think she was a silly old lady, mistaking a dog for a bear, but that she had a bad experience with a bear coming into the Herman W. Block Memorial Library a long time ago and she had never quite gotten over it.

"When did that happen?" I asked her.

"Well," said Miss Franny, "it is a very long story."

"That's okay," I told her. "I am like my mama in that I like to be told stories. But before you start telling it, can Winn-Dixie come in and listen, too? He gets lonely without me."

"Well, I don't know," said Miss Franny. "Dogs are not allowed in the Herman W. Block Memorial Library."

"He'll be good," I told her. "He's a dog who goes to church." And before she could say yes or no, I went outside and got Winn-Dixie, and he came in and lay down with a *"huummmppff"* and a sigh, right at Miss Franny's feet.

She looked down at him and said, "He most certainly is a large dog."

"Yes ma'am," I told her. "He has a large heart, too."

"Well," Miss Franny said. She bent over and gave Winn-Dixie a pat on the head, and Winn-Dixie wagged his tail back and forth and snuffled his nose on her little old-lady feet. "Let me get a chair and sit down so I can tell this story properly.

"Back when Florida was wild, when it consisted of nothing but palmetto trees and mosquitoes so big they could fly away with you," Miss Franny Block started in, "and I was just a little girl no bigger than you, my father, Herman W. Block, told me that I could have anything I wanted for my birthday. Anything at all."

Miss Franny looked around the library. She leaned in close to me. "I don't want to appear prideful," she said, "but my daddy was a very rich man. A very rich man." She nodded and then leaned back and said, "And I was a little girl who loved to read. So I told him, I said, 'Daddy, I would most certainly love to have a library for my birthday, a small little library would be wonderful.'"

"You asked for a whole library?"

"A small one," Miss Franny nodded. "I wanted a little house full of nothing but books and I wanted to share them, too. And I got my wish. My father built me this house, the very one we are sitting in now. And at a very young age, I became a librarian. Yes ma'am."

"What about the bear?"

"What about the bear?" I said.

"Did I mention that Florida was wild in those days?" Miss Franny Block said.

"Uh-huh, you did."

"It was wild. There were wild men and wild women and wild animals."

"Like bears!"

"Yes ma'am. That's right. Now, I have to tell you, I was a little-miss-know-it-all. I was a miss-smarty-pants with my library full of books. Oh, yes ma'am, I thought I knew the answers to everything. Well, one hot Thursday, I was sitting in my library with all the doors and windows open and my nose stuck in a book, when a shadow crossed the desk. And without looking up, yes ma'am, without even looking up, I said, 'Is there a book I can help you find?'

"Well, there was no answer. And I thought it might have been a wild man or a wild woman, scared of all those books and afraid to speak up. But then I became aware of a very peculiar smell, a very strong smell. I raised my eyes slowly. And standing right in front of me was a bear. Yes ma'am. A very large bear."

"How big?" I asked.

"Oh, well," said Miss Franny, "perhaps three times the size of your dog."

"Then what happened?" I asked her.

"Well," said Miss Franny, "I looked at him and he looked at me. He put his big nose up in the air and sniffed and sniffed as if he was trying to decide if a little-miss-know-it-all librarian was what he was in the mood to eat. And I sat there. And then I thought, 'Well, if this bear intends to eat me, I am not going to let it happen without a fight. No ma'am.' So very slowly and very carefully, I raised up the book I was reading."

"Then what happened?"

"Did he come back?"

"What book was that?" I asked.

"Why, it was *War and Peace*, a very large book. I raised it up slowly and then I aimed it carefully and I threw it right at that bear and screamed, 'Be gone!' And do you know what?"

"No ma'am," I said.

"He went. But this is what I will never forget. He took the book with him."

"Nuh-uh," I said.

"Yes ma'am," said Miss Franny. "He snatched it up and ran."

"Did he come back?" I asked.

"No, I never saw him again. Well, the men in town used to tease me about it. They used to say, 'Miss Franny, we saw that bear of yours out in the woods today. He was reading that book and he said it sure was good and would it be all right if he kept it for just another week.' Yes ma'am. They did tease me about it." She sighed. "I imagine I'm the only one left from those days. I imagine I'm the only one that even recalls that bear. All my friends, everyone I knew when I was young, they are all dead and gone."

She sighed again. She looked sad and old and wrinkled. It was the same way I felt sometimes, being friendless in a new town and not having a mama to comfort me. I sighed, too.

Winn-Dixie raised his head off his paws and looked back and forth between me and Miss Franny. He sat up then and showed Miss Franny his teeth.

"Well now, look at that," she said. "That dog is smiling at me."

"It's a talent of his," I told her.

"It is a fine talent," Miss Franny said. "A very fine talent." And she smiled back at Winn-Dixie.

"We could be friends," I said to Miss Franny. "I mean you and me and Winn-Dixie, we could all be friends."

Miss Franny smiled even bigger. "Why, that would be grand," she said, "just grand."

And right at that minute, right when the three of us had decided to be friends, who should come marching into the Herman W. Block Memorial Library but old pinch-faced Amanda Wilkinson. She walked right up to Miss Franny's desk and said, "I finished *Johnny Tremain* and I enjoyed it very much. I would like something even more difficult to read now, because I am an advanced reader."

"Yes dear, I know," said Miss Franny. She got up out of her chair.

Amanda pretended like I wasn't there. She stared right past me. "Are dogs allowed in the library?" she asked Miss Franny as they walked away.

"Certain ones," said Miss Franny, "a select few." And then she turned around and winked at me. I smiled back. I had just made my first friend in Naomi, and nobody was going to mess that up for me, not even old pinch-faced Amanda Wilkinson.

...the three
of us
had decided
to become
friends...

Think Critically

1. How does Miss Franny Block feel after she realizes that the animal outside the window is a dog? CHARACTER'S EMOTIONS

2. Opal tells Miss Franny that Winn-Dixie gets lonely without her. Do you think that dogs feel emotions as people do? Explain. MAKE JUDGMENTS

3. Look back at the author's description of Amanda Wilkinson. How does Opal feel about her? How do you know? DRAW CONCLUSIONS

4. Explain how the author's choice of setting affects the story events. CHARACTER, SETTING, AND PLOT

5. **WRITE** Think about the story that Miss Franny tells Opal. How does sharing this story help them to become friends?
   SHORT RESPONSE

About the Author
Kate DiCamillo

For many years, Kate DiCamillo dreamed of becoming a writer. However, she did not start writing until she began working in the children's section of a book warehouse. She read many children's books there, and she fell in love with them. She began writing two pages every morning before she went to work. Kate DiCamillo says she never feels like sitting down to write, but afterward, she is always glad that she did. Even now that she is a successful author, she still writes two pages every day. It takes her about a year to write a book. Kate DiCamillo's advice for others who are interested in writing is to pay careful attention to the world around you and write a little bit every day.

 www.harcourtschool.com/storytown

Science

NATIONAL GEOGRAPHIC
kids
DARE TO EXPLORE

Silly
Pet
Tricks

Expository Nonfiction

Decoding Dog Speak

by Ruth Musgrave

Would you like to understand your dog's dialogue? How about your cat's chitchat? It's easy. Just use your eyes. Dogs and cats use their ears, tail, head, and body posture to communicate. If you keep "listening," the body language becomes clear.

Sue May, of Yachats, Oregon, found out how important it can be to understand your dog. Every day, she and her golden retriever, Zoe, walked the same neighborhood route to reach a mountain trail.

One day, Zoe started their walk with her tail high, sniffing everything. But at the trail, the dog stopped, refusing to budge. May begged. Zoe blocked her path. May ordered. Zoe dropped her tail, slinked a few steps, and stopped. Finally May decided to go on, leaving Zoe at home.

On the trail alone, May wondered what Zoe's problem was. Within seconds she discovered the answer. Blocking the path was a 250-pound black bear. May backed away unnoticed, quickly reaching home and her smart, alert dog.

What Is Your Dog Trying To Tell You?

I'M *SOOO* HAPPY AND EXCITED!

This dog's happy face tells you everything—he's looking right at you and his ears are relaxed. His mouth is open with his lips pulled back and up in a goofy grin. His body is relaxed, his head is up, and his chest is out.

WHAT'S THAT? I'M CURIOUS.

This puppy shows her curiosity by the tilt of her head, ears perked forward, lips pulled back and up in what looks like a smirk, and a relaxed body.

I LOVE YOU.

With a relaxed body and ears slightly back, this dog shows her love and respect. A puppy gets adults to feed her by licking their mouths. As she grows up, this behavior is repeated toward people to let them know she respects them and is not a threat.

BACK OFF.

This dog is in warning mode. His ears are sticking out. There is a little curl to his lip, his head drops slightly, and he's staring directly at what's bugging him. His body is rigid and there's a rumble deep in his throat.

I'M SCARED.

From head to tail, this dog is telling you she is scared. Her ears are flattened back against her lowered head. Her shoulders and tail are drooped. Eyes looking down, she slinks away trying to make herself as small as possible.

PLAY WITH ME!

By lowering his chest and leaving his rump in the air, this little pup bows, inviting you to play. Ears perked forward, looking directly into the eyes of a potential playmate, the dog's swishing tail fans the air with excitement while he awaits your reply.

Connections

Comparing Texts

1. What can you learn from Opal in "Because of Winn–Dixie" about making new friends?

2. Compare the author's purpose for writing "Because of Winn-Dixie" with the author's purpose for writing "Decoding Dog Speak."

3. The Herman W. Block Memorial Library normally does not allow dogs inside. Should libraries admit dogs? Include reasons for and against allowing dogs in libraries.

Vocabulary Review

Word Webs

Work with a partner. Create a word web for each Vocabulary Word. In the outer circles, write words and phrases that are related to the Vocabulary Word. Tell how each word or phrase in your web is related to the Vocabulary Word.

consisted

intends

prideful

recalls

select

snatched

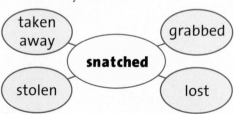

Fluency Practice

Tape-Assisted Reading

Listen to the beginning of "Because of Winn-Dixie" on *Audiotext 5*. Stop the recording after the sentence "I would know him anywhere" on page 549. As you listen, read along silently and track the text with your finger. Pay attention to the reader's intonation. Then listen to the recording a second time, as you read aloud softly, matching your intonation to the reader's voice.

Writing

Write a Story

Think about a dog you have met or would like to meet. Imagine that the dog has helped you in some way. Write a story telling when, where, and how the dog helped you.

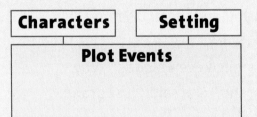

Characters	Setting
Plot Events	

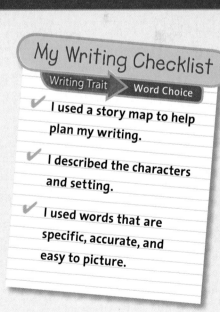

My Writing Checklist

Writing Trait ▶ Word Choice

✔ I used a story map to help plan my writing.

✔ I described the characters and setting.

✔ I used words that are specific, accurate, and easy to picture.

Reading-Writing Connection

Analyze Writer's Craft: Story

A **story** is a work of fiction. It has **characters**, a **setting**, and a series of **plot events**. Characters often face one main conflict, or problem, and find a resolution by the end of the story. When you write stories, you can use the works of authors such as Kate DiCamillo as writing models. Read the passage below from "Because of Winn-Dixie," and look at the way the author writes a conversation between two characters.

Writing Trait

SENTENCE FLUENCY
The writer uses short sentences to create **dialogue**, or conversation, between characters. She begins a new paragraph for each one.

Writing Trait

CONVENTIONS
The writer places quotation marks around a speaker's words. Commas and periods are placed inside the quotation marks.

"Well, now, look at that," she said. "That dog is smiling at me."

"It's a talent of his," I told her.

"It's a fine talent," Miss Franny said. "A very fine talent." And she smiled back at Winn-Dixie.

"We could be friends," I said to Miss Franny. "I mean you and me and Winn-Dixie, we could all be friends."

Miss Franny smiled even bigger. "Why, that would be grand," she said, "just grand."

Story

A **story** is a fictional narrative. A student named Cheryl wrote the story below. Notice how she includes characters, the setting, and plot elements.

Student Writing Model

Just Like Lily
by Cheryl G.

Writing Trait

ORGANIZATION
At the beginning of the story, Cheryl introduces the **setting**, main **characters**, and main **conflict**.

Writing Trait

WORD CHOICE
Cheryl uses **strong verbs**, such as *grabbed* and *pulled*, to vividly describe Lily's actions.

Lily and her parents had moved to Maple Grove in June. It was a quiet, small town. Lily wanted to make friends, but she was the only kid on her new street.

One Saturday at the grocery store, Lily saw a sign on the bulletin board: *Free Puppies to Good Homes*. Lily grabbed her mother's hand and pulled her to the bulletin board.

"Mom, can I please have a puppy?" Lily begged. "I really want one! Please, can't we just go and look?"

Lily's mom laughed softly and said, "Sure, Lily. Write down the address."

They went home, put away the groceries, and drove to the address. It was only four blocks away. Lily saw a red bike leaning against the porch. It looked just like her own bike.

Writing Trait

ORGANIZATION
Cheryl describes a **series of events** that lead toward a resolution of the story's main conflict.

A woman with dark hair opened the door. Behind her stood a girl about Lily's age.

"Hi," said Lily.

"Hi," the girl replied. She had on a t-shirt with a picture of Lily's favorite band.

"Do you like the Maniac Monkeys?" Lily asked.

"They're my favorite!" the girl said.

Lily couldn't believe her luck. The girl's name was Marcy, and she was in the fourth grade—just like Lily! Marcy liked computer games and music—just like Lily! They both loved animals, and they both played softball. In fact, Marcy's dad coached a softball team!

Marcy showed Lily a pile of wiggly black puppies. Lily chose the cutest one to take home.

Cheryl concludes with a **resolution** of the story's main conflict.

Marcy became Lily's best friend. They rode bikes and listened to music together. Lily signed up for the softball team. Thanks to a "free puppies" sign, Lily found *two* new best friends!

Now look at what Cheryl did to prepare to write her story.

Brainstorm Story Ideas

First, Cheryl made an idea web. She wrote different story ideas in the web. Next, she chose the idea she knew the most about.

Organize Information

Then, Cheryl used a story map to plan her story. She included the characters, setting, conflict, plot events, and resolution. The story map helped her plan what would happen at the beginning, in the middle, and at the end of her story.

a dog gets lost

Story Ideas

a girl moves to a new town

a boy finds a treasure map

Characters
Lily and her mom, Marcy

Setting
Maple Grove

Conflict: Lily wants to make friends, but there are no kids on her street.

Plot Events

• Lily sees a sign for free puppies.

• Lily's mom lets her get a puppy.

• When they get the puppy, Lily meets a girl named Marcy who lives four blocks away.

Resolution: Lily and Marcy become best friends.

CONTENTS

Genre: Diary

My **Diary**
from **Here** to **There**

Mi **diario** de aquí hasta allá

Story / Cuento
Amada Irma Pérez

Illustrations / Ilustraciones
Maya Christina Gonzalez

Moving

There's an Orange
Tree Out There

Genre: Poetry

Character, Setting, and Plot

Stories contain three main elements: **character, setting, and plot**. The characters and setting work together to shape the plot. Each event in a story affects the events that follow it. The plot often includes several events that reveal a conflict or problem. At the end of most stories, the conflict or problem is resolved.

Setting	Characters
Plot Events	

Tip

As you read a story, pay attention to the way each event affects the next.

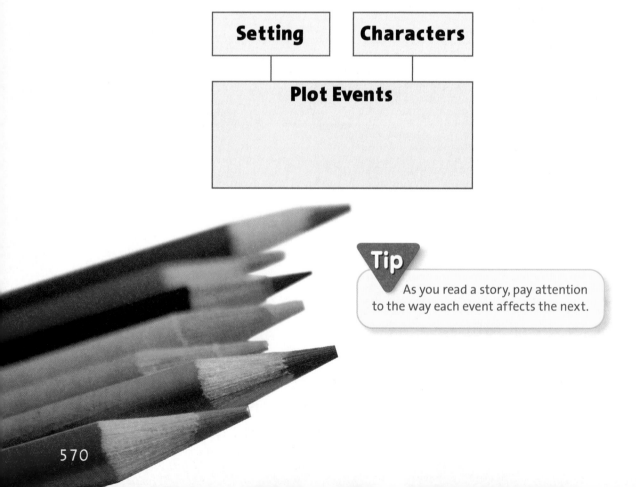

Read the paragraph below. Then look at the graphic organizer. It shows how the characters and the setting work together to shape the plot.

Wai-Ling looked around the classroom. Everything was different here in the United States. She thought that she would never make friends. Then the teacher asked everyone to draw a portrait. Wai-Ling drew Mei-Mei, her best friend back in China. When Wai-Ling finished, two students admired her drawing. They invited her to eat lunch with them. "Maybe I'll make friends here after all," Wai-Ling thought.

Setting A classroom in the United States	**Characters** Wai-Ling, other students, teacher

Plot Events

- Wai-Ling is at a new school and thinks she will never make friends.
- Wai-Ling draws a portrait of her friend Mei-Mei.
- Two students admire Wai-Ling's drawing and invite her to have lunch with them.

Try This!

Look back at the paragraph. How do the characters and setting affect the plot events? How does each plot event affect the one that follows it?

GO online www.harcourtschool.com/storytown

Vocabulary

Build Robust Vocabulary

opportunities

comforted

journey

burst

huddle

recognizes

Adventure in Mexico

Monday, August 22
We're finally in Mexico! We're staying at a place near the beach, so we'll have lots of **opportunities** for swimming.

Wednesday, August 24
Tamika was feeling a bit sick today, so Mom and Dad said we shouldn't go for a boat ride. They said maybe we could go after she's feeling better, which **comforted** me a little.

Thursday, August 25
Today, we visited some pyramids outside town. The **journey** took us two hours by bus.

I thought I'd **burst** with excitement when I climbed a pyramid. I felt as if I had traveled 500 years back in time!

Saturday, August 27

Last night, we were walking to a restaurant, and it began to rain like crazy! The four of us had to **huddle** together in a doorway to stay dry!

Tuesday, September 6

Today was the first day back at school. With my new shirt from Mexico and my new hair wrap that I had done on the beach, I'm surprised that everyone at school still **recognizes** me! I had some difficulty studying tonight. All I could think about was climbing that pyramid!

GO online www.harcourtschool.com/storytown

Word Detective

Your mission this week is to search for Vocabulary Words outside the classroom. You might find them in a book or a magazine, or you might hear them on TV or in a conversation. Each time you see or hear a Vocabulary Word, write it in your vocabulary journal. Make sure you record where you found the word.

My Diary from Here to There

Mi diario de aquí hasta allá

Story / Cuento
Amada Irma Pérez

Illustrations / Ilustraciones
Maya Christina Gonzalez

Diary

Genre Study

A diary is a personal account of the author's day-to-day experiences, ideas, and feelings. As you read, look for

- first-person point of view.

- the author's thoughts about people, places, and events.

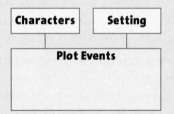

Characters	Setting
Plot Events	

Comprehension Strategy

Use story structure to understand the organization of a story and to make predictions about plot events.

My Diary
from Here to There

by Amada Irma Pérez

illustrated by
Maya Christina Gonzalez

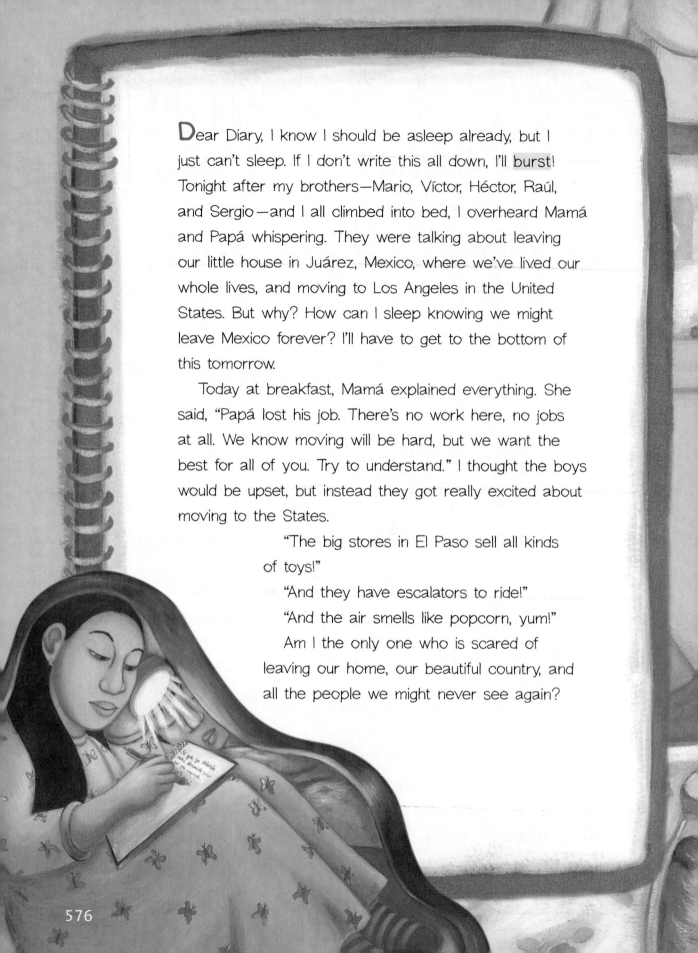

Dear Diary, I know I should be asleep already, but I just can't sleep. If I don't write this all down, I'll burst! Tonight after my brothers—Mario, Víctor, Héctor, Raúl, and Sergio—and I all climbed into bed, I overheard Mamá and Papá whispering. They were talking about leaving our little house in Juárez, Mexico, where we've lived our whole lives, and moving to Los Angeles in the United States. But why? How can I sleep knowing we might leave Mexico forever? I'll have to get to the bottom of this tomorrow.

Today at breakfast, Mamá explained everything. She said, "Papá lost his job. There's no work here, no jobs at all. We know moving will be hard, but we want the best for all of you. Try to understand." I thought the boys would be upset, but instead they got really excited about moving to the States.

"The big stores in El Paso sell all kinds of toys!"

"And they have escalators to ride!"

"And the air smells like popcorn, yum!"

Am I the only one who is scared of leaving our home, our beautiful country, and all the people we might never see again?

My best friend Michi and I walked to the park today. We passed Don Nacho's corner store and the women at the *tortilla* shop, their hands blurring like hummingbird wings as they worked the dough over the griddle.

At the park we braided each other's hair and promised never to forget each other. We each picked out a smooth, heart-shaped stone to remind us always of our friendship, of the little park, of Don Nacho and the *tortilla* shop. I've known Michi since we were little, and I don't think I'll ever find a friend like her in California.

"You're lucky your family will be together over there," Michi said. Her sisters and father work in the U.S. I can't imagine leaving anyone in our family behind.

Ok, Diary, here's the plan—in two weeks we leave for my grandparents' house in Mexicali, right across the border from Calexico, California. We'll stay with them while Papá goes to Los Angeles to look for work. We can only take what will fit in the old car Papá borrowed— we're selling everything else. Meanwhile, the boys build cardboard box cities and act like nothing bothers them. Mamá and Papá keep talking about all the opportunities we'll have in California. But what if we're not allowed to speak Spanish? What if I can't learn English? Will I ever see Michi again? What if we never come back?

Today while we were packing, Papá pulled me aside. He said, "Amada, *m'ija*, I can see how worried you've been. Don't be scared. Everything will be all right."

"But how do you know? What will happen to us?" I said.

He smiled. "*M'ija*, I was born in Arizona, in the States. When I was six—not a big kid like you—my Papá and Mamá moved our family back to Mexico. It was a big change, but we got through it. I know you can, too. You are stronger than you think." I hope he's right. I still need to pack my special rock (and you, Diary!). We leave tomorrow!

579

Our trip was long and hard. At night the desert was so cold we had to huddle together to keep warm. We drove right along the border, across from New Mexico and Arizona. Mexico and the U.S. are two different countries, but they look exactly the same on both sides of the border, with giant saguaros pointing up at the pink-orange sky and enormous clouds. I made a wish on the first star I saw. Soon there were too many stars in the sky to count. Our little house in Juárez already seems so far away.

We arrived in Mexicali late at night and my grandparents Nana and Tata, and all our aunts, uncles and cousins (there must be fifty of them!) welcomed us with a feast of *tamales*, beans, *pan dulce*, and hot chocolate with cinnamon sticks.

It's so good to see them all! Everyone gathered around us and told stories late into the night. We played so much that the boys fell asleep before the last blanket was rolled out onto the floor. But, Diary, I can't sleep. I keep thinking about Papá leaving tomorrow.

Papá left for Los Angeles this morning. Nana comforted Mamá, saying that Papá is a U.S. citizen, so he won't have a problem getting our "green cards" from the U.S. government. Papá told us that we each need a green card to live in the States, because we weren't born there.

I can't believe Papá's gone. Tío Tito keeps trying to make us laugh instead of cry. Tío Raúl let me wear his special *medalla*, and Tío Chato even pulled a silver coin out of my ear. The boys try to copy his tricks but coins just end up flying everywhere. They drive me nuts sometimes, but today it feels good to laugh.

We got a letter from Papá today! I'm pasting it into your pages, Diary.

My dear family,

I have been picking grapes and strawberries in the fields of Delano, 140 miles north of Los Angeles, saving money and always thinking of you. It is hard, tiring work. There is a man here in the fields named César Chávez, who speaks of unions, strikes, and boycotts. These new words hold the hope of better conditions for us farmworkers.

So far, getting your green cards has been difficult, for we are not the only family trying to start a new life here. Please be patient. It won't be long before we are all together again.

Hugs and kisses,
Papá

583

I miss Papá so much—it feels like he left ages ago. It's been tough to stay hopeful. So far we've had to live in three different houses with some of Mamá's sisters. First, the boys broke Tía Tuca's jewelry box and were so noisy she kicked us out. Then, at Nana's house, they kept trying on Tía Nena's high heels and purses. Even Nana herself got mad when they used her pots and pans to make "music." And they keep trying to read what I've written here, and to hide my special rock. Tía Lupe finally took us in, but where will we go if she decides she's had enough of us?

FINALLY! Papá sent our green cards—we're going to cross the border at last! He can't come for us but will meet us in Los Angeles.

The whole family is making a big farewell dinner for us tonight. Even after all the trouble the boys have caused, I think everyone is sad to see us go. Nana even gave me a new journal to write in for when I finish this one. She said, "Never forget who you are and where you are from. Keep your language and culture alive in your diary and in your heart."

We leave this weekend. I'm so excited I can hardly write!

My first time writing in the U.S.A.! We're in San Ysidro, California, waiting for the bus to Los Angeles. Crossing the border in Tijuana was crazy. Everyone was pushing and shoving. There were babies crying, and people fighting to be first in line. We held hands the whole way. When we finally got across, Mario had only one shoe on and his hat had fallen off. I counted everyone and I still had five brothers. Whew!

Papá is meeting us at the bus station in Los Angeles. It's been so long—I hope he recognizes us!

What a long ride! One woman and her children got kicked off the bus when the immigration patrol boarded to check everyone's papers. Mamá held Mario and our green cards close to her heart.

Papá was waiting at the station, just like he promised. We all jumped into his arms and laughed, and Mamá even cried a little. Papá's hugs felt so much better than when he left us in Mexicali!

I wrote to Michi today:

Dear Michi,

I have stories for you! Papá found a job in a factory, and we're living in a creaky old house in El Monte, east of Los Angeles. It's not at all like Juárez. Yesterday everything started shaking and a huge roar was all around us—airplanes, right overhead! Sometimes freight trains rumble past our house like little earthquakes.

Every day I hold my special rock and I think about home— Mexico—and our walks to the park. Papá says we might go back for the holidays in a year or two. Until then, write me!

Missing you,
Amada Irma

Well, Diary, I finally found a place where I can sit and think and write. It may not be the little park in Juárez, but it's pretty. You know, just because I'm far away from Juárez and Michi and my family in Mexicali, it doesn't mean they're not here with me. They're inside my little rock; they're here in your pages and in the language that I speak; and they're in my memories and my heart. Papá was right. I AM stronger than I think—in Mexico, in the States, anywhere.

P.S. I've almost filled this whole journal and can't wait to start my new one. Maybe someday I'll even write a book about our journey!

Think Critically

1. Why do Amada's parents decide to move the family to the United States? NOTE DETAILS

2. What makes Amada realize that she is stronger than she thought? CHARACTER, SETTING, AND PLOT

3. Why do you think Amada keeps a diary of her journey? MAKE INFERENCES

4. Amada feels sad and a little scared about moving to California. How would you feel if you were in Amada's situation? IDENTIFY WITH CHARACTERS

5. **WRITE** Tell how Amada's reaction to the move to California is DIFFERENT from that of her brothers. Be sure to include details and information from the selection. SHORT RESPONSE

About the Author
Amada Irma Pérez

Amada Irma Pérez was born in Mexico. When she was young, her family immigrated to the United States. Amada Irma Pérez uses her life experiences as a basis for her writing. She is a bilingual education teacher who works to create better understanding between people of different cultures. Amada Irma Pérez lives with her husband and children in southern California.

About the Illustrator
Maya Christina Gonzalez

Maya Christina Gonzalez has loved to draw and color for as long as she can remember. When she was young, she would draw her own face on the blank pages at the front or back of coloring books. Today, she helps children express feelings and experiences through art. Maya Christina Gonzalez's home in San Francisco, California, reflects her love of art. There are bright colors everywhere.

 www.harcourtschool.com/storytown

589

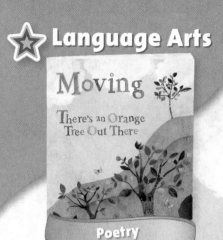

Moving

We are moving away
So I must say good-bye
To my room and my swing
And that sweet part of sky
That sometimes hangs blue
And sometimes hangs gray
Over the fields
Where I used to play.

Good-bye to my old friends
Jason and Sue
They wave from their porches,
Are they crying too?
The moving truck rumbles
Past all that I know—
The school and the woods
And the creek down below.
And everything seems
To be pleading
"Don't go!"

—Eileen Spinelli

There's an Orange Tree Out There

translated from the Spanish by Darwin J. Flakoll

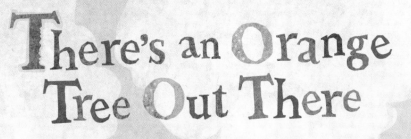

There's an orange tree out there, behind that old,
abandoned garden wall,
but it's not the same orange tree we planted,
and it's a beautiful orange tree
so beautiful it makes us remember
that orange tree we planted
     —in our earth—
before coming to this house
so distant and remote from that one
where we planted an orange tree
and even saw it—like this one—in flower.

—Alfonso Quijada Urías

Connections

Comparing Texts

1. What can you learn from Amada's experience that might help you face a challenge?

2. How is "My Diary from Here to There" like the poems on pages 590–591? How is it different?

3. Amada expresses her thoughts and feelings by writing them in a diary. What are some other ways a person could express thoughts and feelings?

Vocabulary Review

> There were many opportunities for learning on our journey.

Word Pairs

Work with a partner. Write the Vocabulary Words on separate index cards. Place the cards face down. Take turns flipping over two cards and writing a sentence that uses both words. Read the sentence aloud to your partner. You must use the words correctly in the sentence to keep the cards. The partner with the most cards at the end wins.

journey

burst

opportunities

huddle

comforted

recognizes

Fluency Practice

Partner Reading

Your intonation is the way the pitch of your voice rises and falls as you speak. Choose a section from "My Diary from Here to There." Read aloud the text as your partner listens and follows along. Then have your partner give you feedback on your intonation. Read the section aloud again, keeping in mind the feedback your partner gave you. Then switch roles and repeat the activity.

Writing

Write a Paragraph

Imagine that you have just settled with your family in a new town. Write a paragraph that tells about an experience you have had in your new home.

Plot Events
1.
2.
3.

My Writing Checklist

Writing Trait ➤ Word Choice

✔ I used a graphic organizer to plan my writing.

✔ I used vivid words to describe the experience.

✔ I organized the events in the correct order.

CONTENTS

Lesson 23

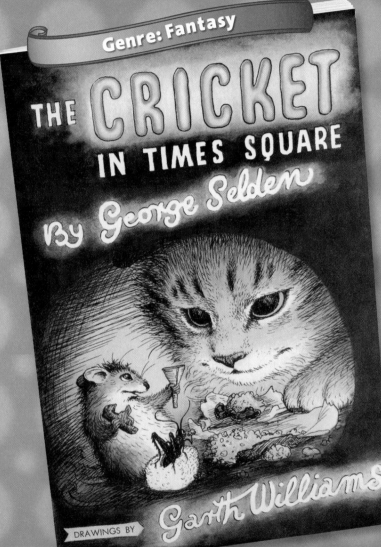

Genre: Fantasy

THE CRICKET IN TIMES SQUARE

By George Selden

DRAWINGS BY Garth Williams

Cricket Thermometer

Genre: Experiment

Focus Skill

Sequence: Story Events

Sequence is the order in which events happen. Authors of fiction stories usually write the **story events** in sequence. An author may use time-order words such as *first, next, then,* and *finally* to show the sequence. Keeping track of the sequence of events can help you understand what you read.

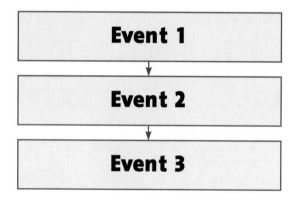

| Event 1 |
| Event 2 |
| Event 3 |

Tip

Sometimes the author does not use time-order words to indicate sequence. Use your own knowledge and clues in the text to identify the order of events.

Read the paragraph below. Then look at the graphic organizer. It shows the sequence of events in the paragraph.

George Gopher wanted to have the longest tunnel on the block. Early in the morning, he started digging. After several hours, he curved his tunnel upward. To his surprise, he found himself directly under the Maytown Library! George gave the problem much thought. He decided he might as well make the best of things. The next day, George got a library card.

Event 1 George started digging his tunnel.

Event 2 George curved his tunnel upward and found himself under the library.

Event 3 George made the best of things and got a library card.

Try This!

Look back at the paragraph. Use the information in the graphic organizer and time-order words to retell the story.

 www.harcourtschool.com/storytown

Vocabulary

- scrounging
- forlornly
- stingy
- pathetic
- noble
- resolved
- fidget
- suspicion

Crumbs for the Taking

Mira Mouse was not happy with the new family that had moved into her house. They kept the kitchen floor much too clean. Every day, Mira spent hours **scrounging** for crumbs, but she found only a few.

One morning, Mira hid behind a plant, **forlornly** gazing at the family as they ate breakfast. Mira's sister Mitsy was visiting, and Mira told her sister about her problem. "This family is very **stingy** with food," she said. She gave a **pathetic** sigh. "Perhaps I'll have to move."

598

Mitsy was a **noble** sort of mouse. She **resolved** to help her sister. Mitsy studied the situation. "Look at the boy **fidget**!" she whispered. "I'll bet he drops a lot of crumbs."

"His parents sweep the floor after breakfast," Mira said sadly, "right after the boy leaves for school."

Mitsy cried, "There's your solution!" When the family left the table, the mice sped to where the boy had eaten, and gathered as many delicious crumbs as they could carry. They made it back into the mouse hole before the parents returned to sweep.

"I have a **suspicion** you won't go hungry anymore," Mitsy said with a grin.

 www.harcourtschool.com/storytown

Word Detective

 Your mission this week is to look for Vocabulary Words outside the classroom. You might hear them on TV or in a conversation, or you might find them in a magazine. Each time you see or hear a Vocabulary Word, write it in your vocabulary journal. Be sure to record where you found the word.

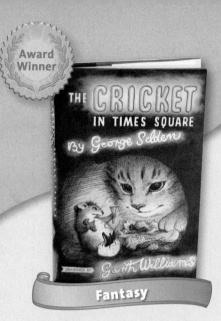

Fantasy

Genre Study

A fantasy is an imaginative story that may have characters and events that are not realistic. As you read, look for

- characters who behave in an unrealistic way.

- story events that happen in time order.

Event 1
Event 2
Event 3
Event 4

Comprehension Strategy

Ask questions as you read and then find the answers in the text.

THE CRICKET
IN TIMES SQUARE

by George Selden

drawings by Garth Williams

Hopping into a picnic basket, Chester Cricket finds himself in New York City—far away from the Connecticut tree stump he calls home. Mario Bellini finds Chester near his parents' newsstand in the Times Square subway station. He begs his parents to let him keep the cricket as a pet. While living in the Bellinis' newsstand, Chester makes friends with two of the residents of the subway station, Harry Cat and Tucker Mouse. Mario buys a cricket cage so Chester can have his own house. One night, Chester's new friends free him from his cage. Tucker Mouse snuggles into Chester's cage to sleep.

Harry Cat purred his chuckle. "Good night, Chester," he said. "I'm going back to the drain pipe, where I can stretch out." He jumped to the floor.

"Good night, Harry," Chester called.

Soft and silent as a shadow, Harry slipped out the opening in the side of the newsstand and glided over to the drain pipe. Chester hopped into his matchbox. He had gotten to like the feeling of the tissue. It was almost like the spongy wood of his old tree stump—and felt much more like home than the cricket cage. Now they each had their own place to sleep.

"Good night, Tucker," Chester said.

"'Night, Chester," Tucker answered.

Chester Cricket burrowed down deeper into the tissue. He was beginning to enjoy life in New York. Just before he fell asleep, he heard Tucker Mouse sighing happily in the cage.

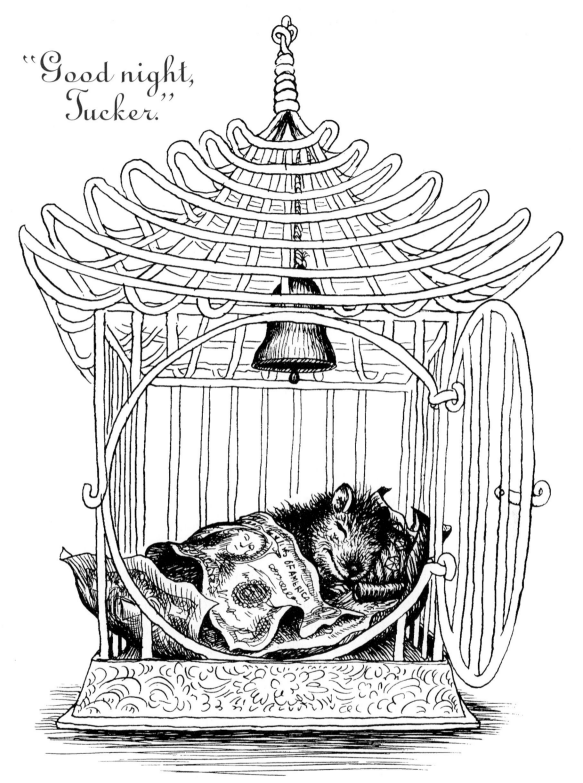

"Good night, Tucker."

"'Night, Chester."

Chester Cricket was having a dream. In his dream he was sitting on top of his stump back in Connecticut, eating a leaf from the willow tree. He would bite off a piece of leaf, chew it up, and swallow it, but for some reason it didn't taste as good as usual. There was something dry and papery about it, and it had a bitter flavor. Still, Chester kept eating, hoping that it would begin to taste better.

A storm came up in his dream. The wind blew clouds of dust across the meadow. They swirled around his stump, and Chester began to sneeze because the dust got in his nose. But he still held on to the leaf. And then he sneezed such a big sneeze that it woke him up.

Chester looked around him. He had been walking in his sleep and he was sitting on the edge of the cash register. The storm had been a gust of air that blew into the newsstand when the shuttle pulled up to the station. He was still choking from the dirt that flew around him. Chester looked down at his two front legs, half expecting to find the willow leaf. But it was no leaf he was holding. It was a two-dollar bill and he had already eaten half of it.

He dropped the bill and leaped over to the cricket cage, where Tucker Mouse was sleeping peacefully. Chester shook the silver bell furiously; it rang like a fire alarm. Tucker jumped out from under his blanket of dollar bills and ran around the cage shouting, "Help! Fire! Murder! Police!"

"Oh oh oh oh," moaned Tucker Mouse. "Not a one-dollar bill—not even a one-dollar bill and a fifty-cent piece—*two dollars* you had to eat! And from the Bellinis too—people who hardly make two dollars in two days."

"What am I going to do?" asked Chester.

"Pack your bags and go to California," said Tucker.

Chester shook his head. "I can't," he said. "They've been so good to me—I can't run away."

Tucker Mouse shrugged his shoulders. "Then stay and take the rap," he said. He crept out of the cage and examined the remains of the money. "There's still half of it left. Maybe we could put tape along the edge and pass it off as a one-dollar bill."

Then he realized where he was and sat down panting. "What is the matter with you, Chester?" he said. "I could have died from fright."

"I just ate half of a two-dollar bill," said Chester.

Tucker stared at him with disbelief. "You did what?" he asked.

"Yes," said Chester, "look." He fetched the ruined two-dollar bill from the cash register. "I dreamed it was a leaf and I ate it."

"No one would believe it," said Chester. He sat down, still forlornly holding the bill. "Oh dear—and things were going along so nicely."

Tucker Mouse put his bedclothes back in the cash register drawer and came to sit beside Chester. "Buck up," he said. "We could still figure something out, maybe."

They both concentrated for a minute. Then Tucker clapped his paws and squeaked, "I got it! Eat the rest of it and they'll never know what happened."

"They'd accuse each other of losing it," said Chester. "I don't want to make any bad feelings between them."

"Oh, you're so honorable!" said Tucker. "It's disgusting."

"Besides, it tastes bad," added Chester.

"Then how about this." Tucker had a new idea. "We could frame the janitor who cleans the station. I'll take the evidence over and plant it in his water closet. He whopped me with a mop last week. I would be glad to see him go to jail for a few days."

"No, no," said Chester. "We can't get somebody else in trouble."

"Then a stranger," said Tucker. "We tip over the tissue, break the glass in the alarm clock, and throw all the small change on the floor. They'll think a thief came in the night. You could even put a bandage on and make out like a hero. I could see it all—"

"No!" Chester interrupted him. "The damage we'd do would cost even more than the two dollars."

Tucker had one more idea: he was going to volunteer to go over and swipe two dollars from the lunch counter. But before he could suggest that, the top of the stand was suddenly lifted off. They had forgotten what time it was. Mama Bellini, who was on duty in the morning, stood towering, frowning down on them. Tucker let out a squeak of fear and jumped down to the floor.

"Catch the mouse!" shouted Mama. She picked up a magazine—very big and heavy—and heaved it after Tucker. It hit him on the left hind leg just as he vanished into the drain pipe.

Chester Cricket sat frozen to the spot. He was caught red-handed, holding the chewed-up two dollars in his front legs. Muttering with rage, Mama Bellini picked him up by his antennae, tossed him into the cricket

cage, and locked the gate behind him. When she had put the newsstand in order, she pulled out her knitting and began to work furiously. But she was so angry she kept dropping her stitches, and that made her angrier still.

Chester crouched in a far corner of the cage. Things had been going so well between Mama and him—but that was all ruined now. He half expected that she would pick him up, cage and all, and throw him onto the shuttle tracks.

At eight-thirty Mario and Papa arrived. Mario wanted to go to Coney Island for a swim today, but before he could even say "Good morning," Mama Bellini stretched out her hand and pointed sternly at Chester. There he was, with the evidence beside him.

A three-cornered conversation began. Mama denounced Chester as a money eater and said further that she suspected him of inviting mice and other unsavory characters into the newsstand at night.

Papa said he didn't think Chester had eaten the two dollars on purpose, and what difference did it make if a mouse or two came in? Mama said he had to go. Papa said he could stay, but he'd have to be kept in the cage. And Mario knew that Chester, like all people who are used to freedom, would rather die than live his life behind bars.

Finally it was decided that since the cricket was Mario's pet, the boy would have to replace the money. And when he had, Chester could come out again. Until then—the cage.

By working part-time delivering groceries, when he wasn't taking care of the newsstand, Mario thought he could earn enough in a couple of weeks to get Chester out of jail. Of course that would mean no swimming at Coney Island, and no movies, and no nothing, but it was worth it. He fed the cricket his breakfast—leftover asparagus tips and a piece of cabbage leaf. Chester had practically no appetite after what had happened. Then, when the cricket was finished, Mario said, "Goodbye," and told him not to worry, and went off to the grocery store to see about his job.

That night, after Papa had shut up the newsstand, Chester was hanging through the gilded bars of his cage. Earlier in the evening Mario had come back to feed him his supper, but then he had to leave right away to get in a few more hours of work. Most of the day Chester had spent inventing hopping games to try to keep himself entertained, but they didn't work, really. He was bored and lonely. The funny thing was that although he had been sleepy and kept wishing it were night, now that it was, he couldn't fall asleep.

Chester heard the soft padding of feet beneath him. Harry Cat sprang up and landed on the shelf. In a moment Tucker Mouse followed him from the stool, groaning with pain. He was still limping in his left hind leg where the magazine had hit him.

"How long is the sentence?" asked Harry.

"Until Mario can pay back the money," sighed Chester.

"Couldn't you get out on bail for the time being?" asked Tucker.

"No," said Chester. "And anyway, nobody has any bail. I'm surprised they let me off that easily."

Harry Cat folded his front paws over each other and rested his head on them. "Let me get this straight," he said. "Does Mario have to work for the money as punishment—or does he just have to get it somewhere?"

"He just has to get it," said Chester. "Why should he be punished? I'm the one who ate the money."

Harry looked at Tucker—a long look, as if he expected the mouse to say something. Tucker began to fidget. "Say, Chester, you want to escape?" he asked. "We can open the cage. You could come and live in the drain pipe."

"No." Chester shook his head. "It wouldn't be fair to Mario. I'll just have to serve out the time."

Harry looked at Tucker again and began tapping one of his paws. "Well?" he said finally.

Tucker moaned and massaged his sore spot. "Oh, my poor leg! That Mama Bellini can sure heave a magazine. Feel the bump, Harry," he offered.

"I felt it already," said Harry. "Now enough of the stalling. You have money."

"Tucker has money?" said Chester Cricket.

Tucker looked nervously from one to the other. "I have my life savings," he said in a pathetic voice.

"He's the richest mouse in New York," said Harry. "Old Money Bags Mouse, he's known as."

"Now wait a minute, Harry," said Tucker. "Let's not make too much from a few nickels and dimes."

"How did you get the money?" asked Chester.

Tucker Mouse cleared his throat and began wringing his two front feet. When he spoke, his voice was all choked up with emotion. "Years ago," he said, "when yet a little mouse I was, tender in age and lacking in experience, I moved from the sweet scenes of my childhood—Tenth Avenue, that is—into the Times Square subway station. And it was here that I learned the value of economicness— which means saving. Many and many an old mouse did I see, crawling away unwanted to a poor mouse's grave, because he had not saved. And I resolved that such a fate would never come to me."

"All of which means that you've got a pile of loot back there in the drain pipe," said Harry Cat.

"Just a minute, please, if you wouldn't mind," said Tucker. "I'll tell it in my own way." His voice became high and pitiful again. "So for all the long years of my youth, when I could have been gamboling—which means playing—with the other mousies, I saved. I saved paper, I saved food, I saved clothing—"

"Save time and get to the point," said Harry.

Tucker gave Harry a sour smile. "And I also saved money," he went on. "In the course of many years of scrounging, it was only natural I should find a certain amount of loose change. Often—oh, often, my friends," Tucker put his hand over his heart, "would I sit in the opening of my drain pipe, watching the human beings and waiting. And whenever one of them dropped a coin—*however small!*—pennies I love—I would dash out, at great peril to life and limb, and bring it back to my house. Ah, when I think of the tramping shoes

and the dangerous galoshes—! Many times have I had my toes stepped on and my whiskers torn off because of these labors. But it was worth it! Oh, it was worth it, my friends, on account of now I have two half dollars, five quarters, two dimes, six nickels, and eighteen pennies tucked away in the drain pipe!"

"Which makes two dollars and ninety-three cents," said Harry Cat, after doing some quick addition.

"And proud I am of it!" said Tucker Mouse.

"If you've got all that, why did you want to sleep on the two dollar bills in the cricket cage?" asked Chester.

"No folding money yet," said Tucker. "It was a new sensation."

"You can get Chester out and still have ninety-three cents left," said Harry Cat.

"But I'll be ruined," whimpered Tucker. "I'll be wiped out. Who will take care of me in my old age?"

"I will!" said Harry. "Now stop acting like a skinflint and let's get the money."

Chester rang the silver bell to get their attention. "I don't think Tucker should have to give up his life's savings," he said. "It's his money and he can do what he wants with it."

Tucker Mouse poked Harry in the ribs. "Listen to the cricket," he said. "Acting noble and making me look like a bum. Of course I'll give the money! Wherever mice are spoken of, never let it be said that Tucker Mouse was stingy with his worldly goods. Besides, I could think of it as rent I pay for sleeping in the cage."

In order that Tucker could keep at least one of each kind of coin, Harry Cat figured out that they should bring over one half dollar, four quarters, one dime, five nickels, and fifteen cents.

That would leave the mouse with a half dollar, a quarter, a dime, a nickel, and three cents.

"It's not a bad beginning," said Tucker. "I could make up the losses in a year, maybe."

The cat and the mouse had to make several trips back and forth between the drain pipe and the newsstand, carrying the money in their mouths. They passed the coins into the cage one by one, and Chester built them up into a column, starting with the half dollar on the bottom and ending with the dime, which was smallest, on top. It was morning by the time they were finished. They had just time enough to share half a hot dog before Mama Bellini was due to open the stand.

Mario came with her. He wanted to feed Chester early and then work all morning until he took over the newsstand at noon. When they lifted off the cover, Mama almost dropped her end. There was Chester sitting on top of the column of change, chirping merrily.

Mama's first suspicion was that the cricket had sneaked out and smuggled all the money from the cash register into the cage. But when she looked in the drawer, the money from the night before was still there.

Mario had the idea that Papa might have left it as a surprise. Mama shook her head. She would certainly have known if he had two dollars to leave anybody.

They asked Paul, the conductor, if he'd seen anyone around the newsstand. He said no. The only thing he'd noticed was that the big cat who sometimes prowled through the station had seemed to be busier than usual last night. And of course they knew that he couldn't have had anything to do with replacing the money.

But whoever left it, Mama Bellini was true to her word. Chester was allowed out of the cage, and no further questions were asked. Although she wouldn't have admitted it for the world, Mama felt the same way about money that Tucker Mouse did. When you had it, you had it—and you didn't bother too much about where it came from.

There was Chester sitting on
top of the column of change,
chirping merrily.

Think Critically

1. Why did Chester eat the two-dollar bill? CAUSE AND EFFECT

2. Why do you think Tucker Mouse takes so long to tell the story about how he saved up his money? DRAW CONCLUSIONS

3. Do you think it is fair of Mama and Papa Bellini to make Mario repay the money that Chester has eaten? Why or why not? MAKE JUDGMENTS

4. Use time-order words to describe how Chester Cricket is able to replace the two dollars. SEQUENCE: STORY EVENTS

5. **WRITE** Which character is more honest—Chester Cricket or Tucker Mouse? Be sure to include details and information from the story to support your answer. SHORT RESPONSE

About the Author

George Selden

George Selden started out as a playwright. A friend suggested that he try writing children's books. George Selden became famous for writing stories about animals who act like humans. His characters show the importance of friendships.

The Cricket in Times Square is an unusual story because of its city setting. Like Chester Cricket, George Selden came from Connecticut. He really heard a cricket chirp in the subway, and it made him homesick for the country. When he was asked to write a sequel, he waited ten years for an idea he thought was good enough. In the end, he wrote six more books about Chester and his friends.

 www.harcourtschool.com/storytown

Cricket Thermometer

°F °C

NH 41

220
200
180
160
140
120
100
80
60
40
20
0
20

110
100
90
80
70
60
50
40
30
20
10
0
10
20
30

Now where did that thermometer run off to? *Chirp, chirp.* Oh! There it is.

What You'll Need:

- watch with second hand or digital watch with second timer
- cricket
- jar
- nylon stocking
- rubber band

What to Do:

1. Place the cricket in a jar and secure the nylon over the top of the jar with a rubber band.
2. Count the number of cricket chirps in 15 seconds.
3. Add forty to the number of counted chirps. This sum equals the air temperature in degrees Fahrenheit.
4. Repeat the above process a few times; verify results with an actual themometer.
5. Release the cricket!

How does this work? Cold weather makes crickets sluggish, as it does many other animals. Crickets chirp more when the weather is warm than when the weather is cold, so you can estimate the temperature based on the activity of a nearby cricket.

Connections

Comparing Texts

1. Tucker Mouse helps his friend, Chester. Describe a time when a friend helped you, or a time when you helped a friend.

2. Compare and contrast "The Cricket in Times Square" with "Cricket Thermometer."

3. Tucker Mouse worked hard to save his money. What are some reasons that people save money?

Vocabulary Review

Word Sort

Sort the Vocabulary Words into categories such as actions or feelings. Work with a small group to compare your sorted words. Then choose two Vocabulary Words in each category and write a sentence that shows why they belong in the same category.

forlornly

fidget

pathetic

resolved

scrounging

noble

stingy

suspicion

Fluency Practice

Partner Reading

Your reading rate is how quickly you can read a text correctly. Work with a partner to choose a portion of "The Cricket in Times Square" to reread aloud. Read the passage as your partner listens and times your reading with a wall clock or a stopwatch. Have your partner give you feedback on your reading rate. Then reread the passage, and try to improve your reading rate. Switch roles and repeat the process.

Writing

Write a Story

Think about two very different animals that might meet and become friends. Write a short story about how the two animals meet.

Event 1

↓

Event 2

↓

Event 3

My Writing Checklist

Writing Trait ➤ Conventions

✓ I used a graphic organizer to help plan my writing.

✓ I described the events in my story in order.

✓ I used correct spelling and grammar in my story.

CONTENTS

Lesson 24

MANGROVE WILDERNESS
NATURE'S NURSERY
TEXT & PHOTOGRAPHS BY BIANCA LAVIES

MANGROVE

Genre: Encyclopedia Article

Focus Skill

Text Structure: Sequence

Authors of expository nonfiction organize their ideas in what are called **text structures**. One text structure authors use is **sequence**.

- Authors of scientific topics use sequence to describe growth or change in nature.
- Authors of historical topics use sequence to explain events in history.

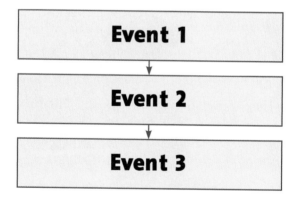

Event 1
Event 2
Event 3

Tip

Look for words that give clues about time passing to help you identify the sequence of ideas.

Read the paragraph. Then look at the graphic organizer below. It shows the sequence of the events in the paragraph.

In summer, a female alligator makes her nest on a raised mound or bank near the water. Then she lays about thirty eggs and covers them with plants and grasses. About nine weeks later, the eggs hatch. For about two years, the baby alligators stay by their mother, often riding on her back or head.

Event 1 In summer, an alligator makes her nest.

Event 2 She lays about thirty eggs.

Event 3 The eggs hatch in about nine weeks.

Try This!

Find one more event from the paragraph that you could add to the chart. Where does this event belong? What clue words help you understand the sequence?

 www.harcourtschool.com/storytown

Vocabulary

Build Robust Vocabulary

- remarkable
- extract
- stealthy
- advantage
- withstand
- suitable

Florida's Great Reefs

Florida's coral reefs are the home of a **remarkable** group of living things. Corals are actually very small animals that live in clusters called *colonies*. Corals eat tiny animals that float through the water. They also **extract** nutrients from plants that live inside their bodies. As individual corals die, new ones grow on top of them. Over time, the buildup of corals grows into a reef.

Coral reefs are very beautiful to look at. The tiny plants that live inside corals can cause them to take on all the colors of the rainbow.

At night, **stealthy** predators such as eels swim around coral reefs, looking for a tasty meal.

Coral reefs benefit people. One **advantage** is that they help protect nearby land from waves and storms. Reefs can help the economy of the places near where they grow. Millions of visitors swim, boat, and snorkel among coral reefs every year.

Coral reefs are easily damaged. They cannot **withstand** a lot of human activity. Powerful storm waves can harm reefs. Damaged corals take a long time to grow back. Some coral reefs are hundreds of years old.

Even under **suitable** conditions, it can take 1,000 years for a reef to grow from 1 foot to 16 feet in height.

 www.harcourtschool.com/storytown

Word Champion

Your challenge this week is to use the Vocabulary Words outside the classroom. Post a list of the words where you can see it easily. Use as many of the words as you can when you talk with family members or friends. For example, you might tell your parents about a remarkable thing you saw. At the end of each day, write in your vocabulary journal the words you used and tell how you used them.

MANGROVE
WILDERNESS
NATURE'S NURSERY

TEXT & PHOTOGRAPHS BY BIANCA LAVIES

Expository Nonfiction

Genre Study

Expository nonfiction gives facts and information about a topic. As you read, look for

- facts and details about a subject or topic.

- text structure—the way ideas and information are organized.

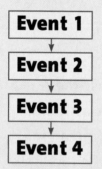

> Event 1
> ↓
> Event 2
> ↓
> Event 3
> ↓
> Event 4

Comprehension Strategy

Ask questions while you read. Then look for the answers in the text.

MANGROVE WILDERNESS

by Bianca Lavies

A frog, a crab, a fish, and a bird—these four creatures, and many more, hunt, seek shelter, and raise their young in forests along the southern coast of Florida. They are part of a vast web of animal life that is supported by a remarkable kind of tree: the red mangrove.

It is an odd-looking tree that seems to stand on stilts, and it grows where few other trees can—in salt water. The stilts are actually the mangrove's roots. They are called *prop roots*, because they help prop, or support, the tree against the ocean's strong waves and tides.

Red mangroves grow in warm tropical regions near the earth's equator. In Florida they flourish along the edges of the swampy Everglades, at the southern tip of the state. There the land is broken up into thousands of small islands by inlets and waterways.

The trees thrive in these inlets, or estuaries, where fresh river water leaves the land and meets the salty ocean tides. The water around the trees takes on a reddish color from the natural dye called *tannin* in their bark.

A red mangrove tree produces about three hundred seeds a year. By no means do all the seeds survive, but if the conditions are suitable, a lone red mangrove like this one will be surrounded by a forest of young trees in about twenty-five years.

The new forest will be a nursery for all kinds of wildlife. Creatures from the tiniest worms to huge birds, like pelicans, will be able to find food, shelter, and safe nesting places among the mangroves' tangled roots and full branches.

Life Cycle of the Mangrove

Bright yellow flowers are the first step in the formation of mangrove seeds. More than a thousand flowers bloom on each mature tree in the spring. After a month, the inch-wide blossoms drop off, leaving behind rust brown fruits the size of plums. Each fruit contains a single seed.

◀ Mature mangrove trees bloom every spring.

631

▲ Mangrove seeds sprout and become seedlings.

In about two months, something unusual happens. The seed inside each fruit sprouts into a seedling. The root end emerges from the fruit first, followed by the stem.

The seeds of most kinds of trees do not begin to sprout until they have fallen off the parent tree and landed on warm, moist earth. If the red mangrove seeds were simply to drop, the salt in the ocean water would keep them from sprouting. So the seeds take advantage of their parent tree's ability to extract nutrients and moisture from the water and soil without taking in any harmful salt. Staying attached to the parent tree, the seeds grow into six-to twelve-inch seedlings that are themselves resistant to salt.

Development of Mangrove Seedlings

▲ A mangrove seedling takes root in the bottom of shallow ocean water.

These cigar-shaped seedlings, called *propagules*, have a store of nutrients to keep them alive after they drop into the water. They are also buoyant and can float away, out of the shade of the parent tree, to areas where they will have more room and sunlight to grow.

When the seedlings fall, some drop like darts, root end first, into the sandy shore or the shallows. These seedlings put down roots near the parent tree. Others float in a horizontal position until their root ends become waterlogged and heavy. The weight pulls the root ends down, and the seedlings float with their stems upright. They may drift for thousands of miles, living up to a year, before they come to shallow water. Then, their root ends bump along the water's bottom. This triggers the growth of a network of small roots that eventually catch in the soil. Scientists believe the red mangroves in Florida are the descendants of seedlings that drifted all the way from Africa.

Growth of the Mangrove

A couple of years ago the tree in this photo was a six- to twelve-inch seedling. Now it is about two feet tall. It will continue to grow several inches a year throughout its life. The average height for a red mangrove in Florida is thirty feet, but if the conditions are good, this tree could grow to be eighty feet tall.

Red mangrove trees grow best in shallow water like that around the oyster bars off Florida's southwest coast. Oyster bars are underwater mounds made up of colonies of living oysters and the shells of their dead predecessors.

The water around these bars, which is often only one or two feet deep, is ideal for red mangroves. The trees actually turn oyster bars and sandbars into islands. As debris in the roots becomes soil, land eventually forms around the trees. Red mangroves that once sprouted around old exposed coral reefs helped to create the islands we call the Florida Keys.

Once the ground is built up around the red mangroves, other kinds of mangroves—black, white, and buttonwood—move in. But red mangroves are usually first, and most often at the water's edge. They seem to be the most successful at growing in tidal salt water, and their strong roots are best able to withstand storm winds and waves, preventing the land around them from being washed into the sea.

▲ Mangrove forests off the coast of Florida

However, storms with extremely high winds, like hurricanes, can uproot even the sturdiest red mangrove trees. Hurricane Andrew swept through southern Florida in 1992, destroying mangrove forests along twenty miles of coastline. But because the seedlings can live for a year in the water, new young trees soon sprouted where the old ones once grew.

635

Life in the Mangrove Forest

The mangrove leaves floating in the picture above are an essential part of the mangrove wilderness food chain. Even before the leaves fall from the mangrove trees, they are food for airborne bacteria and fungi. These microscopic life forms are able to break down a material in the leaf called *cellulose* that many other creatures cannot easily digest. Once the leaves drop into the water, more bacteria and fungi attach to them, making the leaves rich in protein, and good food for larger animals. Small crabs and other crustaceans gnaw at the leaves, breaking them into pepper-speck bits called *detritus*.

Pink shrimps and many kinds of worms, mollusks, and crabs dine on the detritus. They are eaten by small fish, which are in turn eaten by larger fish. The larger fish are themselves eaten by birds, continuing the food chain.

In the photograph bottom right, hundreds of mangrove snapper and other fish hunt for smaller fish among the gray-green shadows of the mangrove roots. Orange sponges, oysters, and other filter feeders cling to the roots, trapping tiny particles of detritus as they strain water through their bodies. We humans eat oysters, fish, shrimps, and other animals from different stages of the food chain supported by the red mangrove trees.

Occasionally an alligator enters the coastal mangrove forests from its inland home in the grassy swamps of the Everglades. A young alligator will eat the many pink shrimps, small fish, and crabs in this rich marine feeding ground.

But a fully grown alligator would visit the mangrove forest in search of big fish and such mammals as a raccoon.

▲ The Everglades rat snake is one of the many inhabitants of a mangrove forest.

In the branches of a red mangrove tree, an Everglades rat snake is waiting silently to snatch a small rodent, bird, or tree frog. A rat snake is a constrictor. When it catches a meal, it does not eat the animal immediately but curls its body around the creature and squeezes until its prey is no longer moving.

At low tide, a raccoon pokes its long nimble fingers among the mangrove roots, searching for crabs. Strong, sharp teeth allow the raccoon to eat hard-shell crabs and other shellfish.

▲ **Green-backed heron**

But this stealthy predator's favorite food is coon oysters, which it can find clinging in huge clusters to the sturdy mangrove roots.

Early in the morning, a green-backed heron stands motionless at the water's edge. The bird has left its roost among the mangrove branches to search for fish, worms, or insects to eat. Nearby, a snowy egret stands equally still, watching for fish or shrimps. Both birds will strike swiftly, grabbing their prey with daggerlike beaks.

Green-backed herons and snowy egrets are just two of more than twenty different kinds of birds that inhabit the red mangrove forests.

▼ Snowy egret

On an island formed by mangroves, two brown pelicans are building their nest. The male collects leaves and sticks from neighboring mangrove trees, preserving the branches of his own. He returns to the nest high in the leafy canopy, and with a clumsy flapping of his wings, he swoops to present the building material to his mate.

The islands are safe nesting places, or rookeries, for birds. The surrounding water offers a measure of protection from the egg-eating raccoons and snakes.

And with so many birds nesting and roosting together, one is sure to spot an enemy, such as a swimming raccoon, in time to squawk a warning to the rest.

These three white ibis (above right) have just landed on the mangrove island where they spend every night. As the day ends, thousands of birds, including herons, egrets, cormorants, frigate birds, and pelicans, arrive at their own special mangrove islands. There is a lot of squawking as the birds compete for a place to perch. Some dive into the water for one last meal, then return to their branches as the light fades.

Suddenly the sun is gone. Silence follows. The birds settle down to sleep and gather strength for another busy day in the red mangrove wilderness.

One of the many birds that spend the night on the mangrove island ▼

THINK CRITICALLY

1. Explain how new mangrove seedlings form.

    TEXT STRUCTURE: SEQUENCE

2. How do red mangroves help create islands such as those in the Florida Keys? CAUSE AND EFFECT

3. Why do you think the author wrote "Mangrove Wilderness"? What is her viewpoint about this topic?
   AUTHOR'S PURPOSE AND PERSPECTIVE

4. Think of a park or forest near where you live. What are some plants and animals that make up the food chain there? PRIOR KNOWLEDGE

5. **WRITE** Scientists believe that the red mangroves in Florida are the descendents of seedlings that came from Africa. Use information and details from the selection to explain:

   - why it is important that red mangrove seedlings stay attached to the parent tree until they are 6 to 12 inches long, and
   - what happens to the seedlings once they fall from the parent tree. EXTENDED RESPONSE

Bianca Lavies

Writer, photographer, and adventurer Bianca Lavies has done things that many people only dream of doing. She once sailed a 30-foot boat all the way from South America to the United States. She has also waded through shark-infested waters and spent time in the company of snakes, spiders, and killer bees in order to get a good photo.

Bianca Lavies says that taking the photographs for "Mangrove Wilderness" was one big, exciting adventure. She guided a small sailboat off the southwest coast of Florida, visiting the mangrove islands there. She lived in a house in a mangrove swamp for two years, sharing her living quarters with three-inch spiders and a coral snake! "Sand flies and fleas feasted on me," she says, "taking their turn in the mangrove food chain."

 www.harcourtschool.com/
storytown

MAN

The **mangrove** is a land-building tree. It lives in marshes, on seashores, and on riverbanks. Its roots let water through, but trap leaves, shells, and driftwood. Slowly, this material forms new soil around the mangrove roots.

Red mangroves grow in salt water. Their roots extend a foot or more into the soil. They are able to absorb water without taking in salt. Bacteria, algae, and fungi attach to the roots. They form the start of a food chain that includes crab, shrimp, and alligators.

Pink shrimp hatch in the Dry Tortuga Islands, one hundred miles off the southwest coast of Florida. They drift on the tides to Florida's mangrove forests where they feed and grow.

GROVE

FLORIDA

Everglades
National Park

Florida has nearly a half-million acres of mangrove forests. White, black, and red mangroves grow in the state. Red mangroves grow thickly along the southern tip of Florida in Everglades National Park.

Connections

Comparing Texts

1. Imagine that you go along with Bianca Lavies as she takes photographs of the mangrove forests. What do you like and dislike about the trip?

2. Name three facts you learned about mangroves from "Mangrove Wilderness" and "Mangrove."

3. Do you think a human being could live in the mangrove community? Explain your answer.

Vocabulary Review

Rate a Situation

Work with a partner. Read aloud each sentence below. Point to the spot on the line that describes how happy you would feel in each situation. Explain your choices.

Least ——————————————————— Most
Happy   Happy

- You had an **advantage** in a game you were playing.

- A dentist had to **extract** one of your teeth.

- People thought you were a **remarkable** person.

advantage

extract

remarkable

stealthy

suitable

withstand

Fluency Practice

Repeated Reading

Your reading rate is how quickly you can read a text correctly. You can improve your reading rate with practice. Choose a passage of three paragraphs from "Mangrove Wilderness." Read the passage aloud once. Then use a stopwatch or wall clock to time your second reading. Set a goal for an improved time. Reread the passage until you reach your goal.

Writing

Write a Nature Log Entry

Imagine that you have just spent 24 hours in a mangrove forest, observing the creatures that live there. Write a nature log entry in which you tell about the animals you saw or heard.

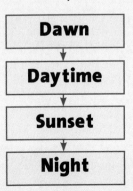

Dawn
↓
Daytime
↓
Sunset
↓
Night

My Writing Checklist

Writing Trait ➤ Conventions

✔ I used a graphic organizer to plan my writing.

✔ I used details from "Mangrove Wilderness" in my entry.

✔ I used correct grammar, spelling, and punctuation.

CONTENTS

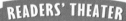

Readers' Theater
TRAVEL SHOW

Welcome to
Chinatown
illustrated by Tomer Hanuka

Amelia's Garden
by Miriam Kirby
illustrated by Sarajo Frieden

Reading Fiction
REALISTIC FICTION

destinations

aspects

vigorously

reconstruct

gorgeous

festive

ornate

symbolize

expectantly

misfortune

Reading for Fluency

When reading a script aloud,

- Match your **intonation** to the character's mood.

- Make sure your **reading rate** is fast enough to hold listeners' attention.

Welcome to Chinatown!

illustrated by Tomer Hanuka

Characters

Kim Richards, Co-host of *New Destinations*

Tom Taylor, Co-host of *New Destinations*

Garrett, History Correspondent

Maria, History Correspondent

Connor, On-the-street Correspondent

Aimee, On-the-street Correspondent

Emily, Shopping and Dining Correspondent

Monica, Shopping and Dining Correspondent

Kim: Hello again, everyone, and welcome to another episode of *New Destinations*! I'm Kim Richards, and with me, as always, is my co-host, Tom Taylor.

Tom: Hi, everyone! Today's new destination is one that's rich in history and culture. Today, Kim and I welcome you to Chinatown!

651

Fluency Tip

To improve your reading rate, practice reading portions of text that have unfamiliar terms.

Kim: We have a great show planned for you! Today, you'll learn about Chinatown's history as part of San Francisco and California. We'll also talk about Chinatown's architecture and other aspects of the area that make it unique.

Tom: Then we'll tell you about some of the interesting things you can do when you visit Chinatown.

Kim: We hope to give you a sense of what it's like to visit and to live in this unusual community.

Tom: You might even become curious enough to want to see for yourself the remarkable things we describe!

Kim: Let's start by turning things over to Garrett and Maria, our history correspondents.

Garrett: Thanks, Kim. There are Chinatowns in major cities all over the world. San Francisco's Chinatown is one of the oldest. It's also the third-largest Chinatown in North America.

Maria: That's right, Garrett. As old as it is, however, this Chinatown is not the one that was built by Chinese immigrants in the 1850s. That Chinatown was destroyed in the 1906 San Francisco earthquake.

Garrett: The earthquake and the fires caused by the earthquake destroyed more than 500 city blocks!

Maria: The first large groups of Chinese immigrants made the journey to the United States in the 1850s. The immigrants came here for opportunities to earn a suitable living by working on the railroads.

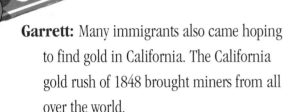

Garrett: Many immigrants also came hoping to find gold in California. The California gold rush of 1848 brought miners from all over the world.

Maria: These first immigrants settled in what is today the heart of Chinatown. They built homes, opened restaurants, and started businesses.

Garrett: After the earthquake, the residents worked vigorously to reconstruct Chinatown. To encourage tourists to visit, they designed the buildings and streets with the features that everyone now recognizes as typical of Chinatown.

Maria: Starting in the 1950s, more groups of Chinese immigrants settled in the United States.

Garrett: The population of San Francisco's Chinatown boomed. New residents built smaller Chinatowns in neighboring areas, but the original Chinatown is still the one tourists visit most often. Back to you, Kim and Tom.

Tom: Thanks, Garrett and Maria. Chinatown is such an interesting place to visit!

Kim: It's a major tourist attraction. Did you know that Chinatown attracts more visitors than San Francisco's famous landmark, the Golden Gate Bridge?

Tom: One of the main streets in Chinatown is Grant Avenue. Our on-the-street correspondents, Connor and Aimee, are there now to tell us what people can see and do on Grant Avenue.

Connor: Thanks, Tom. Here on Grant Avenue colorful lanterns, curved roofs, and gorgeous columns carved from stone all give Chinatown its festive look.

Aimee: They definitely do, Connor! Grant Avenue is also where you'll find the famous Dragon Gate, an arch that stands at the southern entrance to Chinatown. The Dragon Gate gets its name from the two ornate dragon sculptures that sit on top of the arch.

Connor: On Grant Avenue you'll find many restaurants and shops. You can buy the perfect souvenir to remember your visit!

Aimee: Be sure to visit Portsmouth Square, too. There's always something interesting going on there.

Connor: In the mornings, you can watch groups of people practicing *tai chi*. It's a form of Chinese exercise that helps people develop better balance and flexibility.

Aimee: We'll be back a little later in the program to tell you about the Chinese New Year parade, which will be starting here in just a few minutes! For now, let's go back to Kim and Tom.

Kim: Chinatown has many interesting grocery stores and markets. You might be surprised by how different they are from the supermarket where you shop!

654

Tom: Chinatown grocers import many of the items they sell from countries in Asia. They provide the ingredients to area restuarants, where you can eat Vietnamese, Chinese, Thai, and Malaysian food. For a report on all the great food and shopping in Chinatown, let's go to Emily and Monica, live at the Good Luck Grocery on Stockton Street!

Emily: Thank you, Tom! For many years, markets like the Good Luck Grocery were the only places you could get things like jasmine rice from Thailand, oolong tea from China, or oyster sauce from the Philippines.

Monica: A market in Chinatown may also sell fish and other select seafood items. Don't be surprised if you see large aquariums filled with fish, lobsters, and crabs in a Chinatown market. Seafood is a popular ingredient in traditional Chinese recipes.

Emily: Depending on what time of year you visit Chinatown, you might find different things at the market. For example, around the time of the Chinese New Year, usually near the end of January, you'll find many people buying oranges and tangerines.

Monica: In Chinese culture, oranges and tangerines symbolize happiness. People give them as New Year's gifts to friends and relatives. In fact, the Chinese word for "orange," *ju*, sounds a lot like the word for "good luck" in Chinese!

Emily: The markets are not the only places you can buy fruits and vegetables in Chinatown. When you walk down Grant Avenue, you'll see street vendors with carts just about everywhere!

Monica: These merchants also sell newspapers, clothes, and souvenirs. You could spend an entire day just looking at what everyone has for sale.

Emily: You can also go into the many shops that line the street. Like the markets, these shops import much of what they sell from countries in Asia.

Monica: Of course, no visit to Chinatown would be complete without a meal. You'll have no trouble finding a restaurant. The hard part will be choosing which one to try!

Fluency Tip

Practice reading your lines until you can read them at a consistent reading rate.

Emily: Many restaurants in Chinatown serve *dim sum* in the afternoon. *Dim sum* means "heart's delight." *Dim sum* menus offer a lot of choices, but everything comes in small portions, so you can try a lot of different things.

Monica: A typical order consists of steamed buns and dumplings filled with a mixture of beef, chicken, or pork and vegetables. Tea is also served with *dim sum*.

Emily: If you're in a large group, everyone can order different things. Sharing and trying what everyone orders is part of the fun of eating *dim sum*! Kim and Tom, you have to get over here to try this!

Tom: Thanks, Emily! Save us some if you can!

Kim: If you intend to go to Chinatown, think about visiting when the Chinese celebrate the New Year. As you may recall, Emily said earlier that the Chinese New Year usually falls around the end of January.

Tom: Chinese New Year is among the most important traditional Chinese holidays. The celebration lasts for fifteen days. Let's go back now to Connor and Aimee for their report on the parade.

Aimee: Thanks again, Tom. On the first day of the celebration, you'll see throngs of people along the streets. They're expectantly waiting for the Chinese New Year parade and the lion dancers.

Connor: Lion dancing plays an important part in any Chinese New Year celebration. The tradition of the lion dance can be traced back more than a thousand years in Chinese culture!

Aimee: Lion dance performers wear a lion costume, which usually has a very large head. A single performer operates the head, moving its eyes and jaw, while dancing energetically.

Connor: Sometimes a pair of dancers operates a lion costume. The second dancer forms the back and the rear legs of the lion. This requires coordination and practice. The two dancers huddled under the costume must move together perfectly.

Aimee: To those who celebrate the Chinese New Year, the lion symbolizes courage. Performing the lion dance is believed to frighten away misfortune.

Connor: Residents celebrate the fifteenth day of the New Year with the Lantern Festival. On the night of the Lantern Festival, you'll see children everywhere carrying lanterns with many complex shapes and designs.

Aimee: You'll also find parades during the Lantern Festival. Light fills the streets as lanterns of every shape and color brighten the night. Back to you, Kim and Tom.

Tom: Thank you, Aimee! Thanks to all our correspondents for their interesting reports on our show today.

Kim: Thank you for joining us. No matter what time of year you choose to visit Chinatown, you'll have a wonderful experience. We'll see you again soon, on the next episode of *New Destinations*!

Tom: Good bye!

COMPREHENSION STRATEGIES
Review

Reading Fiction

Bridge to Reading for Meaning Realistic fiction has characters, settings, and events that are like people, places, and events in real life. In realistic fiction, a character's actions are affected by his or her motivations, the plot, and the setting. The notes on page 659 point out some features of realistic fiction, including setting, characters, and plot events. How can understanding these features help you read realistic fiction?

Review the Focus Strategies

If you do not understand what you are reading, use the comprehension strategies you learned about in this theme.

 Use Story Structure
Use story structure to understand how the characters, setting, and plot events fit together in a story.

 Ask Questions
As you read, stop to ask yourself questions about the characters, the setting, or the plot events to make sure you understand what you are reading.

As you read "Amelia's Garden" on pages 660–663, think about where and how to use the strategies.

CHARACTERS
Characters are the people in a story. They are like real people, and they often learn a lesson or change by the end of a story.

Amelia's Garden

by Miriam Kirby
illustrated by Sarajo Frieden

To Amelia, it seemed the whole world had traveled to Adams Avenue. Her neighbors came from far away and spoke many languages. Amelia's grandmother said, "All those strange-sounding words, what an awful noise!" Amelia thought the mixed-together voices sounded like music.

Mrs. Yasdani chanted in Persian. Mr. and Mrs. Quon called to their four children in Chinese. Mr. Leder and Mr. Strauss played chess and bickered happily in Hebrew and German. Señor Sanchez always greeted Amelia in Spanish, "¡Buenos dias! (BWAYN•ohs DEE•ahs) Good morning, Amelia."

When Amelia said *buenos dias* to Mrs. Yasdani, she turned away.

Mrs. Quon was leaning out her window, hanging laundry. Amelia shouted, "¡Buenos dias!" Mrs. Quon screeched and dropped a soggy sock on Amelia's head.

That day, Amelia realized her neighbors didn't speak to each other.

Everyone said "hello" to Amelia. They smiled and waved when she walked down the street. Why did people talk to her but not to each other?

Amelia asked her grandmother about it. Gran said, "Peas grow in pods, crows fly in flocks."

"What does that mean?"

Gran explained, "People like people just like themselves. They are afraid of anyone different."

"But Gran, people are just people."

"Yes child, but their different languages make them different."

"That's the silliest thing I've ever heard," said Amelia.

Amelia studied what made people different. She decided people were not alike at all. They only thought they were. Strangest of all, thinking you were the same as a few people made you different from everyone else.

People were like flowers, all of them pretty in their own way. Amelia imagined a garden with nothing but blue petunias. How boring!

She could help her neighborhood be like a garden brimming with every kind of flower.

SETTING
The setting is where and when a story takes place. The authors of realistic fiction use a setting that is real or could be real.

PLOT EVENTS
Plot events are the actions that take place in a story. The characters and the setting affect the plot events.

Apply the Strategies Read this story about Amelia and her neighbors. As you read, use different comprehension strategies, such as asking questions, to help you understand the text.

Amelia's Garden

by Miriam Kirby
illustrated by Sarajo Frieden

To Amelia, it seemed the whole world had traveled to Adams Avenue. Her neighbors came from far away and spoke many languages. Amelia's grandmother said, "All those strange-sounding words, what an awful noise!" Amelia thought the mixed-together voices sounded like music.

Mrs. Yasdani chanted in Persian. Mr. and Mrs. Quon called to their four children in Chinese. Mr. Leder and Mr. Strauss played chess and bickered happily in Hebrew and German. Señor Sanchez always greeted Amelia in Spanish, "¡Buenos dias! (BWAYN•ohs DEE•ahs) Good morning, Amelia."

Pay attention to the characters' words and actions to help you understand the plot. **USE STORY STRUCTURE**

When Amelia said *buenos dias* to Mrs. Yasdani, she turned away.

Mrs. Quon was leaning out her window, hanging laundry. Amelia shouted, "¡Buenos dias!" Mrs. Quon screeched and dropped a soggy sock on Amelia's head.

That day, Amelia realized her neighbors didn't speak to each other.

Everyone said "hello" to Amelia. They smiled and waved when she walked down the street. Why did people talk to her but not to each other?

Amelia asked her grandmother about it. Gran said, "Peas grow in pods, crows fly in flocks."

"What does that mean?"

Gran explained, "People like people just like themselves. They are afraid of anyone different."

"But Gran, people are just people."

"Yes child, but their different languages make them different."

"That's the silliest thing I've ever heard," said Amelia.

Amelia studied what made people different. She decided people were not alike at all. They only thought they were. Strangest of all, thinking you were the same as a few people made you different from everyone else.

People were like flowers, all of them pretty in their own way. Amelia imagined a garden with nothing but blue petunias. How boring!

She could help her neighborhood be like a garden brimming with every kind of flower.

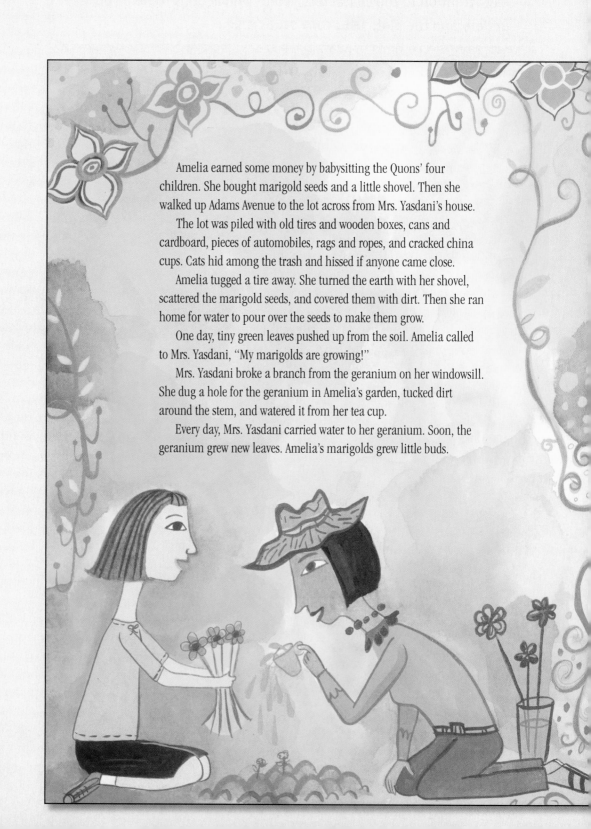

Amelia earned some money by babysitting the Quons' four children. She bought marigold seeds and a little shovel. Then she walked up Adams Avenue to the lot across from Mrs. Yasdani's house.

The lot was piled with old tires and wooden boxes, cans and cardboard, pieces of automobiles, rags and ropes, and cracked china cups. Cats hid among the trash and hissed if anyone came close.

Amelia tugged a tire away. She turned the earth with her shovel, scattered the marigold seeds, and covered them with dirt. Then she ran home for water to pour over the seeds to make them grow.

One day, tiny green leaves pushed up from the soil. Amelia called to Mrs. Yasdani, "My marigolds are growing!"

Mrs. Yasdani broke a branch from the geranium on her windowsill. She dug a hole for the geranium in Amelia's garden, tucked dirt around the stem, and watered it from her tea cup.

Every day, Mrs. Yasdani carried water to her geranium. Soon, the geranium grew new leaves. Amelia's marigolds grew little buds.

Stop and Think

As you read, stop to ask yourself questions about how the characters, the setting, and the plot events work together to tell the story. **ASK QUESTIONS**

Next, Amelia discovered two small palm trees near her marigolds. Señor Sanchez sloshed buckets of water on the trees to keep them green.

Mr. Strauss and Mr. Leder pushed wooden boxes together to make a table and chairs in Amelia's garden. They unfolded their chessboard and played there every afternoon.

Day after day, plants grew taller and the garden grew larger. People admired Amelia's marigolds. Bit by bit, they carried trash away and planted roses and daisies.

Señor Sanchez planted corn. Gran planted blackeyed peas. Mr. Strauss planted tomatoes. Mr. Leder planted lettuce so they could make salads. The Quon children filled stacked tires for blackberry vines.

In Amelia's garden, people talked to each other and smiled. Señor Sanchez learned to say "Ni hao. Ni hao ma?" (NEE•HOW•MAH), which means "Hello, how are you?" in Chinese. Mrs. Quon learned from Mrs. Yasdani that the best part of Persian rice is the golden stuff on the bottom of the pot. Mr. Leder finally beat Mr. Strauss at chess and told everyone—twice, at least.

Gran agreed with Amelia. All those different languages did sound like music when you listened in just the right way.

READING-WRITING
CONNECTION

Lesson 26 ❯

Lesson 27 ❯

Theme 6 Exploring Our World

Diego Rivera, *Sunsets*

CONTENTS

Lesson 26

Main Idea and Details

The **main idea** is the most important idea in a text. **Details** are pieces of information that support the main idea. Often the author states the main idea in a topic sentence. This sentence may appear near the beginning of a nonfiction passage. Identifying the main idea and supporting details in a passage will help you better understand what you read.

Detail	Detail	Detail

Main Idea

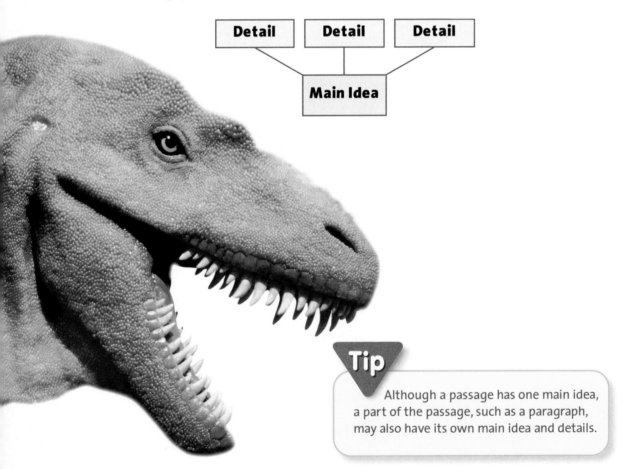

Tip

Although a passage has one main idea, a part of the passage, such as a paragraph, may also have its own main idea and details.

Read the paragraph below. The main idea is stated in the topic sentence. Then look at the graphic organizer. It shows the main idea and three details that support it.

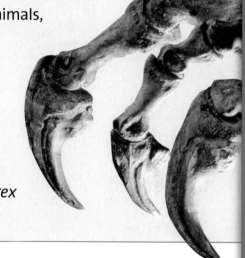

Dinosaurs can be classified by the type of food they ate. Carnivorous dinosaurs ate animals, and herbivorous dinosaurs ate plants. Carnivorous dinosaurs had pointed teeth, sharp claws, and strong jaws for catching and eating animals. Herbivorous dinosaurs had flat teeth for chewing plants. You can probably guess which category *Tyrannosaurus rex* belonged to!

Detail	**Detail**	**Detail**
Some dinosaurs ate plants.	Some dinosaurs ate animals.	Carnivorous dinosaurs had pointed teeth, sharp claws, and strong jaws.

Main Idea

Dinosaurs can be classified by the type of food they ate.

Try This!

Look back at the paragraph about dinosaurs. Find another detail that supports the main idea.

 www.harcourtschool.com/storytown

Vocabulary

Build Robust Vocabulary

- contraption
- submerged
- massive
- eerie
- roamed
- obstacles
- elegant
- complicated

A Look at the Past

What if it were possible to build a **contraption** that would let you take photos of Earth in the distant past? What might you see? You would probably see that most of Earth's surface was **submerged** under a single ocean. Some scientists believe that all of the continents were once joined as a giant supercontinent. An enormous ocean covered the rest of Earth.

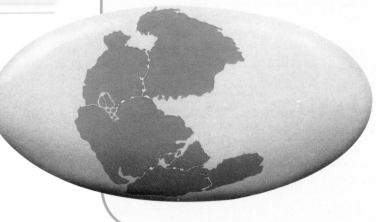

Scientists have named the **massive**, prehistoric supercontinent *Pangaea*.

670

You might find it **eerie** to look in on such a different Earth. However, paleontologists and other scientists would be delighted to be able to see the prehistoric landscape and the creatures that **roamed** across it.

Modern scientists face **obstacles** when they try to make models of extinct animals. They cannot be certain about details such as color, shape, and skin type. Perhaps some of these creatures looked quite **elegant.** With a camera to look back across time, scientists would have a simple way to find answers to **complicated** questions about prehistoric times. Sadly, such a camera exists only in the imagination.

www.harcourtschool.com/storytown

Word Detective

This week, search for the Vocabulary Words around you. Pay attention when you read magazine articles and when you listen to conversations or news broadcasts. In your vocabulary journal, write the Vocabulary Words you see or hear, and list where you found each one.

Expository Nonfiction

Genre Study

Expository nonfiction gives information on a topic in an interesting way. As you read, look for

- information divided into sections with headings.

- photographs and illustrations with captions.

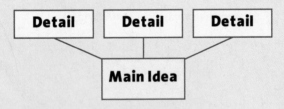

| Detail | Detail | Detail |

| Main Idea |

Comprehension Strategy

While you read, pause to **summarize** difficult sections of text.

672

Dragons and Dinosaurs

by Meg Moss

How do we know we are right when we imagine the past? Well, we really don't. We weren't there. When it comes to dinosaurs, scientists have only bones and fossils—and now computers—to help them understand how these ancient beasts might have looked.

Until very recently, people didn't know what the world was like before humans. They didn't understand that entire species could disappear from the earth, or go extinct.

No human ever saw a living dinosaur, but our ancestors did find—and wonder about—dinosaur bones.

PREHISTORY MYSTERY

Ancient people had their own ways of explaining the strange bones they found. They thought the bones were the remains of giants, dragons, sea monsters, and other creatures you read about today in fairy tales and myths. Consider the legend of the griffin, a fantastic cross between a lion and an eagle once believed to live in the deserts of China. People all over the ancient world—Asia, the Middle East, and Greece and Rome—told stories of these griffins. Each culture imagined them differently, but most ancient art shows them with gigantic beaks, claws, wings, and catlike bodies.

Now take a look at the skull of a small dinosaur we call *Protoceratops*. Scientists have found many of these skulls in the Gobi desert in Mongolia (a region of China), where *Protoceratops* lived about 80 million years ago.

The real *Protoceratops*? Scientists think so, but even if the shape is right, we may never know what color it was. We can only guess based on modern reptiles.

Protoceratops had a huge, birdlike beak designed to chop up the plants it ate and to defend itself. A large "frill" on its head and bony bumps on its cheeks (probably both a form of protective armor) give its skull a monstrous look. Ancient people who saw these skulls guessed that they were the remains of winged, lionlike birds that guarded gold in the desert mountains. They thought they were griffins.

When you look at its skull, it's easy to see why people once thought *Protoceratops* was a fantastic birdlike creature.

The ancient people were not far from the truth. These were the bones of amazing creatures, though not human giants, nor dragons, nor griffins. In the 1800s, scientists began to recognize that ancient bones and fossils belonged to long-extinct animals, which no one, of course, had ever seen. The mystery deepened.

What did these animals really look like? The task of arranging the bones in the proper order and accurately imagining the flesh and muscle that covered them was quite a challenge.

THE TERRIBLE LIZARDS

Pretend for a moment that you have never seen a bicycle before. You have no idea what it does or how it is used.

Now suppose you stumble upon a funny-looking triangular leather thing sticking out of the earth. Next to it lies a curved metal bar with plastic ends.

Farther along, a piece of rubber.

What could these things be? Are they parts of a single contraption? Are they related to anything you know about? How do they fit together? How many, and what, pieces are missing?

This gives you an idea of the questions scientists ask when they find dinosaur bones. Just over a hundred years ago, the first scientists to study them thought these bones belonged to gigantic, ferocious lizards that once roamed the earth.

A brilliant English scientist named Richard Owen recognized that these creatures were different enough from modern reptiles to deserve their own name. He called them dinosaurs, from the Greek for "terrible lizard." Though Owen was correct to group them under one name, he didn't realize that some dinosaurs were small and harmless. And though dinosaurs belong to the reptile family, they are very different from lizards.

"It's a lizard—so its legs must be on the side."

"Sounds good to me."

Today scientists believe *Iguanodon* held its tail straight behind it and walked mostly on all fours.

Iguanodon was among the first dinosaurs to be scientifically described. Its discoverer, Gideon Mantell, believed that the very large teeth and bones he found must have belonged to a huge iguana-like creature whose legs sprawled out to the side like those of a lizard. Mantell thought that the large pointed object his wife discovered was the creature's nose horn. Over the years, scientists changed their minds many times about the appearance of *Iguanodon*. Today we know that it had four straight legs, like a mammal, and could walk either on two hind legs or on all fours. That spiky object mistaken for a horn was really a long, sharp toenail.

"Those guys had it all wrong—the legs go underneath."

"It walked on its hind legs. And this wasn't a horn—it was a toenail!"

"Sounds good to me."

677

THE CASE OF THE DECEPTIVE DINOSAUR

Today we know of more than 1,000 species of dinosaurs, and others are being discovered every year. Paleontologists, scientists who study bones and fossils to learn about the past, have a tough job keeping up with all the bones. When bones are first discovered, it is sometimes difficult to know what animal they belong to.

Is it a new dinosaur or one we already know about? And when the bones of more than one creature are jumbled together, scientists must be careful to separate and identify each animal.

Take the case of poor old *Apatosaurus* (whose name means "deceptive lizard"). Now there's a dinosaur with an identity crisis. This huge 30-ton creature was first discovered and named in 1877. Two years later, the same scientist examined another set of *Apatosaurus* bones and thought they belonged to a different type of dinosaur, which he named *Brontosaurus* (or "thunder lizard"). With its long graceful neck and whiplike tail, *Brontosaurus* became a familiar favorite among dinosaur lovers. But, in 1974, scientists decided that *Brontosaurus* was really *Apatosaurus*— that there was no *Brontosaurus* after all.

Everyone was excited about the discovery of *Apatosaurus*. One newspaper published this picture of the huge creature looking into an 11th-story window.

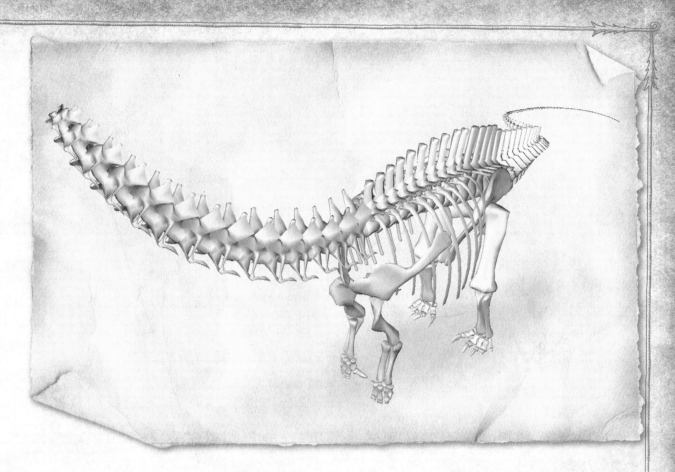

To make matters worse, *Apatosaurus* lost its head. Honestly. Because the original skeleton was found without a head, no one was sure what *Apatosaurus's* skull looked like. For nearly 100 years, models and drawings in museums all over the world showed it with no head or the wrong head. Finally, the skull was located in a museum basement, and *Apatosaurus* could once again hold its head up proudly.

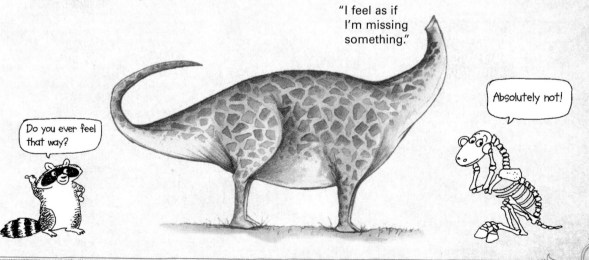

"I feel as if I'm missing something."

Do you ever feel that way?

Absolutely not!

Or maybe not. Recent evidence indicates that *Apatosaurus* and other dinosaurs with long, elegant necks may not have been able to lift their heads far off the ground. For many years, experts believed that these vegetarian dinosaurs reached their necks into the treetops to dine, like giraffes.

Recently, however, computer modeling has revealed that the positioning of their neck bones would have prevented them from raising their heads any higher than about 12 feet. While it may have been able to rear up on its hind legs to snag treetop treats, more often *Apatosaurus* probably reached its long neck across creeks or other obstacles as it grazed for food along the ground.

We finally have a complete picture of *Apatosaurus*, but there's a lot more to learn.

Computer Images

To create these images of *Apatosaurus* and its neck movements, scientists entered information about the size, number, and positioning of the animal's neck bones into a computer, which figured out just how far the dino could move its neck up and down and sideways.

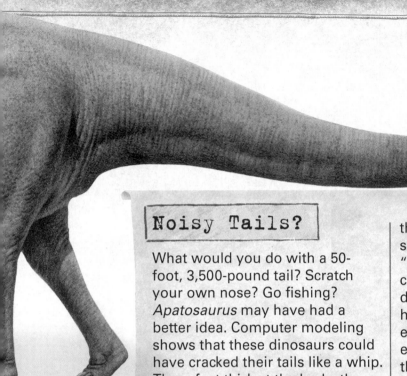

Noisy Tails?

What would you do with a 50-foot, 3,500-pound tail? Scratch your own nose? Go fishing? *Apatosaurus* may have had a better idea. Computer modeling shows that these dinosaurs could have cracked their tails like a whip. Three feet thick at the body, the tail thinned to a narrow tip about the width of a human thumb. As the dino lashed it, a wave of energy would have traveled down to the tip, arriving at a speed faster than that of sound—more than 750 miles per hour. When something moves that fast it "breaks the sound barrier," creating a loud noise. A cracking dino tail would have made a huge, thundering clap—loud enough, perhaps, to scare off an enemy. But some scientists think that such supersonic tail wagging is unlikely because it would have hurt or damaged the dino's tail. After all, they remind us, just because the computer says it was possible doesn't mean it actually happened that way.

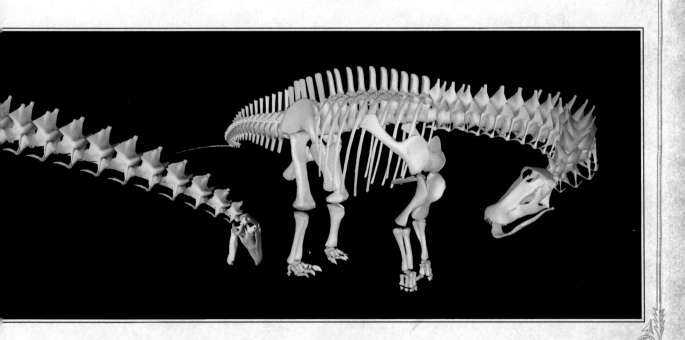

Snorkel? Weapon? Noisemaker? *Parasaurolophus's* curious crest has scientists guessing.

Maybe it's his thinking cap?

LISTENING TO THE BONES

Computers have become a valuable tool to help paleontologists picture dinosaurs better. Scientists can now even hear what dinosaurs might have sounded like. Consider *Parasaurolophus*, an odd-looking fellow. A large, bony crest extended from the top of its head back over its shoulders. Handsome, perhaps, but what did the crest do? Some scientists think it may have been a weapon or even a snorkel, but no evidence supports these ideas.

How about a trombone? When a nearly complete *Parasaurolophus* skull was found in New Mexico, computer scientists and paleontologists joined forces to see if the head crest might actually have been a noisemaker.

"Sounds like a tuba. No, a trombone, definitely a trombone."

Snorkeling Brachiosaurus

Apatosaurus and its cousins—the "long-necks"—weighed more than any other creature that ever lived. For a long time, scientists thought that the only way these huge animals could move their massive bodies must have been in the water. Their long necks would keep their heads up so that they could breathe as they walked along a lake or river bottom, grazing on soft aquatic plants.

But modern scientists wondered: wouldn't the water's pressure collapse the great creature's lungs and disable its heart? Probably so, which made scientists imagine that the long-necks may have wandered on land after all.

New research reveals yet another possibility. Sometimes, along "trackways" where dinosaur footprints have been preserved, scientists find only front footprints. In ancient times, these trackways may have been underwater. Could the long-necks actually float, touching the bottom with only their front feet? That way, they could live in water without their giant bodies being deeply submerged.

Computer modeling shows that this may have been possible, especially since we now know that the creatures had tiny air sacs along their spines that would help them stay afloat. The catch? If they lost contact with the bottom, they would probably tip over.

They took scans of the inside of the crest with special imaging equipment so that they wouldn't have to break it open. Then they used the scans to model a three-dimensional image of the crest. They found that it was filled with a complicated series of hollow tubes and chambers. When the computer created the sounds made by blowing air through the crest, the scientists heard an eerie, deep rumbling tone. Were the scientists hearing a sound not made on earth since the dinosaurs lived here? Who can know?

This computer image shows the complicated tubes and chambers in the fossil of the *Parasaurolophus's* crest.

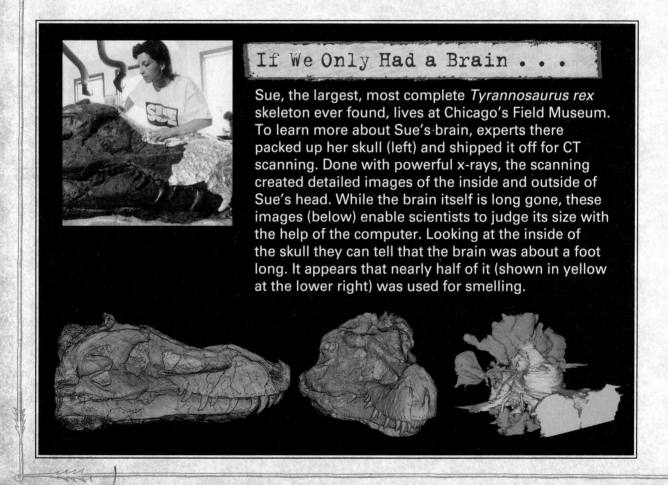

If We Only Had a Brain . . .

Sue, the largest, most complete *Tyrannosaurus rex* skeleton ever found, lives at Chicago's Field Museum. To learn more about Sue's brain, experts there packed up her skull (left) and shipped it off for CT scanning. Done with powerful x-rays, the scanning created detailed images of the inside and outside of Sue's head. While the brain itself is long gone, these images (below) enable scientists to judge its size with the help of the computer. Looking at the inside of the skull they can tell that the brain was about a foot long. It appears that nearly half of it (shown in yellow at the lower right) was used for smelling.

Think Critically

1. What did ancient people believe about the dinosaur bones they found? Why did they believe what they did? **Focus Skill** MAIN IDEA AND DETAILS

2. Does the author think that paleontologists have an easy job? Explain your answer with details from the selection. AUTHOR'S PERSPECTIVE

3. Think back to a time when you came across an object you had never seen before. What did you do to figure out what it was? MAKE CONNECTIONS

4. Do you think that what scientists today believe about dinosaurs will be the same many years from now? Explain. SPECULATE

5. **WRITE** What are some ways in which computers have helped paleontologists learn about dinosaurs? Use details and information from the selection to support your answer. SHORT RESPONSE

Saturday Night at the Dinosaur Stomp

By Carol Diggory Shields
illustrated by Scott Nash

Word went out 'cross the prehistoric slime:
"Hey, dinosaurs, it's rock 'n roll time!
Slick back your scales and get ready to romp
On Saturday night at the Dinosaur Stomp!"

By the lava beds and the tar pit shore,
On the mountaintop and the rain forest floor,
Dinosaurs scrubbed their necks and nails.
They brushed their teeth and curled their tails.
Then—ready, set, go—they trampled and tromped,
Making dinosaur tracks for the Dinosaur Stomp.

Plesiosaurus paddled up with a splash,
A pterodactyl family flew in for the bash.
Protoceratops brought along her eggs,
Diplodocus plodded on big fat legs.
A batch of bouncing babies followed Mama Maiasaur.
The last time she counted, she had twenty-four.

The old ones gathered in a gossiping bunch,
Sitting and sipping sweet Swampwater Punch.
Dinosaurs giggled and shuffled and stared,
Ready to party, but a little bit scared.

Then Iguanodon shouted, "One, two, three!"
Started up the band by waving a tree.
Brachio-, Super-, and Ultrasaurus
Sang, "Doo-bop-a-loo-bop," all in a chorus.
Ankylosaurus drummed on his hard-shelled back,
Boomalacka boomalacka! **Whack! Whack! Whack!**

Pentaceratops stood up to perform
And blasted a tune on his favorite horn.
They played in rhythm, they sang in rhyme,
Dinosaur music in dinosaur time!

Duckbill thought he'd take a chance:
Asked Allosaurus if she'd like to dance.
Tarchia winked at a stegosaur she liked.
They danced together, spike to spike.
The Triassic Twist and the Brontosaurus Bump,
The Raptor Rap and Jurassic Jump.

Tyrannosaurus Rex led a conga line.
Carnosaurs capered close behind.
They rocked and rolled, they twirled and tromped.
There never was a party like the **Dinosaur Stomp.**

The nighttime sky began to glow.
Volcanoes put on a fireworks show.
The ground was rocking—it started to shake.
Those dinosaurs danced up the first earthquake!

The party went on—it was so outrageous,
They stayed up well past the late Cretaceous.

When the Cenozoic dawned they were tired and beat.
They yawned big yawns and put up their feet.
And they're *still* asleep, snoring deep in the swamp.
But they'll be back . . . next **Dinosaur Stomp!**

Connections

Comparing Texts

1. Do you think a paleontologist has an important job? Explain.

2. Compare the information in "Dragons and Dinosaurs" and the poem "Saturday Night at the Dinosaur Stomp." What is the author's purpose in each text?

3. What did you know about how scientists study dinosaur bones before you read "Dragons and Dinosaurs"? What did you learn from the article?

Vocabulary Review

Rate a Situation

Read the sentences below. Point to the spot on the line that shows how pleased you would feel in each situation. Explain your choices.

Most _____ Least
Pleased   Pleased

- You built an interesting **contraption**.
- Your yard was **submerged** in water.
- You were invited to an **elegant** dinner.

contraption

roamed

massive

submerged

elegant

obstacles

complicated

eerie

690

Fluency Practice

Partner Reading

With a partner, practice rereading a portion of "Dragons and Dinosaurs." Read aloud a paragraph as your partner follows along in the text. As you read, focus on accuracy. Ask your partner to tell you if you have misread any words. Then trade roles and follow along as your partner reads the paragraph aloud. Take turns rereading until each of you can read the paragraph with accuracy.

Writing

Write a Letter

Imagine that you have recently helped a paleontologist dig up bones of a now-extinct animal. Write a letter to a friend describing what the animal might have looked like.

My Writing Checklist

Writing Trait → Sentence Fluency

✓ I used a graphic organizer to plan my writing.

✓ I used a variety of sentence types to keep my writing interesting.

✓ I used information from more than one resource.

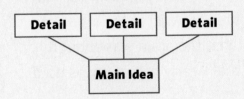

| Detail | Detail | Detail |

Main Idea

Analyze Writer's Craft: Expository Nonfiction

Expository nonfiction gives facts about a topic. It may include **headings, diagrams, photographs,** and **captions.** When you write expository nonfiction, you can use the works of authors such as Meg Moss as writing models. The passage below is from "Dragons and Dinosaurs." As you read it, look for ways to improve your own writing.

> The author begins this section of information with a clever **heading** that grabs the reader's interest.

Writing Trait

ORGANIZATION
In this paragraph, the author describes a series of steps in a process.

If We Only Had a Brain...

Sue, the largest most complete *Tyrannosaurus rex* skeleton ever found, lives at Chicago's Field Museum. To learn more about Sue's brain, experts there packed up her skull and shipped it off for CT scanning. Done with powerful x-rays, the scanning created detailed images of the inside and outside of Sue's head. While the brain itself is long gone, these images enable scientists to judge its size with the help of the computer. Looking at the inside of the skull they can tell that the brain was about a foot long. It appears that nearly half of it was used for smelling.

Research Report

A **research report** is a type of expository nonfiction. It gives information about a topic. A research report includes a list of the books, articles, and websites the writer used to find the information. As you read Alex's research report, notice the **text features** and **text organization** he used.

Student Writing Model

The La Brea Tar Pits
by Alex G.

Every year, thousands of people visit the La Brea Tar Pits in Los Angeles, California, to see an amazing collection of fossils. Over thousands of years, animals became trapped in these pools of sticky asphalt. Millions of fossils have been found in the tar. People have benefited from the tar pits in many ways, especially by learning about the past.

Formation of the Tar Pits

Los Angeles sits on top of rich deposits of oil. This underground oil rose to the surface when cracks formed in the earth's crust thousands of years ago. In low areas, the oil created sticky black pools of asphalt, an extremely thick liquid made of oil. Animals tried to walk across the solid-looking pools and became stuck. They slowly sank in, and the asphalt preserved their bones.

Fossils in the Pits

Scientists have found millions of fossils in the La Brea Tar Pits, including mammals, birds, and insects. The bones of mammals such as saber-toothed cats, mammoths, and ancient camels have been found there. The tar pits have also preserved more than 100,000 bird fossils. Fossils of many insects, including two species of extinct beetles, have also been recovered from the La Brea Tar Pits.

Writing Trait

SENTENCE FLUENCY
Alex varies the **types of sentences** in his report. He begins this paragraph by asking a question.

The **conclusion** paragraph sums up the supporting ideas. Then it explains why the topic is important.

Writing Trait

CONVENTIONS
Book and magazine titles are underlined or printed in italic type. Titles of magazine and online articles are placed in quotation marks.

Benefits to Humans

How have these thick black pools of asphalt been useful to humans? The Chumash tribe of Native Americans used the sticky stuff for waterproofing canoes. After the Civil War, workers mined oil and asphalt from the pits. Thousands of people have visited the museum at the tar pits and have learned from its educational programs.

Scientists are still learning how the La Brea tar pits were formed. They continue to study the millions of fossils they have found there. This amazing place still benefits the people who study it. The La Brea treasures will keep scientists busy for many years to come.

List of Sources

Bahn, Paul and Lister, Adrian.
Mammoths.
Diane Books, 1998.

"Mammoth Mammals."
National Geographic Explorer.
Nov./Dec. 2004: 16–21.

"The La Brea Exploration Guide."
Natural History Museum of
Los Angeles County,
September 18, 2002.

Now look at what Alex did to prepare to write his research report.

Notes

Alex used note cards to write down information from a variety of sources. He copied the complete website addresses of online sources onto his note cards. He wrote down each book's title, authors, publisher, city, and year. He also copied the name of the author and the title of each magazine article, the magazine's name, and the issue in which the article appeared.

La Brea Fossils
Mammals–
   • mammoths
   • saber-toothed cats
   • camels

"The La Brea Exploration Guide." Natural
History Museum of Los Angeles County,
http://tarpits.org/education/guide/index.html,
September 18, 2002.

Outline

Then Alex created an outline to organize the information for his report. The outline shows the order in which Alex plans to include ideas in his introduction, three subtopics, and conclusion.

Title: The La Brea Tar Pits

  I. Introduction
    A. Background
    B. Supporting ideas

  II. Formation of the tar pits
    A. Oil seeps to surface
    B. Animals get trapped

  III. Fossils
    A. Mammals
    B. Birds
    C. Insects

  IV. Usefulness to humans
    A. Native people
    B. Miners
    C. Visitors
    D. Scientists

  V. Conclusion
    A. Sum up supporting ideas
    B. Importance of topic

CONTENTS

Lesson 27

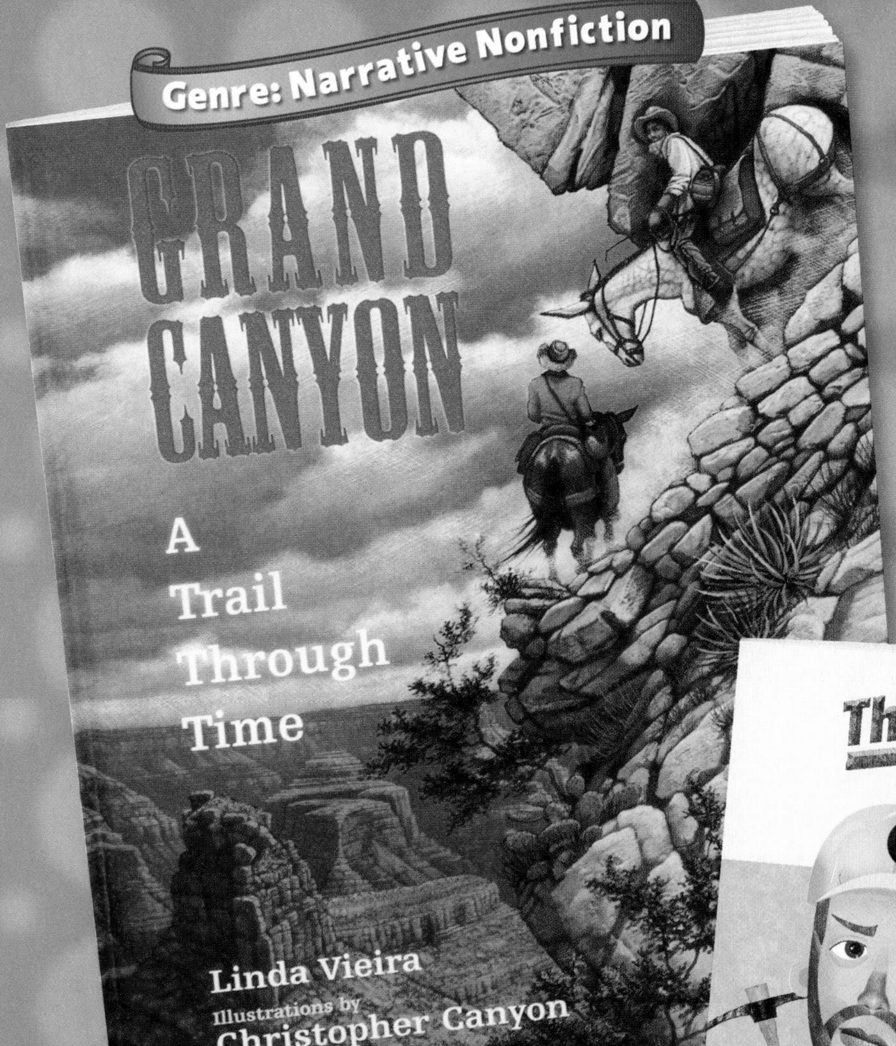
Genre: Narrative Nonfiction
GRAND CANYON
A Trail Through Time
Linda Vieira
Illustrations by
Christopher Canyon

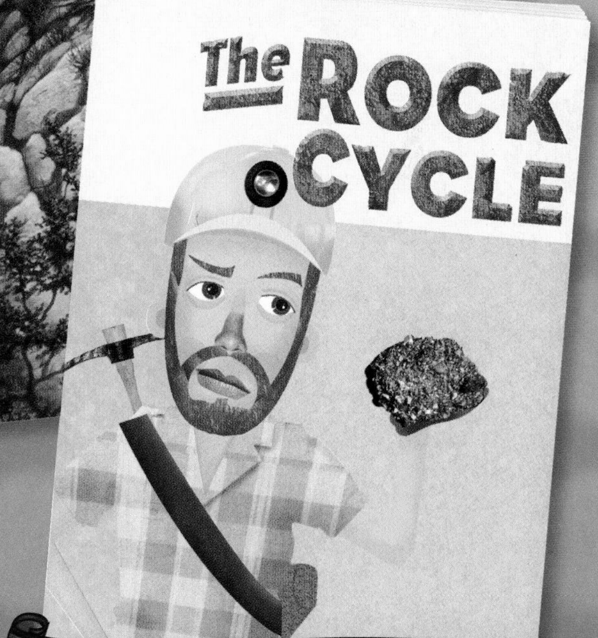
The ROCK CYCLE
Genre: Expository Nonfiction

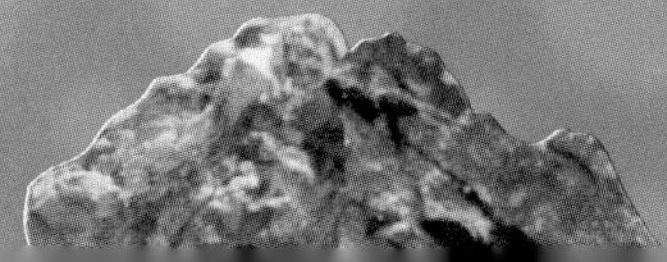

Focus Skill

Main Idea and Details

You have learned that nonfiction selections have **main ideas** supported by **details**. Sometimes a passage does not clearly state the main idea in one sentence. You can use details as clues to figure out the main idea. Ask yourself what important idea the details tell about.

Detail	Detail	Detail

Main Idea

Tip

Group together details on the same topic to help you determine the main idea of a passage.

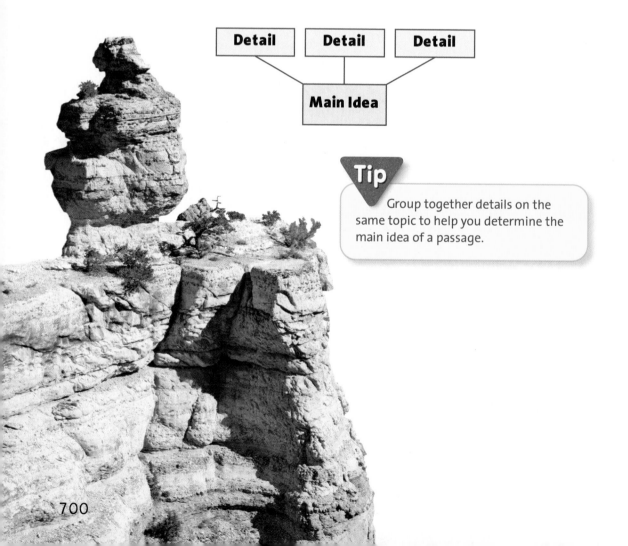

Read the paragraph below. Then look at the graphic organizer. It shows how supporting details can help you figure out a main idea that is not directly stated in the text.

You hike the steep trail to the bottom of the Grand Canyon. There you come upon a Havasupai village. You wonder how the people can live in such a dry area. You talk with them and learn the answer. For centuries, the Havasupai have used the water of the Colorado River to irrigate crops. Today, they also earn money from tourism.

Detail
The land at the bottom of the Grand Canyon is very dry.

Detail
The Havasupai live at the bottom of the Grand Canyon.

Detail
The Havasupai grow crops with water from the Colorado River.

Main Idea
The Havasupai have developed a way of life that allows them to live in a very dry place.

Try This!

Reread the paragraph about the Havasupai to find another detail supporting the main idea.

www.harcourtschool.com/storytown

Vocabulary

embedded

distant

cascading

ancient

eroding

glistens

sentries

weary

The Amazing Power of Rivers

Throughout the world, rivers have created landforms that amaze travelers. In the American Southwest, the Colorado River has carved the Grand Canyon out of layers of colorful rock. It has exposed rock **embedded** with fossils.

In East Africa, the Zambezi River has created another natural wonder. Visitors to this **distant** place are rewarded with an amazing sight. The broad, gently flowing Zambezi suddenly pours over cliffs. The **cascading** waters form Victoria Falls, one of the largest waterfalls in the world.

The falling water drops into a deep canyon. It then roars through a narrow gorge. Since **ancient** times, the river has been **eroding** the rock there. Sun and mist create rainbows above the gorge. Wet rock **glistens** where sunshine reaches it.

You can see more than rock and water near Victoria Falls. Hippos wallow and antelopes leap. Baboons patrol paths as if they were **sentries**. Lions prowl nearby. You may be **weary** after all the hiking you'll be doing to see it all, but you will always remember the trip!

 www.harcourtschool.com/storytown

Word Champion

This week, use the Vocabulary Words outside your classroom. Keep the list of words in a place where you can see it. Use as many of the words as you can when you talk with family members and friends. For example, you might talk about a distant land that you would like to visit. Write in your vocabulary journal the words you used and how you used them.

GRAND CANYON
A Trail Through Time

Linda Vieira
Illustrations by
Christopher Canyon

Narrative Nonfiction

Genre Study

Narrative nonfiction tells about people, things, events, or places that are real. As you read, look for

- factual information that tells a story.

- paragraphs organized by main idea and details.

Detail	Detail	Detail

Main Idea

Comprehension Strategy

Focus Strategy

Pause while you read to **summarize** sections of text.

GRAND CANYON

A TRAIL THROUGH TIME

BY LINDA VIEIRA

ILLUSTRATED BY CHRISTOPHER CANYON

A predawn storm rumbles over Grand Canyon National Park. Cracks of lightning shatter the dark sky, flashing above an enormous plateau of peaks, valleys, and trenches where ancient mountains once stood. The deepest trench is called the Grand Canyon, one of the Seven Natural Wonders of the World.

Dawn comes, bringing daylight to spires and buttes standing like sentries on the plateau, worn down by weathering and erosion. Coyotes teach their pups to hunt for food in thick forests along the edges of the Canyon.

Thousands of visitors from all over the world have come to view the splendor of the Grand Canyon. In campgrounds and lodges near the north and south rims, they prepare for the day's activities.

The morning sun climbs above distant mountains, revealing cliffs hanging over the Colorado River at the bottom of the Grand Canyon. The river took almost six million years to carve the Canyon, creating a channel about one mile deep and more than 275 miles long. Wind and water wore down its steep sides, widening the chasm between the cliffs. A raven glides across the opening, making lazy circles over the river far below.

The sun chases away shadows on the craggy rocks thousands of feet below the rims. Pack mules begin a five-hour trip down to the deepest part of the Canyon. They follow each other along a twisted, ten-mile trail to the riverbed. Clouds of dust follow them as voices from the top fade away.

Canyon visitors along the trail peer with curiosity at symbols of people and animals that were painted on a boulder by Havasupai Indians long ago. Havasupai still live in the Canyon today, tending their flocks and farms in the summertime, hunting small game and gathering nuts and berries in the winter months.

As the sun moves higher in the sky, smaller side canyons with rocks layered like multicolored ribbons come into view. Bighorn sheep walk easily along the steep walls of the canyons, looking for food in hidden pockets of soil. Wildflowers stand around them in patches of purple and pink.

The mules continue down the trail to the inner gorge. They carry their riders past layers of rock that display millions of years of the Earth's geologic history. A canyon wren looks for bits of brush to line its nest, hidden in a rocky crevice just off the trail. It searches for twigs and grasses up and down the Canyon walls, flying past fossils of fish teeth and seashells.

The noonday sun glistens on a hidden creek near a granary built into the Canyon wall by Anasazi Indians almost 1,000 years ago. Squirrels chase through the now-empty granary, where crops and plants had been stored for food and trade.

A lizard scurries off the trail. It climbs over fossils of prehistoric trilobites, embedded in layers of shale millions of years ago when the land was covered by a primeval sea. After the mules pass, the lizard creeps out from its hiding place to soak up the warmth of the sun.

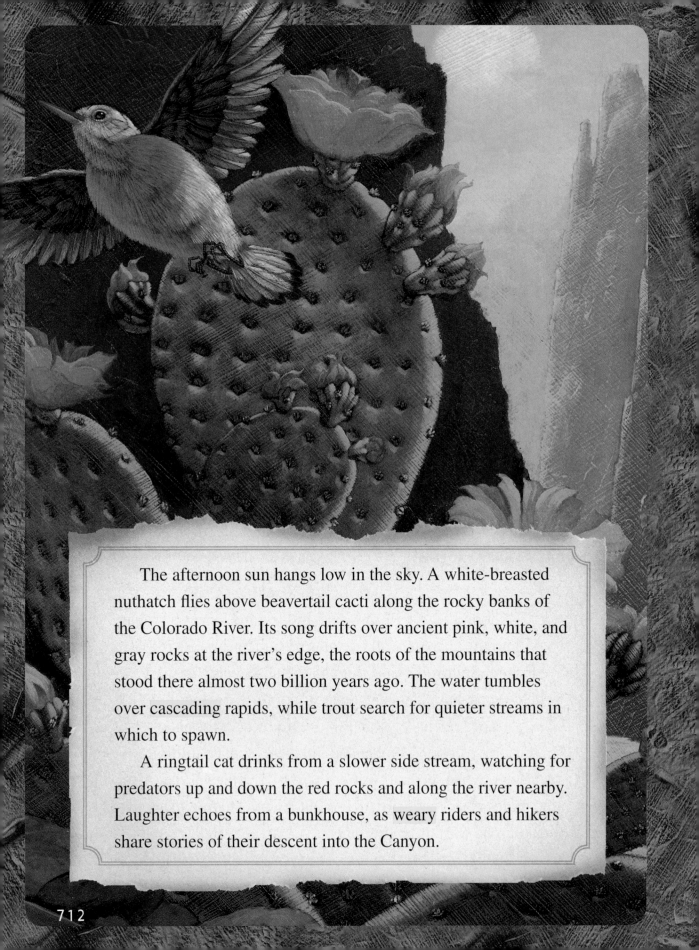

The afternoon sun hangs low in the sky. A white-breasted nuthatch flies above beavertail cacti along the rocky banks of the Colorado River. Its song drifts over ancient pink, white, and gray rocks at the river's edge, the roots of the mountains that stood there almost two billion years ago. The water tumbles over cascading rapids, while trout search for quieter streams in which to spawn.

A ringtail cat drinks from a slower side stream, watching for predators up and down the red rocks and along the river nearby. Laughter echoes from a bunkhouse, as weary riders and hikers share stories of their descent into the Canyon.

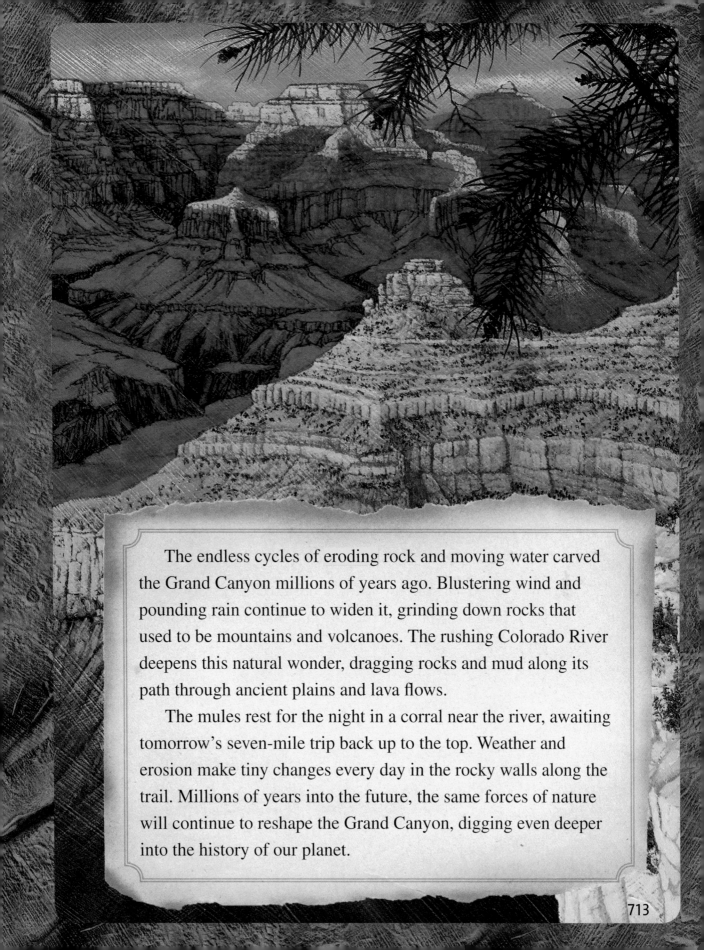

The endless cycles of eroding rock and moving water carved the Grand Canyon millions of years ago. Blustering wind and pounding rain continue to widen it, grinding down rocks that used to be mountains and volcanoes. The rushing Colorado River deepens this natural wonder, dragging rocks and mud along its path through ancient plains and lava flows.

The mules rest for the night in a corral near the river, awaiting tomorrow's seven-mile trip back up to the top. Weather and erosion make tiny changes every day in the rocky walls along the trail. Millions of years into the future, the same forces of nature will continue to reshape the Grand Canyon, digging even deeper into the history of our planet.

Think Critically

1 Reread the first paragraph on page 713. What is the main idea of this paragraph? What details helped you figure out the main idea? MAIN IDEA AND DETAILS

2 How do weather and water erode rock? CAUSE AND EFFECT

3 Why do you think the author wrote the selection? How do you think she feels about the Grand Canyon? AUTHOR'S PURPOSE AND PERSPECTIVE

4 Think about a visit you have made to a natural area or a park. How do you think the effects of weather may change that area over time? PRIOR KNOWLEDGE

5 WRITE What can you learn about Earth's history from the Grand Canyon? Use details and information from the selection to support your answer. SHORT RESPONSE

ABOUT THE AUTHOR
LINDA VIEIRA

ABOUT THE ILLUSTRATOR
CHRISTOPHER CANYON

Linda Vieira says she has been writing her entire life. When she was younger and had a hard time understanding something, she would write it down to make it easier. Later, as an elementary school teacher, she would do the same for her students. Linda Vieira enjoys writing books, such as *Grand Canyon*, that combine science and history. *Grand Canyon* is the second book she has worked on with illustrator Christopher Canyon.

Award-winning illustrator Christopher Canyon loves to draw, read, and make music. He says creating children's books is a way to do his favorite things. When not working on a book, he loves playing guitar and singing with his family. He also visits schools and libraries to share his art with others. His advice to young artists is to have fun and celebrate their creativity. He lives in Columbus, Ohio, with his wife, Jeanette, and their cat, Goppy.

www.harcourtschool.com/storytown

The ROCK CYCLE

Expository Nonfiction

You might think that rocks never move or change, but did you know that rocks are always changing and moving? Forces of nature, such as heat and erosion, have created mountains, canyons, and volcanoes. If you look closely at the layers that make up the walls of the Grand Canyon, you can see different types of rocks. Read on to learn how nature formed these rocks.

◀ Halite is a type of sedimentary rock. It is the natural form of table salt.

◀ Granite and obsidian are types of igneous rocks.

SEDIMENTARY ROCKS

Sediment is pieces of rock that have been broken down and moved. Water, wind, and ice break down rock and then carry the sediment. When the wind or water slows down, the sediment falls to the surface. It piles up in layers. The layers get pressed together. Water, carrying minerals, moves through the sediment. Over time, the minerals cause the sediment to stick together.

IGNEOUS ROCKS

Igneous rocks form when melted rock cools and hardens. Deep inside Earth, it is so hot that some rock is liquid, like syrup. This melted rock is called *magma*. Inside Earth's crust, magma cools slowly. Volcanic eruptions release magma. When magma reaches Earth's surface, it is called *lava*. When the lava cools and hardens, it becomes igneous rock.

The ROCK CYCLE

MAGMA
(molten rock)

cooling and becoming solid

IGNEOUS
(cooled, hardened lava)

weathering and movement

SEDIMENT
(tiny bits of rock)

settling and pressing together

SEDIMENTARY
(compacted sediment)

pressure and heat

METAMORPHIC
(changed by heat, pressure)

◄ Marble and slate are metamorphic rocks.

METAMORPHIC ROCKS

Metamorphic rock is rock that has changed from another type of rock. It can form from any other type of rock, including other metamorphic rock.

Heat and pressure form this type of rock. For example, when mountains form, plates that make up Earth's surface push together. Rock near the surface can get pushed down during this process. Pressure on the rock squeezes it. If the pressure is great enough, minerals in the rock change, forming metamorphic rock.

Connections

Comparing Texts

1. How would you describe the Grand Canyon to someone who has never seen or read about it?

2. How is "Grand Canyon: A Trail Through Time" similar to and different from "The Rock Cycle"?

3. If you could visit any distant place, where would you go and why?

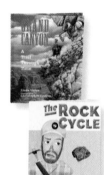

Vocabulary Review

Word Webs

Write a Vocabulary Word in the center of a word web. Around the word, write related words and phrases. Tell how each word or phrase is related to the Vocabulary Word.

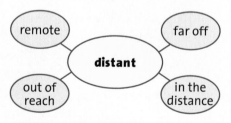

ancient

distant

sentries

glistens

embedded

cascading

weary

eroding

Fluency Practice

Partner Reading

Work with a partner. Choose four paragraphs from "Grand Canyon: A Trail Through Time." Take turns reading aloud the paragraphs. Give each other feedback about the accuracy of your reading. Reread the paragraphs aloud until you can both read with accuracy.

Writing

Write a Descriptive Paragraph

Imagine that while visiting the Grand Canyon, you saw one of the animals mentioned in the selection. Write a descriptive paragraph about the animal and its habitat.

Detail	Detail	Detail

Main Idea

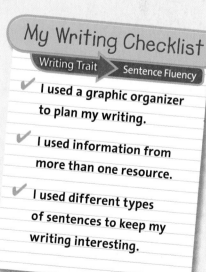

My Writing Checklist

Writing Trait ▶ Sentence Fluency

✔ I used a graphic organizer to plan my writing.

✔ I used information from more than one resource.

✔ I used different types of sentences to keep my writing interesting.

CONTENTS

Lesson 28

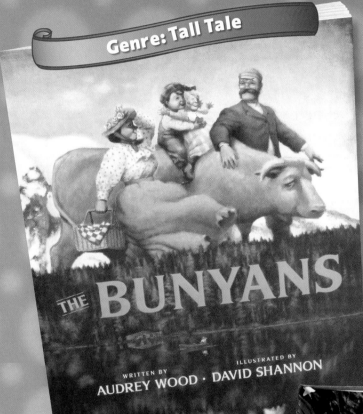

Genre: Tall Tale

THE BUNYANS

WRITTEN BY
AUDREY WOOD · DAVID SHANNON

ILLUSTRATED BY

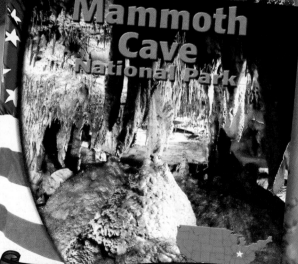

Mammoth Cave National Park

Genre: Expository Nonfiction

Focus Skill

Figurative Language

Authors use phrases that make their writing more interesting and help readers picture the events. These phrases often include **figurative language**. In figurative language, the meaning of a group of words may be different from the words' individual meanings.

- A **simile** is a comparison that uses *like* or *as*.
  The man is as strong as an ox.
- A **metaphor** describes a thing as something else.
  The rainbow was a bright ribbon across the sky.
- An **idiom** is a word group with a special meaning.
  Jen spilled the beans about the surprise party.
- **Personification** gives human qualities to an animal or object.
  The marbles tried to escape.
- **Hyperbole** is an obvious exaggeration.
  I must have seen a million birds that day.

Tip

The word *simile* is related to the word *similar,* meaning "like." This can help you remember that a simile contains the word *like* or *as.*

Read the paragraph below. Then look at the graphic organizer. It lists types and examples of figurative language from the paragraph.

According to legend, Pecos Bill fell from a covered wagon and was raised by coyotes. He grew up to be the best cowhand in the West. One day a mean-spirited cyclone threatened to tear out the grass and scatter Bill's cattle to the ends of the earth. Mad as a hornet, Bill grabbed the cyclone by the tail and swung it high into the sky. The stormy sea of grass turned smooth. "I made short work of that twister," he said.

Figurative Language	Example
Simile	mad as a hornet
Metaphor	stormy sea of grass
Idiom	made short work of
Personification	mean-spirited cyclone
Hyperbole	to the ends of the earth

Try This!

Rewrite the second sentence of the paragraph using a type of figurative language listed in the graphic organizer.

 www.harcourtschool.com/storytown

Vocabulary

Build Robust Vocabulary

- scenic
- colossal
- illusion
- hearty
- behemoth
- fanciful
- cordially

A Giant Turns Ten

Today was the greatest day of my life! For my tenth birthday, Mom and Dad promised me a swimming party at a place full of **scenic** wonders. Wow, did they deliver! Dad broke the top off a **colossal** cone-shaped mountain and filled the mountain with water. Mom said it looked like a crater on the moon. I named it *Crater Lake.*

Dad carried me down to the lake on his shoulders. Being on his shoulders gave me the **illusion** that I could touch the clouds.

When we got back, Mom had a **hearty** meal waiting for us. She had made sixteen buckets of mashed potatoes and enough biscuits for a **behemoth**.

When I opened my first gift from Mom and Dad, I could not hide my disappointment. I'd had the **fanciful** idea that I'd get one of those shiny comets that race through the sky. "Thanks," I said **cordially,** as I tried on the necktie.

That night, the stars twinkled as I opened the other gift they had given me. I couldn't believe my eyes! It was my very own comet! I was so excited, I raced along the shore with the comet streaming behind me like a kite. I think I'll throw it in a curve around the sun.

 www.harcourtschool.com/storytown

Word Scribe

 Your goal this week is to use the Vocabulary Words in writing. Write sentences in your vocabulary journal that show the meaning of the words. For example, you might write about a menu for a hearty meal or share a fanciful thought. Share your sentences with your classmates.

Award Winner

THE BUNYANS

WRITTEN BY AUDREY WOOD · ILLUSTRATED BY DAVID SHANNON

Tall Tale

Genre Study

A tall tale is a humorous story about impossible or exaggerated events. As you read, look for

- events that could not happen in real life.

- American folk heroes and legends.

Characters	Setting

Plot Events

Comprehension Strategy

Monitor comprehension by **rereading** sections of text you did not understand.

THE BUNYANS

BY
AUDREY WOOD

ILLUSTRATED BY
DAVID SHANNON

ow I suppose that you have heard about the mighty logger Paul Bunyan and his great blue ox named Babe. In the early days of our country, Paul and Babe cleared the land for the settlers, so farms and cities could spring up. And you probably know that Paul was taller than a redwood tree, stronger than fifty grizzly bears, and smarter than a library full of books. But you may not know that Paul was married and had two fine children.

One day when Paul Bunyan was out clearing a road through the forests of Kentucky, a great pounding began to shake the earth. Looking around, Paul discovered an enormous hole in the side of a hill. The lumberjack pulled up an acre of dry cane and fashioned a torch to light his way.

Paul climbed inside the hole and followed the sound underground for miles, until he came to a large cavern glistening with crystals. By the flickering light of his torch, he saw a gigantic woman banging a behemoth pickax against a wall.

It was love at first sight.

"I'm Carrie McIntie," the gigantic woman said. "I was sitting on the hill when my lucky wishbone fell down a crack into the earth. I've been digging all day trying to find it."

With a grin on his face as wide as the Missouri River, Paul reached into his shirt pocket. "I've got one too," he said, pulling out his lucky wishbone. "Marry me, Carrie, and we'll share mine."

Carrie agreed, and their wedding invitations were mailed out right away.

The invitations were so large, only one needed to be sent to each state. Everyone could read them for miles!

The invitations said: *You are cordially invited to the mammoth wedding of Paul Bunyan and Carrie McIntie.* The couple were married in the enormous crystal chamber that Carrie had carved, and after the ceremony, folks began to call it "Mammoth Cave." The giantess had dug more than two hundred miles, making it the longest cave in the world, so the name fit perfectly.

Paul and Carrie settled down on a farm in Maine, and soon there were two new Bunyans. While Pa Bunyan traveled with his logging crew, Ma Bunyan worked the farm and cared for their jumbo boy, named Little Jean, and their gigantic girl, named Teeny.

One morning when Pa Bunyan was home between jobs, Ma Bunyan cooked up a hearty breakfast of pancakes and syrup. Teeny was wrestling with her big purple puma named Slink and accidentally dumped a silo of syrup on her head.

Teeny's hair was so sweet, bears crawled into it and burrowed deep in her curls. Try as they might, Pa and Ma Bunyan couldn't wash them out.

"We'll need a forceful shower of water to get rid of those varmints!" Ma Bunyan declared.

Pa Bunyan had an idea. He placed his daughter on Babe, and he led them to the Niagara River in Canada. The gargantuan father scooped out a huge hole in the middle of the riverbed. As the great river roared down into the deep hole, Teeny cried out in delight, "Niagara falls!" Teeny showered in the waterfall, and the pesky bears were washed downstream.

When Little Jean was five, he wanted to work too, so he followed his pa out to his logging camp in Montana. Thinking his son was too young to do much of anything, Paul set Little Jean down in a barren canyon in Utah to play for the day. When the lumberjack went to fetch him, he couldn't believe his eyes. Little Jean had carved the canyon into a wonderland of fanciful shapes.

Pa Bunyan got tongue-tied and said, "That's a mighty brice nanyon, coy, I mean, a mighty nice canyon, boy!" Somehow part of the mix-up stuck.

To this day the canyon is known as Bryce Canyon.

After all that sculpting, Little Jean's shoes were full of sand. Pa knew Ma Bunyan wouldn't want her clean floors dirtied up, so he told Little Jean to sit down and empty out his shoes.

The sand from Little Jean's shoes blew away on the eastern wind and settled down a state away. It covered a valley ten miles long, making sand dunes eight hundred feet high. Everyone knows that's how the Great Sand Dunes of Colorado came to be.

One summer, Little Jean and Teeny wanted to go to the beach.

Ma Bunyan told them to follow a river to the ocean. But all the rivers flowed west back then, so they missed the Atlantic Ocean and ended up on the other side of the country instead.

Ma Bunyan tracked them out to the Pacific Ocean, where she found Teeny riding on the backs of two blue whales and Little Jean carving out fifty zigzag miles of the California coast.

When Ma Bunyan saw what her son had done, she exclaimed, "What's the big idea, sir!?" From that time on, the scenic area was known as Big Sur.

Ma Bunyan knew she had to put up a barrier to remind her children not to wander off too far. So, on the way home, everyone pitched in and built the Rocky Mountains. Teeny gathered up and sorted out all the rivers, letting some flow east and others west. After that, the children had no trouble following the eastern rivers down to the Atlantic Ocean. And when they wanted to go out exploring, Ma Bunyan would call out, "Now don't cross the Continental Divide, children!"

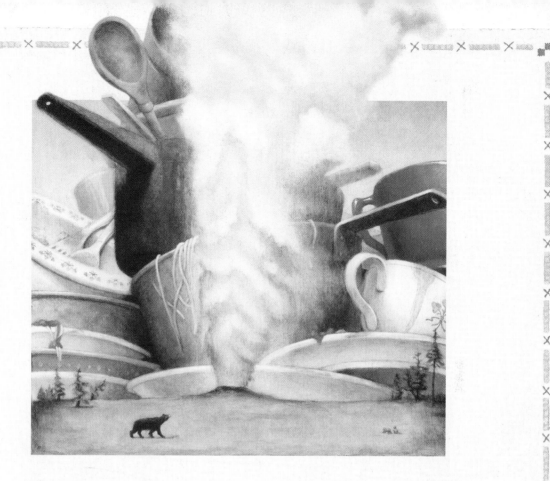

The best thing about camping is sleeping outdoors, and the worst thing is not having enough hot water. That's why the Bunyans always camped in Wyoming. By the time their camping years were over, Ma Bunyan had poked more than three hundred holes in the ground with her pickax and released tons of hot water from geysers. But Ma got tired of poking so many holes, so she made a geyser that blew every hour on the hour. After that, there was a steady supply of hot water to keep the giants' clothes and dishes sparkling clean.

Teeny named the geyser Old Faithful, and to this day, Old Faithful still blows its top every hour in Yellowstone National Park.

As our great country grew up, so did the Bunyan children. When the kids left home, Ma and Pa Bunyan retired to a wilderness area, where they still live happily.

Teeny hitched a ride on a whale over to England and became a famous fashion designer. Her colorful skirts made from air balloons and her breezy blouses cut from ship sails were a sensation at the first World's Fair in London.

Little Jean traveled to Venice, Italy, where he studied astronomy and art. Every day, the gondoliers would take their passengers down the Grand Canal to watch the giant artist chiseling his marble sculptures.

After graduation, Little Jean decided to explore new lands, as his parents had done. So he took two great jumps and one flying leap and bounded up into outer space.

In 1976, the year of our country's bicentennial, a spacecraft sent by the National Aeronautics and Space Administration was on a mission to study Mars. The spacecraft was named *Viking I*, and it took many photographs of the surface of the planet. One mysterious photo looked like a face carved out of colossal rock.

Some say the photograph is not a face, but an illusion caused by light and shadows on the rock. Others think the famous "Martian face" is just the spitting image of Little Jean Bunyan. If that's so, who knows what he's up to on the other planets. Only time will tell!

THINK CRITICALLY

1. Why does Mrs. Bunyan create Old Faithful? CAUSE AND EFFECT

2. According to the story, the rock formation on Mars is the spitting image of Little Jean. What kind of figurative language is the phrase *spitting image*, and what does it mean? FIGURATIVE LANGUAGE

3. What details does the author give to show that Little Jean and Teeny are not ordinary children? AUTHOR'S CRAFT

4. What kinds of difficulties would you have if you were as big as Teeny or Little Jean? MAKE CONNECTIONS

5. WRITE Both of the Bunyan children are creative. How does the author tell you this? Use details and information from the story to support your answer. SHORT RESPONSE

AUDREY WOOD

Audrey Wood and her sisters were raised in an artistic family. Her great-grandfather, grandfather, and father were all artists. When Audrey Wood was very young, her father painted murals at the circus, and young Audrey became friends with some of the circus performers. They thought she would grow up to be a trapeze artist! As an adult, she chose a career in art, but she also wrote stories. When she began reading picture books to her two-year-old son, she started thinking seriously about writing books for children. Now Audrey Wood is both an author and an illustrator of children's books.

DAVID SHANNON

David Shannon says that he draws many of the same subjects today that he drew as a child—pirates, knights, and baseball players. His popular book *No, David!* is based on a book he first drew when he was five—*no* and *David* were the only words he could spell! David Shannon grew up in Spokane, Washington. He now lives in Los Angeles with his wife and daughter.

GO online www.harcourtschool.com/storytown

MAMMOTH CAVE

NATIONAL PARK

Mammoth Cave is the world's longest cave. It has more than 360 miles (580 kilometers) of mapped cave passages. Mammoth Cave is three times longer than any known cave in the world.

Mammoth Cave National Park covers 53,000 acres (21,000 hectares) in Kentucky. About 1.7 million people visit the park every year.

The area above and around Mammoth Cave is filled with forests, springs, and sinkholes. The ground falls in where sinkholes form. The huge cave is underneath these sinkholes.

In 1941, the U.S. government made the area of Mammoth Cave a national park. The government creates national parks to protect special natural areas. People cannot build or hunt on park lands. But they can camp, hike, and view the wildlife and scenery in the park.

How Mammoth Cave Formed

Millions of years ago, a shallow sea covered the Mammoth Cave area. Tiny animals that lived in the sea left behind skeletons. Over time, the skeletons formed a layer of limestone.

After the sea dried up, a river dumped sand on the limestone. The sand became sandstone. Over time, the limestone and sandstone layers started to crack.

Rain and riverwater mixed with chemicals in the air and soil. This mixture formed acid. The acid leaked into the cracks. Over many years, acid broke down the limestone underground. This process created a series of caves.

Dripping water helped cave formations develop. Many strange and beautiful cave formations are found within Mammoth Cave. Stalactite formations hang from the cave's ceiling. Stalagmites rise from the ground.

Activities

Most people come to the park to tour Mammoth Cave. Some tours take visitors to the most interesting cave formations. One tour takes visitors into the cave using lanterns. The "Trog Tour" is just for children. Kids crawl, slither, and climb through narrow cave openings.

Visitors to Mammoth Cave also enjoy camping, hiking, mountain biking, canoeing, fishing, and rock climbing.

Cave formations, such as stalactites and columns, form over time from dripping water.

Connections

Comparing Texts

1. Imagine that you are a giant like Little Jean or Teeny. What would you like about being that size? What wouldn't you like about it?

2. Compare and contrast the descriptions of how Mammoth Cave was formed in "The Bunyans" and in "Mammoth Cave National Park."

3. What kind of safety rule might Mrs. Bunyan have told Teeny before she crossed the ocean?

Vocabulary Review

Word Sort

Work with a partner. Copy the words on a separate sheet of paper, and decide in which of the three categories below each Vocabulary Word belongs. Write the words where they belong, and then compare lists. Explain your choices. Some words may fit in more than one category.

Size	Personality	View

behemoth

cordially

hearty

fanciful

scenic

colossal

illusion

Fluency Practice

Tape-Assisted Reading

When you read with expression, you use your voice to express the feelings of the characters in a story. Listen carefully to a recording of the first three paragraphs of "The Bunyans" on *Audiotext 6*. Pay close attention to the reader's expression as you read along silently. Then reread the paragraphs aloud, and try to match the reader's expression. Continue until you have read all three paragraphs.

Writing

Write a Tall Tale

Think of a place outdoors in your community, such as a park or a beach. Imagine how it might have formed. Write a tall tale about how that place came to be.

Figurative Language	Example in Tall Tale

My Writing Checklist

Writing Trait ▸ Organization

✓ I used a chart to organize my ideas.

✓ I used figurative language to make my story lively and interesting.

✓ I used sensory details to help readers picture the place.

CONTENTS

Lesson 29

JOHN MUIR
and STICKEEN

An Icy Adventure
with a No-Good D...

by JULIE DUNLAP AND MARYBETH LORBIECKI   illustrated by BILL FARNSWORT...

JOHN MUIR
EXTREME EXPLORER

by Crystal Hubbard
illustrated by Nenad Jakesevic

Louisville
KENTUCKY
VIRGINIA
NORTH
CAROLINA
SOUTH
CAROLINA

Figurative Language

You have learned that authors may use **figurative language** to help readers clearly picture what is happening in a story. Words and phrases used as figurative language may have a literal, or direct, meaning that is different from the meaning they have in the story. You can use context clues to understand the meaning of figurative language, such as an **idiom.** To understand the meaning of a **simile** or a **metaphor**, think about the two things the author is comparing.

Figurative Language	Example	Meaning

Tip

The word part *hyper* means "above" or "beyond." This can help you remember that hyperbole is exaggeration.

Read the paragraph below. The graphic organizer shows the meaning of five examples of figurative language in the paragraph.

Joanna woke up at the crack of dawn. The cabin was cozy, but ice crystals covered the windows like frosty lace. Outside, the sun touched the frozen ground. Joanna's brother, Joe, was still snoring a bassoon solo. "I wouldn't want to sleep my days away like Joe," thought Joanna.

Figurative Language	Example	Meaning
Idiom	at the crack of dawn	at the first sign of daylight
Simile	ice crystals covered the windows like frosty lace	The ice crystals looked like lace on the windows.
Personification	sun touched the frozen ground	sunlight was on the ground
Metaphor	snoring a bassoon solo	snoring loudly and deeply
Hyperbole	sleep my days away	waste my days sleeping

Try This!

Find another example of figurative language in the paragraph. What is the literal meaning of the words? What is their meaning in the paragraph?

 www.harcourtschool.com/storytown

Vocabulary

Build Robust Vocabulary

- determined
- dainty
- pitiful
- dedicated
- coddled
- endured
- memorable

Snow Camp Diary

March 2 Today, my Alaskan snow camp adventure began. What a disaster! Six of us are happy to be here, but one is not. Beatrice seems **determined** to have a rotten time. On our first hike, she took **dainty** little steps in the snow. Each time she sank in past her ankles, she made a **pitiful** whimper. She is also a **dedicated** complainer. First, she's too cold. Then, she's hungry. Then, she's tired. I wonder why she came to camp at all.

We got into shape at snow camp by taking several short hikes.

March 4 Tomorrow, we are going to hike to a stream and build a snow cave. Derek, our counselor, called a meeting. "No one will be **coddled** on our hike," he said. "You will all enjoy a fine adventure, and I want you to work together." As if I hadn't **endured** enough of Beatrice already, Derek turned to me. "You and Bea will be partners," he said.

March 5 I don't know what happened, but Beatrice has come around! We worked really well together. Our snow cave was awesome! I'm happily surprised to say that this trip will be one of my most **memorable** experiences.

We all worked together to build this snow cave.

 www.harcourtschool.com/storytown

Word Detective

Your mission this week is to look for the Vocabulary Words outside your classroom. Pay attention when you are reading stories and articles about people's experiences. Write in your vocabulary journal the words you find. Be sure to record where you found each word.

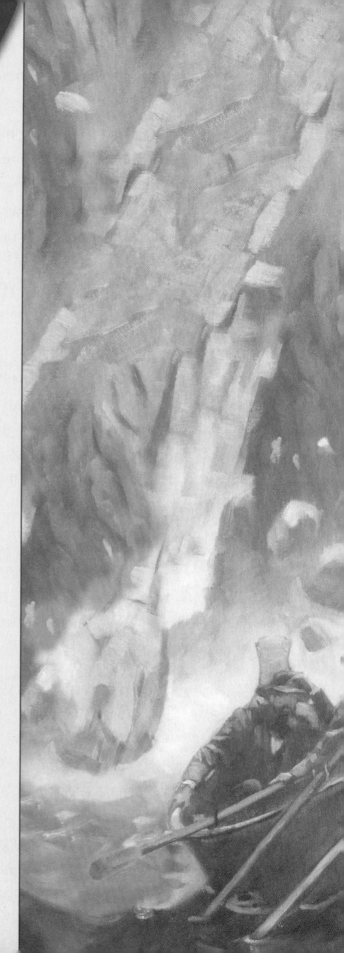

Genre Study

Historical fiction is set in the past and portrays people, places, and events that did happen or could have happened. As you read, look for

- actual historical figures and settings.

- historical events told in time order.

First
↓
Next
↓
Then
↓
Finally

Comprehension Strategy

Focus Strategy

Monitor comprehension while you read by stopping to **reread** parts of the text that you did not understand.

JOHN MUIR AND STICKEEN

An Icy Adventure with a No-Good Dog

by *Julie Dunlap* and
Marybeth Lorbiecki

illustrated by *Bill Farnsworth*

COME ALONG ON A TRIP TO ALASKA

It's 1880 and few American citizens have ventured up into Alaska, unless they are after gold. But John Muir isn't after gold, he's after ice! He is out to map glaciers—age-old rivers of slowly moving ice.

And he wants nothing to do with pets—especially the no-good, stubborn, troublemaking dog, Stickeen, that his friend wants to bring along. This is the true story of Muir's voyage, based on his writings and journals.

John Muir was born in Scotland in 1838. He spoke with an accent and used many Scottish expressions, like "ye" instead of "you."

At the time of this Alaska trip, John Muir was not famous. He hadn't yet convinced President Roosevelt to create a national park in California or helped to start the Sierra Club—a group dedicated to wilderness adventures and protecting wild places. But he had been a farmer, inventor, and wanderer through swamps, across prairies, and over mountains.

Muir had even herded sheep so he could live day and night in the mountains. He learned to hate the sheep and cattle for gobbling and trampling the mountain meadows. John was sure tame animals had lost the quick brains and bold spirits he admired in wild ones.

That is, until one determined dog changed his mind.

John Muir stared at his friend's dog. Silky hair. Dainty paws. And darkness in his eyes, like weather that could turn on you.

"Yer pet doesn't belong on this trip," John complained. "He'll need care like a baby."

Hall Young just laughed. "Stickeen's a wonder of a dog, Muir. He can swim like a seal, stand cold like a bear."

John scoffed. But the dog jumped into the boat. That's how much Stickeen cared for John Muir's opinion.

"Ut-ha! Pull!" The expedition was off—to map Alaska's glaciers.

The men leaned into their oars. John jotted notes and sketched. He drew gulls slicing through the breeze and porpoises arching above the waves. This was the life!

Then a thunderous crack echoed—CRRRRRRRRCH! A chunk of glacier slammed into the water. Icy waves shot up. The canoe rocked.

Everyone fought to keep the canoe from tipping. Everyone except Stickeen, his snout on the prow.

The waters finally quieted.

John glanced at the sopping-wet dog. Just as I thought. A lazy, coddled pet, waiting for a towel-rub.

Stickeen saw John's eyes on him. He crawled under Muir's legs, then shook himself dry.

Hall and the crew hooted while John dripped.

At every landing, Stickeen was the first out. The dog went where he wanted and ignored all calls to leave. At the last moment, there would be Stickeen, paddling to catch up.

He's not my problem, thought John.

His mind was on the wild mountains of ice. Muir had such a crazy love of glaciers, the natives called him *Glate Ankow*, "Ice Chief."

At each camp, John tramped into the forest and over mountains, scribbling notes along the way. And who began tagging along?

Stickeen!

"Get on with ye," John shouted. "Ye're not fit for the wild!" He waved his arms. He threw pinecones. He ignored the dog.

Nothing worked.

Every day, there he'd be, that dog, following Muir. Not close enough to be friendly. Never a tail wag. Never a lick or a look or a bark of greetings.

Stickeen seemed as cold and silent as a glacier.

One night, John and Lot left camp in the dark to catch supper. Thousands of salmon fins churned the stream into silver fire. Then from a far bank came a steady comet-like blaze toward them—like a huge beast chasing the fishermen. Lot rowed hard.

Inches from the boat, the "monster" lifted its head. Muir roared with laughter. "Stickeen!"

What a puzzle was that bothering little dog.

The last morning in Glacier Bay was as wild and dark as an angry grizzly. Tomorrow, the expedition would have to turn for home. The ice called to Muir, rousing him from a deep sleep. He slipped from the tent, careful not to wake the others or Stickeen.

Not far from camp, John spotted a shadow slipping behind him through the trees.

"Go back to camp and have yer breakfast!" John yelled. "This storm will kill ye!"

But Muir should have known. Stickeen was more stubborn than he. Beaten, John offered the drenched dog a bit of his biscuit.

John hiked up rocky slopes, leaving the dog to do as he wished. A shaft of sun split the storm. Ahead stood the king of glaciers!

Hacking ice-steps with his ax, Muir climbed the blue wall. Stickeen scrambled after. On top, an endless sheet of ice stretched before them.

John hiked and sketched for hours, with an eye on the sky. He skipped over small ice cracks and zigzagged around deep crevasses. Stickeen followed.

The clouds blackened again. Muir had to hurry back to camp or face a night on the glacier without tent or fire. He ran hard through the swarming snow, the dog close at his heels. Both were hungry, soaked, and aching from cold.

Then John stopped. Stickeen looked up at him. It was as if the dog knew.

Muir was lost.

Backtracking, John used lines in the ice and wind direction to find his way. Stickeen tracked him like a trooper. At one broad gash, Muir peered down, down, down. Only one spot was narrow enough to leap across. And the far side was much lower. If he jumped down, he could never jump back up.

John hurdled across and down, wobbling on the slippery edge. Stickeen landed after Muir, not a hair to spare. But he trotted on, unrattled. Did nothing scare this dog?

Within minutes, the widest crack yet blocked their way. They were marooned on an island of ice.

Kneeling, John saw one slim chance of escape. Far below, a sagging sliver of ice bridged the chasm. Could it hold their weight? Stickeen nudged his shoulder. "Hush yer fears, wee beastie," John crooned softly.

Chip, chip, chip. He carved one heel hold, then another, down the ice-canyon's wall.

Ever so slowly, Muir lowered his body onto the sagging bridge.

It held.

Stickeen paced the rim. He began to whimper.

Legs dangling, John shaved flat the ice before him. He hitched himself forward, smoothing a path two-paws wide.

Mournful cries called to him from above.

Somehow, John's cold-clumsy hands cut a ladder up the other side of the canyon and he hauled himself out of danger. But he didn't rejoice.

He looked back for the dog. Could that pitiful creature, wailing and pacing, be Stickeen? "Come on, come on," Muir pleaded. "Ye can do it, wee boy!"

Then Stickeen lay down. His howls dipped and screeched.

John tried ordering him. "Stop yer nonsense!"

Shaking, Stickeen replied with more miserable wails.

Time was running out. With nightfall, Stickeen would likely fall or freeze to death. Could John return to camp for help and grope his way back in the dark?

No. The dog had to do it on his own. Now.

"Stickeen, poor boy," Muir said. "Don't ye see there's nothing I can do!"

The dog did not stir.

It was the last thing in the world he wanted to do, but John turned and walked away.

Stickeen's howls pierced the wind as Muir's back disappeared in the swirling gloom.

Stickeen's cries and shivers drained away. He pressed himself against the ice and slid his front paws, then his back, over the edge. Hair by hair, down each step.

Then a final sliding of muscle and fur, and he made it to the little bridge of ice.

But how far he still had to go! His tail fell to half mast. His body began to shake, more fiercely than before. The wind sharpened, nearly pushing Stickeen off the ice bridge.

Then the dog glanced up at the rim.

John was peering down. He had never really left.

The dog's tail flew over his back. Steady as the pelting snow, Stickeen moved over John's bridge-way path.

But at the wall, Stickeen stopped and eyed the towering cliff.

Dogs are poor climbers, John knew.

Would Stickeen try?

Stickeen launched skyward, scrabbling up the wall and over the top. "Well done," John cheered. "Well done, my boy!" He reached out for the dog, but Stickeen whizzed past, whirling, dancing, rolling head over heels. Squealing, the dog spun and charged at John, nearly knocking him down. A gleam in Stickeen's eyes shouted, "Saved! Saved at last!"

Nothing could frighten them now. All the cracks they met seemed puny and easily hopped.

Through the darkness, they spotted Lot's campfire.

Stickeen staggered to a blanket by the fire.

The men rubbed John dry as he spun out the tale of their storm battle for life. Stickeen had proven that his spirit was as fine as any wild creature's—or any human's.

"Yon's a brave doggie," John declared, nodding to Stickeen. Stickeen answered with a heavy thump of his tail.

For the rest of their voyage, the dog sat by John in the canoe by day and slept by his side at night. Stickeen and the Ice Chief endured many more adventures on the trip south.

At Sitka, Alaska, John had to leave his companions to catch a steamship home to California. The crew had to hold the struggling dog while John stepped onto the pier. Stickeen stood in the canoe—howling, howling—his mournful good-bye carried on the winds.

John never forgot his brave friend. Muir devoted himself to protecting wild lands, talking to presidents, giving speeches, and writing books about our need for nature's freedom and beauty. But he always had time to tell his favorite tale of Stickeen's struggle for life on the ice in Glacier Bay. He called their adventure "the most memorable of all my wild days."

In two books written late in life, *Stickeen* and *My Boyhood and Youth*, Muir urged readers to love all of the Earth's creatures, both wild and tame. Stickeen had shown something to Muir. Animals were much more like humans than John had thought. In Stickeen, the Ice Chief had found his kindred spirit.

THINK CRITICALLY

1. Why did John Muir and his crew go to Alaska? NOTE DETAILS

2. Did the authors clearly show what Stickeen was feeling and thinking? Give some examples from the story to support your answer. AUTHOR'S CRAFT

3. In your experience, are dogs normally as brave as Stickeen was? Explain. PRIOR KNOWLEDGE

4. The authors write that the last morning in Glacier Bay "was as wild and dark as an angry grizzly." What kind of figurative language is this phrase? What does it mean?
   Focus Skill FIGURATIVE LANGUAGE

5. **WRITE** John Muir's feelings about Stickeen changed during the story. Use information and details from the story to explain:
   - how John Muir felt about Stickeen at the beginning of the story, and
   - what happened on the trip to make Muir's feelings about Stickeen change. EXTENDED RESPONSE

About the Authors
JULIE DUNLAP

Julie Dunlap (right) has written picture books, biographies, and natural history books for young people of all ages. She studied forestry and the environment in college. Julie Dunlap also volunteers as a naturalist in Columbia, Maryland, where she lives with her family.

MARYBETH LORBIECKI

Marybeth Lorbiecki (left) was born in Germany and grew up in Minnesota. She likes writing about history and nature, and she believes young readers should have a wide range of literature available to them.

About the Illustrator
BILL FARNSWORTH

Before he starts painting, Bill Farnsworth researches his subjects and takes photographs of the things he plans to draw. Many of his illustrations, portraits, and landscapes have the look and feel of photographs.

 www.harcourtschool.com/storytown

JOHN MUIR
EXTREME EXPLORER

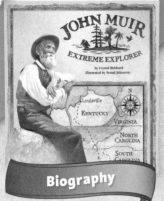

JOHN MUIR
EXTREME EXPLORER
by Crystal Hubbard
illustrated by Nenad Jakesevic

by **Crystal Hubbard**
illustrated by **Nenad Jakesevic**

Scottish explorer John Muir climbed glaciers and mountain peaks with only a walking stick and a pair of boots. When Muir decided to explore Florida, he did it as simply as he could—he walked.

Muir left Louisville, Kentucky, on September 1, 1867. He planned to walk a thousand miles to Cedar Keys, Florida. He took only the gray suit he had on, a change of clothes, and three books. A lot of people thought Muir was insane. Why would anyone walk so far just to look at plants? On October 15, Muir reached northeastern Florida. He decided that the walk was worth every step. He saw plants and land that were strange and new to him. Florida was more exciting than Muir had imagined.

Muir set off immediately to explore groves of trees he had never before seen. In his journal, Muir described Florida as a "watery and vine-tied land" because of the swampy coast and vine-covered trees.

From the northeastern corner of Florida, Muir made his way southwest to the Gulf Coast. There he saw his first palmetto. The palmetto plant looks like a cross between a broomstick and a palm tree. Muir hiked through miles of alligator-filled swamps to see a grove of palmettos that was seven miles long.

Muir had very little money. Strangers often shared their meals with him. Sometimes they gave him a place to sleep at night.

Muir spent a long time exploring the islands of the Cedar Keys. He drew the junipers, long-leafed pines, and oaks that grew there. He observed herons, pelicans, and mockingbirds. He collected samples of colorful flowers in the marshes and swamps.

The streams and rivers of Florida confused Muir. He expected them to run downhill, to a lake or an ocean. Instead, Florida's waters seemed to stand still.

Muir left Florida and spent some time exploring Cuba. He missed living in the United States, though, and in 1868 he sailed to California. There he discovered new mountains, valleys, and forests to explore.

Muir observed many birds while exploring the Cedar Keys.

Connections

Comparing Texts

1. Would you have liked exploring Glacier Bay by canoe with John Muir and Stickeen? Explain.

2. Compare "John Muir and Stickeen" with "John Muir: Extreme Explorer." How is the information in the selections alike? How is it different?

3. How have explorers like John Muir added to our knowledge of the world?

Vocabulary Review

They endured the difficult training because they were determined to win.

Word Pairs

Work with a partner. Write each Vocabulary Word on a separate index card, and place the cards face down. Take turns flipping over two cards and writing a sentence that uses both words. Read aloud the sentence to your partner. If you have used both words correctly, keep the cards. The student who has more cards at the end wins.

dedicated

determined

dainty

coddled

pitiful

endured

memorable

Fluency Practice

Partner Reading

With a partner, choose two paragraphs from "John Muir and Stickeen" to reread. Read the paragraphs aloud as your partner listens. Ask your partner for feedback about your expression. Then reread the passage, keeping your partner's feedback in mind. Switch roles, and listen as your partner reads.

Writing

Write a Letter

Imagine that you went along on John Muir's expedition. Use your imagination, along with information from the selection, to write a letter to a friend describing the expedition.

First
↓
Next
↓
Then
↓
Finally

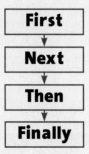

My Writing Checklist

Writing Trait ▸ Organization

✔ I used a graphic organizer to plan my writing.

✔ I organized the events I described in time order.

✔ I used figurative language in my writing to make the descriptions lively and interesting.

CONTENTS

Lesson 30
Theme Review and Vocabulary Builder

Readers' Theater
INFORMATIONAL NARRATIVE

Discovering the Atocha
FLORIDA
illustrated by Dave Stevenson

Content-Area Reading
SCIENCE TEXTBOOK

YOUR Science TEXTBOOK

distinguished

verify

discern

dubious

descend

frantically

estimate

vicinity

abruptly

scrutinize

Reading for Fluency

When reading a script aloud,

- Practice reading each word correctly until you can read your lines with **accuracy**.

- Read with **expression** that matches your character's personality and emotion.

Discovering the Atocha

FLORIDA

Characters

Narrator 1

Narrator 2

Juan, crew member

Taffi, Mel's daughter

Minna, crew member

Mel Fisher

Dolores, Mel's wife

Duncan, Mel's chief underwater archaeologist

Kane, Mel's son

Narrator 1: The story you are about to hear is based on true events.

Narrator 2: In 1985, distinguished treasure hunter and underwater explorer Mel Fisher, along with his "golden crew," his dedicated team of explorers, discovered the wreck of the Spanish galleon *Atocha* (uh•TOH•chuh).

Narrator 1: The *Atocha* sank after being caught in a hurricane in 1622. At the time, the ship was heavily laden with treasure and bound for Spain.

Narrator 2: For more than 360 years, the wreck and all its treasure lay hidden beneath the waters just 20 miles west of Key West, Florida.

Narrator 1: Mel Fisher began exploratory dives for the *Atocha* in 1969, after reading about it in a guidebook for divers seeking treasure.

Narrator 2: His discovery of the *Atocha* on July 20, 1985, completed a search that had lasted more than fifteen years.

Narrator 1: We begin our story in 1975. Mel Fisher and his team are diving near the Key of Matecumbe (ma•tuh•KUM•bee), continuing their search.

Narrator 2: Mel, his daughter Taffi, and two members of his crew, Juan and Minna, swim to the surface. They look frustrated.

Juan: We've searched all the waters around this key.

Taffi: We've been at this twice a day for the past nine months.

Minna: Six coral reefs, hundreds of starfish, and probably a million fish . . . but no sign of any treasure.

Juan: There's no trace of a shipwreck or even a single gold doubloon down there.

Mel: I think you're right. There's no shipwreck down there.

Taffi: Dad, you aren't giving up, are you?

Mel: I never give up. All I meant is that the *Atocha* isn't here.

Minna: So where do we search next?

Mel: Where do you think? The rest of the islands!

Juan: There are 882 islands in the Keys! Exploring them all would take a colossal amount of time.

Minna: We can't keep doing two dives a day, year after year.

Mel: Don't worry. I've got an idea that doesn't involve diving. We're going to fly instead!

Narrator 1: Later that day, Mel tells his family and crew about his plan as they all fly in a plane above the Marquesas (mar•KAY•suhz) Keys.

Taffi: I still don't understand why you couldn't tell us your plan on the ship, Dad.

Juan: Flying above the water is certainly easier than scuba diving.

Mel: I've been doing more research about the hurricane that sank the *Atocha*.

Juan: Have you learned something new?

Mel: I have a hunch, and flying above the Keys is the only way I can verify it. We're going to take a very close look at the Marquesas Keys.

Minna: There's no way the *Atocha* would have sailed in the direction of the Marquesas Keys.

Mel: True, but the hurricane might have driven the ship there.

Taffi: The Marquesas Keys are in the middle of nowhere, Dad!

Mel: That's why no one has ever searched there before. Take a close look, everybody!

Dolores: I see a coral reef to the east and three more to the west. Are there any more, Kane? You dove in this area recently.

Kane: There are reefs north and south of here, also.

Juan: No one would try to sail a small ship here, let alone a galleon like the *Atocha*.

Dolores: Yes, a ship would hit a reef and sink fast. So what's your idea, Mel?

Mel: Everyone knows that the hurricane forced the *Atocha* off course. If my hunch is correct, the storm smashed the ship into the Marquesas Keys!

Kane: Dad, with all the reefs in the Marquesas Keys, the *Atocha* would never have had a chance.

Mel: Exactly! That's why we're going to search for the *Atocha* right here! Today may be the day. . . .

Narrator 1: Our story now moves forward five years, to 1980. Mel and his crew have spent those years searching the Marquesas Keys.

Narrator 2: Juan, Dolores, Minna, Kane, and Duncan are scuba diving. Mel and Taffi are aboard Mel's ship, the *Dauntless*, waiting for them to surface. When the divers come out of the water, they look frustrated.

Dolores: The water is really murky.

Kane: I keep thinking I'm seeing shapes, but they're just illusions from all the silt floating around.

Duncan: My metal detector senses something in the sand.

Minna: The water is so cloudy that we can't discern anything!

Narrator 1: Mel lugs a box to the edge of the boat. A long hose is attached to it.

Mel: This should help with the silt.

Duncan: And just what is that?

Dolores: That's the contraption Mel's been perfecting for years now.

Narrator 2: Duncan points at the box in Mel's hand, a dubious look on his face.

Duncan: It looks like a mailbox with a hose attached.

Mel: It should help us see better under water.

Juan: Tell him how it works, Mel.

Mel: A motor inside pumps clear water down to the part of the ocean floor we're searching.

Duncan: Let's give it a try. Anything will help at this point.

Fluency Tip

Practice reading aloud unfamiliar words until you can read them with accuracy.

Narrator 1: Duncan lowers the box into the sea. The divers jump into the water again. Mel accompanies them. They stay under just long enough to see whether Mel's invention works. Then they surface.

Juan: It works! The machine clears away the murky water. Now we'll be able to see!

Kane: Great job, Dad!

Narrator 1: The divers descend again and slowly sweep their metal detectors over the ocean floor. Suddenly, Minna's metal detector beeps loudly.

Narrator 2: The divers realize that something is embedded in the sand. Excited, they start digging frantically. They uncover a long, rusty metal tube. The divers surface.

Kane: Just a rusty old pipe. Oh well, we've endured plenty of disappointments before.

Minna: I guess someone dumped that tube overboard.

Mel: It's not a pipe, and it's not a tube. I think it's part of a weapon.

Kane: A weapon! A cannon from an old ship!

Duncan: If the cannon is Spanish, I'll be able to recognize the design.

Juan: It's very rusty. It's been eroding under water for a long time.

Duncan: I estimate that this piece has been under water for at least a century—maybe much longer.

Minna: Could it possibly be from the *Atocha*?

Mel: Let's go back down and take a closer look. Maybe the shipwreck is in the vicinity. Today may be the day!

Narrator 1: It is now 1985. Juan, Kane, and Minna continue to make dives. Mel works from their home base, recording the crew's findings. Dolores, Taffi, and Duncan are with him.

Narrator 2: When Juan is below, he stops abruptly. He signals with his hands to the other divers, pointing above them. The others nod their heads, and they all swim up to the surface.

Juan: Something went wrong with my metal detector. It won't stop beeping. I was scanning the coral reef, and the machine began beeping like crazy.

Minna: We should go down and scrutinize that reef again.

Juan: I think you're right. Let's look again.

Narrator 1: Minna, Kane, and Juan dive down to the coral reef. They see a square object. Then the metal detector begins beeping.

Narrator 2: The divers push the sand

away. Something golden glistens in the water.

Narrator 1: The divers swim back to the surface.

Juan: You were right, Minna! That isn't part of the reef . . . it's a block of solid gold!

Kane: And the sand dune we were standing on . . . it's not a dune!

Minna: We must have been standing on the wreck of the *Atocha*!

Juan: We've got to tell Mel right away!

Narrator 2: Meanwhile, back in his office, Mel sits at his desk, studying a map of the Keys. Suddenly, his two-way radio crackles to life.

Kane: Hello, Unit 1, this is Unit 11. Dad, are you there?

Mel: Go ahead, Kane.

Kane: Put away the charts. We've got the

Mother Lode!

Mel: The whole wreck? Where? Where are you?

Narrator 2: Dolores, Taffi, and Duncan rush into the office.

Dolores: Mel, what's happened? Is something wrong?

Mel: They found the wreck!

Taffi: Where are they, Dad?

Mel: They're aboard the *Dauntless*.

Dolores: This is great! Mel, your dream has come true! You've overcome all obstacles.

Mel: We've all been after this goal for a long time.

Duncan: Yes, and we've had many memorable adventures!

Taffi: We certainly have!

Mel: You all know, though, that the work is just beginning.

Duncan: You're right. There's so much to learn from everything that's down there.

Dolores: The artifacts will have to be restored and preserved, too. We have to share all of this with the world.

Narrator 1: The lengthy search was over, but the journey of discovery was just beginning. To this day, artifacts and treasures from the *Atocha* are being recovered, analyzed, and preserved.

COMPREHENSION STRATEGIES
Review

Reading a Science Textbook

Bridge to Content-Area Reading Science textbooks
are examples of expository nonfiction. Expository
nonfiction explains facts and information about a topic.
The notes on page 785 point out some features of a science
textbook, including headings, highlighted words, and
questions. How can you use these features to skim and scan
a science lesson?

Review the Focus Strategies

If you do not understand what you are reading, use the
comprehension strategies you learned about in this theme.

Summarize
As you read, pause to summarize the most important ideas
in the text. You can summarize after reading a paragraph, a
section of text, or a complete text.

Monitor Comprehension: Reread
Monitor comprehension while you read. Reread any sections
of text that you did not understand.

As you read the pages from a science textbook on pages
786-789, think about where and how you can use
comprehension strategies.

HEADINGS

Headings give the topic of each section of text.

Reading in Science

VOCABULARY
producer p. 166
consumer p. 166
herbivore p. 168
carnivore p. 168
omnivore p. 168
decomposer p. 170

SCIENCE CONCEPTS
▶ how living things use the energy from sunlight
▶ how living things get energy from other living things

READING FOCUS SKILL
MAIN IDEA AND DETAILS
Look for details about the movement of energy among living things.

Producers and Consumers

Most living things on Earth get the energy to live from sunlight. Green plants and algae (AL•jee) use energy in sunlight, plus water and carbon dioxide, to make their own food. Any living thing that can make its own food is called a **producer**. Producers can be as small as a tiny moss or as large as a huge redwood tree.

Some animals, such as deer and cattle, get the energy they need to live by eating plants. When these animals eat, the energy stored in the plants moves into the animals' bodies.

Not all animals eat plants. Lions and hawks, for example, get the energy they need by eating other animals.

An animal that eats plants or other animals is called a **consumer**. Consumers can't make their own food, so they must eat other living things.

These plants are using energy in sunlight to produce food. Without sunlight, the plants would die.

Horse

Which animal gets its energy directly from producers? Which one gets its energy from other consumers? Which one gets its energy from both?

Florida panther

Some consumers eat the same kind of food all year. Horses, for example, eat grass during warm weather. During winter, they eat hay, a kind of dried grass.

Other consumers eat different things in different seasons. For example, black bears eat grass in spring. Later on, they might eat birds' eggs. Bears might also dig up tasty roots or eat fish from streams. In fall, bears eat ripe berries.

Florida panthers eat other consumers, but their diet varies. Mostly, panthers consume wild hogs, which are easy for them to catch. Another favorite meal is deer. Panthers also eat rabbits, raccoons, rats, birds, and sometimes, even alligators.

MAIN IDEA AND DETAILS What is a producer? What is a consumer? Give two examples of each.

Black bear

166

167

HIGHLIGHTED WORDS

Important vocabulary to know is highlighted.

QUESTIONS

Questions help you check your understanding of the text.

Apply the Strategies Read these pages about producers and consumers from a science textbook. As you read, use comprehension strategies, such as rereading, to help you understand the text.

Reading in Science

VOCABULARY
producer p. 166
consumer p. 166
herbivore p. 168
carnivore p. 168
omnivore p. 168
decomposer p. 170

SCIENCE CONCEPTS
▶ how living things use the energy from sunlight
▶ how living things get energy from other living things

READING FOCUS SKILL
MAIN IDEA AND DETAILS
Look for details about the movement of energy among living things.

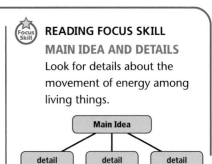

Producers and Consumers

Most living things on Earth get the energy to live from sunlight. Green plants and algae (AL•jee) use energy in sunlight, plus water and carbon dioxide, to make their own food. Any living thing that can make its own food is called a **producer**. Producers can be as small as a tiny moss or as large as a huge redwood tree.

Some animals, such as deer and cattle, get the energy they need to live by eating plants. When these animals eat, the energy stored in the plants moves into the animals' bodies.

Not all animals eat plants. Lions and hawks, for example, get the energy they need by eating other animals.

An animal that eats plants or other animals is called a **consumer**. Consumers can't make their own food, so they must eat other living things.

These plants are using energy in sunlight to produce food. Without sunlight, the plants would die.

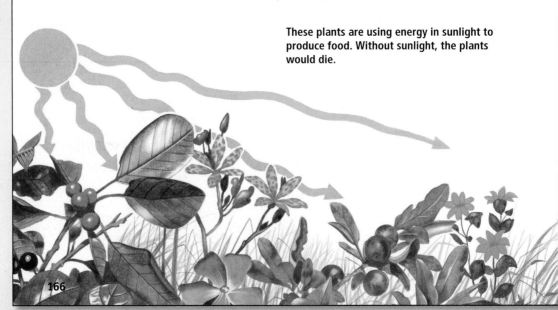

166

Stop and Think

Go back and reread any parts of this text that you had trouble understanding. **MONITOR COMPREHENSION: REREAD**

Horse

Which animal gets its energy directly from producers? Which one gets its energy from other consumers? Which one gets its energy from both?

Florida panther

Some consumers eat the same kind of food all year. Horses, for example, eat grass during warm weather. During winter, they eat hay, a kind of dried grass.

Other consumers eat different things in different seasons. For example, black bears eat grass in spring. Later on, they might eat birds' eggs. Bears might also dig up tasty roots or eat fish from streams. In fall, bears eat ripe berries.

Florida panthers eat other consumers, but their diet varies. Mostly, panthers consume wild hogs, which are easy for them to catch. Another favorite meal is deer. Panthers also eat rabbits, raccoons, rats, birds, and sometimes, even alligators.

 MAIN IDEA AND DETAILS What is a producer? What is a consumer? Give two examples of each.

Black bear

167

Kinds of Consumers

Consumers are not all the same. In fact, there are three kinds—herbivores, carnivores, and omnivores.

A **herbivore** is an animal that eats only plants, or producers. Horses are herbivores. So are giraffes, squirrels, and rabbits.

A **carnivore** is an animal that eats only other animals. The Florida panther and the lion are carnivores. A carnivore can be as large as a whale or as small as a frog.

An **omnivore** is an animal that eats both plants and other animals. That is, omnivores eat both producers and other consumers. Bears and hyenas are omnivores. Do any omnivores live in your home?

Producers and all three kinds of consumers can be found living in water. Algae are producers that live in water. They use sunlight to make their own food. Tadpoles, small fish, and other small herbivores eat algae. Larger fish that are carnivores eat the tadpoles. Some animals, including green sea turtles, are omnivores. Green sea turtles eat seaweed, algae, and fish. In fact, algae makes the flesh of the green sea turtle green!

 MAIN IDEA AND DETAILS Name the three kinds of consumers. Give two examples of each.

This diagram shows how kinds of consumers get energy to live.

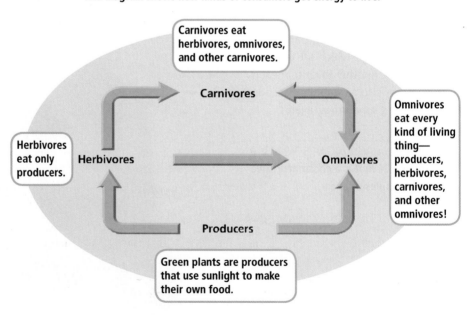

Carnivores eat herbivores, omnivores, and other carnivores.

Omnivores eat every kind of living thing—producers, herbivores, carnivores, and other omnivores!

Herbivores eat only producers.

Green plants are producers that use sunlight to make their own food.

Carnivores

Herbivores

Omnivores

Producers

168

Stop and Think

Pause to summarize the important ideas in the text.

SUMMARIZE

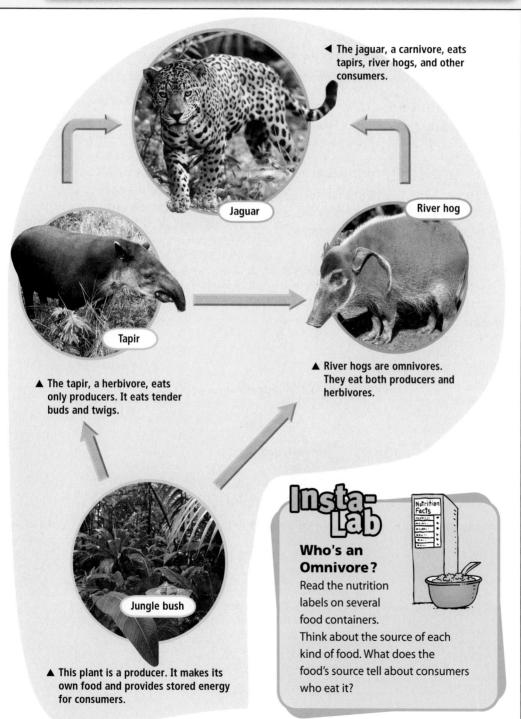

◀ The jaguar, a carnivore, eats tapirs, river hogs, and other consumers.

Jaguar

River hog

Tapir

▲ River hogs are omnivores. They eat both producers and herbivores.

▲ The tapir, a herbivore, eats only producers. It eats tender buds and twigs.

Jungle bush

▲ This plant is a producer. It makes its own food and provides stored energy for consumers.

Insta-Lab

Who's an Omnivore?

Read the nutrition labels on several food containers.

Think about the source of each kind of food. What does the food's source tell about consumers who eat it?

169

Using the Glossary

Like a dictionary, this glossary lists words in alphabetical order. To find a word, look it up by its first letter or letters.

To save time, use the **guide words** at the top of each page. These show you the first and last words on the page. Look at the guide words to see if your word falls between them alphabetically.

Here is an example of a glossary entry:

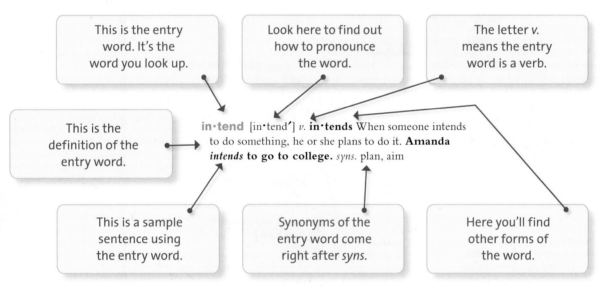

This is the entry word. It's the word you look up.	Look here to find out how to pronounce the word.	The letter v. means the entry word is a verb.

in·tend [in·tend′] *v.* **in·tends** When someone intends to do something, he or she plans to do it. **Amanda *intends* to go to college.** *syns.* plan, aim

This is the definition of the entry word.		
This is a sample sentence using the entry word.	Synonyms of the entry word come right after *syns*.	Here you'll find other forms of the word.

Word Origins

Throughout the glossary, you will find notes about word origins, or how words get started and change. Words often have interesting backgrounds that can help you remember what they mean. Here is an example of a word origin note:

> **Word Origins**
>
> **jostle** *Jostle* comes from the word *joust*, the root of the Old French word *jousten*. It originally came from the Latin word *juxtare*, meaning "to come together." When people bump into each other, they jostle each other.

Pronunciation

The pronunciation in brackets is a respelling that shows how the word is pronounced. The **pronunciation** key explains what the symbols in a respelling mean. A shortened pronunciation key appears on every other page of the glossary.

PRONUNCIATION KEY

a	add, map	m	move, seem	u	up, done
ā	ace, rate	n	nice, tin	û(r)	burn, term
â(r)	care, air	ng	ring, song	yo͞o	fuse, few
ä	palm, father	o	odd, hot	v	vain, eve
b	bat, rub	ō	open, so	w	win, away
ch	check, catch	ô	order, jaw	y	yet, yearn
d	dog, rod	oi	oil, boy	z	zest, muse
e	end, pet	ou	pout, now	zh	vision, pleasure
ē	equal, tree	o͝o	took, full	ə	the schwa, an
f	fit, half	o͞o	pool, food		unstressed vowel
g	go, log	p	pit, stop		representing the
h	hope, hate	r	run, poor		sound spelled
i	it, give	s	see, pass		*a* in *above*
ī	ice, write	sh	sure, rush		*e* in *sicken*
j	joy, ledge	t	talk, sit		*i* in *possible*
k	cool, take	th	thin, both		*o* in *melon*
l	look, rule	t̶h̶	this, bathe		*u* in *circus*

Other symbols:
- · separates words into syllables
- ´ indicates heavy stress on a syllable
- ˏ indicates light stress on a syllable

Abbreviations: *adj.* **adjective,** *adv.* **adverb,** *conj.* **conjunction,** *interj.* **interjection,** *n.* **noun,** *prep.* **preposition,** *pron.* **pronoun,** *syn.* **synonym,** *v.* **verb**

A

a·brupt·ly [ə·brupt′lē] *adv.* If you do something abruptly, you do it very suddenly. **The baseball game ended *abruptly* when it started to rain.** *syns.* suddenly, unexpectedly

---
Word Origins

abrupt The word a*brupt* comes from the Latin *abruptus,* meaning "broken off or disconnected." The word parts are *ab-* "off" + *ruptus* "break." It originally referred to a rupture or fracture of an arm or a leg. Something that happens abruptly happens in a seemingly broken and disconnected way.

ACADEMIC LANGUAGE

accuracy When you read with *accuracy,* you read without any mistakes.

ac·cus·ing [ə·kyoo′zing] *adj.* When you look at someone in an accusing way, you are showing that you think he or she has done something wrong. **The judge gave Victor an *accusing* look when he thought Victor was guilty.** *syn.* blaming

ad·van·tage [ad·van′tij] *n.* When someone takes advantage of something, he or she makes good use of it. **Nellie and Janine take *advantage* of their neighbor's knowledge of woodworking by asking him for advice on building a birdhouse.** *syns.* benefit, use

al·ter [ôl′tər] *v.* **al·tered** When something has been altered, it has been changed. **Darnel *altered* the look of the old sofa by covering it with new fabric.** *syns.* change, modify

an·ces·tor [an′ses′·tər] *n.* **an·ces·tors** The people who came before you in your family are your ancestors. **Alice's *ancestors* came to this country from Poland.** *syn.* forebear

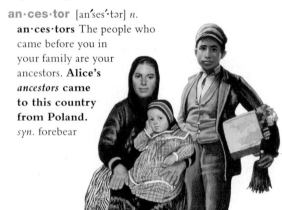

ancestor

an·cient [ān′shənt] *adj.* Something ancient is very, very old. **Scientists in China have discovered the ruins of an *ancient* city that is more than two thousand years old.** *syn.* old

an·noy [ə·noi′] *v.* **an·noyed** To be annoyed means to be somewhat angry about something. **Rachel was *annoyed* when Mary spilled hot chocolate on her homework.** *syn.* irritate

anx·ious·ly [angk′shəs·lē] *adv.* If you waited anxiously for something, you worried about how it would turn out. **As Mr. Donovan handed out the report cards, Leroy waited *anxiously*.** *syns.* nervously, uneasily

as·pect [as′pekt′] *n.* **as·pects** The aspects of a place or thing are its features and elements. **The test has two *aspects,* the reading section and the writing section.** *syns.* feature, part

at·ten·tive [ə·ten′tiv] *adj.* If someone is attentive, that person is carefully listening to or watching something. **The students were *attentive* as they watched the video about the food chain.** *syns.* alert, focused

ACADEMIC LANGUAGE

autobiography An *autobiography* is a person's account of his or her own life. Autobiographies use the first-person point of view.

a·vert [ə·vûrt′] *v.* **a·vert·ed** If you averted your eyes, you looked away from something instead of directly at it. **During the eclipse, María *averted* her eyes from the sun.** *syn.* turn away

a·void [ə·void′] *v.* If you avoid a person or thing, you keep away from them. **Chico knows how to *avoid* getting tagged while running from third base to home plate.** *syn.* escape

B

bar·ri·er [bar′·ē·ər] *n.* **bar·ri·ers** Barriers are objects or people that keep you from moving ahead. **The police put up *barriers* to prevent cars from driving on Main Street during the parade.** *syns.* obstacle, fence

beam [bēm′] *v.* **beams** Someone who beams is grinning. **Denisha *beams* with pride when her hockey team wins the game.** *syn.* smile

be·he·moth [bi·hē′məth] *n.* Something called a behemoth is extremely large. **Scientists describe the prehistoric sloth as a hairy *behemoth*.** *syn.* giant

━━ Word Origins ━━

behemoth *Behemoth* is a Latin word that came from the Hebrew word *b'hemoth,* a plural form of the word *b'hemah,* meaning "beast." The Hebrew word, most likely a version of the Egyptian word *pehemau,* literally means "water-ox," the name for the hippopotamus. The hippopotamus, whose habitat was the Nile River, was the "beast" most feared by the Egyptians, who used the river daily for transportation and trade.

ACADEMIC LANGUAGE

biography A *biography* is the story of a real person's life that is written by another person.

bond [bänd] *n.* A bond is a feeling or interest that unites two or more people or groups. **The twins, Carmen and Isabella, have such a close *bond* that they seem to know each other's thoughts.** *syns.* link, relationship

boun·ti·ful [boun′ti·fəl] *adj.* If you had a bountiful amount of something, you would have a lot of it. **The harvest was so *bountiful* that Maggie's family was eating corn for months.** *syns.* plentiful, abundant

bril·liant [bril′yənt] *adj.* Things that are brilliant are very bright and often shiny. **Emanuel's mom got a necklace with a *brilliant* blue gemstone for her birthday.** *syns.* dazzling, sparkling

burst [bûrst] *v.* When a person feels ready to burst if he or she doesn't say something, it means that the person is very excited and cannot wait to say that thing. **Lamont felt that he would *burst* if he didn't announce his invitation to attend the International Science Fair.** *syn.* erupt

C

cas·cade [kas·kād′] *v.* **cas·cad·ing** Cascading water falls or rushes downward very fast. **A *cascading* waterfall flows over Luis's rock garden.** *syn.* flow

cease [sēs′] *v.* If you cease to do something, you stop doing it. **Takara is going to *cease* watching television during the week of exams.** *syns.* stop, quit

cher·ish [cher′ish] *v.* If you cherish something, it means a lot to you and you care for it lovingly. **Grandparents *cherish* their grandchildren and delight in their visits.** *syns.* treasure, value

FACT FILE

cherish *Cherish* comes from Old French and means "to hold dear." Some state courts have put the word *cherish* into their state constitutions, requiring the government to "cherish education." By this they mean not only to value education but also to support it financially. By law, a state must cherish education by funding it through taxes.

clus·ter [kləs′tər] *n.* **clus·ters** Clusters are small groups of people or things that are close together. **We bought two *clusters* of grapes for an afternoon snack.** *syn.* bunch

cluster

cod·dle [kä′dəl] *v.* **cod·dled** Someone who has been coddled has been treated too kindly or protected too much. **Fred's mother *coddled* him and wouldn't let him play outside.** *syns.* pamper, overprotect

co·los·sal [kə·lä′səl] *adj.* Something that is colossal is huge. **Many apartment buildings and office buildings in large cities are *colossal* skyscrapers.** *syns.* huge, enormous

FACT FILE

colossal The Colossus was one of the Seven Wonders of the Ancient World. This huge statue, which stood at the entrance to the harbor of the Mediterranean island of Rhodes in Greece, was 120 feet high. It was said to be so large that ships could sail between its legs. The word *colossus* comes from the Greek word *kolossos,* meaning "large." Without the statue of the Colossus of Rhodes, the English language would never have included the word *colossal.*

a	add	e	end	o	odd	o͞o	pool	oi	oil	th	this		
ā	ace	ē	equal	ō	open	u	up	ou	pout	zh	vision	ə =	*a* in *above*
â	care	i	it	ô	order	û	burn	ng	ring				*e* in *sicken*
ä	palm	ī	ice	o͝o	took	yo͞o	fuse	th	thin				*i* in *possible*
													o in *melon*
													u in *circus*

com·fort [kum′fərt] *v.* **com·fort·ed** If a person comforted a friend, he or she helped that friend feel better about something. **When Jane didn't do well on the test, Lisa *comforted* her by promising to help her study for the next one.** *syns.* console, reassure

com·mence [kə·mens′] *v.* **com·menced** Something that has commenced has begun. **Zack *commenced* doing his homework but was distracted from it when his friend Jacob called.** *syns.* begin, start

com·pli·cat·ed [käm′plə·kā′ted] *adj.* Something that is complicated has many parts that are connected in ways that make it hard to understand. **The engine of a car is a type of *complicated* machinery.** *syns.* complex, intricate

com·pre·hend [käm′pri·hend′] *v.* If you comprehend something, you understand it. **Mother couldn't *comprehend* why Natasha didn't like wearing a uniform to school.** *syns.* understand, grasp

> **― Word Origins ―**
>
> **comprehend** The word *comprehend* comes from the Latin verb *comprehendere,* meaning "to grasp or seize." The word parts are *com-,* meaning "completely," and *prehendere,* meaning "to catch hold of or seize." In 1340, the meaning changed to "to grasp with the mind." A person who comprehends something has grasped its meaning.

con·fi·dent·ly [kän′fə·dənt·lē] *adv.* When you do something confidently, you are sure about what you are doing. **Sharrita *confidently* entered the spelling bee.** *syns.* self-assuredly, assertively

con·found [kən·found′] *v.* If you confound a person, you surprise or confuse him or her. **Toshi knew she could *confound* her sister by telling her she didn't want to borrow her clothes anymore.** *syns.* confuse, bewilder

con·sist [kən·sist′] *v.* **con·sist·ed** If something consisted of several things, it was made up of those things. **The fruit in the basket *consisted* of bananas, apples, and peaches.** *syns.* comprise, include

con·stant [kän′stənt] *adj.* If something is constant, it happens without stopping. **The *constant* breeze from the ocean is delightful in the summertime.** *syns.* steady, continuous

con·ster·na·tion [kän′stər·nā′shən] *n.* Someone who feels consternation is upset or worried about what is happening. **Bret's *consternation* that the ship might sink did not go away until he was safe on shore.** *syns.* concern, worry

con·tract [kən·trakt′] *v.* To contract means to get smaller by shrinking. **In his report, Pedro explained that heating metal makes it get bigger and that cooling metal makes it *contract*.** *syns.* decrease, shrink

con·tra·dict [kän′trə·dikt′] *v.* **con·tra·dict·ing** Contradicting someone is saying that what the person has said is wrong. **Lupita was *contradicting* Marissa's statements about the advantages of going to a private school.** *syns.* disagree, refute

con·trap·tion [kən·trap′shən] *n.* A contraption is a strange-looking machine or device. **For the science fair, the fourth-grade team built a *contraption* for measuring and pouring chemicals.** *syns.* device, machine

cor·dial·ly [kôr′jəl·ē] *adv.* To say something cordially is to say it in a warm, friendly way. **Elena *cordially* answered the tourists' questions.** *syns.* pleasantly, kindly

crane [krān] *v.* **craned** If you craned your neck, you stretched it to let you see or hear something better. **When the concert started, Akio *craned* his neck to better see the performers.** *syn.* stretch

cringe [krinj] *v.* **cringed** If you cringed, you moved or flinched slightly because of discomfort or fear. **Latisha *cringed* when the dentist started drilling one of her teeth.** *syns.* flinch, wince

cu·li·nar·y [kə′lə·ner′ē] *adj.* Culinary skills or tools are related to cooking. **The chef specialized in making desserts that were *culinary* masterpieces.** *syn.* cooking

culinary

D

dain·ty [dān′tē] *adj.* Something that is dainty is small and delicate. **Alberto was afraid of breaking the *dainty* china cup.** *syns.* delicate, fancy

---

Word Origins

dainty The word *dainty* is related to the Latin words *dignus,* meaning "worthy," and *dignitas,* meaning "worth or beauty." Old French changed the Latin word to *daintie* and gave it the meanings of "price or value" and "delicacy or pleasure." The adjective was first recorded in 1300, meaning "choice or excellent." Over time, its meaning changed to "delicately pretty." Lace makes a wedding gown look dainty, or delicately pretty.

dart [därt] *v.* **dart·ed** An animal that darted moved suddenly and quickly in a particular direction. **The rabbit wandered into the yard, but when it saw the cat, it *darted* back into the woods.** *syn.* rush

dash [dash] *v.* **dashed** If someone dashed away, he or she quickly and suddenly ran away. **Matthew *dashed* away in a split second when he spotted his younger sister coming out to play.** *syns.* hurry, run

FACT FILE

dash The word *dash* came from a Scandinavian source, but it has a varied history of meanings. The oldest sense is found in the phrases *dash to pieces* and *dashed hopes.* Then followed the meanings "to move quickly" and "to write hurriedly." The term *dashboard,* which refers to a part of an automobile, came from an earlier use in 1846 to refer to the board in front of a carriage that stopped mud from being dashed, or splashed, into the vehicle by the horse's hoofs.

de·cep·tive [di·sep´tiv] *adj.* A deceptive person or thing tries to make you believe something that is not true. **Brenda's mom realized the advertisement was *deceptive* when it stated that the washing machine would work forever.** *syn.* misleading

de·clare [di·klâr´] *v.* **de·clared** Something that has been declared has been announced in a clear way. **Serena's mom *declared* that dinner would be ready by 6 o'clock.** *syns.* state, announce

ded·i·cate [de´di·kāt´] *v.* **ded·i·cat·ed** If you are dedicated to achieving a goal, you are devoting yourself to that purpose. **Derrick's teacher is *dedicated* to improving the math scores of the class.** *syns.* devote, commit

de·lec·ta·ble [di·lek´tə·bəl] *adj.* A food described as delectable tastes very good. **Lydia baked a *delectable* cake for the party.** *syns.* tasty, delicious

delectable

del·i·cate [de´li·kət] *adj.* If something is done in a delicate way, it is done with great care so that nothing is broken or hurt. **With a *delicate* touch, José removed the new dishes from the carton.** *syn.* fragile

de·prive [di·prīv´] *v.* **de·priv·ing** If someone is depriving you of something, the person is keeping you from having it. **Mom was *depriving* Karl of the last piece of cake until he finished his homework.**

depth [depth´] *n.* **depths** The depths of something are its deepest parts. **Scientists in a minisub found a new species of fish in the *depths* of the ocean.**

de·scend [di·send´] *v.* When you descend, you move downward. **With the elevator broken, Takashi wondered how long it would take to *descend* the fifteen floors by using the stairs.** *syn.* fall

des·ti·na·tion [des´tə·nā´shən] *n.* **des·ti·na·tions** Destinations are the places people are going to. **The travelers took the shuttle bus from the airport to their *destinations*.**

de·ter·mined [di·tûr´mind] *adj.* A determined person will do everything possible to try to accomplish a task. **Felipe is a *determined* tennis player who practices hitting the tennis ball every day.** *syns.* persistent, resolute

---

a	add	e	end	o	odd	o͞o	pool	oi	oil	th	this		a in *above*
ā	ace	ē	equal	ō	open	u	up	ou	pout	zh	vision		e in *sicken*
â	care	i	it	ô	order	û	burn	ng	ring			ə =	i in *possible*
ä	palm	ī	ice	o͝o	took	yo͞o	fuse	th	thin				o in *melon*
													u in *circus*

dis·cern [di·sûrn′] v. If you discern things, you are aware of them and are able to tell differences between them. **Tia learned to *discern* between a real friend and someone who just wanted to use her things.** *syns.* distinguish, perceive

dis·cour·age [dis·kûr′ij] v. **dis·cour·aged** If something discouraged you, it made you believe things weren't going to turn out as you hoped. **Charles was hoping to earn money for a bike, but the lack of after-school jobs *discouraged* him.** *syn.* dishearten

dis·tant [dis′tənt] adj. Something distant is very far away. **Sam doesn't see his friend John much, since he moved to a *distant* town.** *syns.* far, remote

dis·tin·guished [dis·ting′gwisht] adj. A distinguished person stands out from others in a job or field of work. **Carl Sagan, a *distinguished* astronomy professor, was invited to speak at many scientific conventions.** *syns.* famous, prominent

dis·tressed [dis·trest′] adj. Someone who is distressed feels very sad and helpless. **Kana was *distressed* to learn that her favorite teacher was leaving.** *syns.* upset, troubled

down·cast [doun′kast′] adj. Someone who is downcast is feeling sad and has no hope. **Gabriela was *downcast* when a blizzard ruined her vacation plans.** *syns.* dejected, depressed

drab [drab] adj. Something drab looks dull and lacks color. **Awan's living room looks *drab* because all the walls and furniture are in shades of brown.** *syns.* dull, plain

drudg·er·y [drə′jə·rē] n. Drudgery is hard and unpleasant or boring work. **Cleaning my room is *drudgery* to me.** *syn.* toil

du·bi·ous [doo′bē·əs] adj. A person who is dubious is doubtful or unsure about something. **Debra's coach was *dubious* about her ability to finish the ten-mile race.** *syns.* doubtful, uncertain

---

E

---

ee·rie [ir′ē] adj. Something that is eerie is strange and makes people feel afraid. **The local cemetery at night has an *eerie* atmosphere.** *syns.* creepy, weird

el·e·gant [el′ə·gənt] adj. Something elegant is graceful and pleasing to look at. **The design of Molly's dress is *elegant*.** *syn.* tasteful

em·bed [im·bed′] v. **em·bed·ded** If an object is embedded in something, it is stuck firmly in it. **A splinter was *embedded* in Gusto's finger.** *syns.* stick, entrench

en·cir·cle [in·sûr′kəl] v. To encircle a place means to surround it. **Bonnie's plan is to *encircle* the area with traps and wait to see if the ants take the bait.** *syns.* surround, circle

en·dure [in·door′] v. **en·dured** Someone who has endured hardships has used personal strength to survive them. **Because she had inner strength, Cynthia *endured* the difficult times in her life.** *syns.* survive, outlast

e·rod·ing [i·rō′ding] adj. Something that is eroding is being slowly scraped away a little at a time, often by the force of moving water or strong wind. **During the hurricane, the already *eroding* beach lost more sand.** *syns.* weather, wear

e·rup·tion [i·rup′shən] n. An eruption happens when something bursts through a surface. **The volcanic *eruption* sent thick clouds of smoke into the sky.** *syn.* explosion

eruption

es·ti·mate [es′tə·māt] v. When you estimate an amount of something, you make a careful guess about how many things there are in it. **Tim tried to *estimate* the cost of the bike to make sure he had enough money to buy it.** *syns.* approximate, guess

ex·ist [ig·zist′] v. **ex·ists** When something exists, it is a real thing that is present in the world. **Ben found where ants *exist* in his apartment by following their trail to the bread in the cabinet.** *syns.* live, survive

ex·ot·ic [ig·zä′tik] adj. Something exotic is unusual and interesting because it came from a faraway place. **Some people consider dates and hummus from the Middle East *exotic* foods.** *syn.* unusual

ex·pec·tant·ly [ik·spek′tənt·lē] adv. When you wait expectantly for something, you eagerly look forward to it. **Alisha was *expectantly* awaiting a letter from her grandfather.** *syns.* hopefully, eagerly

ex·pose [ik·spōz′] v. **ex·posed** A thing that has been exposed has been uncovered and has lost its protection from its surroundings. **The hurricane blew off the garage roof and *exposed* the car to the wind and rain.** *syn.* uncover

ex·ten·sive [ik·sten′siv] *adj.* Something extensive includes a large amount of things. **Kioshi's mother's plans to remodel the kitchen were *extensive* and included new appliances, new cabinets, and new flooring.** *syns.* large, sizable

ex·tract [ik·strakt′] *v.* When you extract something, you carefully pull it out of something else. **The dentist will *extract* two of Stan's teeth.** *syns.* remove, extricate

ex·u·ber·ant [ig·zoo′bər·ənt] *adj.* If someone is exuberant, he or she is full of excitement, energy, and happiness. **Mauricio is *exuberant* about doing a comedy sketch in which he can use lots of facial expressions.** *syns.* enthusiastic, excited

fan·ci·ful [fan′si·fəl] *adj.* Something that is fanciful is not real but comes from the imagination. **In her journal, Lakeisha wrote about her *fanciful* journey to the moon.** *syns.* imaginary, whimsical

fas·ci·nate [fa′sə·nāt′] *v.* **fas·ci·nat·ed** When you are fascinated by something, you are very interested in it and pay close attention to it. **The kitten is *fascinated* by the colorful fish in the aquarium.** *syn.* enthrall

fes·tive [fes′tiv] *adj.* Something that is festive is colorful and exciting. **The holidays are *festive* in Dario's village, as families celebrate with special foods, singing, and dancing.** *syns.* exciting, merry

fidg·et [fi′jət] *v.* People might fidget, or move around restlessly, when they are bored or nervous. **At the movies, Patrice and Frankie annoy everyone when they *fidget* and won't sit still.** *syns.* squirm, move

fierce [firs] *adj.* A fierce person or animal is angry, violent, or ready to attack. **A possum can be *fierce*, attacking with its very sharp teeth.** *syns.* aggressive, violent

flex·i·ble [flek′sə·bəl] *adj.* Something is flexible if it can bend or be bent easily. **Ryan used a *flexible* cord to bundle a stack of newspapers.** *syns.* supple, limber

flinch [flinch′] *v.* **flinched** If a person flinched, he or she quickly moved away from something dangerous or painful. **Aneko *flinched* as the doctor injected the flu vaccine into her arm.** *syns.* recoil, cringe

fluke [flook] *n.* A fluke is something unusual that happens by accident. **It was just a *fluke* that Dad found my ring when he was mowing the lawn.** *syn.* coincidence

foist [foist′] *v.* **foist·ed** If something is foisted on you, it is given to you whether you want it or not. **It was not Dan's turn to do the dishes, but the job was *foisted* on him when his brother became sick.** *syns.* impose, force

forge [fôrj] *v.* **forged** If you forged something together, you did it with great effort and you hope it lasts a long time. **Consuela and Daphne *forged* a new work schedule to organize the tasks on the farm.** *syns.* create, build

a	add	e	end	o	odd	$\overline{oo}$	pool	oi	oil	th	this		a in *above*
ā	ace	ē	equal	ō	open	u	up	ou	pout	zh	vision		e in *sicken*
â	care	i	it	ô	order	û	burn	ng	ring			ə =	i in *possible*
ä	palm	ī	ice	$\overline{oo}$	took	yōō	fuse	th	thin				o in *melon*
													u in *circus*

for·lorn·ly [fôr·lôrn′lē] *adv.* If you do something forlornly, you do it in a way that shows you feel sad and lonely. **After her guests left, Aponi looked around** *forlornly* **at the empty house.** *syns.* sadly, unhappily

fra·gile [fra′jəl] *adj.* If a thing is fragile, it is easily broken or damaged. **Jenny's mom has special cups that she uses only on special occasions because they are very** *fragile*. *syns.* delicate, frail

fragile

fran·ti·cal·ly [fran′ti·kə·lē] *adv.* To behave frantically is to behave in a wild, energetic way. **When the bus took the turn too fast, Shen and Jason** *frantically* **grabbed something to hold on to.** *syns.* anxiously, worriedly

> **ACADEMIC LANGUAGE**
>
> **functional text** *Functional text* is writing used in everyday life, such as letters, manuals, and directions.

fu·ry [fyoor′ē] *n.* Fury is extremely strong anger. **When Jack didn't get his way, he stomped out of the room in a** *fury*. *syns.* anger, wrath

G

gape [gāp] *v.* **gaped** If you gaped at something, you stared open-mouthed in surprise. **As the parade passed by, the crowd** *gaped* **at the gigantic balloon characters.** *syns.* stare, gawk

glare [glâr] *v.* **glared** If you glared at someone, you stared at the person in an angry way. **Ramon** *glared* **at Francisco after Francisco laughed at him for slipping in the mud.** *syn.* glower

glis·ten [glis′ən] *v.* **glis·tens** Something that glistens looks wet and shiny. **The lake** *glistens* **in the sunlight every morning.** *syns.* gleam, sparkle

gloat [glōt] *v.* **gloat·ed** If someone gloated, he or she bragged about something in a mean way. **Showing poor sportsmanship, the winning team** *gloated* **over its victory.** *syn.* revel

gor·geous [gôr′jəs] *adj.* A gorgeous person or thing is attractive and stunning. **The princess looked** *gorgeous* **in her gown as she entered the ballroom.** *syns.* beautiful, stunning

> **FACT FILE**
>
> **gorgeous** *Gorgeous* has roots in the Latin word *gurga*, which became the Old French word *gorge*, meaning "throat." *Gorgeous* was borrowed from the Old French word *gorgias*, meaning "fashionable, elegant, or fond of wearing jewelry." Since a necklace is jewelry worn around the throat, beautiful jewelry came to be described as *gorgeous*.

grace·ful [grās′fəl] *adj.* If a person is graceful, he or she moves in a smooth way that is nice to look at. **A ballet dancer is** *graceful*. *syns.* elegant, pleasing

gra·cious [grā′shəs] *adj.* Someone who is gracious is pleasant and polite. **Camila was very** *gracious* **as she welcomed her guests and made them feel at home.** *syns.* courteous, sociable

grad·u·al·ly [gra′jə·wəl·ē] *adj.* Something that happens gradually happens very slowly over time. **Asad is learning his multiplication facts** *gradually* **by memorizing a different set of facts each week.** *syns.* slowly, progressively

gui·dance [gī′dəns] *n.* Someone who gives guidance provides help and advice. **With her dancing teacher's** *guidance,* **Annette learned the new tap routine.** *syns.* supervision, direction

H

heart·y [här′tē] *adj.* If a meal is hearty, it is satisfying and includes plenty of good food. **We always have** *hearty* **meals at our family reunions.** *syns.* filling, plentiful

her·mit [hər′mət] *n.* A hermit is a person who lives alone, often far from a community. **Far from the city's malls, traffic, and crowds, the** *hermit* **felt comfortable in his country home.** *syns.* loner, recluse

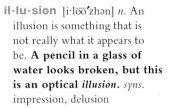

Word Origins

hermit The word *hermit* has roots in the Greek word *eremos,* meaning "uninhabited." It is also related to the Greek words *eremia,* meaning "desert or solitude," and *eremites,* meaning "person of the desert." Latin changed the Greek *eremites* to *ermita,* and Old French changed *ermita* to *(h)eremit.* The hermit crab is known for its solitary habits, seldom leaving its borrowed shell.

ACADEMIC LANGUAGE

historical fiction *Historical fiction* stories are set in the past and portray people, places, and events that did happen or could have happened.

hoax [hōks] *n.* **hoax·er** Someone who tries to trick people is a hoaxer. **Kelley is a *hoaxer* who pretends to be asleep when she's not.** *syn.* trick

---

FACT FILE

hoax The phrase *hocus-pocus* is believed to have been invented by magicians to make them sound impressive when performing tricks. Although this phrase is made up of meaningless rhyming words, from *hocus* has come the word *hoax,* meaning "a mischievous trick."

---

hoist [hoist] *v.* To hoist something is to raise it, often with mechanical help. **Archie and Mike know when to *hoist* the sails and let the wind guide the boat.** *syns.* lift, raise

---

ACADEMIC LANGUAGE

how-to article A *how-to article* gives step-by-step instructions for completing a task or project.

hud·dle [hə′dəl] *v.* When people huddle together, they gather close to each other in a tight group. **The animals *huddled* together in the cold barn to stay warm.** *syns.* cluster, crowd

---

I

il·lu·sion [i·lo͞o′zhən] *n.* An illusion is something that is not really what it appears to be. **A pencil in a glass of water looks broken, but this is an optical *illusion.*** *syns.* impression, delusion

illusion

FACT FILE

illusion *Illusion* comes from the Latin *illusionem,* a combination of *il-,* meaning "at" + *ludere,* meaning "to play." Old French changed the meaning to "mocking," or making someone look ridiculous, either playfully or harmfully. *Illusion* entered the English language in 1350 with the meaning "mockery." Then, in 1380, *illusion* changed to mean "misleading appearance." Optical illusions mislead the senses into perceiving what is not real.

---

im·me·di·ate [i·mē′dē·ət] *adj.* An immediate event is one that happens right away. **Julio knew an *immediate* response was needed to explain how the carpet got so dirty.** *syns.* instant, instantaneous

im·press [im·pres′] *v.* **im·pressed** To be impressed with someone means to admire that person. **Evan was *impressed* when his friend Tanya won first prize at the science fair.** *syn.* awe

in·ad·ver·tent·ly [i′nəd·ver′tent·lē] *adv.* If you do something inadvertently, you do it without meaning to. **The bus stopped so suddenly that Annabelle *inadvertently* stepped on Ricardo's foot.** *syns.* unintentionally, accidentally

in·fest [in·fest′] *v.* **in·fest·ed** If insects or animals infest a place, they are there in large numbers and usually cause damage. **When the large tree fell over, we realized that it had been *infested* by termites.** *syn.* overrun

---

a	add	e	end	o	odd	o͞o	pool	oi	oil	th	this		*a* in *above*
ā	ace	ē	equal	ō	open	u	up	ou	pout	zh	vision		*e* in *sicken*
â	care	i	it	ô	order	û	burn	ng	ring			ə =	*i* in *possible*
ä	palm	ī	ice	o͝o	took	yo͞o	fuse	th	thin				*o* in *melon*
													u in *circus*

in·sist [in·sist′] *v.* **in·sist·ed** If you insisted on something, you said it very firmly and you refused to change your mind. **Bobby's mother** *insisted* **that he put on a clean shirt before dinner.**

—— **Word Origins** ——

insist The word *insist* has roots in the Latin word *insistere,* meaning "persist, dwell upon, or stand upon." Its word parts are *in-,* meaning "upon," + *sistere,* meaning "to take a stand." Someone who insists on something takes a stand on it, or feels strongly and firmly about it.

in·spect [in·spekt′] *v.* **in·spect·ing** Someone who is inspecting something is looking at it very carefully. **Dad is** *inspecting* **the car before we start our vacation.** *syns.* examine, scrutinize

in·spire [in·spīr′] *v.* **in·spires** If something inspires you, it makes you excited about doing something good. **Dustin's social studies teacher** *inspires* **the class to volunteer in the community.** *syns.* motivate, encourage

in·stall [in·stôl′] *v.* **in·stalled** If you installed a piece of equipment, you put it in to make it ready for use. **Mr. Sims** *installed* **the new dishwasher at Myra's house.** *syns.* connect, fit

in·tend [in·tend′] *v.* **in·tends** When someone intends to do something, he or she plans to do it. **Amanda** *intends* **to take her dog for a walk this afternoon.** *syns.* plan, aim

in·ten·tion [in·ten′shən] *n.* **in·ten·tions** Intentions are ideas about what a person means to do. **The teacher has the best** *intentions* **of helping her students increase their reading rates.** *syn.* purpose

in·ter·ro·ga·tion [in·ter′ə·gā′shən] *n.* An interrogation is a long period of intense questioning to get information from someone. **The thief was taken to the police station for** *interrogation* **about other robberies in the neighborhood.** *syns.* questioning, grilling

in·ter·val [in′tər·vəl] *n.* **in·ter·vals** Something that happens at regular intervals is repeated over and over with a certain amount of time in between. **Lanh's schedule at school is divided into six** *intervals,* **starting with math.** *syns.* gap, period

in·trep·id [in·tre′pəd] *adj.* A person who is intrepid acts brave because he or she has no fear. **The** *intrepid* **explorers ventured far from home, not knowing what awaited them.** *syns.* fearless, brave

jos·tle [jä′səl] *v.* **jos·tling** If the people in a crowd push or knock against you, they are jostling you. **The runners were** *jostling* **for position before the race.** *syns.* push, shove

jostle

—— **Word Origins** ——

jostle *Jostle* comes from *joust,* the root of the Old French word *jousten.* It originally came from the Latin word *juxtare,* meaning "to come together." When people bump into each other, they jostle each other.

jour·ney [jûr′nē] *n.* A journey is a trip from one place to another that usually takes a long time. **Would you like to take a** *journey* **to the moon some day?** *syns.* trip, voyage

—— **Word Origins** ——

journey *Journey* comes from the Old French word *journée,* meaning "a day's work or travel." Its root word is *jour,* meaning "day." It originated from the Latin word *diurnum,* meaning "a day." The original sense of a journey was a trip that took a day's time.

L

FACT FILE

legend In Latin, *legere* means "to read" and *legenda* were "things to be read." Centuries ago, *legenda*, or legends, were narratives about saints or martyrs and were intended to glorify people in a religious way. When fictional elements were added to the stories, the meaning of *legends* changed to "fanciful tales from the past." Today a person may be called a "legend in his own time," and a *legendary* person may have outstanding accomplishments that seem "larger than life."

leg·en·dar·y [lej′ənd·âr·ē] *adj.* Someone who is legendary has a special fame for something he or she has done. **Eugenie Clark is *legendary* for swimming with sharks to study them.** *syns.* famous, renowned

loom [lo͞om] *v.* **loom·ing** When an event is looming, it seems likely to happen soon. **When Paulita got a toothache, she knew that a visit to the dentist was *looming*.** *syn.* threaten

lum·ber [lum′bər] *v.* **lum·bers** When a person or an animal lumbers, it moves in a slow and clumsy way. **A large, heavy animal, such as a bear or an elephant, *lumbers* when it moves.**

lure [lo͝or] *v.* **lures** If something lures you, it makes you want to go to it, even though it is dangerous or could get you in trouble. **Hoshi felt the deep, dark forest *lure* him to explore its paths.** *syns.* entice, tempt

lurk [lûrk] *v.* **lurked** If something lurked somewhere, it waited there quietly hidden, usually before doing something bad. **When night came, the lion that *lurked* near the water hole made its attack.** *syn.* skulk

M

ACADEMIC LANGUAGE

magazine article A *magazine article* gives information on a topic and usually includes photographs with captions.

mag·nif·i·cent [mag·nif′ə·sənt] *adj.* Something magnificent is very beautiful and impressive. **The Eiffel Tower is *magnificent* when it is lit up at night.** *syns.* superb, splendid

mas·sive [mas′iv] *adj.* Something massive is very large and heavy. **Dinosaurs were *massive* creatures.** *syns.* enormous, solid

ma·ture [mə·cho͝or′] *adj.* A mature person or animal is fully grown and behaves like an adult. **Dad says my brother is not *mature* enough to own a car.** *syns.* adult, grown

magnificent

mem·o·ra·ble [mem′ər·ə·bəl] *adj.* If something is memorable, it is worth remembering or easy to remember. **The student concert was a *memorable* event for Fernando's family.** *syn.* unforgettable

mim·ic [mi′mik] *v.* If you mimic a person or thing, you try to act or look exactly like that person or thing. **Rochelle and Valerie tried to *mimic* Juliet's hairstyle.** *syns.* imitate, copy

mis·chie·vous [mis′chi·vəs] *adj.* Someone who is mischievous likes to play tricks on other people. **Sometimes Beth's *mischievous* little brother draws pictures on her homework.** *syn.* impish

mis·er·a·ble [miz′ər·ə·bəl] *adj.* A person who feels miserable feels uncomfortable and unhappy. **When Sue had chicken pox, she was itchy and *miserable*.** *syns.* uncomfortable, unhappy

mis·for·tune [mis·fôr′chən] *n.* Misfortune is something unlucky or unpleasant that happens to someone. **The storm brought *misfortune* when the bridge collapsed and people were stranded.** *syns.* disaster, hardship

a	add	e	end	o	odd	o͞o	pool	oi	oil	th	this		a in *above*
ā	ace	ē	equal	ō	open	u	up	ou	pout	zh	vision	ə =	e in *sicken*
â	care	i	it	ô	order	û	burn	ng	ring				i in *possible*
ä	palm	ī	ice	o͝o	took	yo͞o	fuse	th	thin				o in *melon*
													u in *circus*

mon·i·tor [mon′ə·tər] *v.* When you monitor something, you regularly check its progress. **Uncle Charlie will help us *monitor* the growth of the tomato plants.** *syns.* watch, observe

mut·ter [mut′ər] *v.* **mut·tered** If you muttered, you said something very quietly because you did not want it to be heard. **Jimar *muttered* about her disappointment in her team's loss.** *syns.* murmur, mumble

ACADEMIC LANGUAGE

mystery A *mystery* is a story that centers on answering questions such as *Who did it?, Where is it?,* or *What happened?*

ACADEMIC LANGUAGE

narrative nonfiction *Narrative nonfiction* tells about people, things, events, or places that are real.

narrative poem A *narrative poem* is a poem that tells a story. Narrative poetry often contains figurative language.

nim·ble [nim′bəl] *adj.* If someone is nimble, he or she moves quickly, lightly, and easily. **Acrobats exercise every day to stay *nimble*.** *syns.* quick, lively

no·ble [nō′bəl] *adj.* If you describe someone as noble, you think that person is honest and unselfish. **Thao did a *noble* deed when he shopped for his elderly neighbor after the ice storm.** *syns.* generous, gallant

nur·ture [nûr′chər] *v.* If you nurture a living thing, you care for it while it is growing and developing. **The mother bear will *nurture* her cubs until they can survive on their own.** *syns.* cultivate, nourish

ob·sta·cle [ob′stə·kəl] *n.* **ob·sta·cles** Obstacles are things that get in your way when you are going somewhere or trying to reach a goal. **Delays caused by traffic and a shortage of parking spaces were *obstacles* to getting Inez to her recital on time.** *syns.* impediment, barrier

obstacle

ob·vi·ous [ob′vē·əs] *adj.* If something is obvious, it is so easily seen or understood that no one has to explain it. **When Clayton's mom entered the living room, it was *obvious* that the dog had torn apart the sofa cushions.** *syns.* apparent, evident

oc·ca·sion·al·ly [ə·kā′zhən·əl·ē] *adv.* If something happens occasionally, it happens once in a while. **Raul *occasionally* goes camping with his family.** *syn.* sometimes

om·i·nous [om′ə·nəs] *adj* Something ominous is a sign of trouble or a warning that something bad is going to happen. **At the opening of the play, the audience heard an *ominous* sound just before the scenery came tumbling down.** *syns.* threatening, menacing

op·por·tu·ni·ty [op′·ər·tōō′nə·tē] *n.* **op·por·tu·ni·ties** Opportunities are chances to do something you want to do. **Keith and Polly are looking for *opportunities* to do volunteer work in a hospital.** *syn.* chance

or·nate [ôr·nāt′] *adj.* Something that is ornate is decorated with a lot of complicated patterns. **During ceremonies, some kings and queens wear *ornate* garments and jewels.** *syns.* fancy, elaborate

ornate

P

ACADEMIC LANGUAGE

pace Reading at an appropriate *pace* means reading with smoothness and consistency, not too quickly or too slowly.

pact [pakt] *n.* A pact is an agreement between people or countries in which they promise to do certain things. **Rob and Leron made a *pact* to be partners on the science project.** *syns.* deal, agreement

par·ti·ci·pate [pär·tis′ə·pāt′] *v.* If you participate in a game, you are involved in it. **To become a well-rounded athlete, William will *participate* in a different sport each season.** *syns.* partake, join

par·tic·u·lar [pər·tik′yə·lər] *adj.* Something that is particular is one specific thing of its kind. **A boxer is a *particular* breed of dog.** *syn.* specific

pa·thet·ic [pə·thet′ik] *adj.* A person or thing that is pathetic is sad or helpless. You usually feel sorry for pathetic people or things. **The drenched kitten looked *pathetic*.** *syns.* pitiable, sad

pe·cul·iar [pi·kyōōl′yər] *adj.* Something that is peculiar is strange and unusual, usually not in a good way. **The basketball coach was breathing in a very *peculiar* way, so Florence called for help.** *syns.* odd, strange

pen·sive [pen′siv] *adj.* Someone who is pensive is thinking deeply about something. **After reading the book, Nikko was *pensive*, reliving the events in his mind.** *syn.* thoughtful

— Word Origins —

pensive The word *pensive* has roots in the Latin word *pensare,* meaning "to weigh or to consider." It also is related to the Latin word *pendere,* meaning "to hang or weigh." In jewelry, *pendants* are like little weights that hang down from a necklace. Old French changed *pensare* to *penser,* with the meaning "to think," from which came the adjective *pensif.* English borrowed this word, and it became *pensive.* A pensive person is "weighed down" in thought.

per·fect [pər·fekt′] *v.* To perfect something is to improve it so that it is the best it can be. **Lucy had to *perfect* her piano solo before the concert.** *syn.* polish

ACADEMIC LANGUAGE

phrasing *Phrasing* is grouping words into meaningful "chunks," or phrases, when you read aloud.

pit·i·ful [pit′i·fəl] *adj.* If something is pitiful, it is so sad and weak that people feel sorry for it. **The dog acted *pitiful* so people would feed it.** *syns.* sad, pathetic

ACADEMIC LANGUAGE

play A *play* is a story that is meant to be performed for an audience. Plays often include stage directions that tell the characters how to act. Plays may be broken up into acts and scenes.

pli·a·ble [plī′ə·bəl] *adj.* Something that is pliable is easy to move or bend without breaking. **Jeff made a bowl out of the clay while it was still *pliable*.** *syn.* flexible

plunge [plunj] *v.* If you plunge into something, you rush into it suddenly. **Enrique *plunged* into the water to find his sister's bracelet.** *syn.* dive

ACADEMIC LANGUAGE

poetry *Poetry* is a form of expressive writing in verse.

pounce [pouns] *v.* **pounced** A person or animal that pounced on something jumped on it eagerly to take it. **When Mario dropped the toy mouse, the cat *pounced* on it.** *syns.* swoop, jump

ACADEMIC LANGUAGE

pourquoi tale A *pourquoi tale* is an imaginative story that tells how or why something came to be. Pourquoi tales usually describe how things came to be in nature.

a	add	e	end	o	odd	o͞o	pool	oi	oil	th	this
ā	ace	ē	equal	ō	open	u	up	ou	pout	zh	vision
â	care	i	it	ô	order	û	burn	ng	ring		
ä	palm	ī	ice	o͞o	took	yo͞o	fuse	th	thin		

ə = { a in *above*
e in *sicken*
i in *possible*
o in *melon*
u in *circus* }

pred·a·tor [prĕd'ə·tər] *n.* **pred·a·tors** Predators are animals that kill and eat other animals. **Zebras live together in herds to protect themselves from** *predators* **such as lions.** *syn.* attacker

predator

pre·serve [pri·zûrv'] *v.* To preserve something is to keep it from being harmed or changed. **The government helps** *preserve* **the natural areas by making laws to protect the wildlife in them.** *syns.* protect, maintain

pride·ful [prīd'fəl] *adj.* A person is prideful if he or she feels very satisfied because of something he or she has done. **Justin felt** *prideful* **after winning first-prize at the science fair.** *syns.* vain, haughty

pris·tine [pris'tēn'] *adj.* If a place is pristine, it is clean and untouched. **Iliana's family was happy to be moving from the crowded city to the** *pristine* **countryside.** *syns.* pure, unspoiled

priv·i·lege [priv'ə·lij] *n.* A privilege is a special advantage or right that only certain people can have. **Hinto and Tehya had earned the** *privilege* **of extra computer time.** *syns.* advantage, benefit

---

Q

quea·sy [kwē'zē] *adj.* If you feel queasy, you have a sick feeling in your stomach. **When the teacher announced a pop quiz, Earl felt** *queasy.* *syns.* sick, nauseous

quest [kwest] *n.* A quest is a journey with a specific purpose. **The knight began his** *quest* **to find the missing princess.** *syn.* mission

---

R

re·call [ri·kôl'] *v.* **re·calls** When a person recalls something, he or she remembers it. **Armando** *recalls* **the fun he had on his eighth birthday.** *syns.* remember, recollect

rec·og·nize [rĕ'kig·nīz] *v.* **rec·og·niz·es** If someone recognizes you, it means they know who you are when they see you. **Nori's teacher** *recognizes* **him in the mall and says hello.** *syns.* know, identify

re·con·struct [rē'·kən·strukt'] *v.* To reconstruct something that has been damaged or destroyed means to rebuild it. **The earthquake survivors have begun to** *reconstruct* **their damaged homes.** *syns.* restore, repair

re·cruit [ri·krōōt'] *v.* When you recruit someone, you get him or her to join a group for a special purpose. **Dad had to** *recruit* **Rashan and Tyrone to help him put together the new cabinet.** *syn.* enlist

re·lent·less [ri·lent'ləs] *adj.* Someone who is relentless in trying to do something keeps at it and refuses to give up. **The climber was** *relentless* **in his attempt to reach the mountaintop.** *syns.* persistent, unyielding

re·luc·tant [ri·luk'tənt] *adj.* If someone is reluctant to do something, he or she does not want to do it. **Denise was** *reluctant* **to tell her parents about her low math score.** *syn.* hesitant

re·mark·a·ble [ri·mär'kə·bəl] *adj.* A remarkable thing is something very special in a way that makes other people notice it. **Charlene's** *remarkable* **drawings of her favorite cartoon characters won first place in the art contest.** *syns.* extraordinary, outstanding

rem·i·nis·cent [rĕm'·ə·nis'ənt] *adj.* If something is reminiscent of something else, it brings back memories of that other time or place. **Grandfather said that the Thanksgiving feast was** *reminiscent* **of holiday meals long ago.** *syns.* evocative, suggestive

re·sem·ble [ri·zem′bəl] *v.* **re·sem·bles** If one person or thing resembles another, the two look similar. **Everyone says that my sister *resembles* me.**

resemble

re·solve [ri·zolv′] *v.* **re·solved** When you have resolved to do something, you have made up your mind to do it. **John *resolved* to learn to drive by his sixteenth birthday.** *syns.* decide, vow

FACT FILE

resolve The word *resolve* is from the Latin word *resolvere,* meaning "to loosen or undo." It is related to the word *solve,* whose meaning "explain or answer" came about in 1533 and became related to the word *solution.* The term's mathematical use was recognized in 1737. A problem can be answered by "undoing" it part by part until it is solved.

re·sound [ri·zound′] *v.* **re·sound·ed** If a place resounded with a sound, it became filled with that sound. **The empty house *resounded* with laughter after the family moved in.** *syns.* echo, reverberate

re·source·ful [ri·sôrs′fəl] *adj.* A resourceful person is good at finding ways to solve problems. **Without enough money for real flowers, the *resourceful* decorator made paper roses.** *syns.* ingenious, inventive

re·spon·si·ble [ri·spon′sə·bəl] *adj.* If someone is responsible, that person can be trusted to do a job on his or her own. **Lian would be allowed to get a dog only if he agreed to be *responsible* for taking care of it.** *syns.* accountable, answerable

re·veal [ri·vēl′] *v.* **re·vealed** When something is revealed, it was hidden but can now be seen. **As Roger got closer to the huge sculpture, the lines connecting the pieces were *revealed*.** *syns.* disclose, divulge

— **Word Origins** —

reveal The word *reveal* has origins in the Latin word *revelare,* meaning "to uncover or disclose." *Revelare* literally means "to unveil," from *re-,* which can mean "opposite of," and *velare,* meaning "to veil or cover." Old French changed *revelare* to *reveler,* which English borrowed. To uncover something is to reveal it.

roam [rōm] *v.* **roamed** If a creature roamed an area, it wandered around there. **At one time, herds of buffalo *roamed* the Great Plains.** *syns.* wander, travel

rouse [rouz] *v.* **roused** If you roused someone, you woke up or alerted that person. **The alarm clock *roused* Ginny so she wouldn't be late for school.** *syns.* awaken, stir

rum·ple [rum′pəl] *adj.* **rum·pled** Something is rumpled if it is wrinkled or messy. **Kareem fell asleep on the long ride, and when he woke up, his shirt was *rumpled*.** *syn.* wrinkle

S

scan [skan] *v.* To scan a place is to look carefully over the entire area for something specific. **Rosalie had to *scan* the crowd in the auditorium to find where her dad was sitting.** *syn.* skim

sce·nic [sē′nik] *adj.* A scenic place has lovely natural features, such as trees, cliffs, or bodies of water. **Juan stopped the car so that he could enjoy the *scenic* ocean view.** *syn.* picturesque

scenic

a add	e end	o odd	o͞o pool	oi oil	th this	
ā ace	ē equal	ō open	u up	ou pout	zh vision	
â care	i it	ô order	û burn	ng ring		ə =
ä palm	ī ice	o͝o took	yo͞o fuse	th thin		

ə = { *a* in *above* / *e* in *sicken* / *i* in *possible* / *o* in *melon* / *u* in *circus* }

scoff [skof] *v.* **scoffed** If you scoffed at something, you spoke about it in a mocking or critical way. **Eloise *scoffed* at Hubert's suggestion that they dress up to go to the football game.** *syns.* mock, ridicule

scrounge [skrounj] *v.* **scroung·ing** If an animal is scrounging, it is looking around trying to find food. **The hungry dog was *scrounging* through the garbage cans for food.** *syn.* rummage

scru·ti·nize [skrōō′tə·nīz′] *v.* When you scrutinize something, you examine it carefully to find out some information about it. **Mom thought she saw a tiny bug, so she decided to *scrutinize* the lettuce before using it.** *syns.* examine, inspect

sea·soned [sē′zənd] *adj.* A person who is seasoned at something has a lot of experience with that thing. **After working with the cook in the restaurant for several months, Salma felt she was a *seasoned* chef.** *syns.* experienced, skilled

se·lect [sə·lekt′] *adj.* A select group is one that is special and among the best of its kind. **The owner of the orange grove made up a boxful of *select* oranges for his special guests.** *syns.* best, elite

self-as·sur·ance [self′·ə·shoor′əns] *n.* People who have self-assurance are confident and sure of themselves. **The coach gives the team members a pep talk before the game to give them *self-assurance.*** *syn.* confidence

sen·try [sen′trē] *n.* **sen·tries** Sentries are people who stand as guards around a camp, building, or other area. **The king posted *sentries* around his castle.** *syns.* guard, patrol

se·rene·ly [si·rēn′lē] *adv.* If something is done serenely, it is done in a calm and quiet way. **The day seemed peaceful as Leon sat *serenely* under the tree, watching the sunset.** *syns.* calmly, peacefully

siz·zle [siz′əl] *v.* **siz·zles** If something sizzles, it is very hot and makes a hissing sound. **When the bacon *sizzles,* the egg cooks, and the toast is done, it's time for breakfast.** *syns.* crackle, sputter

skep·ti·cal·ly [skep′ti·kə·lē] *adv.* If you speak skeptically about something, you express doubt about whether it is true. **Francine's father listened *skeptically* to her excuses for not doing homework.** *syns.* doubtfully, unbelievingly

slick [slik] *adj.* If something is slick, it is presented in an attractive way. **Eleanora's new black computer monitor looks *slick.*** *syns.* impressive, striking

smol·der [smōl′dər] *v.* **smol·der·ing** Something smoldering is burning slowly from the inside, without flames. **After the fire was out, the cabin was still *smoldering.*** *syn.* burn

snatch [snach] *v.* **snatched** If you snatched something, you grabbed it or pulled it away quickly. **Joan walked into the playroom and *snatched* her teddy bear out of her younger brother's hands.** *syns.* grab, seize

snick·er [snik′ər] *v.* **snick·er·ing** Snickering is laughing quietly in an unkind way at what someone says or does. **We heard Miguel *snickering* when Rendrick poured juice instead of syrup on his pancakes by mistake.** *syns.* mock, scoff

sol·emn·ly [sol′əm·lē] *adv.* When you say something solemnly, you say it in a very serious way. **Mrs. Pressman spoke *solemnly* as she told the students about their classmate's accident.** *syns.* seriously, somberly

sol·i·tar·y [sol′ə·târ′·ē] *adj.* To live in a solitary way is to be alone most of the time. **The guidance counselor spoke with Harriet about changing her *solitary* way of life.** *syns.* lonely, aloof

--- Word Origins ---

solitary The word *solitary* originates from the Latin word *solitarius,* meaning "alone or lonely." It has roots in *solitas,* meaning "loneliness," and *solus,* meaning "alone."

spar·kle [spär′kəl] *v.* **spar·kling** Something that is sparkling is shining, clear, and bright. **The jewel was so shiny, it was *sparkling.*** *syn.* twinkle

sparkle

stat·ure [stach′ər] *n.* A person's stature is his or her height. **Ramona may be small in *stature,* but she has big ideas.** *syns.* height, size

stealth·y [stel′thē] *adj.* A stealthy animal is one that stays quiet and hidden as it moves about, so that others do not notice it. **The turkeys did not notice the *stealthy* fox hiding behind the rock, lying in wait to make its move.** *syns.* sneaky, furtive

stern [stûrn] *adj.* Someone who is stern is very serious and strict. **Belita's aunt is very *stern* about making visitors take off their shoes before entering her house.** *syn.* strict

stin·gy [stin′jē] *adj.* Someone who is stingy doesn't like to spend money or share what they have. **Karly thinks her brother is *stingy* because he won't give her money when the ice-cream truck comes around.** *syn.* miserly

stroll [strōl] *v.* To stroll is to walk in a slow, relaxed way. **On Sundays, Chim and Felix *stroll* in the park with their families.** *syns.* walk, amble

stun [stun] *v.* **stunned** When someone is stunned by something amazing, he or she is shocked and sometimes even speechless. **The announcement that she had been given the lead part in the play *stunned* Jean.** *syns.* shock, amaze

sub·merge [səb·mûrj′] *adj.* **sub·merged** If something is submerged, it is beneath the surface of a body of water. **The boys couldn't reach the watch because it was *submerged* at the bottom of the pool.** *syn.* immersed

--- **Word Origins** ---

submerge The word *submerge* comes from the Latin word *submergere,* meaning "to sink or to overwhelm." It is made of two parts: *sub-,* meaning "under," + *mergere,* meaning "to plunge, dip, or immerse." *Submerge* is commonly used in connection with submarines, which travel underwater.

suit·a·ble [sōō′tə·bəl] *adj.* Something is suitable if it is right for whatever it is being used for. **That purple velvet robe will make a *suitable* costume for the king in the play.** *syn.* appropriate

surge [sûrj] *n.* If you feel a surge of a particular feeling, you feel it suddenly and very strongly. **I felt a *surge* of "spring fever" as I took out the camping gear.** *syn.* gush

sur·ren·der [sə·ren′dər] *v.* When you surrender, you stop fighting something or someone. **Amy and Tamecia refused to *surrender* to the rule that girls are not allowed on the football team.** *syns.* relinquish, concede

--- **Word Origins** ---

surrender The word *surrender* comes from the Old French word *surrendre,* meaning "to give up or deliver over." It is made up of two parts: *sur-,* meaning "over," + *rendre,* meaning "to give back." A considerate young person will surrender his or her seat on a bus to an older person.

sus·pi·cion [sə·spish′ən] *n.* If you think someone is guilty of doing something wrong, you have a suspicion about him or her. **When Brent's lunch money was missing, he had a *suspicion* that his sister had raided his backpack.**

swerve [swûrv] *v.* **swerved** If a car swerved, it turned suddenly to avoid hitting something. **The car *swerved* to avoid hitting the deer that had suddenly jumped across the road.** *syn.* veer

sym·bo·lize [sim′bəl·īz′] *v.* If an animal or object symbolizes something, it represents that thing. **On the American flag, the thirteen stripes *symbolize* the original 13 states, and the 50 stars stand for the current number of states.** *syn.* represent

symbolize

ACADEMIC LANGUAGE

tall tale A *tall tale* is a humorous story about impossible or exaggerated happenings. Many tall tales are stories about American folk heroes and legends.

taut [tôt] *adj.* Something that is taut has been stretched or pulled very tightly. **When Margaret's mother makes the beds, she pulls the sheets *taut*.** *syns.* tight, firm

ACADEMIC LANGUAGE

textbook *Textbooks* are organized by chapter titles and headings within chapters. They provide information without the author's opinions.

tim·id [tim′id] *adj.* A timid person is shy and unsure of himself or herself. **Wally was so *timid* that he was afraid to enter the room if he was late for class.** *syns.* shy, hesitant

a add	e end	o odd	o͞o pool	oi oil	th this	a in *above*
ā ace	ē equal	ō open	u up	ou pout	zh vision	e in *sicken*
â care	i it	ô order	û burn	ng ring		ə = { i in *possible*
ä palm	ī ice	o͝o took	yo͞o fuse	th thin		o in *melon*
						u in *circus*

tink·er [ting′kər] *v.* When you tinker with something, you try to fix or adjust it. **Alita doesn't want Doug to *tinker* with any of the musical instruments.** *syn.* meddle

trait [trāt] *n.* **traits** Traits are particular qualities or characteristics of a person or thing. **Vincente's sister has *traits,* such as being quiet and shy, which are very different from his own loud mannerisms.** *syns.* characteristic, feature

— Word Origins —

trait The word *trait* comes from the Latin word *tractus,* meaning "a drawing." It later came to mean "a drawn line or feature." The sense of the word further extended to mean "a particular feature or distinguishing quality." Middle French borrowed it and made it *trait.* People can be described by their personality traits.

tram·ple [tram′pəl] *v.* **tram·pled** If you trampled something, you stepped on it very hard and damaged it. **Nick walked carefully through the flowerbed so that the plants would not get *trampled.*** *syn.* crush

treach·er·ous [trech′ər·əs] *adj.* Something treacherous is dangerous and unpredictable. **Emilio knew it was a *treacherous* situation when he saw the cottonmouth snake in the yard.** *syns.* dangerous, unsafe

— Word Origins —

treachery The word *treachery* comes from the Old French word *trecherie,* meaning "deceit or cheating." It is related to *trique,* meaning "trick." Playing a mean trick on a person is using treachery to mislead him or her.

trem·ble [trem′bəl] *v.* **trem·bling** If something is trembling, it is shaking slightly. **Jalissa was *trembling* as she told the park ranger she had seen a bobcat.** *syns.* wobble, shake

U

un·doubt·ed·ly [un′dou′tid·lē] *adv.* If something will undoubtedly happen, it will definitely happen. **Social studies will *undoubtedly* be Hien's favorite subject this year, as it was last year.** *syns.* unquestionably, doubtlessly

u·nique [yo̅o̅·nēk′] *adj.* Something is unique if it is the only one of its kind. **Actresses attending award shows want their gowns to be *unique.*** *syns.* exclusive, distinctive

FACT FILE

unique The word *unique* was not commonly used until 1850. From the Latin word *unus,* meaning "one," it became *unicus,* meaning "single." It was then borrowed by the French, who changed it to *unique,* meaning "solitary." Its original meaning in English was "one of a kind," but through extended meanings, things that are unusual, rare, or distinctive are now called unique. For example, an unusual piece of jewelry may be called "unique," even though similar pieces exist.

un·tan·gle [un′·tang′gəl] *v.* **un·tan·gled** If you untangled something, you untied knots in it or straightened it if it was twisted. **Eva patiently *untangled* the yarn from the ball that her cat had played with.** *syn.* unravel

V

vast [vast] *adj.* Something that is vast is so wide it would be hard to get across it. **The Grand Canyon is a *vast* North American landmark.** *syns.* huge, enormous

ven·ture [ven′chər] *n.* A new venture is a project that is exciting and even risky. **The brothers were excited about their new business *venture,* selling frozen pizzas.** *syn.* project

— Word Origins —

venture The word *venture* is a shortened form of *adventure. Adventure* comes from the Latin *aventura* and is related to *advenire,* meaning "to come about." Originally, the meaning was "to arrive," but Middle English changed it to "a risky undertaking." It has the general sense of being a daring project.

ver·i·fy [ver′ə·fī′] *v.* If you verify something, you check to make sure that it is true by using very careful research. **Kishawn used an encyclopedia to *verify* information about the largest fish in the world.** *syns.* confirm, prove

vi·cin·i·ty [vi·sin′ə·tē] *n.* If something is in the vicinity, it is nearby. **Yoshi lives in the *vicinity* of the school.** *syns.* neighborhood, locality

— Word Origins —

vicinity The word *vicinity* comes from the Latin word *vicinitas,* meaning "neighborhood." *Vicinitas* is related to *vicus,* meaning "a group of houses." Neighbors live in a group of houses that make up a neighborhood.

vig·or·ous·ly [vig′ər·əs·lē] *adv.* If you do something vigorously, you do it with energy and enthusiasm. **Bonita *vigorously* mixed the batter so the cake wouldn't be lumpy.** *syns.* forcefully, energetically

viv·id [viv′id] *adj.* Something that is vivid has very bright colors. **Tina chose *vivid* pinks and yellows for her painting of spring flowers.** *syns.* bright, colorful

— Word Origins —

vivid The word *vivid* is from the Latin word *vividus,* meaning "animated or lively." It is related to the Latin word *vivus,* meaning "alive." The word has come to mean "something strong and clear." This meaning was extended to colors in 1665. In writing, teachers suggest using *vivid* verbs and adjectives to produce strong and colorful mental images.

vul·ner·a·ble [vul′nər·ə·bəl] *adj.* A person or an animal that is vulnerable is weak and unprotected and at risk of being harmed. **Ocean fish are *vulnerable* to shark attacks.** *syns.* defenseless, susceptible

— **W** —

wea·ry [wir′ē] *adj.* If you are weary, you are very tired from working hard at something and you want to stop. **The camper was *weary* from hiking all day.** *syns.* tired, exhausted

with·stand [with·stand′] *v.* If you withstand a difficult time, you are able to get through it all right. **Jamie was able to *withstand* his teammates' teasing after he struck out last night.** *syns.* endure, survive

a	add	e	end	o	odd	o͞o	pool	oi	oil	t͟h	this		a in *above*
ā	ace	ē	equal	ō	open	u	up	ou	pout	zh	vision	ə =	e in *sicken*
â	care	i	it	ô	order	û	burn	ng	ring				i in *possible*
ä	palm	ī	ice	o͝o	took	yo͞o	fuse	th	thin				o in *melon*
													u in *circus*

Index of Titles and Authors

Page numbers in green refer to biographical information.

Acknowledgments

For permission to reprint copyrighted material, grateful acknowledgment is made to the following sources:

Angel Island Association: From *Kai's Journey to Gold Mountain: An Angel Island Story* by Katrina Saltonstall Currier, illustrated by Gabhor Utomo. Copyright © 2005 by Angel Island Association.

Boyds Mills Press, Inc.: "Moving" from *Where Is the Night Train Going* by Eileen Spinelli. Text copyright © 1996 by Eileen Spinelli. Published by Wordsong, an imprint of Boyds Mills Press.

Candlewick Press, Inc., Cambridge, MA: From *Because of Winn-Dixie* by Kate DiCamillo. Text copyright © 2000 by Kate DiCamillo. *Saturday Night at the Dinosaur Stomp* by Carol Diggory Shields, illustrated by Scott Nash. Text copyright © 1997 by Carol Diggory Shields; illustrations copyright © 1997 by Scott Nash.

Capstone Press: From *Mammoth Cave National Park* by Mike Graf. Text copyright © 2004 by Capstone Press.

Carus Publishing Company, 30 Grove St., Suite C, Peterborough, NH 03458: "Make a Movie Machine" by Nick D'Alto, cover illustration by Jack Desrocher from *Cobblestone: Discover American History* Magazine, January 2005. Copyright © 2005 by Carus Publishing Company. From "Summertime Star Parties" in *Odyssey: Adventures in Science* Magazine, May 2002. Text copyright © 2002 by Cobblestone Publishing Company.

Children's Better Health Institute, Indianapolis, IN: Adapted from "Three Little Pigs Revisited" by Kok Heong McNaughton from *Children's Digest* Magazine, January/February 2004. Text copyright © 1987 by Children's Better Health Institute, Benjamin Franklin Literary & Medical Society, Inc.

Children's Book Press, San Francisco, CA, www.childrensbookpress.org: *My Diary From Here to There* by Amada Irma Pérez, illustrated by Maya Christina Gonzalez. Text copyright © 2002 by Amada Irma Pérez; illustrations copyright © 2002 by Maya Christina Gonzalez. From *Just Like Me,* edited by Harriet Rohmer. Text and illustrations copyright © 1997 by Tomie Arai, Carmen Lomas Garza, Nancy Hom, George Littlechild, Stephen Von Mason, Mira Reisberg, Elly Simmons, Daryl Wells, and Michele Wood; overall book project copyright © 1997 by Harriet Rohmer.

Chronicle Books, LLC, San Francisco, ChronicleBooks.com: "Hard Cheese" from *Unwitting Wisdom: An Anthology of Aesop's Fables* by Helen Ward. Copyright © 2004 by Helen Ward.

Creative Education: From *Mimicry and Camouflage* by Mary Hoff. Text copyright © 2003 by Creative Education.

The Cricket Magazine Group, a division of Carus Publishing Company: "The Little Fly and the Great Moose" by Janeen R. Adil, cover illustration by Matt Faulkner from *Spider* Magazine, August 1999. Text and illustration copyright © 1999 by Carus Publishing Company. From "Dragons and Dinosaurs" by Meg Moss, illustrated by Ariane Elsammak in *ASK* Magazine, September 2004. Text and illustrations © 2004 by Carus Publishing Company. "Cricket Thermometer" and cover illustration by Nicholas Debon from *Cricket* Magazine, May 2002. Copyright © 2002 by Carus Publishing Company.

Curbstone Press: "There's an Orange Tree Out There" by Alfonso Quijada Urías. Text copyright © 1991. Distributed by Consortium.

Dutton Children's Books, a Division of Penguin Young Readers Group, A Member of Penguin Group (USA) Inc., 345 Hudson St., New York, NY 10014: From *Mangrove Wilderness* by Bianca Lavies. Copyright © 1994 by Bianca Lavies.

Farrar, Straus and Giroux, LLC: From "The Cricket Cage" and "Tucker's Life's Savings" in *The Cricket in Times Square* by George Selden, illustrated by Garth Williams. Text copyright © 1960 by George Selden Thompson and Garth Williams; copyright renewed 1988 by George Selden Thompson.

Harcourt, Inc.: "The Chameleon," "The Glass Frog," and "The Poison-Dart Frogs" from *Lizards, Frogs, and Polliwogs* by Douglas Florian. Copyright © 2001 by Douglas Florian.

HarperCollins Publishers: *Fire Storm* by Jean Craighead George, illustrated by Wendell Minor. Text copyright © 2003 by Julie Productions Inc.; illustrations copyright © 2003 by Wendell Minor. *Danitra Brown Leaves Town* by Nikki Grimes, illustrated by Floyd Cooper. Text copyright © 2002 by Nikki Grimes; illustrations copyright © 2002 by Floyd Cooper. From *The Hot & Cold Summer* by Johanna Hurwitz. Text copyright © 1984 by Johanna Hurwitz. From *Mountains* by Seymour Simon. Text copyright © 1994 by Seymour Simon. From *Justin and the Best Biscuits in the World* by Mildred Pitts Walter. Text copyright © 1986 by Mildred Pitts Walter. From *On the Banks of Plum Creek* by Laura Ingalls Wilder, illustrated by Garth Williams. Text copyright 1937, 1965 by Little House Heritage Trust; illustrations copyright 1953, 1981 by Garth Williams.

Frances C. Hodgkins: "To the Top of the World" by David Breashears and Fran Hodgkins from *Boys' Life* Magazine, May 1999. Published by Boy Scouts of America.

Houghton Mifflin Company: *The Stranger* by Chris Van Allsburg. Copyright © 1986 by Chris Van Allsburg.

Lerner Publications Company, a division of Lerner Publishing Group: From *Weaving a California Tradition: A Native American Basketmaker* by Linda Yamane, photographs by Dugan Aguilar. Copyright © 1997 by Lerner Publications Company.

Mike Makley: "The New Kid" by Mike Makley.

Millbrook Press, Inc., a division of Lerner Publishing Group: *I Am an Artist* by Pat Lowery Collins. Text copyright © 1992 by Pat Lowery Collins.

National Geographic Society: "Decoding Dog Speak" by Ruth Musgrave from *National Geographic Kids* Magazine, March 2006. Text copyright © 2006 by National Geographic Society. "Flame Busters" by R. G. Schmidt from *National Geographic WORLD* Magazine, June 1999. Text copyright © 1999 by National Geographic Society.

National Wildlife Federation®: "Wonder Weaver" by Ellen Holtzen from *Ranger Rick®* Magazine, October 2001. Text copyright 2001 by the National Wildlife Federation.

Philomel Books, A Division of Penguin Young Readers Group, A Member of Penguin Group (USA) Inc., 345 Hudson St., New York, NY 10014: From *So You Want to Be an Inventor?* by Judith St. George, illustrated by David Small. Text copyright © 2002 by Judith St. George; illustrations copyright © 2002 by David Small.

PLAYS/Sterling Partners, Inc., PO Box 600160, Newton, MA 02460: *Three Little Cyberpigs* by Jane Tesh from *Plays: The Drama Magazine for Young People*, March 2000. Text © 2000 by Plays, Inc.

QA International, www.qa-international.com: From *Scholastic Atlas of Weather.* Copyright © 2006 by QA International.

Marian Reiner: "Secret Talk" from *A Word or Two with You* by Eve Merriam. Text copyright © 1981 by Eve Merriam. Published by Atheneum.

Scholastic Inc.: Juan Verdades: The Man Who Couldn't Tell a Lie by Joe Hayes, illustrated by Joseph Daniel Fiedler. Text copyright © 2001 by Joe Hayes; illustrations copyright © 2001 by Joseph Daniel Fiedler. Published by Orchard Books. *The Bunyans* by Audrey Wood, illustrated by David Shannon. Text copyright © 1996 by Audrey Wood; illustrations copyright © 1996 by David Shannon. Cover illustration from *Scholastic Atlas of Weather.* Illustration copyright © 2004 by Scholastic Inc. Published by Scholastic Reference.

Simon & Schuster Books for Young Readers, an Imprint of Simon & Schuster Children's Publishing Division: Mighty Jackie by Marissa Moss, illustrated by C. F. Payne. Text copyright © 2004 by Marissa Moss; illustrations copyright © 2004 by C. F. Payne. *Hewitt Anderson's Great Big Life* by Jerdine Nolen, illustrated by Kadir Nelson. Text copyright © 2005 by Jerdine Nolen; illustrations copyright © 2005 by Kadir Nelson.

Skipping Stones, Inc.: "My Japanese Sister" by Emily Bernier from *Skipping Stones* Magazine, November/December 2000. Text copyright © 2000 by Skipping Stones.

T & N Children's Publishing: John Muir and Stickeen: An Icy Adventure with a No-Good Dog by Julie Dunlap and Marybeth Lorbiecki, illustrated by Bill Farnsworth. Text © 2004 by Julie Dunlap and Marybeth Lorbiecki; illustrations © 2004 by Bill Farnsworth.

Texas Red Songs: Lyrics from "Hats Off to the Cowboy" by Red Steagall. Lyrics © 1989 by Texas Red Songs.

University of Washington Press: Untitled poem from Lai, Lim, and Yung's *Island: Poetry and History of Chinese Immigrants on Angel Island, 1910-1940.*

Walker Publishing Company, Inc.: From *Homesteading: Settling America's Heartland* by Dorothy Hinshaw Patent, photographs by William Muñoz. Text copyright © 1998 by Dorothy Hinshaw Patent; photographs copyright © 1998 by William Muñoz.
Grand Canyon: A Trail Through Time by Linda Vieira, illustrated by Christopher Canyon. Text copyright © 1997 by Linda Vieira; illustrations copyright © 1997 by Christopher Canyon.

Photo Credits

Placement Key: (t) top; (b) bottom; (l) left; (r) right; (c) center; (bg) background; (fg) foreground; (i) inset

18 (c) Goodacre; 56 (bc) PhotoDisc; 77 (tr) Artville; 82 (tr) ImageDJ / Alamy; 105 (tr) Digital Stock; 130 (br) TongRo Image Stock / Alamy; 131 (br) Gary Conner / PhotoEdit; 131 (bl) Gary Conner / PhotoEdit; 154 (t) Jason Kasumovic/ Shutterstock; 234 (bc) Dana White / PhotoEdit; 261 (tr) Mashpee carrying basket, from Massachusetts (plant fibre), American School/Private Collection, © Boltin Picture Library/ Bridgeman Art Library; 282 (bl) Royalty Free/Corbis; 284 (cr) Steve Hopkin/Getty; 285 (tr) Stephen Frink/zefa/Corbis; 286 (c) Dick Jacobs; 289 (bl) Jim Rowan; 290 (bl) Robert Krupp/ Root Resources; 291 (c) Dick Jacobs; 293 (t) Tom Myers; 294 (bl) Jim Rowan; 294 (tr) Jim Rowan; 295 (br) Jim Rowan; 295 (tr) Kenny Bahr/Image Finders; 296 (tc) Tom Stack; 297 (t) Dick Jacobs; 297 (br) Jim Rowan; 298 (t) Thomas Kitchin/ Tom Stack & Associates; 299 (r) Jeff Daly/Visuals Unlimited; 300 (tr) Photodisc RF; 305 (tr) Alamy Images; 315 (tr) Imelda Medina/Corbis; 332 (cr) Robert Schauer; 334 (tl) Robert Schauer; 341 (tr) Val Corbett/Getty Images; 342 (cr) Alamy Images; 342 (bl) AP Images; 343 (tr) Gary Moon/Superstock; 358 (c) Dan Helms/NGS; 359 (cr) Dan Helms/NGS; 360 (tl) Dan Helms/NGS; 360 (cl) Dan Helms/NGS; 360 (bc) Dan Helms/NGS; 361 (cr) Dan Helms/NGS; 386 (tr) StockTrek; 387 (r) StockTrek; 444 (bl) Heather Angel/Natural Visions; 445 (tr) Adam Parker/Alamy images; 465 (tr) agefotostock; 491 (tr) Leonid Serebrennikov/Alamy Images; 538 (c) Images. com/CORBIS; 542 (bl) PhotoDisc; 544 (t) Frank Boellmann/ Shutterstock; 544 (cr) Getty; 545 Phil Schermeister/CORBIS; 572 (cr) Medioimages; 572 (bl) PhotoDisc; 573 (tr) Digital Vision; 622 (bc) National Geographic; 625 (tr) Digital Vision; 628 (c) Photodisc Green; 664 (c) Schalkwijk / Art Resource, NY; 670 (cr) Royalty-Free/Corbis; 671 (tr) Science Faction; 691 (tr) Kevin Schafer/Corbis; 700 (c) Photodisc Red; 703 (cr) PhotoDisc; 719 (tr) PhotoDisc RF; 725 (tr) StockTrek; 747 (tr) Sandy Macys / Alamy; 771 (t) Lonely Planet Images; 771 (br) National Geographic.

All other photos © Harcourt School Publishers. Harcourt photos provided by Harcourt Index, Harcourt IPR, and Harcourt Photographers: Weronica Ankarorn, Eric Camden, Doug DuKane, Ken Kinsie, April Riehm and Steve Williams.

Illustration Credits, Cover Art; James Shepherd, Background art by: Laura and Eric Ovresat, Artlab, Inc.